The Adventure of Religious Pluralism
in Early Modern France

KW-406-890

Keith Cameron
Mark Greengrass
Penny Roberts
(eds)

The Adventure of Religious Pluralism in Early Modern France

Papers from the Exeter conference,
April 1999

PETER LANG

Oxford · Bern · Berlin · Bruxelles · Frankfurt am Main · New York · Wien

Die Deutsche Bibliothek – CIP-Einheitsaufnahme

The adventure of religious pluralism in early modern France :
papers from the Exeter conference, April 1999 / Keith Cameron ... (ed.). –
Oxford ; Bern ; Berlin ; Bruxelles ; Frankfurt am Main ; New York ; Wien :
Lang, 2000
ISBN 3-906758-71-0

British Library and Library of Congress Cataloguing-in-Publication Data:
A catalogue record for this book is available from *The British Library*,
Great Britain, and from *The Library of Congress*, USA

Cover design: Thomas Jaberg, Peter Lang AG

ISBN 3-906758-71-0
US-ISBN 0-8204-5084-7

© Peter Lang AG, European Academic Publishers, Bern 2000
Jupiterstr. 15, Postfach, 3000 Bern 15, Switzerland; info@peterlang.com

Printed in Germany

Foreword

> A man may say on one side, that to give the people the reins to entertain every man his own opinion, is to scatter and sow division, and, as it were, to lend a hand to augment it, there being no legal impediment or restraint to stop or hinder their career; but, on the other side, a man may also say, that to give the people the reins to entertain every man his opinion, is to mollify and appease them by facility and toleration, and to dull the point which is whetted and made sharper by singularity, novelty, and difficulty: and I think it is better for the honour of the devotion of our kings, that not having been able to do what they would, they have made a show of being willing to do what they could (Montaigne, *Essais*, II, XIX, transl. Charles Cotton).[1]

In his inimitable way, Montaigne summed up, in 1580, French political actions to come to terms with the Protestant presence within the kingdom of France. Although none of the kings would have said they believed wholeheartedly in religious tolerance and pluralism, they were forced to admit the necessity of trying to find a peaceful outcome to the hostile alternative of not recognising the faith of others. Similarly, almost twenty years later, the Edict of Nantes was an expedient based more upon the urgency of contemporary politics than on a principle of understanding and tolerance.

Nevertheless from 1562 onwards, there was a series of royal Edicts, culminating in the Edict of Nantes, which sought to find an acceptable solution to Religious Pluralism in France. In spite of the research efforts of scholars, there still remains a huge question mark over what exactly happened and what was practised during the troubled years of the second half of the sixteenth and during the seventeenth centuries.

---

1   'On peut dire, d'un costé, que de lâcher la bride aux pars d'entretenir leur opinion, c'est espandre et semer la division; c'est préter quasi la main à l'augmenter, n'y ayant aucune barriere ny coercion des loix qui bride et empesche sa course. Mais, d'austre costé, on diroit aussi que de lascher la bride aux pars d'entretenir leur opinion, c'est les amolir et relâcher par la facilité et par l'aisance, et que c'est émousser l'éguillon qui s'affine par la rareté, la nouvelleté et la difficulté. Et si, croy mieux, pour l'honneur de la devotion de nos rois, c'est que, n'ayans peu ce qu'ils vouloient, ils ont fait semblant de vouloir ce qu'ils pouvoient' (Montaigne: *Essais*, II, XIX).

To practise a religion contrary to the practices of those of the established government and church in the sixteenth century demanded great courage. To stand up for one's convictions could lead to persecution, ostracism and death. The adventure of Religious Pluralism in this turbulent period was lived at a personal, local, national and international level.

At the personal level, Calvin, as early as 1544, had published his *Excuse de Jehan Calvin, A Messieurs les Nicodemites, sur la complaincte qu'ilz font de sa trop grand'rigueur*, in which he had lambasted those who were hypocritical in their beliefs in the face of the world to save their own skins, if not their souls. The starting point of his argument is 'un homme fidele conversant entre les papistes ne peut communiquer leurs superstitions, sans offenser Dieu' and it raises the question of how many French or English persons (to overlook the English dimension would be folly), pretended to belong to one religion whereas their hearts and their beliefs were convinced of another truth?

At the national level, the King and his *Parlement* issued Edicts which embodied the Royal intent, but to what extent were these Edicts carried out locally in the provinces, many of which were many days journey from the capital? How different was life in the towns of France after the promulgation of an Edict from what it was before?

At an international level, what do we know about the intervention of England, the Germanic powers, Italy and Spain in French politics? There is the diplomatic historical account and then there is the nuanced reality. How powerful were the English Catholic refugees in France in fomenting opposition to Protestantism in general and to Religious Pluralism in particular? What was the effect of the publication of polemical tracts on attitudes and political events?

The above are all thorny questions which demand careful research to provide the essential perspective to what we already know. The papers in this volume address some of the problems, such as the Edicts and their effectiveness as regards Religious Pluralism. As our documentation of the period is defective, it is important to take into account the literary and polemical perspective, which we have tried to do. How pluralism actually worked at municipal level is an area which needs even further exploration. Some of the papers in this volume contribute towards the picture but there is still much to be done. As for Religious Pluralism after the Edict of Nantes, the papers given here only touch at the subject but nevertheless indicate some of the fascinating avenues of research which are being followed, e.g., its influence on architecture, religious orders, attitude towards other religions, dynastic matches, etc. What happened in England where a royal decree transformed the country from Roman Catholicism to Anglican Catholicism is of more than passing interest. It provides a picture, by analogy, of what religious life in France may have been like in some areas in the late sixteenth century.

The chapters in this volume started their existence as papers at a colloquium held on 19-21 April, at the University of Exeter in 1999 and which was supported by the French Embassy. If the colloquium was such a success, much of the credit must go to the organising powers of Lindy Ayubi. It was an international gathering with scholars from Canada, France, Italy, the UK and the USA. What was encouraging was the richness of the viewpoints and the contribution made by young researchers. The collection is imperfect in its coverage, but it provides a wide spectrum of important points which make a valuable contribution to our knowledge of the period. New questions are raised and readers of this volume are challenged to solve them.

Keith Cameron
Exeter

Editorial note: The full bibliography for this volume may be consulted on the Internet at http://www.ex.ac.uk/french/pluralism/bibliog.html

Table of Contents

Part 1

Religious Pluralism in Practice

ALAIN TALLON

Gallicanism and Religious Pluralism in France in the Sixteenth Century*

Religious pluralism in a unitarian State is a novelty specific to France in the sixteenth and seventeenth centuries. Despite the recent replacing of religious peace agreements within their European context,[1] and the valleys of the Vaud obtaining, weapons in hand, a certain tolerance from the Duke of Savoy even before the January edict (Cavour agreements, June 5, 1561), only the kingdom of France attempted to implement a legal coexistence of religious beliefs on a wide and united geographical scale. This 'French exception' has caused much ink to flow, but seldom has its singularity been placed alongside another, much earlier phenomenon particular to the kingdom: since the fourteenth century, France claimed to possess, within the universal Church, a certain number of specific privileges, the rights of the Gallican Church. This Gallicanism became one of the constitutive elements of French national consciousness, despite its being expressed in very different ways: the Gallicanism of the king was not that of Parlement, the universities or the clergy. Nevertheless all these tendencies, while on occasions being opposed one to the other, such as in the case of the Bologna concordat, possess a common basis: the affirmation of the Christian supremacy of France, and of the conformity of the Gallican Church with that of the time of the apostles. This certainty explains the stormy attitude of Their Very Christian monarchs and subjects in their relationships with the papacy. But beyond such anti-Roman squabbles, Gallicanism was a sanctification of the French nation, source of its cohesion and unity. Could this unity survive religious pluralism? In the tradition of the work of Mario Turchetti[2] – who barely touches on the Gallican aspect – it is this tension between the

---

*   Translated from the French by Elizabeth Kapff.
1.   Christin, O. (1997), *La paix de religion. L'autonomisation de la raison politique au XVIe siècle,* Paris: Seuil.
2.   (1984) *Concordia o tolleranza? François Bauduin (1520-1573) e i moyenneurs,* Geneva: Droz.

Gallican ideal of a single Church and the reality of religious pluralism which the present article will address, particularly in the years 1560-1563 which saw the monarchy hesitate before the adoption of a policy of tolerance.

Gallican pride still held sway into the mid-1550s, one of its essential components being that France, alone amongst Christian kingdoms, had never known heresy. Indeed, Saint Jerome asserted in his treatise *Contra Vigilantium*: 'Gaul alone has no monsters', a sentence which became almost proverbial in Gallican rhetoric. Given this context, the blinkered view of French leaders in relation to the growth of the Reform is understandable. For a long time sovereigns, their entourage and the leaders of the French clergy considered it as merely a German phenomenon, and most unlikely to affect the kingdom of France. The Gallican superiority complex remained unaffected by the early manifestations of religious dissidence within the kingdom, and repression was deemed to be sufficient response. In 1548 Cardinal Du Bellay felt justified in informing Henri II that 'the very best of theology is to be found in your kingdom' and that 'your Gallican Church is the greatest, the most whole and the least contaminated in respect of faith and morality'.[3] In 1550, Charles de Marillac, French ambassador to the court of Charles the Fifth of Spain, suggested that the king should oppose the meeting of a council called for by the Emperor to settle the German religious crisis, since France had no need for it, still less so 'your Church which remains catholic and without taint of these [Lutheran] doctrines'.[4] Rude was the awakening when the authorities became aware of the new religious situation. For a growing number of the king's subjects, to be French no longer meant to be a member of the ancient Gallican Church. Religious unity which, coupled with loyalty to the Crown, cemented the French nation together, was cast into doubt and repression on its own was unable to remedy the situation, especially as the death of Henri II weakened the monarchy.

The religious crisis, far from dispelling Gallican ideology, seemed to act as a stimulant: after all, had not all this come to pass because of ecclesiastical abuses in general, and those of Rome in particular, denounced by Gallicanism for the last three hundred years? Was not the

---

3.   Ribier, G. (ed.) (1666), *Lettres et mémoires d'Estat des roys, princes, ambassadeurs et autres ministres sous les règnes de François premier, Henri II, et François II (...)*, Paris: François Clouzier et la Veuve Aubouyn, t. 2, p. 164, letter from Rome, 14 September 1548.
4.   *Ibid.*, p. 280. Letter dated 22 July 1550.

only way to restore harmony to return to the moral purity of apostolic times, preserved by the Gallican Church – according to itself – more effectively than any other? The vast majority of those in power felt this to be the case. For them, the monarchy alone could prevent a religious pluralism which would be incompatible with political order, and maintain the old Gallican unity of faith. The natural inclination of Gallicanism in these crisis years would seem to tend towards a solution in the Anglican mould.

Affinities between these two ecclesiologies certainly exist,[5] and became apparent from the very beginning of the crisis between Rome and Henry VIII. After the Boulogne/Calais meeting in October 1532, the stand taken by the English and French sovereigns against Charles the Fifth and Clement VII aroused a certain degree of hope amongst Protestants: François I was apparently going to convene the clergy at Christmas in order to establish a Gallican patriarchate independent of Rome.[6] Ill-founded though this rumour proved to be, it accurately represented the attitude of the king, who sent the Cardinals Gramont and Tournon to Clement VII with a threatening brief.[7] Tensions were released when the Pope turned away from alliance with the Emperor, but the Gallican patriarchate remained a choice weapon for the French monarchy whenever relations with Rome became strained. Such a novel approach must be emphasised here: previously, sovereigns preferred to call for a council to be convened.[8] But the failure of the council of Pisa, and above all the mistrust of François I and his successors regarding an assembly which might threaten their control over the Gallican Church, led to the French abandoning in part their preference for such councils. The theme of the patriarchate reappeared at regular intervals during the 1530s and 1540s,

---

5. Salmon, J. H. M. (1987), 'Gallicanism and Anglicanism in the age of the Counter-Reformation', *Renaissance and Revolt. Essays in the intellectual and social history of early modern France*, Cambridge: Cambridge University Press, pp. 155-188. See also Bouwsma, W. J. (1971), 'Gallicanism and the Nature of Christendom', Molho, A. and Tedeschi, J. (eds), *Renaissance studies in honour of Hans Baron*, Florence: Sansoni, pp. 809-830.
6. Herminjard, A. L. (ed.) (1878), *Correspondance des Réformateurs dans les pays de langue française*, Geneva: H. Georg, t. II, p. 464, letter from Thomas *** (Italus) to Guillaume Farel, Bâle, 9 December 1532.
7. Hamy, A. (1898), *Entrevue de François Ier avec Henry VIII à Boulogne-sur-mer*, Paris, p. CCLXXV *et seq.*
8. Gazzaniga, J.-L. (1984), 'L'appel au concile dans la politique gallicane de la monarchie de Charles VII à Louis XII', *Bulletin de littérature ecclésiastique*, 85: pp. 111-129.

keenly observed by Henry VIII who hoped to win France over to the
anti-Roman side.[9]

The lessening in importance of the council and its replacement by
the patriarchate is evident at the time of the Gallican crisis in 1551. After
having talked of calling a national council, Henri II had the intention of
creating a patriarch, the plan of which formed the object of a memorable
seance of the king's council in August 1551. The cardinal of Lorraine
appealed to the king's conscience and appeared to convince him not to
continue with this initiative.[10] Short-lived though it was, this crisis of
1551 is nevertheless revealing: as Marc Venard has shown, the monarchy was unveiling a project of Gallican Reform, undeniably connected to
a wish for counter-reformation. The rupture with the Pope in no way indicates that the king felt any leanings towards Protestantism. On the
contrary, the edict of Châteaubriant, dated June 27, 1551, reinforces
measures of repression. This point lies at the heart of our argument: the
Gallicanism of the king was by its very essence intolerant, not only because it had to prove its orthodoxy in order to justify its rupture with
Rome, but above all because as it identified itself exclusively with the
monarchy, the imperative of religious unity became all the more crucial.

Ten years after the Gallican crisis, the affirmation of royal power
over the Gallican Church seemed to be the only way to avoid religious
pluralism. But to maintain Gallican unity, the monarchy not only had to
be involved in ecclesiastical organisation, but also to resolve liturgical
conflicts and questions of dogma. The temptation to follow the Anglican
model was without doubt most attractive during these first years of the
1560s in France. At the end of 1561, a member of the Parlement, Paul de
Foix, praised the results of the policy of religious colloquia, which he
attributed, interestingly enough, to the English sovereigns: 'and indeed

---

9.   In 1538, at the time of the proposed marriage between Henry VIII and Marie de
      Guise, the king of England advised François I to establish a patriarch in France, and
      asked him to nominate the cardinal Jean de Lorraine. Castillon, L. de and Marillac,
      C. de (1885), *Correspondance politique de MM. de Castillon et de Marillac, am-
      bassadeurs de France en Angleterre 1537-1542*, Kaulek, J. (ed.), Paris: Félix Alcan,
      p. 61, Castillon to the king, London, 19 June 1538.
10.   Lestocquoy, J. (ed.) (1966), *Correspondance des nonces en France Dandino, Della
      Torre et Trivultio (1546-1551)*, Rome-Paris: Presses de l'université grégorienne-E
      de Boccard, p. 507. On the Gallican crisis, see Romier, L. (1911-1912), 'La crise
      gallicane de 1551', *Revue historique*, 108: pp. 225-250 and 109: pp. 27-55, and Ve-
      nard, M. (1981), 'Une Réforme gallicane? Le projet de concile national de 1551',
      Revue d'histoire de l'Eglise de France, 47: pp. 201-225.

behold the Saxons and English, who by their nature have always been given to factions and sedition, living in great unity and harmony'.[11] To achieve a similar exemplary unity, the king of France could and would have to reorganise the Gallican Church. Overtly Erastian treatises increased dramatically from 1560 onwards. Of course they did not all explicitly allude to the English example, choosing rather to refer to Gallican history, and above all to this mythical golden age supposedly represented by the period of the Franks.[12] A '*Traicté de la puissance et authorité des roys*', published by Claude Gousté in 1561, by royal command according to the author, readily takes up this example, together with those of the king of Israel and of the Christian Emperors, in order to assert: 'The grandeur of royalty occupies the first and most eminent position in the Church'; 'the overall responsibility for the Church and Kingdom belongs with the king as ordained by God; thus it follows that, after God, he is the general governor of the Churches'.[13] The king can, therefore, call national councils, preside over them and even require the participation of his officials as 'a part of the royal corps'.[14] French leaders, and above all Michel de l'Hospital, whilst not stating it categorically, shared this conviction that the king should reform the Gallican Church in order to maintain religious unity.

But what kind of reform exactly? Once again, the Anglican model had its followers, notably those in the entourage of Odet de Châtillon, a figure who remains poorly understood,[15] whose religious stance is all too often judged to be that of his brothers. This cardinal, together with certain French bishops such as Jean de Monluc and Jean de Saint-Gelais, dreamed of a Gallican Church which would preserve the old episcopal structure whilst adopting the theology and a certain number of liturgical

---

11. Smith, M. C. (1993), 'Paul de Foix and Freedom of Conscience', *Bibliothèque d'Humanisme et Renaissance*, 55, p. 313.
12. Salmon, J. H. M. (1990), 'Clovis and Constantine. The Uses of History in Sixteenth-Century Gallicanism', *Journal of Ecclesiastical History*, 41: pp. 584-605.
13. Gousté, C. (1561), *Traicté de la puissance et authorité des roys, et de par qui doyvent estre commandez les diettes ou conciles solennels de l'Eglise...*, no place of publication, fo. 14 and 15 v°.
14. *Ibid.*, fo. 61 v°.
15. T. Wanegffelen only refers to him in one note, (1997), *Ni Rome ni Genève. Des fidèles entre deux chaires en France au XVIe siècle*, Paris: Honoré Champion, pp. 186-187. He explains this by writing 'les sources d'une étude de la sensibilité et l'évolution religieuses du cardinal de Châtillon font défaut'. This is true for direct sources, but inferences can at least be made from indirect sources.

practices of the Reform. Thus would the Reform take root in France in the footsteps of the Gallican tradition and this continuity of ecclesiastical ministries, starting with the episcopate, would enable them to take issue with Catholic attacks on the unrecognised status of ministers of the Reform.[16] Châtillon, wanting to keep his benefices and persisting in wearing his cardinal's habit, even after his condemnation by Rome, intended thereby to place the new Church he so wished for on a firm and unquestioned footing in the steps of Gallican history. This desire for continuity even countenanced maintaining the supremacy of Rome. It was to Pius IV that Châtillon and friends sent their programme for reform of the Church and still in 1564, when the papal nuncio required him and his brother to submit to the decrees of the council of Trent, the disgraced cardinal gave the answer that he wished to maintain complete papal authority in France, particularly in the matter of benefices.[17] The dialogue was soon broken off, but remains indicative of Châtillon's ecclesiology, far removed from strict calvinist orthodoxy. It could be better compared with that of one such as James the First declaring to Parliament on the 19th March 1604: 'I acknowledge the Romane Church to be our Mother Church, although defiled with some infirmities and corruption, as the Iews were when they crucified Christ'.[18] These abuses were clearly outlined in the programme of reform sent to Pius IV at the end of 1561, and which had no doubt been previously submitted to the Queen Regent in or after August 1561.[19] It conjures up a picture of a reformed

16. This forms the crux of Claude d'Espence's argument against the Reform in his speech at the Poissy colloquium, Evennett, H. O. (1930), 'Claude d'Espence et son Discours du colloque de Poissy', *Revue historique*, 164, pp. 61-64. He had already tackled Bucer on this question at Strasbourg in 1546, and later Calvin during his visit to Geneva in 1548 when returning from the council of Bologna. Espence, C. d' (1568), *Apologie contenant ample discours, exposition, response et deffense de deux conférences avec les ministres extraordinaires de le Religion prétendue réformée en ce Royaume*, Paris: Nicolas Chesneau, p. 142 sq.
17. BAV, Patetta 1153, fo. 293 v°, Santa Croce to Gallio, Paris, 23 January 1564.
18. Patterson, W. B. (1997), *King James VI and I and the reunion of Christendom*, Cambridge: Cambridge University Press, p. 35.
19. De Thou mentions that Catherine de Medici herself had apparently sent a very similar programme in her name in August 1561, (1734), *Histoire universelle depuis 1543 jusqu'en 1607*, t. 4, (1560-1564), London, pp. 78-79. He seems to have confused her plan with its actual realisation. The Queen Mother would never have committed herself thus far, and the correspondence of the nuncio Santa Croce or that of the legate Hippolyte d'Este shows clearly that the programme was not sent to Rome until after the failure of Poissy, and only in the name of Châtillon, and that of his friends, BAV, Patetta 1153, fo. 7 v°, Santa Croce to Borromée, Poissy, 15 No-

Gallican Church capable of maintaining the religious unity of the kingdom.

From the very beginning of the text, the Pope finds himself being reminded of the distressing discord in the kingdom of France, which the authors are convinced that he will wish to remedy by all possible means. A quarter of the kingdom has broken itself off from communion with the Church, and amongst this number are gentlemen of good family, educated men, wealthy citizens and others of some social standing, as well as soldiers and other ordinary people with some experience of the world. Such a party thus possesses military force, intellectual power and financial wherewithal, which makes a return to unity through the exercise of force impossible. A civil war would, moreover, ruin the kingdom and leave it a prey to neighbouring states, and the weakening of France would only harm the Holy See which would thereby lose its main supporter.

A peaceful return to unity was possible, as the Christians who had broken away from the Church were neither anabaptists nor heretics. They shared the same creed and recognised the decrees of the first six ecumenical councils. 'Differences of opinion should not prevent all Christians being within the Church, under the obedience of the Holy See, just as in antiquity the various ways of celebrating Easter, of organising fasts and ceremonies, as much in the administration of sacraments as in the ways of serving God, did not prevent all from being Christians communicating one with another.' This would moreover be the means to achieve a general reconciliation of Christendom. Even if that was unattainable, the French ills had to be remedied, to avoid an exodus of those still remaining within the Church. The programme of reform was as follows: remove all images from altars and locate them in places certain not to incite idolatry; reform baptism ceremonies, making the procedure of exorcism at least optional; give communion under both kinds to the laity, prepare them to receive the sacrament through prayers and exhortations in French, but abolish any adoration of the Eucharist; authorise the use of French in Mass, during which all participants must receive communion; authorise the singing of psalms and prayers in French, following directives issued by the bishop of each diocese.

---

vember 1561. The Italian version of the text is published in (1967), *Concilium Tridentinum*, t. XIII, Fribourg-en-Brisgau: Herder, pp. 517-525.

Such a programme may appear utterly utopic, but it must be remembered that it was in fact religious pluralism which seemed so in the eyes of contemporaries. Upholding Gallican unity by means of such a compromise was not the isolated plan of Cardinal Châtillon and certain other prelates seduced by the Reform. Catherine de Medici, albeit with extreme caution, conducted a policy inspired by the same principles in her convening of the assembly of Poissy and organising the Saint-Germain talks. Even after the Edict of January and the start of the civil war, she continued to cherish hopes, witness her instructions to the French ambassadors at the council of Trent and those given to the Cardinal of Lorraine some months later. The Queen Regent requested the fathers of the council not to 'stubbornly insist on such things as pertain to civil rather than divine law, which things can without offending the conscience be left alone and changed, in order to accommodate more easily those who have broken away from us and our Church'.[20] The points in question were communion under both kinds, the use of French in the liturgy and the singing of psalms.[21] The same desire for the reunification of Christendom through a greater autonomy of national Churches is to be found in the Cardinal of Lorraine, who was nevertheless an enemy of the Châtillons and held at a distance by the Queen Mother. This shared concern thereby explains the entire religious policy of the cardinal, from the Amboise conspiracy to his visit to the council of Trent, and notably his negotiations with the Lutheran princes of Germany.[22] In June 1561, he proposed to them an agreement on the doctrine of the sacraments by returning to the practices of the ancient Church, without adhering to overly constrictive formulations of dogma.[23] At Poissy, the cardinal even stated to Bèze: 'As far as transubstantiation is concerned, I do not believe a schism exists in the Church'.[24] At the meeting in Saverne with the Duke of Wurtemberg in February 1562, he went so far as to make significant

---

20. Tallon, A. (1997), *La France et le concile de Trente, 1518-1563,* Rome: Ecole française de Rome, p. 832.

21. *Ibid.*, pp. 836-837.

22. Tallon, A. (1997), 'Les Guise, pionniers de l'œcuménisme?' in *Homo Religiosus. Autour de Jean Delumeau,* Paris: Fayard, pp. 361-367.

23. The text is edited by Evennett, H. O. (1930), *The cardinal of Lorraine and the council of Trent,* Cambridge: University Press, pp. 485-497 and in *Concilium Tridentinum,* t. XIII, pp. 464-497.

24. Aubert, H., Meylan, H. and Dufour, A. (eds) (1960), *Correspondance de Théodore de Bèze,* Geneva: Droz, t. 3, p. 134 sq., letter from Bèze to Calvin, Saint-Germain-en-Laye, 25 August 1561.

concessions, taken rather too quickly by his interlocutors to be a conversion to Lutheranism.[25] In fact, as a good Gallican, the cardinal wanted to restore the unity of the universal Church by granting extensive national autonomy. Each individual Church, while remaining in communion with the others and respecting the primacy of the Roman See, would be able to settle on the liturgical formulations, and even those of dogma, best suited to its situation. Of course, Lorraine had no intention of going as far as Cardinal Châtillon and was much more concerned to keep within the perspectives of Christendom. But the principle of his religious policy remained the same.

Such programmes did not exist merely as ideas, but took concrete shape in initiatives on the part of certain priests attempting to apply them. The most famous is that of Antonio Carracciolo, bishop of Troyes, who tried to become the bishop of Protestants as well as Catholics.[26] His failure is well-known, as is that of the liturgical experiments undertaken by Odet de Châtillon and his curate Louis Bouteiller in the diocese of Beauvais. This failure is traditionally interpreted as that of a 'third way' easy to link with Christian humanism, despite the vagueness of this notion. But this third way is above all a Gallican one, which explains why Geneva no less than Rome felt unable to identify with this Gallican Church as remodelled by Châtillon, or even with the projects of the Cardinal of Lorraine. Papal rejection was undoubtedly the most significant factor, leaving the king to stand alone in the search for a solution which would maintain Gallican unity; and the absence of Rome's collaboration seemed to point towards the English model.

However, it was this very model which constituted the principal reason for its failure to attract France. No in-depth study has been undertaken on the French view of England's religious evolution, but it does appear to have been a somewhat negative one. The first reason is simply due to the persistence of old antagonism, which was hardly alle-

---

25. Muntz, A. (ed.) (1855), 'Entrevue du duc Christophe de Wurtemberg avec les Guise à Saverne', *Bulletin de la société d'histoire du protestantisme français*, 4: pp. 184-196.

26. On Carracciolo, see the ground-breaking thesis of Roserot de Melin, J. (1923), *Antonio Carracciolo, évêque de Troyes (1515?-1570)*, Paris: Letouzey et Ané, and the more recent works of Johnson, Burns L. T. (1994), 'The politics of Conversion: John Calvin and the bishop of Troyes', *The Sixteenth Century Journal*, 25: pp. 809-822, and of Wanegffelen, T., *op. cit.*, pp. 229-253. For the lack of results in the field, Roberts, P. (1996), *A city in conflict. Troyes during the French wars of religion*, Manchester: Manchester University Press, p. 64 sq.

viated at all by the new rivalry with the Habsburgs. The English were still the enemy as of old. At the States General at Orléans, Michel de l'Hospital expressed his horror at the discord within the kingdom caused by religion: 'See how a Frenchman and an Englishman of the same religion are more friendly than two citizens of the same town, subject to the same overlord, but who are of different religions'.[27] It was no coincidence that the chancellor took as his example the anglo-huguenot alliance: strong religious feeling led to connections with one's country's arch enemies. After the peace of Amboise, when Catherine de Medici attempted to reconcile Catholics and Huguenots, she deployed troops which had just been confronting each other on the battlefield, against Le Havre, occupied by Elizabeth. The winning back of Le Havre on July 30, 1563 was presented by the monarchy as proof of France's regained solidarity in a war with foreigners,[28] a constantly recurring theme during the wars of religion, but first used against the English rather than the Spanish.

This animosity explains why the majority of the French considered the Anglican Reformation to be a counter-model. In France, Henry VIII was seen as a tyrant in the grip of seriously unbalanced behaviour. Charles de Marillac, French ambassador to London, criticised the Anglican bishops in these terms: 'So that they appear to be good and faithful ministers, when dealing with real obedience, they allow their king to interpret, add, subtract and do more, in the matter of divine law, than the apostles, their vicar apostolics and successors ever dared undertake; so that through their fine reasoning, everything he says must be taken as the law of God or oracle of the prophets, and they want not only to attribute to him the obedience due to a king, to whom belongs all honour, obedience and service here on earth, but also to make of him a veritable statue for idolatry'.[29] The execution of Fisher shocked the French court, according to the evidence – no doubt biased – of the nuncio Rodolfo Pio di Carpi: the king, Cardinal Du Bellay and Admiral Chabot de Brion told him of their disgust, and Pio di Carpi was able to conclude that the long alliance with England was no more than a memory as a result of Henry

---

27. L'Hospital, M. de (1993), *Discours pour la majorité de Charles IX et trois autres discours*, Descimon, R. (ed.), Paris: Imprimerie Nationale, pp. 83-84.
28. See L'Hospital's speech at Rouen in *Ibid.*, p. 99 sq.
29. Castillon, L. de and Marillac, C. de, *op. cit.*, p. 211, Marillac to Montmorency, London, 6 August 1540.

VIII's religious policy.[30] The death of Thomas More caused even more lasting condemnation: decades later, Jacques Auguste de Thou, notwithstanding his great admiration for Henry VIII and the Anglican model, noted that Edward VI 'died on the same day that Henry his father had had Thomas Morus beheaded; as though the unjust death of such a great man demanded expiation by that of Henry's own son'.[31] The English example discredited any notion of a State Church in the eyes of the very people, jurists and humanists, who might have been its natural allies.

This discredit was still in evidence during the Gallican crisis of 1551, and undoubtedly affected the outcome of the conflict. Cardinal Jean Du Bellay, hardly a sympathiser with the Holy See, left court 'on the pretext of my continuing fever, so as not to witness what will happen there'. Indeed, as he wrote to the abbé de Mannes: 'There is no doubt that if the Pope does not think long and hard, and soon, and does not make some changes to what he has done, things here in France will become extremely difficult for him, and I cannot but consider that, whoever might win or lose, he will have thereby caused the ruin of the Holy See. Because although the intention of the king is not to withdraw from obedience to the Church, but only from Julius, its minister, nevertheless I see clearly what will happen eventually. The start of it in England was slow, perhaps even more gentle than it is here now. But the end was as we have seen. The marriage between their king [Edward VI] and the eldest daughter of our king was agreed on, and the treaties drawn up. Too many things will be seen to bear a similar stamp. In short, the Pope will be able to boast of having ruined the Holy See for ever.'[32] While Du Bellay made Julius III entirely responsible for the conflict, he nonetheless disapproved of the plan for an independent patriarchate, explicitly backing up his argument with reference to the English religious evolution.

Of course, in 1561-62, voices could be heard pointing out that at least England had safeguarded its religious unity. Still more numerous,

---

30. Lestocquoy, J. (ed.) (1961), *Correspondance des nonces en France. Carpi et Ferrerio 1535-1540*, Rome-Paris: Presses de l'université grégorienne-E de Boccard, p. 47, Carpi to Ricalcato, La Fère, 4 July 1535.

31. Thou, J.-A. de, *op. cit.*, t. 2, p. 405.

32. (1903), Letter to the abbé de Mannes, 18 August 1551, *Revue de la Renaissance*, 4, pp. 176-177.

however, were those emphasising the persistent Catholic opposition.[33] The French ambassadors seized every opportunity to call attention to its existence, if necessary exaggerating its importance. Bertrand de La Motte-Fénelon, giving his account of the 1569 Catholic uprising in the north, saw in it a just punishment for a queen who had done her utmost to prevent the re-establishment of religious unity in France, thereby causing the civil wars, and who was henceforth suffering the same troubles in her realm.[34] The illusion of religious unanimity through a Church of the State was dissipated, and with it the last vestiges of the Anglican temptation.

The English counter-example was not the only factor preventing the king from imposing on rival denominations his conception of religious unity. The very diversity of Gallicanism did not lend itself easily to an Erastian solution. This was evident at the Poissy assembly. Much more than a hypothetical religious dialogue, this assembly convened by the king was to redefine the relationship between the monarchy and the Gallican Church, within the new framework of the political and religious crisis. This essential aspect has been neglected by historians who too often sum up the assembly as an abortive discussion between ministers and prelates.[35] But at Poissy it was above all a question of knowing whether the regent and her advisers could reform the Gallican Church and to what extent the French prelates would agree to collaborate with temporal power in order to maintain French religious unity, which included compromises rejected by the Papacy. The answer was clear right from the start of the assembly's negotiations: in reply to the very ambiguous opening speech of Michel de L'Hospital on July 30, 1561, the prelates declared that they were not a national council, but a simple assembly, and that all their resolutions were to be submitted to the

---

33. La Boétie, in 1561, writes thus: 'Je sçay bien qu'il y a grand nombre d'hommes en Angleterre qui, en leur cœur, ne sauroint approuver la religion de leur royne et qui tiennent l'esglize romaine pour la vraye et appostolicque'. La Boétie bases his argument on the absence of places of worship for Catholics in England, maintaining that French Protestants should therefore be forbidden them, (1983), *Mémoire sur la pacification des troubles*, Smith, M. (ed.), Geneva: Droz, p. 94.

34. (1838) *Correspondance de Bertrand de Salignac de la Mothe-Fénelon, ambassadeur de France en Angleterre de 1568 à 1575*, Paris-Leipzig: Brockaus et Avenarius, t. 2, p. 397, letter to the king, London, 17 December 1569.

35. The ecumenical perspective of Nugent, D. (1974), *Ecumenism in the Age of the Reformation: the Colloquy of Poissy*, Cambridge (Mass.): Harvard University Press, seems to me to be anachronistic.

judgement of the Pope.[36] Thus the Gallican episcopate asserted its refusal to accept without question the wishes of the monarchy, these moreover being expressed with such caution that all clarity was lost. L'Hospital's evasion, in refusing to give Cardinal de Tournon the written version of his speech, is in this sense significant. In spite of promises of submission to the Holy See, Châtillon and his friends were relegated to the sidelines. After the appearance of Théodore de Bèze, Lorraine, who had the responsibility of answering the reformer, began his speech by reminding the king that sovereigns are members of the Church, and not its leaders. Thus episcopal Gallicanism warded off the encroachment of royal Gallicanism. Inspired by a moderate episcopalianism, the articles of reform proposed by the French prelates dealt only with ecclesiastical disciplines. Many of the points raised at Poissy were, moreover, taken up again at Trent, which was to facilitate the rallying of ecclesiastical Gallicanism with the Tridentine Reform. Etienne Pasquier neatly evaluated the legacy of Poissy when he asserted: 'The assembly is over; after its break-up, we quite openly possessed three different religions in France: one whose preaching resounded the name of Christ, another echoing the name of Jesus in its synagogues and a third, that of us traditional Catholics, we who in our Churches recognise the merit of our faith in the unique name of Jesus Christ'.[37] The only nuance we can add to this statement concerns the reality of the existence of a Church of traditional Catholics, to be understood as that of royal Gallicanism. In actual fact, this latter was unable to establish itself firmly in the face of ecclesiastical Gallicanism.

This split between the two Gallicanisms was the real foundation stone of religious pluralism in France. The Gallican Church having rejected unity imposed by the monarchy, it remained to this latter only to orchestrate the peaceful coexistence of the two denominations. Unity was not renounced without strong opposition, notably that of the Parlements who set themselves up as the bastion of the united Gallican tradition, which the monarchy appeared to be abandoning.[38] Those in power, however, had not lost all hope of a return to unity sometime in

36. Roserot de Melin, J. (1921-1922), 'Etudes sur les relations du Saint-Siège et de l'Eglise de France dans la seconde moitié du XVIᵉ siècle. I: Rome et Poissy', *Mélanges d'archéologie et d'histoire de l'Ecole française de Rome*, 39, pp. 94-95.
37. Pasquier, E. (1982), *Le Catéchisme des Jésuites*, Sutto, C. (ed.), Sherbrooke: éditions de l'université, pp. 144-145.
38. Daubresse, S. (1998), 'Le Parlement de Paris et l'édit du 17 janvier 1562', *Revue historique*, 299: pp. 515-547.

the future, sooner or later, and nearly all contemporary texts written in defence of the new policy of tolerance agreed that this solution was but a last resort, after the failure of all the others. This is evident in the opinions submitted to the regent at the time of the preparation of the January edict by Parlement's Arnaud Du Ferrier, Paul de Foix and Christophe de Harlay. The latter two stressed the fact that it was only necessity that compelled tolerance, a return to unity being infinitely preferable.[39] For Harlay, the desire to authorise only the religion of one's forefathers was a laudable one, certainly, but unenforceable: 'I do not know the Judge who would dare try to lay hands on ten or twelve thousand men gathered together'.[40] Like Paul de Foix, he learnt his lesson from the failure of Poissy: the prelates merely made 'canons to preserve their grandeur, authority, plurality of benefices and privileges' [41] and gave proof of their inability to reform the Church, just like the Pope and the General Council. It was therefore up to the king to do it, according to Harlay, even though he took advantage of the occasion to repeat all Parlement's criticisms of royal Gallicanism since 1516: 'It is absolutely fitting that the Church which was devastated and deformed by Kings who shamefully handed out benefices, should be reformed by a King'.[42] This reform pending – since it would take considerable time – one could not do other than concede churches for the Protestants.

Arnaud Du Ferrier's view is distinguishable from that of the others due to his total absence of nostalgia for a single Church. Religious diversity held nothing monstrous for him, and he felt that coercion on matters of conscience was the root cause of the troubles. Du Ferrier reminded people that forcing those who were reformed to live according to the Catholic faith would be to deny Gallicanism: 'The faith of the Gallican Church [is] in several aspects contrary to the faith of the Church of Rome, such as in procurations, annates, dispensations, transferral of sees, and other powers claimed by the Pope against the honour of God, and the holy decrees and councils of the Church, which the Gallican Church, the Sorbonne and parliament have never approved'.[43] In a decidedly

---

39. See these writings in BN, Fr. 4766, fo. 24 v°-35 v°, studied and edited in part by Smith, M. C., (1994) 'Paul de Foix', *op. cit.*, et 'Early French Advocates of Religious Freedom', *The Sixteenth Century Journal*, 25, pp. 40-46.
40. BN, Fr. 4766, fo. 34.
41. *Ibid.*
42. *Ibid.*, fo. 35.
43. *Ibid.*, fo. 26 v°.

original manner, Du Ferrier here reverses the traditional relationship between national Gallican consciousness and religious pluralism: far from destroying the French nation, this pluralism confirms it in its independence from Rome.

Such a postulate implied a painful reappraisal of all the founding myths of Gallicanism. Though not sharing Du Ferrier's positive vision of religious pluralism, Paul de Foix and Christophe de Harlay likewise emphasised the precedent set not only by Christian, but also Jewish and pagan history, in the matter of religious tolerance. Out of the same tendency towards historical reappraisal came the rediscovery of heresies in France's past. Already at the States General of Orléans, Michel de L'Hospital had had no hesitation in unearthing the Albigensian precedent,[44] even though it contradicted Saint Jerome and Gallican pride in its entirety. This was only the first step of a reconsideration of the whole Gallican past, which was to be the work of erudite Gallicanism in the second half of the century. Whilst these scholarly Gallicanists, who were linked with judicial circles, usually took a hostile stance in relation to religious pluralism, nevertheless their concern to reassess French history can also be explained by this new fact, that of the coexistence of religious beliefs, and the need thereby to adapt the founding myths of national consciousness.[45]

These diverse Gallicanisms thus played very different roles in the evolution towards a religious pluralism of which none of them, however, approved. Due to the political crisis, royal Gallicanism was no more able than was the Gallicanism of Parlement to impose the solution of a Church of the State, a concept in any event seriously devalued by the Anglican counter-model. Ecclesiastical Gallicanism rejected it completely and reasserted its twofold allegiance to the Pope and the king, the prerequisite of its twofold liberty in the face of royal and pontifical absolutism. But the reassertion of the freedom of the Gallican Church also liberated the monarchy, which could not accept religious pluralism in the framework of a Church of the State. Resistance to the attractions of the Anglican example on the part of the Gallican Church meant that those in power were able to organise the coexistence of different religious beliefs,

---

44. L'Hospital, M. de, *op. cit.*, p. 86.
45. On this last point, see Parsons, J. (1997), *Church and Magistrate in Early Modern France. Politics, Ideology and the Gallican Liberties, 1550-1615*, Ph.D, John Hopkins University. I am extremely grateful to Jotham Parsons for having passed on to me his unpublished work.

on the grounds that this was inevitable. In this sense, the Gallican exception explains the French exception of legally recognised tolerance in Reformation Europe and, paradoxically, it is the fidelity to Rome, 'in spite of it all', of the French episcopate, or rather the old balance between papacy and monarchy, to which Protestantism owes its official acknowledgement. In refusing any pact, the Gallican Church had made a policy of tolerance unavoidable.

Nostalgia for a single Church did not, however, disappear; on the contrary, it was even the origin of the logic of extermination of part of French Catholicism, and not only of the mythical 'ultramontane party'. But, when the murderous passions of the civil war subsided, religious pluralism was not really under threat from the anti-Protestant tirades of the Gallican Church or the never-ending complaints from Rome, and it became incorporated into the interplay of coexisting religious beliefs far more swiftly and easily than its displays of indignation might have led to suppose.[46] In a kind of ritual, the protests of the Pope and the French clergy confirmed the monarch in his comfortable role as arbiter. The real threat for religious pluralism came from the periodical return of Erastianism, with the king wanting to change his role of arbiter to that of leader. The moments of tension between Rome and the monarchy, those when rumours of a Gallican patriarchate resurfaced, were also those when the monarchy attempted to re-establish a single religion in France. This axiom holds true up until its last manifestation, that of the revocation of the edict of Nantes in the heat of the crisis between Louis XIV and Innocent XI. The complex relations between Gallicanism in its different guises and religious pluralism were brought to a close at that time, in an inverted 'French exception' which, like the first, was the envy of few in Europe.

46. Tallon, A. (1998), 'Rome et les premiers édits de tolérance d'après la correspondance du nonce Santa Croce', Grandjean, M. and Roussel, B. (eds) (1598), *Coexister dans l'intolérance. L'édit de Nantes*, Paris-Geneva: Labor et Fides, pp. 339-352.

PENNY ROBERTS

Religious Pluralism in Practice:
The Enforcement of the Edicts of Pacification[1]

The edicts of pacification which punctuated the French Wars of Religion represent a unique attempt to bring about a *modus vivendi* between the faiths in a country particularly riven by the confessional tensions stirred up by the Reformation. This essay concentrates on the first years of the attempted reconciliation of Huguenot and Catholic which were to prove decisive in shaping the course of the pacification process up to and including the 1598 Edict of Nantes. Indeed, it is arguable that the Edict of Nantes cannot be understood without reference back to the experience of the attempts at peace of the previous thirty-seven years, of which it was a continuation, as well as a significant beneficiary. Since the early 1560s the pacification of the confessionally-divided realm had become the main concern of crown business. A major factor in the enforcement of such a policy was the appointment of commissioners to oversee and en-sure the implementation of the terms of the edicts throughout the provinces. In addition, the role of provincial governors, as well as that of the local judiciary and royal officials was to prove decisive, whether in assisting or obstructing the commissioners in their work. As discussed elsewhere in this volume, the impact of local tensions and disputes was also influential with regard to the acceptance of the terms of the peace in a particular province or town.[2] The problems which faced the commis-sioners in enforcing the royal will in the localities, and their ultimate failure to do so, can go some way to demonstrating why the goal of re-ligious pluralism was never to be fully realised in sixteenth-century France. In view of its flaws, it is perhaps more remarkable that the crown

---

1. The relevant edicts discussed in this paper are: Edict of Saint-Germain (January 1562); Edict of Amboise (March 1563); Edict of Lonjumeau (March 1568); Edict of Saint-Germain (August 1570); Peace of Monsieur (May 1576); Peace of Fleix (No-vember 1580); Edict of Nantes (April 1598).
2. See the essays by Conner and Watson in this volume.

persevered with such a policy than that successive commissions failed in brokering the peace.

It is evident that religious pluralism in sixteenth-century France was not to involve anything like equal recognition of the 'new' Protestant faith, or true 'toleration' as we would understand it.[3] The edicts represented no more than a means by which to return the realm to peace by bringing an end to the divisions between the faiths which had first led to civil war, as stated in their preambles and, indeed, argued by historians since. Nevertheless, by according the Reformed Church in France some status, however restrictive, the edicts provided a tacit acknowledgement of its right to exist and so lent it a legitimacy which had not been their primary intention. Yet for the Huguenots too, the edicts were a mixed blessing: on the one hand granting them certain rights and privileges, whilst on the other imposing strict limitations upon them. As both sides sought to present themselves to the crown as the more loyal upholders of the edicts, so these inherent contradictions were reinforced, and the Huguenots' room for manoeuvre, in particular, was restricted. From their inception, therefore, the edicts generated antagonism on both sides: Catholics considering the terms far too generous and Huguenots that they fell far short of meeting their needs. This was the atmosphere which confronted the commissioners who were sent out by the crown to implement the edicts in the provinces of France. But before turning to a more detailed examination of these commissions, and in particular the problems which the commissioners faced in enforcing their charge, it is first necessary to consider briefly the initiation of this process on the eve of the religious wars.

The first commissions specifically to deal with the implementation of the terms of an edict were sent out following the publication of the Edict of Saint-Germain on 17 January 1562, just six weeks prior to the outbreak of hostilities between the faiths which later became known as the first civil war. It is notable that, on this occasion, the commissions appear to have been confined to the particularly troublesome provinces of the south and west: to Provence, Languedoc and Guyenne. Such was the intensity of the existing confessional divisions in these regions that the commissioners were to find their task impeded at almost every turn. Furthermore, they were to prove so unsuccessful in reconciling the trou-

---

3.   For contemporary definitions of concord and tolerance see Turchetti, M. (1991), 'Religious Concord and Political Tolerance', *Sixteenth Century Journal*, 22: 15-25.

bles in Provence that it was to be the only province to gain exemption from the subsequent edict of 1563 regarding the establishment of official sites for Reformed worship, despite the appeals of other areas who claimed that their case for exemption was just as good.[4] Nevertheless, whatever its other difficulties, the impact of the 1562 edict was to prove short-lived as a result of the outbreak of armed conflict in the spring of that year. It was not until twelve months later with the ending of the first war that another edict, that of Amboise and the first of the so-called edicts of pacification, was published by the crown, establishing a pattern of provision and resistance that was to continue into the next century.

The commissions of 1563 were officially inaugurated by a royal declaration of 18 June outlining the specific duties that the commissioners were expected to undertake.[5] These appear straightforward enough. First, they were to ensure the enforcement of the provisions of an edict where they were not already established, including the disarming of the faiths, the freeing of religious prisoners, the return of or compensation for property taken, the reinstatement of Huguenots to office and ecclesiastics to benefices, and the provision of sites for Reformed worship and burial. Equally, they were to bring to justice those who contravened these provisions, as well as to arbitrate in any outstanding disputes. But the problems that the commissioners faced were many and various: local dynamics and a past history of tension (especially in those towns which had suffered badly during the first war); differing interpretations of the edicts by both sides in their own self interest, itself a reflection of the lack of clarity in some of the articles which further complicated its enforcement; and obstruction by governors, parlements and municipal authorities who were supposed to assist the commissioners in execution of their charge.

Thus, beyond the contents of their provisions, the most important aspect of the edicts was to be the nature of their enforcement, or rather the attitude and authority of their enforcers. The task of enforcing the edicts was initially entrusted to the leading military commanders of the day (notably in 1563 the *maréchaux* de Bourdillon, Montmorency and

---

4. On the Provence commission, see Bibliothèque Nationale, Paris (hereafter BN) MS fr. 3186, fos. 53-5r; 3189, fo. 58r; Archives Départementales (hereafter AD) des Bouches-du Rhône (annexe), B 3328, fos. 754-85r.
5. BN Imprimés, F 46824 (Actes Royaux), no. 3.

Vieilleville), assisted by the provincial governors and their lieutenants.[6] This might not seem to have been the most auspicious choice, considering that these were the same individuals who were to lead royal forces against the Huguenots in the ensuing wars. Yet both sides seemed willing to set aside their differences in their concern to enforce the edicts: the *maréchaux* and governors as representatives of the crown, and the Huguenots both to demonstrate their loyalty and, probably more so, because their position in many areas was often favoured by the edicts. However, the need for a more judicially-minded resolution to the problems of enforcement resulted in the subsequent appointment of commissioners to assist the commanders. They were to be drawn from among the councillors of the French *parlements*, as well as other high-ranking royal officials, notably the *maîtres des requêtes*. The paperwork that these commissions generated – correspondence and reports, as well as petitions to the crown from both faiths – forms the bulk of our evidence relating to the practicalities and problems of enforcing the edicts in the localities.

In many ways the actions of those charged with enforcing the edicts reveal very prosaic concerns. For the military commanders in the provinces their primary concern was security, and they were, on the whole, not prepared to compromise on this issue whatever the contents of the edicts, as reflected in the tension between the needs of war and pacification described by the governor of Burgundy, Gaspard de Saulx-Tavannes. He complained that the commissioners sent to enforce the Edict of Amboise of 1563 in the towns under his jurisdiction were in fact endangering the security of a frontier province through issues such as disarmament, whereas the commissioners argued that they were simply enforcing the royal will as stated in the edict.[7] Local authorities – both members of the royal administration and municipal officials – were also instructed to assist the commissioners in their enforcement, but shared the military's concerns over security. For them, too, the keeping of order was of primary importance. Only if this could be guaranteed were they prepared to accept the concessions granted to the minority (usually Huguenot) faith.

---

6. On the appointment of the *maréchaux*, see La Ferrière, H. de (1885) *Lettres de Catherine des Médicis*. 10 vols, Paris, vol. II, p. 42 (18 May 1563); BN MS fr. 20507, fos. 101-2r.

7. BN MS fr. 4634, fo. 129; 4635, fos. 13-14r.

It is evident that the royal commissioners, as members of the judiciary, viewed their charge as primarily one of enforcing the law as defined by the edicts. This brought them into conflict not only with the local authorities, military and administrative, but also with both faiths who interpreted the purpose of the edicts rather more broadly than the strict observation of their terms allowed. It is clear that many, both Catholic and Huguenot, were to be disappointed by the contents and enforcement of the edicts. This was due not least to the lack of clarity in their provisions, which the commissioners themselves found hard to interpret once faced with the realities on the ground. It is not surprising then that some did not feel that the commissioners got it right, or indeed believed that they were using their own judgement rather than enforcing the law. However, whilst the commissioners were not infrequently accused of failing in their charge, on closer examination they do appear, on the whole, to have been unwavering in upholding the terms of their commissions. A couple of examples should suffice to illustrate this point.

The remonstrances to the crown in 1563 by the Huguenot nobility of the region of Le Mans, in which the commissioner Gabriel Myron was singled out as being 'le plus pernicieux, injuste & miserable homme que la terre porte', emphasise his professional arrogance rather than confessional bias, concluding that he 'n'est pas tant dévotieux papiste que méchant juge', acting therefore through malice rather than religious zeal.[8] This reflects the general view of the remonstrances that those sent to enforce the edicts 'se sont estimez plus sages que l'Edict de pacification', judging not according to the equity of the law but 'selon leurs passions particulières'. Interestingly, the petitioners of Le Maine also believed that previous commissions to the region had been deputed by the 'papists' in place of more moderate appointees. As it turns out, one of those about whom they were complaining, Jean Lavau, was a chief suspect on a Parisian police report of 1562, which accused him of attending Huguenot assemblies at which he received the sacrament.[9] This does not sit at all comfortably with accusations that he and his colleague favoured Catholics and turned a deaf ear to the complaints of, and a blind eye to the crimes committed against, Huguenots, rather than keep-

---

8. In Sécousse, D.-F. (ed.) (1743) *Mémoires de Condé*. 6 vols, Paris, vol. V, pp. 301-27, esp. 302-10.
9. BN, MS fr. 4047, fos. 8-10r. See also Taber, L. (1990) 'Research Note: Religious Dissent within the Parlement of Paris in the Mid-Sixteenth Century: A Reassessment', *French Historical Studies*, 16: 684-99 (esp. 'Appendix', 699).

ing a balance between the faiths. So how can we explain such a discrepancy? One way of doing so is to consider the terms of their commission; for although they are accused of having violated the edict, the commissioners' suppression of judicial actions against past misdemeanours is entirely consistent with the edict's instruction for how to go about reconciling the faiths: that only crimes which had been committed since the edict was published should be prosecuted. Indeed, in other situations, commissioners would complain that the faiths were bent on using their commissions as a means for exacting vengeance on their adversaries for offences committed during the war, contrary to the royal will that past enmities should be forgotten and that the faiths should live henceforth in peace. Here, it does seem to be a matter of the distinction between the hopes and expectations of the faiths that justice would be seen to be done for all crimes against them and the commissioners' observation of the letter of the law as instituted by the edict.

An earlier example can serve to highlight the problems inherent in the interpretation of the edicts, as well as the tensions between the royal commissioners and vested local interests. In early 1562, Nicolas Compaing along with Guillaume Girard, had been sent to enforce the Edict of January in the province of Guyenne. However, the two men were to be accused of favouritism towards the Huguenots, having fallen out with the provincial military commanders, Monluc and Burie, as well as members of the local nobility and clergy, over their interpretation of the edict with regard to the provision of Huguenot ministers. Disillusionment set in quickly; for whilst on 1 February Burie could state that Compaing was highly regarded and beyond suspicion so that 'j(e l)'aymerais myeulx en ma compagnie que cent harquebusiers', by 18 March he and Girard had been replaced in their duties by two councillors from the parlement of Bordeaux.[10] With hindsight, Blaise de Monluc emphasised the commissioners' religious bias in his memoirs, as well as revealing another (and perhaps more influential) cause of his growing distrust and hostility towards them. Whilst remarking on the commissioners' arrogant refusal to obey royal directives, Monluc adds that Compaing and Girard claimed 'qu'ilz estoient les principaux commissaires, et que nous n'avions authorité aulcune, sinon de leur tenir main forte à l'execution de leurs

---

10. BN MS fr. 3186, fos. 1, 36-7r.

arrestz'.[11] Monluc retorted that, as he understood it, the commissioners were answerable to the commanders and not the other way around.

The issue of clashes over precedence with regard to the edicts is also familiar from the commissioners' relations with other local authorities. In particular, members of provincial parlements (and sometimes municipal authorities) might feel that their authority was being eroded or undermined by the commissioners' activities. This was in turn reinforced by royal insistence that, although they should assist the commissioners in the execution of the edicts, these officials were not otherwise to be given the details of any of the cases being pursued, which in the event of difficulty were to be referred back to the *conseil privé*. The councillors of the parlement of Bordeaux protested against this state of affairs as early as March 1562, attempting to convince the king that everyone's best interests would be served by employing the existing local judiciary as his predecessors had done.[12] The first edict to end a war, the Edict of Amboise generated particular controversy during its period of enforcement from 1563 to 1566. At Toulouse, Grenoble and Châlon-sur-Saône, disagreement arose over the commissioners' attempts to restore confiscated property to the towns' Huguenots, with the authorities defending the rights of those who had bought the property in good faith during the troubles and disputing the legality of the commissioners' position.[13] Tensions also flared in Toulouse as well as in Lyon over the reintegration of Huguenots to office; whereas judicial sensitivities in Valence were offended by the overriding of municipal privilege.[14] Despite such complaints, on the whole the local authorities complied with the edicts and those sent to enforce them, using the official channels to protest against those decisions they thought detrimental to keeping order. The commissioners, for their part, argued that it was not their own will but that of the king which they were enforcing, which none, therefore, could contradict.

What is most striking for our purposes in the case of Compaing and Girard versus Burie and Monluc in Guyenne, however, is not so much

---

11. Ruble, A. de (ed.) (1866) *Commentaires et Lettres de Blaise de Monluc, Maréchal de France.* 5 vols, Paris, vol. II, pp. 360, 364-65.
12. BN MS fr. 3159, fos. 39-40.
13. Archives Municipales de (hereafter AM) Toulouse, AA 127, fos. 126-9; GG 830. AM Grenoble, BB 23, fo. 123. On Châlon, see BN MS fr. 4637.
14. On Toulouse, see AD de la Haute-Garonne, B 57, fos. 65-9, 72-4r. AM Lyon, BB 83, fos. 132-3. Archives Communales de Valence, BB 6, fos. 239-40.

the issue of jurisdictional precedence but the difference of opinion over the interpretation of the 1562 edict. According to the commissioners, the commanders had decided that, where there had been no Huguenot minister previously, one should not now be permitted, despite the fact that this ran contrary to the tenor of the edict. For, as the commissioners pointed out, it clearly penalised those who had actually obeyed earlier royal prohibitions on having a minister and holding services, instead of allowing them to benefit from the edict. They requested that a declaration be sent to clarify this point since 'aultrement il demeureroit beaucoup de personnes sans religion'.[15] Only a few days earlier, the commanders had stated their position. They declared that there were already too many ministers and sites of worship in Guyenne, also requested clarification of the edict's terms, and expressed their hope that they could chase out the newly established ministers.[16] The Cardinal of Armagnac also added his voice to the rising complaints against the commissioners, confirming that they had been granting permission to all those who had asked them to establish a minister in their town, even though, he argued, 'suyvant l'edict', the consent of the local lord, the priest and the churchwardens was necessary.[17] In fact, according to the terms of the edict, this restriction was accurate in the case of ministers travelling from place to place preaching, but not as a general rule for those who were in residence.[18] Whilst it appears, therefore, that on this occasion the commissioners had the letter of the edict correct, nevertheless, the complaints of the local authorities were sufficient to undermine the execution of their charge.

Aside from clashes over precedence with local officials and doubts about the impartiality of the commissioners, other contentious issues threatened to jeopardise, and certainly impeded the progress of the commissions in reconciling the faiths. These included the designation of sites for Reformed worship and burial, and the return of property confiscated

---

15. BN MS fr. 3189, fo. 59 (17 Mar.).
16. BN MS fr. 3186, fos. 60-1r (13 Mar.).
17. BN MS fr. 3159, fo. 41r (15 Mar.).
18. For the text of the 1562 edict, see Fontanon, A. (1585) *Les Edicts et Ordonnances des roys de France*. 2nd edn, Paris, vol. IV, pp. 1053-1055; and Stegmann, A. (1979) *Edits des Guerres de Religion* (1979), pp. 8-14, and specifically on this issue, p. 12.

and sold during the troubles.[19] It was not only Huguenots who sought restitution and compensation; Catholics did so too, in Protestant strongholds such as at La Rochelle, and in Orléans after its occupation in 1562-63. In claim and counter-claim, the faiths competed to present themselves to the commissioners and the crown as the moderates, the voice of reason, in each dispute, as reflected in the arguments they employed, in their concern, as Christin has shown, to stay within the law.[20] Equally, the dynamic of the confessional balance in a region could affect the sorts of obstructions which the commissioners faced as well as the nature of their attempts at pacification.

In 1563, René de Bourgneuf and Pierre de Masparrault conducted a four-month expedition through Poitou, Aunis, La Rochelle and Saintonge, a region notorious for the defiance of its Huguenot inhabitants who in many communities held the upper hand. The commissioners visited the main towns of the region and reported back on their attempts to enforce the Edict of Amboise.[21] They were to find themselves dealing with a delicate situation in which both faiths had to be persuaded to forget past enmities and to respect the authority of their commission. In particular, Catholic clergy continued to be victimised and terrorised by local Huguenots preventing the effective restoration of Catholic worship. In neighbouring Guyenne, Antoine Fumée and Jerosme Angenoust, faced non-cooperation from a different source, the parlement of Bordeaux, who (as we have seen) had appealed unsuccessfully to play a more participatory role in enforcing the 1562 edict. This stalemate continued for about a month. However, although Fumée reported with relief on 6 September 1563 that the parlement was now complying with their commission, he was also worried by the sheer volume of the caseload

---

19. I have written elsewhere about the disputes surrounding sites for Reformed worship and burial: Roberts, P. (1998) 'The Most Crucial Battle of the Wars of Religion? The Conflict over Sites for Reformed Worship in Sixteenth-Century France', *Archiv für Reformationsgeschichte* 89: 247-267; and Roberts, P. (2000) 'Contesting Sacred Space: Burial Disputes in Sixteenth-Century France', in B. Gordon and P. Marshall (eds), *The Place of the Dead: Death and Remembrance in Late Medieval and Early Modern Europe*. Cambridge: Cambridge University Press, pp. 131-148.

20. Christin, O. (1997) *La paix de religion: l'autonomisation de la raison politique au XVIe siècle*. Paris: Editions du Seuil, p. 104.

21. For the commissioners' correspondence with the crown: BN MS fr. 15878, fos. 110, 141-142r, 209-210. Barthélemy, E. de (1877) 'Lettres historiques du XVIe siècle', *Archives historiques de la Saintonge et de l'Aunis* 4: 296-297 (this letter is wrongly dated to 1569).

which they now faced.[22] Furthermore, Fumée lamented, he was now to be left to undertake the commission on his own as a result of Ange-noust's departure, 'tant pource qu'il craignoit de tomber malade que pource qu'il a desesperé qu'entre tant de contrarietez de ceux qui vous debvoyent faire obeyr, et avec tant de menasses que l'on nous a faict', there was little more that he could do.

Illness and other forms of adversity also disrupted other commissions. A neat solution was found in the case of those sent to the contiguous south-eastern provinces of Provence and Dauphiné in 1563 by ordering the remaining healthy members of each, Jacques Phelippeaux and Jessé de Bauquemare, to team up and undertake the commissions jointly.[23] However, such a solution also reflects how enormous could be the task that faced the commissioners in trying to cover large areas at a time of slow communications and difficult transport conditions. In 1570, Philippes Gourreau and François Pin, were assigned to a huge area encompassing the Orléanais, Touraine, Chartrain, Le Maine, Berry, Poitou, Aunis, Anjou and Brittany, reflecting a general shift in policy towards fewer and more geographically wide-ranging commissions.[24] Undertaking such charges could even prove life-threatening, as Jacques de Bauquemare discovered when he was shot at in the course of his duties in Languedoc in 1563, the culmination of longstanding tensions with local groups. Following this incident, the king commented that if the incident was not dealt with effectively it might deter others from serving in this capacity.[25] Further deterrents faced by the commissioners included financial problems, since they were often expected to meet the initial costs of a commission themselves, although the crown promised them reimbursement. The unreliability of the royal finances is reflected in the repeated appeals which demonstrate the difficulties encountered in recovering their expenses, as Jessé de Bauquemare and Phelippeaux were to find.[26] Even where commissions were successful, the crown had to rely on local officials to maintain the good work since long-term enforcement proved problematic. As a result, in 1565, the crown was to establish specific commissions or *chambres neutres* (fore-

---

22. BN MS fr. 15878, fos. 98-9r, 112r, 130.
23. AD de l'Isère, B 2379, fo. 290.
24. BN Imprimés, F 2177.
25. BN MS fr. 3204, fo. 10.
26. BN MS fr. 15879, fo. 146r; 15880, 37r.

runners of the *chambres mi-parties*) of councillors from the provincial parlements to deal with outstanding disputes.[27]

In conclusion, it is necessary to consider how the pacification process developed during its first decade, and what this can tell us of changing crown policy or as a presage of what was to follow, not only in 1598, but in the intervening years which also witnessed repeated attempts to establish a lasting peace between the faiths. The 1563 edict was perhaps the most ambitious of the edicts in practice and thus, for this reason as well as others, of particular interest. Notably, it represented the first attempt to establish a nationwide commission for the enforcement of an edict (the enforcement of 1562, as we have seen, was mainly confined to the particularly troublesome provinces of the south and west). It was also perhaps the most optimistic of the edicts in terms of what could be achieved, as well as the approach of the crown to the establishment of a lasting peace between the faiths. Later commissions were to be more pruned back, with fewer commissioners dealing with larger areas. Furthermore, it lasted for four years, during the lull between the first and second wars; France would not see such a long opportunity for the enforcement of a religious peace until Nantes some thirty-five years later. This holds true despite the evident exception of the Peace of Fleix of 1580, for arguably by this time the situation had changed, with the negotiations being mainly directed towards the provinces of the south and west where the Huguenot minority was then concentrated. In 1563 Huguenot strength was still considerable throughout the country before the movement was pushed back on the defensive to its south-western strongholds, though it can be argued that its erosion was already evident, not least with regard to the commissions' inability to enforce the provisions of the 1563 edict.

In view of these points, we can see the limitations of the commissions sent out to enforce the edicts of Longjumeau and Saint-Germain in 1568 and 1570 respectively. Although they were constituted on much the same lines as those of 1563, and with similar personnel, there was too little time for the royal will to be enforced effectively. The commissions of 1570 did not begin implementing the peace until the beginning of 1571, and were brought to an abrupt end by the 1572 massacres of Saint

---

27. On the establishment of a *chambre neutre* in Provence, see AD des Bouches-du-Rhône, B 3331, fos. 107-110, which mentions their earlier establishment in the jurisdictions of the parlements of Paris, Toulouse, Bordeaux and Dijon.

Bartholomew. Indeed, it can also be argued that royal enthusiasm for establishing cordial confessional relations had waned as a result of the Conspiracy of Meaux of 1567 which led to the second war. The incident made Catherine de Medici in particular distrustful of the Huguenot leadership for its part in the plot to kidnap the king.[28] Although the process re-established some of its momentum under Henry III, notably in 1576 and 1580, it was soon to be subsumed into the wars of the League and the renewed confessional antagonism which accompanied this conflict.[29]

It is undoubtedly true that the Edict of Nantes was to establish a long-lasting if uneasy and fragile solution to the troubles, but in essence it was a product of these earlier attempts to establish peace, and imitated many of the same strategies to bring about confessional reconciliation. Thus we see the re-establishment of the judicial commissions, including the setting-up of panels comprising judges of both faiths (along the lines of the earlier *chambres neutres* and *chambres mi-parties* of the 1560s and 1570s), the designation of sites and limited freedom of worship as well as other legal rights for Huguenots, the reconciliation of outstanding disputes, the granting of security towns and so on. The Edict of Nantes, as is often stated, also emphasised the temporary nature of the religious toleration which it espoused. No more than its predecessors did it envisage religious pluralism as anything but a means by which to end civil unrest in France. It is arguable that it was only more successful than earlier edicts because of the military and financial exhaustion of both sides in the conflict (and the French people in general faced by renewed economic crisis), as well as the peculiar personal guarantee by the first of the new dynasty of Catholic Bourbon kings, Henry IV, until recently leader of the Huguenots.[30] Furthermore, lessons had clearly been learned from earlier efforts at confessional reconciliation, for instance through greater clarification of the edict's terms, although it should also not be forgotten that it was in no way exempt from the sorts of obstruction which had limited the impact of its predecessors.[31]

---

28. On the Conspiracy of Meaux as a watershed in crown/Huguenot relations, see Knecht, R. J. (1998) *Catherine de' Medici*. London and New York: Longman, esp. pp. 121-122.
29. On the 1576 Peace of Monsieur, see Greengrass in next chapter.
30. Although see the discussion of this point in Trim chapter.
31. On this point see Hickey in this volume; and the most recent research on the edict, Greengrass, 'Epilogue'.

In some ways, then, the Edict of Nantes can be seen as justifying the policy of pacification that had been pursued by the crown, however intermittently, since the early 1560s, and without which Nantes itself could surely not have been implemented. This was due in no small part to the efforts of successive groups of commissioners who, despite determined opposition to their presence, conducted trials and settled disputes in the provinces to the best of their ability. It was through their exertions that the French crown was able to put into practice its chosen policy of allowing religious pluralism within its borders, in an experiment without either precedent or parallel. Although their achievements may have been limited, and were often eroded by subsequent events, the commissions demonstrated the crown's determination to see its edicts, with their tentative recognition of religious diversity, enforced.

MARK GREENGRASS

Pluralism and Equality: The Peace of Monsieur, May 1576

Although it is the pacification at Nantes that is the legislative high-water mark of French's adventure in pluralism, the peace of Monsieur of 6 May 1576 was, in fact, the most ambitious attempt at religious pluralism attempted by the French monarchy before the end of the eighteenth century. It only lasted seven months – but it was unique amongst the edicts of pacification in three respects. It emerged from, and was negotiated and accepted on the basis of, a unique degree of royal weakness. It had a different juridical basis from the other edicts of pacification, and one that was particularly threatening to the catholic majority. In consequence, it was the only edict of pacification to be overthrown quickly, overtly and demonstrably by public reactions to it. All three aspects bear further investigation since it was on the painful lessons of the earlier edicts of pacification that Nantes' success would be based.

Negotiating from Weakness

The basis for the negotiations leading up to the edict of Beaulieu were laid in the armistice agreed at Champigny-sur-Veude on 21 November 1575.[1] The politics of the situation is readily disentangled.[2] Armistices are often flimsy affairs. This one had been hastily constructed in talks

---

1. La Ferrière, Hector de and Puchesse, Gustave Baguenault de (ed.) (1880-1905) *Lettres de Catherine de Médicis* [hereafter *Lettres*] 9 vols Paris, 5, pp. 161-165 for the text of the truce; François, Michel etc (1959) (eds) *Lettres de Henri III roi de Fance* [hereafter *Henri III*]. 4 vols Paris, 2, Nos 1576 *et seq.* for the king's encouragement of it.
2. It is briefly analysed in Chevallier, Pierre (1985) *Henri III* Paris, pp. 305-324; Holt, Mack P. (1986) *The Duke of Anjou and the Politique Struggle during the Wars of Religion* Cambridge pp. 56-69.

held between the king's brother, Alençon and Catherine de Médicis, its prime architect. Alençon negotiated on behalf of the 'confederates' (as they termed themselves). These were the princely and protestant forces led by Alençon and his allies, the prince of Condé, the marshal Henri de Montmorency-Damville in Languedoc, his brother Guillaume de Thoré, and Johann Casimir of the Palatinate. The armistice tottered because the king was weak. In return for a six-month truce, he had agreed to pay half a million *livres* to the confederates' German mercenaries so long as they withdrew back across the Rhine. Six important Loire citadels were handed over to confederate troops who would be supplied and paid for the duration of the truce by the king. For his part, the king agreed to license all his foreign troops, save for his Swiss guards and his Corsicans. Plenipotentiaries would meet, it was agreed, in January 1576 and they must arrive at a definitive peace before 24 June, just over six months later when the armistice would run out.

Catherine had no illusions as to the crown's danger. She knew that the king had mortgaged his capital and credit since his accession.[3] The confederate's mercenaries were on French soil and could not be defeated by force.[4] She estimated that the mercenaries would badly damage the heartlands of eastern catholic France and that royal forces would arrive too late to stop them. So she would divide the confederates, beginning with the most amenable of them – the king's younger brother himself. Alençon's military host was small, his treasury empty, and, although perhaps not unsympathetic to the confederate cause, he hesitated to throw in his lot with a foreign army.[5] Then it would be the turn of Montmorency-Damville. She persuaded him to despatch his secretary Mathurin Charretier to her in December 1575 and held out the distant prospect of the marquisate of Saluzzo for him in exchange for his gov-

---

3. See Greengrass, Mark, 'Pieces of the jigsaw: French royal finances under the last Valois, 1574-1589' in R. J. Bonney and M. Ormrod (eds) (1999), *Crises, revolutions and self-sustained growth. Essays in European fiscal history, 1130-1830* Gloucester pp. 140-172; 'Faytes travaller avoyr de l'argent, car, en tous événemens, yl vous en fault et non peu' she urged the king in October 1575, aware of the precariousness of the king's finances and resources. Crosby, Allan James (ed.) (1880) *Calendar of State Papers, Foreign Series, of the reign of Elizabeth, 1575-1577* London p. 178 (Dale to Sir Thomas Smith and Francis Walsingham, 10 Nov 1575: 'It was concluded in Council that the King must of necessity accord to anything that might be demanded for lack of means to make war').
4. *Lettres*, 5, p. 145.
5. Holt, pp. 57-59.

ernment of Languedoc. She would talk as little as possible about the general terms for a settlement and concentrate instead on the particular demands of the various confederate princes – always the preferred tactic of the crown in peace negotiations during the civil wars. She would urge the king to stress aristocratic duty.[6] Above all, she urged dissimulation, talked of political 'transmutation'; 'yl set [i.e. se] fault transmeuer, non ceulement disimuler'.[7] 'Ballé li belles paroles, car y fault contenter tout le monde' was her advice.[8] Hide your true sentiments, cultivate what friends you can, play for time; 'et n'é plus temps de dire je ne puis dissimuler'.[9] But she knew that there were other voices in council, especially after the duke of Guise's rout of the small contingent of 2,000 protestant confederate forces from Germany led by Montmorency-Thoré in early October 1575 near Dormans. These siren voices intimated that the king should lead an anti-protestant crusade.[10] The rumours of a League were already to be heard in January 1576, picked up and doubtless magnified by the English ambassador in Paris, that seismograph of distant tectonic shifts amidst the Guise clan.[11]

The confederate French aristocrats – Condé, Thoré, Montmorency-Damville, Alençon – knew that finesse was the art of the moment. They should appear to be flexible and proclaim their loyalty to the king whilst seeking the high ground – proclaiming the general principles of an honest peace coupled with the reform of the kingdom.[12] They should refer

---

6. This was assisted by the sudden release of François, duc de Montmorency and Cossé on 2 October 1575.
7. *Lettres*, 5, p. 147.
8. *Ibid.*, p. 145.
9. *Ibid.*, p. 148.
10. *Ibid.*, p. 159. The queen mother was almost certainly referring to the duke of Guise, who had arrived back at court on 6 November, half his face sheathed in velvet and hardly able to speak from the wound sustained at Dormans. He was accompanied by other members of the Guise clan as well as the dukes of Nevers, Nemours and the Chancellor Birague (*Cal.S.P.For.*, *op.cit.*, pp. 179; 189).
11. 'There is a secret ligue made betwene the dukes of Guyse, Nemours, Nevers, Mayne and the rest of that house together with the Chancellor both defensiue against [the] Q[ueen] mother and offensiue against all that would haue any peace to employe them selfes by all meanes both to let the peace if they may and if it be made to haue forces in a readynes to begin a sharp war a fresh...' – Dr Dale to Walsingham and Smith, c.January 1576; PRO SP70/137 fo. 41.
12. As Casimir put it, glossing his instructions to his negotiations on 8 January 1576, they were to negotiate: 'pour l'aduancement de l'honneur et gloire de dieu restablissement de la france et paix et tranquillité non seulement de la france mays aussi des

all peace terms for approval to a wider forum. That way they would be less readily divided. At the same time, they knew that Casimir had his own agenda. There were Palatine debts to be settled going back to before 1570. His troops had mustered and were ready to march. But the confederates were determined to keep their armies in the field during the armistice. The memories of the 'meschante, petite paix qui ne dura que six moys' of Longjumeau less than a decade earlier, when they had felt betrayed as a result of a naïve disarmament, remained fresh.[13]

These were the strategies of both sides as they were played out in the months to May 1576. Playing for time, as Catherine advised, only worked if your opponents did not know your weaknesses. But the confederates did and they suspected the king, especially after the suspected poisoning of Alençon on 26 December and the flight of the king of Navarre from the court six weeks later on 5 February 1576. They heard the opposition on the ground from the inhabitants of La Charité and Angoulême, sustained by their governors, to the surrender of their strongholds to the protestants.[14] Despite the efforts of Gaspard de Schomberg in December 1575, succeded by Bellièvre and Missery, to negotiate with Casimir and Condé to get them to disperse, they failed. At least 20,000 in strength, the forces made a rendez-vous with those from the Swiss cantons around Metz at Christmas 1575.[15] On 9 January 1576 they crossed the Meuse; on 20 January they were pillaging in the vicinity of Dijon. Alençon, still hesitating over the armistice, received a delegation from Montmorency-Damville's secretary, Charretier. He had, so the memorandum Charretier presented to him, been duped in the armistice. He should make head for the south-west, join common cause with the 'catholiques unis', muster and then return to join the mercenaries at the Loire.[16] Alençon took the advice and the confederate forces eventually conjoined in March 1576 near Moulins, one of the largest armies of the French civil wars. Henri III desperately sought funds from individuals in the *chambre des comptes* and *parlement* of Paris and other 'welthy

---

aultres Royaulmes et prouinces...' (PRO SP70/137 fo. 6; Johann Casimir to Dr Dale, Camp de Chastelet).
13. Noue, François de La (1967) *Discours politique & militaires* Ed. F.E. Sutcliffe. Geneva, p. 712.
14. This opposition made itself felt in December 1575; see *Henri III*, 2, Nos 1619; 1621.
15. 8,000 horse, 6,000 Swiss and 7,000 *arquebusiers* according to reports from Cologne to Walsingham of 22 December – *Cal.S.P.For, op.cit.*, p. 207.
16. BN MS Fr 3354 fos. 59 *et seq.* ['Avis'].

men'.[17] He put the young and inexperienced duke of Mayenne in overall command of what forces he could muster.[18] With the confederates ready to march north towards Paris and impose terms on the king, Paris and St Denis prepared their defences.

The confederates proposed terms for peace in 93 articles that they drew up at Moulins in early March.[19] The origins for these articles lay, as Professor Sutherland noted, in petitions from the protestant Midi three years previously.[20] Isolated from their co-religionists to the north that had accepted the peace of La Rochelle in July 1573, the protestants of Languedoc met at Montauban on 25 August 1573.[21] Reflecting their numerical strength and the fluidity of protestant allegiances in the Midi, they demanded the most complete freedom of rights of religious worship, judicial equality before the sovereign courts and equal access to offices and educational institutions.[22] Even the proposed tribunals to investigate those engaged in massacres were to be 'en égal et pareil nombre des deux religions'. These clauses were reflected in the Moulins demands and reinforced by Casimir. His political experience had been in the framework of a smaller, unitary principality where pluralism could be imposed from a set of predetermined principles.[23] His deputies even proposed that, in places where there were several churches, the protestants should have the use of one or more of them, according to their

---

17. PRO SP70/137 fo. 60 (Dale to Burghley, 31 Jan 1576).
18. *Ibid.*, fol. 120 (Willes to Walsingham, 22 Feb 1576).
19. Bibliothèque de l'Institut de France MS Godefroy 95 fos. 10-28
20. Sutherland, N.M., (1980) *The Huguenot Struggle for Recognition* (New Haven and London), p. 228. I am grateful to Professor Sutherland for reemphasising the point in the discussions during and after the colloquium at which this paper was first presented.
21. The text is printed in Haag, Emile (ed.) (1846-1859) *La France Protestante* 10 vols Paris, 10, pp. 114-121; a contemporary copy, misdated and miscalendared, but also providing the 30 signatures to the petition and the king's reply of 18 Oct 1573 (Villers-Cotterets) is noted in *Cal. S.P.For.*, (1572-74) (London, 1876), pp. 456-458.
22. 'Et en ce faisant, ordonner que... l'exercice de leurs religion et discipline ecclésiastique sera libre à tousjours et partout en ce royaume, tant public que privé.'
23. His proposals were made ostensibly to prevent the kind of piecemeal collapse in the peace that had occurred in earlier efforts: 'considerant la pauurete de ceulx de la relligion et que legalite requise entre les deux parties pour conseruer paix et amitie ny est pas obserué ...' (PRO SP70/137 fo. ['Articles propounded...', Vansac, 1 March 1576]).

numerical strength. Where there was only one church, both confessions should share it.[24]

The king's reactions were negative.[25] He merely offered terms similar to those that applied in 1570.[26] There followed lengthy discussions in council with the king present.[27] A deal was almost struck on 31 March but it broke down three days later. Negotiations involving so many parties were bound to be difficult. On 13 April, the king agreed to the equality of worship and *mi-partie* tribunals.[28] Catherine de Médicis brokered the final negotiations, first at Nemours (uncomfortably close to the confederate army), later around Sens. The final draft of replies to the 93 articles was signed by Catherine de Médicis, Alençon, Navarre, Condé and Casimir on 2 May. The king added his signature to it four days later without further consultation from his council and the deed was done.[29]

The Edict of Beaulieu

The edict itself has a singularity that is often not recognised. Its short, abrupt preamble does little to prepare one for the considerable novelty

---

24. *Ibid*, article 2: 'Et pour faire led*it* exercise oultre la permission a eulx donne cy dessus lesdits de la relligion seront es lieux la ou y a plusieurs temples accommodes d'un ou plusieurs selon le nombre des auditeurs attendu quils ont este constraints par leurs predecesseurs aussy bien que par les Catholiques, et la ou n'y en a qu'un ils s'en pourront acomoder alternatiuement sans preiudice a la liberte den pouuoir construire de nouueaux si bon leur semble autant que leur seront necessaire'.

25. *Ibid.*, fo. 267 'the king him self hath brase out in great passions of late which he hath not ben wont to doe that he would aduenture crowne and life and all rather than he woulde condiscend to those demandes' (Dale to Smith and Walsingham, 25 March 1576).

26. *Ibid.*, fo. 276 et seq.

27. 'L'occupation que j'ai eue continuelle depuis quelques jours à délibérer sur le cahier qui m'a été présenté par les députés pour y faire réponse a été cause que je n'ai répondu à vos dépêches qu'à mesure que je les ai reçues' [Henri III to François de Mandelot, 28 March 1576].

28. *Cal.S.P.For.*, *op.cit.*, p. 308 ['Answers of the King of France to the Deputies'].

29. MS Godefroy 95 fos. 50-62.

that lies within it.[30] Some of the clauses reflected earlier edicts, especially that of St-Germain (1570). Like the latter, it was issued in the form of a royal charter, sealed with green wax and dated only by the month, 'perpetual and irrevocable'. This legal formality was essential to an edict that began with clauses that granted extensive clauses of perpetual amnesty.

Thereafter, however, the edict diverges fundamentally from the clauses of the edicts of pacification before and after it. In 1570, the key clauses which shaped the freedom of worship granted to protestants were organised into restricted categories that could be justified within the confines of particular privileges in sixteenth-century France. There were rights of worship allowed to Huguenot gentlemen whose estates had rights of *haute-justice*. Such a right could readily be seen as not much more than a small extension of a nobleman's legal rights and inheritance. There were clauses in 1570 that allowed the right of worship at two locations in each government in the kingdom. These would be determined by royal commissioners whose task was to decide the least controversial places for such worship to take place, a reflection of a privilege accorded by the king's pleasure. Then, there were rights to worship in locations where protestants could prove that, at a particular date, they had already established *de facto* rights of worship.[31]

In 1576, however, there is an entirely different perception of how to legislate for a religious minority. The edict does not work in terms of categories of privilege. Instead, it proclaims a genuine religious pluralism, unrestricted by place and unfettered by legal definition:

> 'Et pour ne laisser aucune occasion de troubles & differends entre nos subiects, auons permis & permettons l'exercice libre, public, & general de la religion pretendue reformee par toutes les villes & lieux de nostre Royaume, & pays de nostre obeissance & protection, sans restriction de temps & personnes, ne pareillement de lieu & places ...'[32]

---

30. The main body of the edict is contained in Fontanon, Antoine *Les edicts et ordonnances des roys de France, depuis St Loys: auec les verifications, modification, et declarations sur icelles*. Revised edition of the original 1580 compilation, undertaken by G. Michel with a table by E. Girard (ed.) (1611) 4 [bound in 3] vols. Paris, 3, 307-315. The 'articles particuliers' are summarised in *Cal.S.P.For.*, *op.cit.*, pp. 327-329.
31. Garrisson, F. (1950) *Essai sur les commissions d'application de l'édit de Nantes* Montpellier.
32. Fontanon, *op.cit.*, p. 307 [art. 3].

The principle it enunciates is not privilege but equality. The protestants were to be 'compatriotes' with the catholics, just as they had been 'concitoyens' with their confederate allies, the *catholiques unis*. The protestants were to have the same rights to sites of worship as catholics. There would be no need for commissioners for its execution because there would be no arrangements on the ground where the crown was obliged to mediate. This was presented as a way of avoiding the legal chicanery that had surrounded the implementation of previous edicts. There would be no need to assemble complex documentation, attend hearings before commissioners, prepare appeals to the privy council when decisions went against them, fight for their legal rights.

The principle of equality was extended to other areas of the edict as well, especially the legal system. Each sovereign court was to establish a chamber of the edict that would be equally bi-confessional, 'mi-partie'.[33] These courts would have specially created protestant judges 'aux mesmes gages, honneurs, auctoritez, prerogatiues, que nos autres Conseillers ...'. These clauses were in addition to the more familiar articles on the open and equal access to royal offices. There were various articles in the edict of Beaulieu that made it distinctive, not least the famous clause 58 that guaranteed the summoning of the estates general of the realm within six months. But it is the novelty of its juridical basis that lay at the heart of the reactions that it generated and the memories it left.

The memories emerge, three years later in February 1579. Once again, Catherine de Médicis was about to negotiate a peace with a protestant delegation, this time at Nérac. In their memorandum to the king on the eve of the negotiations, the protestants alluded to their difficulties with the peace of Bergerac; 'la continuation des dissentions et discordes civiles proceddant des défiances que la malice du temps et la passion et animosité d'aucuns turbulans et faccieulx espritz ont entreprins et qui produisent encores tous les jours les désordres, confusions et attentatz qui se voyent en plusieurs endroitz...'.[34] These were provoked because Bergerac, unlike Etigny, was based on specified privileges, complex to enforce and creative of local dissension. 'Ce qui ne procèdde d'ailleurs que de l'inégalité qui a esté par cy-devant entre les subjectz de ceste cou-

---

33. *Ibid.*, p. 309 [art. 18-20].
34. *Lettres de Catherine de Médicis*, 6, pp. 417 *et seq.* ('Articles présentés au roi', 4 February 1579).

ronne, non seulement en faictz politicques, mais encores plus au faict de la religion. Car tout ainsy que le vray moien d'une concorde entre plusieurs de mesme obéyssance, concitoiens d'ung royaume et compatriotes est l'égalité mère et nourisse de paix, aussy par le contraire de l'inégalité provient le mespris de ceulx qui sont moings favoriz'.[35] They wanted a return to the edict of Beaulieu: 'qu'il plaise de monstrer en tout une bonne et esgalle volunté envers tous ses subjectz, tout ainsy que le requiert d'eux et luy est deue pareille et esgalle obéissance, et ostant par ce moyen toutes occasions de deffiances'. As at Beaulieu, they wanted 'l'exercice libre publicq et général de la religion réfformée par toutes les villes et lieux de son royaume... sans aucune restriction de temps de personnes ny de lieux ...'. They wanted the equality that Bergerac had tempered, not least in the proposed *chambre* for Guyenne whose installation was still proving so difficult.[36]. In February 1579 they went beyond what had been granted at Beaulieu, requesting various *mi-partie* senechalcy and presidial courts as well as a share of the tithe for the maintenance of the pastorate.[37] Catherine de Médicis, to whom the petition was remitted for answer, rejected all these demands on the grounds that they were not within the letter, or spirit of the peace of Bergerac, unlike Beaulieu, the peace from which the crown pulled back decisively in 1577.

Initial reactions to the edict of Beaulieu amongst royalist catholics were mixed and ambiguous, especially in terms of its registration before the sovereign courts. Efforts were made to stifle any debate over the legal principles. In Paris, the king visited the *parlement* on 14 May. There was no debate. The king made a speech and the edict was published. It is possible that an undated copy of a speech in the king's own hand, including various corrections that he made to it, should be ascribed to this moment.[38] If so, it is a fascinating document. It reveals the king's subtle

---

35. *Ibid.*, p. 419.
36. 'Et comme la justice esgallement et bien administrée est l'ung des principaulx moyens pour entretenir la paix, aussi l'inégalle administration et distribution d'icelle et l'impunité proposée aux maleings, qui sont par ce moyen enhardiz à toutes sinistres actions, est grandement dangereuse et pernicieuze'. Cf Brives-Cazes, Emile (1874) *La Chambre de justice de Guyenne en 1583-1584* Bordeaux; Brives-Cazes, Emile "Le parlement de Bordeaux et la chambre de justice de Guyenne en 1582", *Actes de l'Académie impériale des sciences, belles-lettres et arts de Bordeaux* 27.Series 3 (1866), pp. 335-395; pp. 421-498.
37. *Lettres de Catherine de Médicis*, 6, pp. 418-421.
38. BN MS Fr 16512 fos. 288-290.

grasp of *realpolitik*, his political sophistication as he developed the arguments of political prudence and necessity. At the same time, the speech made clear that the king's heart was not in it, that it was an act negotiated by and attributed to his mother and one which he accepted as a necessity. The speech reflected none of the principles in the edict because there was no commitment to them. The debate thereafter focused not on the principles of the edict at all but on the offense to judicial privilege, in particular the creation of new offices for the protestant judges. On 1 June the king insisted that the court register the necessary letters patent for these.[39] The court prevaricated until 5 June arguing that, having not been allowed to debate the registration of the edict of pacification, it could not proceed to debate and publish the chamber that was a consequence of it. The objection brought the king before them once more on 7 June where he spent almost an hour before the letters patent were finally registered. There is something of a paradox in the fact that Beaulieu, the most radical of the edicts of pacification, received its legal enactment more rapidly than the other edicts of pacification in the wars of religion.

There is little doubt as to the reasons for this despatch. The German mercenary army under Johann Casimir was still on French soil. It refused to depart until the huge sum that the king had agreed to satisfy his debts had been paid. The king was due to deliver 1,700,000 *livres*, part of the 3 million indemnity and debt to which he was contracted, on or before 6 June 1576 at Frankfurt.[40] Not to have registered the edict by that date would have given him an additional reason to delay his withdrawal. As it was, the king knew already by 22 May that he simply could not raise that sum. The desperate financial contortions that the king was forced to resort to reveal the state of crisis that the Peace of Monsieur left in its wake. They culminated in the 'trageiocomedie' (as Dr Dale, the English ambassador described it) of Pomponne de Bellièvre, the king's *surintendant des finances*, arriving at Casimir's camp empty-handed. It was, thought Dale, 'more marvail the Reistres toke not their penyworthes of him'.[41] Under virtual house-arrest, Bellièvre negotiated a convention

---

39. Maugis, Edouard (1914) *Histoire du Parlement de Paris de l'avènement des rois Valois à la mort d'Henri IV*. 2 vols. Paris, 2, pp. 45-47.
40. *Cal.S.P.For., op.cit.*, p. 338 (Dale to Burghley, Paris, 5 June 1576).
41. PRO SP70/139 fol. 1 (Dale to Burghley, 6 July 1576).

with Casimir, signed by Bellièvre on 5 July 1576.[42] But the mercenaries would not finally leave France before the first week of August.[43]

By that date, other *parlements* had followed suit, especially those affected by Casimir's army. In Rouen, the edict arrived accompanied by letters from the king requiring its immediate registration: 'Toutes autres choses délaissées ayez à en faire les poursuytes et réquisitions nécessaires, avec telle et si vive instance, que nostre vouloir et intention soyent, en cest endroict, effectuéz et accompliz, sans différer ny le mectre en longueur, et sans y user d'aulcune restriction ou modiffication'.[44] It was registered on 22 May. In Dijon, it arrived on 26 May and enacted two days later, the fact being emphasised by a printed publication immediately afterwards.[45] In Bordeaux, too, it was not contested when it was registered on the same day as that of Dijon under the watchful eye of Monluc.[46] In Toulouse, on the other hand, there is no sign that it was ever accepted.[47] In all the courts, the difficulties would come at a later stage with the reception of protestant judges into their tribunals. This process was only beginning, however, by the time the edict itself was abrogated.[48]

---

42. See P. Chevallier, *op.cit.*, and, more recently, Poncet, Olivier (1999) *Pomponne de Bellièvre* Paris, pp. 87 et seq. The terms of the convention are summarised in PRO SP70/139 fo. 5. The details of the efforts to settle the Palatine debt are fascinating for what they reveal of the credit operations of the French monarchy at this date and deserve a fuller analysis.

43. *Henri III*, 3, No. 1982 (Henri III to Bellièvre, 15 Aug. 1576, Paris).

44. Floquet, A. (1840-1842) *Histoire du Parlement de Normandie* 7 vols Rouen, 4, pp. 161-162.

45. Drouot, Henri (1937) *La première ligue en Bourgogne et les débuts de Mayenne* Dijon, p. 83.

46. Portes, Charles Bon François Boscheron des (1878) *Histoire du parlement de Bordeaux (1451-1790)* 2 vols. Bordeaux, 1, p. 260.

47. Lafaille, Germain de (1687-1701) *Annales de la ville de Toulouse depuis la réunion de la conté de Toulouse à la Couronne ...* 2 vols. Toulouse, 2, p. 343: 'Je ne sçay si la même publication s'en fit au Parlement de Toulouse, ny s'il fût registré; car je n'en ay pû trouver sur le Registre'.

48. The difficulties in Paris were already apparent, however, by August, when the king wrote to the prince of Condé saying that the chamber for the edict 'seroit ja en exercice si ceulx qui ont esté a la nomination de mon frere pourveus des offices de conseillers en lad dicte court pour y servir se feussent presentez, ce qu'ils n'ont encore faict' (*Henri III*, 3, No. 1989, Henri III to Condé, 19 Aug 1576). The court had refused to receive Guillaume Dauvet, sieur d'Arennes as president of the *chambre* on the grounds that a president could not be accepted until all the councillors had first been investigated and accepted (Maugis, *op.cit.*, p. 47). The king wrote from Charleval to his privy council on the matter on the 25 June: 's'il semble que il y en

By that date, there was beginning to be more substantive criticisms of the underlying principles of equality in the edict. It is perhaps in this context that we should interpret parts of Bodin's famous treatise, published at that moment, especially the last section of it. He does not mention the edict but he outlines his prescription for achieving a proper distribution of justice. It should be undertaken, he says, not 'arithmetically' but 'geometrically'. 'Never was', he wrote, 'a commonweal where all the citizens were equals in rights and prerogatives'.[49] He returns to emphasise the point in the concluding section that may be a commentary on the Edict of Beaulieu. An arithmetic state, he writes, is governed by laws under which all are treated equally, a principle which would 'ruinate and destroy estates and Commonweals'. But if it is transformed into a harmonic pattern the result will 'serve well to preserve and maintain the same'.[50]

The Péronne Manifesto

The beginnings of the collapse of the Peace of Monsieur came a month after its publication. The immediate public reactions to the peace reveal a discrepancy between public acceptance and private antipathy. Its publication was not generally delayed.[51] In private, things were different. The principle of equality meant protestant worship in the walls of the major towns of France from which it had been excluded. In his private journal Pépin, canon of Dijon Cathedral, recorded that it was 'la paix la plus pauvre et la plus inique qui fût jamais'. But, with the recent memories of

---

ait qui veullent par ce moyen renversser ce qui a esté fait pour le bien et repos de mon royaume tant ilz sont passionnez en leur fait particulier, je m'asseure que lesdits Presidents comme ceux qui tiennent les premiers lieux de ceste Compagnie et qui ont aussy pluys de cognoissance que nuls autres deds causes qui m'ont meu d'accorder laditte Chambre, aulcuns d'iceulx ayant assisté à tout ce qui en a esté fait et traité, feront tousjours comme ils doivent tout ce qu'ils pourront pour l'execution de ma volonté ...' (*Henri III*, 2, No. 1914, pp. 458-459).

49. *Ibid.*, p. 49.
50. *Ibid.*, p. 761.
51. Ventadour, one of the confederates, apparently delayed its publication in the Limousin on the grounds that it did not reflect what had been agreed with Monsieur – *Cal.S.P.For.*, *op.cit.*, p. 338 (1 June 1576).

the pillage of Nuits and elsewhere by the mercenaries close by the city in January, it was not the moment to say so in public.[52] From Rouen, the cathedral chapter despatched a canon to the cardinal of Bourbon to negotiate an exemption for their city.[53] In Paris, there was a Te Deum to celebrate the coming of peace. As a significant gesture, the cathedral canons at Notre Dame boycotted the service; 'la disans estre plustost vn preparatif & recommencement qu'vn appaisement de troubles, & qu'au lieu de Te Deum, il estoit plus expedient chanter Tedium'.[54] Elsewhere, vocal opposition to the edict was muted and anonymous. Protestants complained of the activities of preachers at Troyes and around Chartres who denounced the peace and compared the king's capitulation adversely with Don John of Austria's flamboyant arrival in the Netherlands to lead the Spanish assault on the patriot opposition.[55]

Private antipathy became publicly demonstrable, however, in places where the protestants were given rights of garrison. Angoulême and Bourges, where the truce had already revealed antipathy, were joined by Péronne in Picardy. In the *articles particuliers*, the king granted the governorship of Picardy to Condé, where Péronne was a garrison town. Its catholicity was already well-known. After the peace of 1563, the town successfully petitioned the privy council through two local seigneurs, the seigneurs d'Estourmel and d'Happlaincourt, to prevent protestant worship there.[56] It was from Péronne that two texts emerged which have become known as the Péronne Manifesto. The first we know only from two contemporary pamphlet versions.[57] It is issued in the name of the 'prélats, sieurs, gentilshommes, capitaines et soldats, habitans des villes et plat pays de Picardie'. They were resolved to take oath to employ

52. Garnier, Joseph (ed.) (1864) *Livre de souvenance de Pépin, chanoine de la sainte-chapelle de cette ville [Dijon]* Dijon, p. 22.
53. Floquet, *op.cit.*, p. 161. The cardinal eventually promised to come 'l'un des prochain jours, et y faire quelque séjour, pour tascher, par tous moyens, à faire cesser les presches introduictes en ceste ville'; this he would do in an extraordinary, and public, gesture on 23 July 1576 when he marched in upon a protestant service and ascended the pulpit to preach before the assembled congregation. (*Ibid.*, pp. 165-166).
54. Préau, Gabriel du (1583) *Histoire de l'estat et svcces de l'église dressee en forme de chroniqve generalle et vniverselle* 2 vols. Paris, 2, fo. 625.
55. PRO SP70/139 fo. 45 (Dr Wyer to Henri III, n.d. [c.25 July 1576]).
56. Dournel, Jules (1879) *Histoire générale de Péronne*, Péronne, p. 20.
57. *Conspiration faicte en Picardie sous fausses & meschantes calomnies contre l'edict de pacification*, no place, 1576; *Articles de la ligue & association de quelques Catholiques ennemis de la paix establie en France* (n.p., 1576).

themeselves to the last drop of their blood 'pour la conservation de ladicte ville et de toute la province en l'obéissance du roi et en l'observance de l'Eglise catholique apostolique et romaine'. To do so, they established a 'saincte et chrestienne union, parfaicte intelligence et correspondance de tous les fidèles, loyaux et bons subjects du roi'. A local militia was envisaged under this a military chief who would also be advised by a council which would keep in contact with others in the province as well as its cross-border neighbours in the Southern Netherlands. They would keep a gentleman at court and a secret roll of signatories to the League. The second text, published alongside the first only by La Popelinière, Mathieu, Palma Cayet and d'Aubigné, amplified the arrangements for a confederation with other provinces.[58] For twenty years, though, doubts have existed about these texts' authenticity.[59] Manfred Orléa pointed out that there are no signed originals. The printed versions have no provenance. Protestant historians, notably La Popelinière, first published them. Could this not be protestant propaganda, repackaging protestant confederative ideas in catholic wrapping? If so, these publications were designed to strengthen the king's resolve to maintain the peace. The protestants would be loyal *compatriotes* against those who sought to disrupt it.

There is evidence, however, to suggest that they were based on documents that emerged from a meeting that we can date, whose membership we can glimpse, and whose context should lead us towards accepting their veracity. The fact that the catholic Claude Matthieu also published the second of the two manifestoes in 1594 gives some cause to doubt that it was uniquely a protestant tradition.[60] More significantly, however, we have the evidence of a contemporary historian from Péronne, a cathedral canon of the city, Gabriel du Préau. In 1583, he

---

58. Popelinière, [Henri Lancelot Voisin de La] (1581) *L'histoire de France Enrichie des plus notables occurrances suruenuz ez Prouinces de l'Europe & pays voisins, ... depuis l'an 1550 iusques à ces temps* 2 vols. La Rochelle, 2, fos. 319-321; d'Aubigné, Agrippa. *Histoire universelle* Ed. Alphonse de Ruble (1886-1897) 9 vols. Paris, 5, pp;. 97-108; Mathieu, Claude *Histoire des derniers troubles...* fos. 9-12; Cayet, Palma *Chronologie novenaire* Ed. Michaud and Poujoulat (1888) Vol. 12. Paris, pp. 13-14.

59. Orléa, Manfred (1980) *La noblesse aux Etats généraux de 1576 et 1588* Paris, pp. 37-38; cf Carroll, Stuart (1998) *Noble Power during the French Wars of Religion. The Guise Affinity and the Catholic Cause in Normandy* Cambridge, p. 163.

60. Matthieu, Pierre (1596) *Histoire des derniers troubles de France. Sous les regnes des rois tres chrestiens Henri III ... & Henri IIII* Lyon, fos. 9-13.

published an enormous 'general and universal' history of the 'state and success of the church'.[61] Du Préau's history reworked La Popelinière's account and its privilege mentioned that it was to be stocked in preference to the latter.

Du Préau gives a detailed account of the events in Péronne in May-June 1576 in which he had played a part. Condé was reintegrated into his government on 9 May. The sieur d'Humières was despatched to transfer authority to him in Picardy's towns. Three days later, the *échevins* in Péronne received a courrier from the Spanish ambassador about the strategic implications of a protestant garrison there and warned them to 'adviser diligemment à leurs affaires, & à pourvoir au contraire desdits accords'.[62] The following day, the town decided to send a delegation to the king. Du Préau was part of it. Their petition was to exempt the town from Condé's command 'ou bien que vostre plaisir soit leur donner terme de six mois pour eux retirer de ladite ville auec leurs femmes, biens, & familles, & prendre demeure ailleurs'.

Du Préau describes how they sought access to the king, first through one of the king's favourites (St-Luc) and then through the duke of Guise and the chancellor 'qui tous deux promirent s'employer pour ladite ville de bonne affection, signamment ledict sieur de Guise'.[63] They gained permission to wait upon the king in the antichamber as he went to Mass and present their petition. Henri promised it would receive attention. Getting a decision out of council, however, proved impossible. They were 'renvoyez de Cayphe à Pilate'. When they waited on the king a third time as he left the council chamber, he told them irritably that they should attend their turn '& leur fit declarer par autres qu'il se facheoit de si frequentes interpellations'. D'Humières passed them on to Villeroy who 'avoit charge & commandement de sa maiesté'. They stood outside Villeroy's lodgings until sunset and, the next day, waited until 3pm, by which time they were told he was unwell. It was back to d'Humières, and to way-lay other councillors in the king's antichamber whom they might badger for a decision. Eventually Villeroy's *commis*, Jules Gassot, told them that they could expect Condé to satisfy them and treat them with great favour.[64] When they met d'Humières later the same day it was

---

61. Préau, Gabriel du (1583) *Histoire de l'estat et svcces de l'église dressee en forme de chroniqve generale et vniverselle* 2 vols. Paris.

62. *Ibid.*, 2, fo. 624.

63. *Ibid.*, 2, fo. 625.

64. *Ibid.*, 2, fo. 626.

apparent that this was soft soap. The king's decision was final. They must obey the edict and allow Condé to reside in the city as specified in its terms. The one concession was that Condé would specifically ensure that the Catholic religion was given equal protection in the city along with the protestant faith. Otherwise, the garrison must be withdrawn and Biron had instructions to see to it. Their discontent was manifest. They had no reply to their original request (threat?) that those who wished should be allowed to leave the city. They had nothing in writing. They returned to Péronne via Senlis and shared their discontents with the *échevins* there. Nothing was said in public, but privately they 'entendirent de plusieurs d'entre les habitans, que puis que les choses estoient telles, plustost ils mourroient sur les remparts de leur ville, que de souffrir l'observance d'une religion du tout contrariant aux sainctes commandemens de Dieu & de son Eglise'.

The following Saturday, the local nobility assembled in Péronne and, alarmed by the delegate's report, decided to send envoys to court themselves. By the time they set off on 25 May, they knew that they had the support of 'grand nombre d'autres tant de la Noblesse de Picardie que d'ailleurs'. Meanwhile a commissioner from Biron, master of the king's artillery, arrived in Péronne to organise the dispersal of the magazine at Péronne castle. His authority was questioned and the town refused to let him carry out his instructions. Two further sets of instructions were issued, the third dated 27 May. When the latter arrived, the town inhabitants decided to postpone any decision until d'Humières arrived back from court. But the day before (4 June) he was due back, the town decided to take control of the castle itself. They placed it in the hands of *hommes d'armes* from the duke d'Aumale's company to public acclamation.

The next day, 5 June, Péronne saw arrivals from all quarters. Hearing of what had happened at the castle, local seigneurs, especially Michel d'Estourmel and Jacques Happlaincourt, 'qui sur tous les autres, comme les plus proches voisins de la ville, favorisoient les Peronnois' entred the town. Estourmel was proud of his family's traditions. His father had defended the town in 1536. His brother-in-law was *avocat du roi*, town clerk of Péronne. He entered with his grandson and following, followed at 2pm by Happlaincourt, 'en grande apparade, suyvi de trente- cinq ou quarente chevaux fort bien en couche, & grand nombre de Gentilshommes tous marchans en belle ordonnance de guerre'.[65] Happlaincourt was the duc d'Aumale's ensign and would become governor of the duchy of Guise in 1580.[66] These forces were the sinister welcome that greeted d'Humières back from court with instructions to enforce royal will and ensure the loyalty of its population. Arriving in the market square, d'Humières met the assembled ranks of Picard noblemen and 'ne se peut contenir de dire qu'on ne l'avoit voulu laisser entrer qu'avec de cinq ou dix cheuaux, & que neantmoins on laissoit bien entrer les autres avec autant qu'ils vouloient, dont on coniectura en luy quelque petite pique & emulation contre ceux de la ville'.

D'Humières descended from his horse and began heated debate with his opponents. The king 'leur tint parolles assez aigres & rigoureuses pour la surprinse & emparement qu'on avoit fait du chasteau'. France needed peace. The prince of Condé was 'fort amyable, doux & gratieux'. He would protected the town. They would not be vexed with impositions and subsidies. Their religion was guaranteed. They were in direct infringement of royal orders, their rebellion 'une preparation d'une haine à iamais contre iceluy pays'.[67] In reply Happlaincourt and others countered that they sought to protect the king and the 'bien public'. If the full strategic significance of Péronne had been appreciated it would never have been surrendered into the hands of Condé. The peace was false because everyone knew that 'elle seroit finalement cause de guerres & de troubles plus aspres que iamais'.

These debates 'rendirent aucuns d'entr'eux fort perplex & pensifs'. D'Humières had done something to secure the loyalties of the inhabitants and the surrounding nobility. Decisions about the castle's command were remitted until the following day, 6 June, when, following his success, d'Humières summoned a general meeting. The churchmen declared that they would follow the will of the nobility.[68] But the latter was clearly divided until two gentlemen arrived and turned the tide. One, Monsieur de Gomeron, was the governor of Ham; the other was the seigneur de Sainte-Marie, governor of Dourlans. Both were strongholds like

---

65. *Ibid.*, 2, fo. 630.
66. Carroll, *op.cit.*, p. 260.
67. Du Préau, *op.cit.*, 2, fo. 630 verso.
68. There were already, according to du Préau, daily preachings '& publiquemment sur le marché deuant la crois iournellement' for the safety of the city in catholic hands, preachings which quickly spread throughout the province and towards Paris (fo. 632).

Péronne. They declared their support for the Peronnois 'd'un si heroique & vertueux courage, que lesdits seigneurs de Humieres & de Clermont [his lieutenant] les ayans ouys en leurs defenses & allegations, furent contraincts de temporiser pour l'heure, de peur d'une esmotion populaire'.

It was following this meeting that d'Estourmel and Happlaincourt rallied the nobility in another meeting of the estates summoned to the house where they were staying. There, after much discussion, they agreed the wording of a covenant of association, which may have been already have been drafted by Happlaincourt the previous day at his country house. Although du Préau does not provide the exact terms of the league, he cites one critical phrase from the first manifesto.[69] The details of the proposed articles of Association may not have been exactly as we have them in the published pamphlets, but that there was such a document, and that it contained something fairly close to them, must be regarded as probable.

Conclusion

The progress of the League of Péronne through the remainder of 1576 is another subject. It spread like clover in grass, underneath the veneer of apparent public compliance with the terms of Beaulieu, in reality exploiting the personal, private antipathies that existed to such an extensive, unmonitored, undelimited religious pluralism. We can trace it in Champagne and through to the edges of Burgundy to the east and west to Normandy and Brittany. Whether the Guises were responsible for its spread is difficult to document; but many contemporaries believed it to

---

69. 'Finalement fut de tous tant en general qu'en particulier conclu & determiné, qu'il falloit faire paroistre qu'ils n'estoient autres que bons & vrays Catholiques, seruiteurs de Dieu & du Roy: & que pour la defense de la foy que leurs predecesseurs auoient tousiours iusques adonc suyuie & maintenue, ils estoient tous tres-contens de mourir, si besoing en estoit. Et à ceste cause, qu'il leur convenoit tous d'vn accord tenir & s'opposer de toute leur puissance & credit à l'entreprise de ceux qui par fiction se vouloient emparer de leur ville...'.

be so.[70] But, as the Péronne affair demonstrated, there were many ways in which a grandee could give a steer to events on the ground. The fact of the matter was that it was the Peace of Monsieur that had created the circumstances in which this could happen. Its failure was to be a comprehensive and humiliating lesson for the French crown in the legislative limits of religious pluralism in sixteenth-century France and it would not be lost in the more successful and enduring adventures in legislative pluralism that followed in 1577 and 1598.

---

70. E.g. *Cal.S.P.For.*, *op.cit.*, pp. 359 – 15 Aug 1576 ('It is known that the Duke of Guise is to be the head of it, both by the report of themselves – yet they will not name him, but that he is as great as was the Admiral – and also by the standing of the Guise in subscribing the Edict of Pacifiction. The Queen Mother is much troubled with that matter, for she understands the first request of this league will be that the King should take the government of his realm into his own hand, and not suffer it to be governed by his mother...').

DANIEL HICKEY

Enforcing the Edict of Nantes: The 1599 Commissions and Local Elites in Dauphiné and Poitou-Aunis

Over the last half-century, a number of historians and several different schools of historical thought have tried to explain the introduction of a conciliation dynamic that eventually led to the ending of the conflict and violence that had marked the French Wars of Religion. Most of the major studies produced have concentrated upon the decade of the 1590s, seeing it as the critical period for the introduction of the tolerance and compromise which led to the eventual Edict of Nantes in 1598.[1] This contribution will attempt to revisit the view that the 1590s and the Edict of Nantes really constituted the final turning point, marking the pacification of the kingdom. Concentrating upon the Commissions set up to execute the edict in 1599, it will try to show that in practical terms the relevant clauses were not simply 'executed', but were negotiated at the local, provincial and regional levels and that they took considerable time to implement. Local elites mediated or brokered the terms that could be accepted by their compatriots and the peace-making process advanced gradually, differing significantly from one region to another.

1. The Edict of Nantes:

Historians have always been ill at ease with the 1598 breaking point. When looking closely at the edict, it becomes clear that there were few new ideas for creating this conciliation dynamic. The vast majority of the 92 public and 56 secret articles repeat elements of previous treaties, notably the 1577

---

1. Exceptions are Bercé, Y-M (1992) *La naissance dramatique de l'absolutisme, 1598-1661*. Vol 3 of Nouvelle histoire de la France Moderne. Paris: Seuil, which does not see 1598 as the final break in the religious wars, Greengrass, M. (1995) *France in the Age of Henri IV, the Struggle for Stability*, 2nd ed. London and New York: Longman, and Holt, M. *(1995) The French Wars of Religion, 1562-1629*, 'New Approaches to European History'. Cambridge: Cambridge University Press.

pacification of Poitiers and the edicts signed at Nérac (1579) and at Fleix (1580).[2] The amalgam of text which constitutes the Edict of Nantes begins with an amnesty for acts committed since 1585 and in articles 3 to 5 the Roman Catholic religion is officially restored: Catholic services are to be reestablished in all parts of the kingdom. In articles 6 to 16 of the published edict and in articles 1 to 23 of the secret agreements the text goes on to ensure a certain organisation and to recognise certain privileges for the protestants. They are to benefit from a certain *liberté de conscience*, excluding them from any obligation to assist at Catholic ceremonies, to follow processions, to contribute to the construction or repair of Catholic churches or buildings. However, they were to pay the *dîme* on their holdings.

Due to the frequent conflicts in interpretation between the published edict and the attached *brevet,* many of the most critical issues to be decided were left to the commissioners who were to be named by the Crown and sent into the different regions. It is significant that the criteria for the nomination of these men were never specified in the edict. They were first referred to in article 4 when they were given the mandate to decide where the religious structures, notably the Huguenot temples were to be placed in each locality. In article 12 they were given the mandate to impose their decisions on *recalcitrant princes, seigneurs, gentilhommes et villes catholiques*. In article 28 they were to decide on the location of Catholic and Protestant cemeteries and on the restitution of Catholic cemeteries confiscated during the war years. Their powers were even more present in the secret articles. Secret article 6 extended and specified the previously noted article 4: the secret clause clearly stated that the Huguenot religious structures were only to be located in villages or faubourgs around the major towns and it was left to the commissioners to choose where they were to be placed. Secret article 10 clarified the publicly announced article 27 which had specified that Huguenots were to be assured access to public office in the major cities and towns. Under the clarification it was left to the commissioners to decide how to carry out this clause. They were therefore expected to go beyond the principles specified in the edict and to rule on the delicate religious and civil problems which confronted each community. The remainder of this paper will examine their work in two of the most

---

2.   The full text of the published edict, the secret articles and the *brevet* can be found in Mousnier, R. (1964) *L'assassinat d'Henri IV*. Paris: Gallimard, pp. 294-334.

deeply affected regions of the kingdom, Dauphiné in the south-east and Poitou-Aunis in the center west.

2. The Commissions for the Execution of the Edict of Nantes:

The Commissions for the execution of the Edict of Nantes, set up in 1599, were one of the major initiatives taken to break the cycle of local violence produced by the wars. The work of the commissioners reveals what they saw as the fundamental reasons behind the continuing causes of conflict and the ways in which they tried to deal with them. From 1599 on, hearings were conducted in almost every region of France by commissioners named to ensure the execution of different clauses of the 1598 edict. Although there were no clauses in the Edict concerning the nominations or mandates of the commissioners to be named, the previous Edicts of Ambroise (1563) and of Saint-Germain-en-Laye had both called for a royal commissioner to visit communities and to arbitrate disputes. Within that tradition, these men and the actions they took were seen to be within the realm of the legal system although there were frequent disputes between the Crown and the Parlements as to the exact nature of their power.[3] Under the Edict of Nantes this tradition continued and the commissioners named were generally *Maîtres de requêtes* or *Conseillers d'Etat*. In the case of Dauphiné the commissioners were the Catholic Méry de Vic, *Conseiller d'Etat* and Intendant for the Lyonnais who was frequently named as the king's representative in Dauphiné, and the Protestant leader, François de Bonne, Duke of Lesdiguières, who was *Lieutenant-général* of the province.

Both of them conducted their visits in the company of Ennemond de Rabot, President of the Parlement of Grenoble.[4] In Poitou-Aunis, as in Dauphiné, the Crown named the *Lieutenant-général* of Poitou to the commission. He was Jean de Beaudéan, Sieur de Parabière, a Huguenot. The second commissioner was Martin Langlois, *maître de requête* in the Parlement de Paris. In Poitou, perhaps because there was no local Parlement, they were accompanied by no third commissioner.

---

3.   Benoît, E. (1970) *Histoire de l'Edit de Nantes*, 5 vols. Paris, 1859: repr., Geneva: Slatkine Reprints, I, pp. 298-299. On the application of the Edict of Nantes in the different regions of France, recent contributions are, Garrisson, F. (1964) *Essai sur les commissions d'application de l'Edit de Nantes: le règne de Henri IV*, tome I. Montpellier: Déhan.

4.   Rabut, E. (1987) *Le Roi, l'Eglise et le Temple. L'exécution de l'Edit de Nantes en Dauphiné* Grenoble: La pensée sauvage, pp. 14-15.

Since the violence that had marked the Wars of Religion was seen as coming directly from the issues dividing local communities,[5] in executing the Edict, the commissioners were to go to the communities where there had been the most difficulties and to hear the complaints of the Protestants and Catholics in order to resolve their differences. In so doing they again followed the procedures that had been envisaged by the previous peace treaties and the edicts negotiated during the long period of the Wars of Religion. The pacification process outlined in all of these documents – and in the Edict of Nantes – depended heavily on building bridges with the local notables who were perceived as the keys to reducing community violence. But, there were major differences between these previous efforts and the 1599 experience. First, there was the fact that for the execution of the Edict of Nantes both a Catholic and Protestant commissioner were to be present according to the royal letters establishing the commissions[6] whereas in the past it had not been clear that a member of each of the religious communities should be present. Second, the geographic areas to be covered by the commissioners were more limited allowing them to concentrate more systematically on the cities, towns and regions to be pacified.

2.1. The Commission in Dauphiné:

As was frequently the case with such early modern commissions, despite a common mandate, uniform procedures and a similar personnel, the approach, operations and goals of these commissions varied considerably between Dauphiné and Poitou-Aunis. In Dauphiné the mandate, procedure and personnel can be reconstituted from the minutes left by the secretary of the commission Jean-Antoine Putod.[7] The document he composed shows that the commissioners in Dauphiné frequently used delegates in carrying out their visits, especially to the isolated Protestant communities. This was particularly the case for the Huguenot-dominated mountainous areas in the South-West (Nyons and the Baronnies). There, Lesdiguières drew upon men from the ranks of the regional Huguenot notables: Pierre de La Baume,

---

5.   Recent historical work has confirmed the opinion of the negotiators of the Edict. See Davis, N. Z. (1975) 'The Rites of Violence,' in *Society and Culture in Early Modern France*. Stanford: Stanford University Press, pp. 152-188.
6.   Garrisson, F., p. 50.
7.   Putod, J.-A. 'Minute du proces verbal faict en Daulphiné sur l'execution de l'edict de Nantes', in Rabut, p. 21.

conseiller to the Parlement, René de la Tour, *sénéchal* of Valentinois and former Captain of War, Louis de Grammont, seigneur de Vachières, the Sieur d'Alençon, Captain Isaac Bar and Charles de Vesc, seigneur de Comps. These men, who were called upon to intervene in more difficult cases, were close to the local Huguenot elites and in a good position to convince them to accord concessions to their Catholic neighbors.

The three commissioners met with representatives from each religious community in the towns where the implementation of the edict posed the most difficulty. They held hearings in eleven different towns and their delegates met with representatives from four other communities (see Map 1). The minutes of these visits began on the 25 October 1599, when the mandate given to the three commissioners was transcribed into the document, and they concluded on the 6 February 1601 with a series of ordinances issued to decide appeals lodged against previous decisions.

The organisation of the visits by the commissioners in Dauphiné was essentially the same from one town to another. Influenced by the role assumed by Lesdiguières in the province during the years following the capitulation of the Catholic League, the visits to implement the terms of the edict were surrounded by major festivities. In the case of Montélimar, the *Lieutenant-général* arrived with de Vic and de Rabot on 11 November escorted by 300-400 cavalry. Upon their arrival, the commissioners convened the town elite, explained their mandate, read the relevant sections of the Edict and discussed how they were to be implemented. Their goal was the restitution of Catholic worship in the town, and they arrived with proposals to pay for the construction of a new Huguenot temple and to restore the Sainte-Croix church which the Huguenots had used during the wars. The representatives of both communities agreed to respect this compromise, after which the Catholic community ordered a general procession through the town to the sound of church bells. Notary Gayet, obviously of Catholic persuasion, recorded these events, noting that this was the first time in fourteen years that so many bells had tolled. He wrote that over 6,000 Catholics took part in the procession as d'Illins and de Vic, but not Lesdiguières, followed the Bishop of Viviers to the church for a high mass. Henri IV's confessor, Père Cotton preached and twelve musicians from Grignan and Viviers were brought in to play for the event.[8]

---

8.   Notaire Gayet, cited in Lacroix, A. (1973) *L'Arrondissement de Montélimar, Géographie, Histoire, Statistique*, vol. 6. Valence, 1882, Paris: Editions du Palais Royal, pp. 202-204.

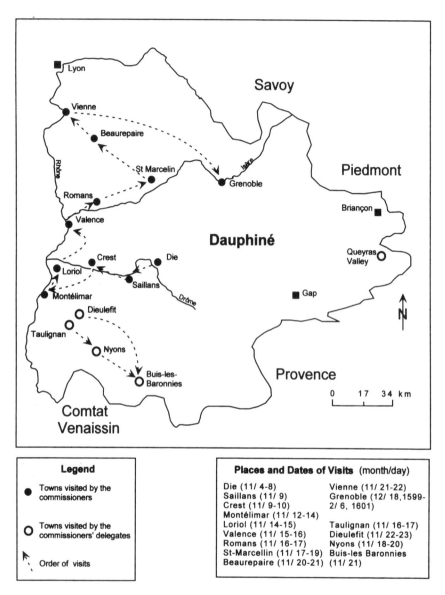

Savoy

Piedmont

Dauphiné

Provence

Comtat
Venaissin

Map 1: Execution of the Edict of Nantes in the Province of Dauphiné, 1599.

The negotiations to implement the terms of the edict did not always go as smoothly as our Catholic observer in Montélimar indicates. Indeed, one wonders if a Protestant observer to the Montélimar festivities would have presented the same version as Gayot. The main sources of conflict during the commissioners visits developed out of the principal claims of each camp. For the Huguenots, articles 8, 11 and 20 concerning the reestablishment of Protestant services was always one of the first questions to be treated. The Protestant community was also interested in using article 10, allowing villages that had possessed Huguenot services before 1577 to reestablish them: enquiries were to be carried out to determine if services could be reestablished on that basis at Châtonnay, Taulignan, Venterol, Tulette, La Pègre and Buis-les-Baronnies.[9] The Huguenots had also obtained secret article 6 which specifically treated the bailliage of Viennois: it ordered that Protestant services should be allowed in three towns (Romans, Beaurepaire and Saint Marcellin) rather than in the two normally allowed in secret article 11. In most localities there was little opposition to the establishment or reestablishment of these services, the exception being Gap where the Bishop consistently presented objections to the new religion and succeeded in blocking the reestablishment of Huguenot services in the town right up to 1606.[10]

In examining closely the questions brought up in each town meeting, it becomes evident that the commissioners and local elite groups were interested in resolving issues related to the separation of church buildings, cemeteries, church bells, the restitution of buildings and holdings confiscated from Catholic parishes or monasteries as well as in reestablishing Huguenot worship in communities where services had previously existed. But, above and beyond the issues which one associates with implementing the edict are a whole series of directives aimed at reestablishing the ground rules for community harmony and at separating what was considered to be within the sphere of community interest from what was seen as a sphere of religious activity (See Graph 1).[11] These ground rules are evident when the commissioners or their delegates treated the question of church bells. Everywhere they ordered that the bell should be left on the town church to ring out the hours, summon inhabitants to council meetings or alert them of

---

9. Putod, pp. 153-154, 158-168 and 179-190.
10. *Ibid.*, pp. 140-143 and 203-205.
11. *Ibid.*, pp. 51-227.

impending danger. Catholics and Protestants were each to procure additional bells to summon faithful to their respective church services. Even more apparent in this attempt to define religious and civic spheres were the rules concerning community assemblies. In every community except Vienne, the commissioners gave orders concerning the formation of assemblies. To ensure the representation of both religious groups, they imposed quotas on representation in town councils, except that of Beaurepaire where they argued that each community was numerous enough to be able to elect its own representatives to town meetings. In other cases in accordance with secret article 10, the town councils were to be divided: Protestants were to be given one-tenth of the seats in Grenoble, a quarter in St-Marcellin, Crest and Romans, one-third in Chabeuil and Buis, half in Gap, two-thirds in Loriol, Montélimar, Dieulefit, Nyons, Die and nine-tenths of the seats in Valence. In some cases, such as Buis, the initial order had not specified the exact division and it took two appeals of the Huguenot population before the commissioners gave them the right to elect one-third of the council.

It is obvious that the commissioners felt that it was necessary to lay down clear ground rules for the constitution of representative community political assemblies as a means of ensuring the participation of the elite of each religious group in the decision-making process and eventually bringing them to work with one another. This process of bringing the community elite to work together appears to have been one of the principal goals of the Lesdiguières-de Vic-Rabot visits. In addition to trying to bring the notables to collaborate with each other on the town councils, they were told to work together to manage community hospitals and colleges in which religion was not to be taught. In effect, continuing the logic of establishing separate public and religious spheres, the commissioners regularly ordered each group to be responsible for teaching religion its own children.

Order was the other goal which can be clearly identified in the *corpus* and the commissioners denounced a whole series of public manifestations associated with the contestation of civil or religious authorities. Charivaris, Abbeys of Misrule, public balls were placed in the same category as gambling, taverns, or duels. In these interventions, the commissioners can be seen as positioning themselves clearly behind municipal officials in try-

Table 1: Subjects treated in meetings between commissioners-delegates for the implementation of the Edict of Nantes, 1599–1601.

	Commissioners												Delegates			
	Grenoble	Die	Saillants	Crest	Montélimar	Loriol	Valence	Romans	St Marcellin	Vienne	Beaurepaire		Buis-les-Baronnies	Taulignan	Dieulefit	Nyons
Restitution / reconstruction of Catholic church or monastery	●	●		●	●		●								●	●
Reestablishment of Catholic services	●	●											●			●
Public processions of Catholics restored	●				●										●	
Reestablishment of Protestant services				●										●		●
Temples to be rebuilt- public buildings to be used in interim				●	●			●	●				●		●	●
Separate cemeteries for each group				●		●		●		●			●	●	●	●
Separate church bells for each group	●	●											●	●	●	●
Reestablishment of municipal governments with quotas established for each group	●	●	●	●	●	●	●	●	●				●	●	●	●
Representation for each group w / o quotas										●						
College to be established to teach both groups / no religion	●			●											●	
Each group responsible for teaching religion to its children	●			●	●		●		●				●			
Hospital to be managed by representatives of each group					●	●	●	●	●		●					
Gambling and taverns forbidden during Catholic and Protestant services				●			●									
Charivaris, Abbeys of Misrule, public balls forbidden					●		●		●							●
Public assemblies of both religious communities forbidden in absence of their leaders													●			
Duels are forbidden					●											

ing to eliminate what were seen as activities providing occasions for the expression of discord and the outbreak of violence.[12] Finally, in each town they visited, the commissioners convened a second meeting at the end of their visit to announce their decisions to the town elite and to ask for an oath of obedience from the community leaders that they would *soigneusement et fidelement garder et observer ledit edit de Nantes en tous ses poincts, ensemble les reglementz par nous faitz...*

It is clear that the power and authority of local elites was reinforced by these judgements and that just as Gregory Hanlon has argued for Bordeaux, one could wonder whether local issues of precedence and power were not just as fundamental to explaining the outbreaks of violence as religious convictions.[13] It is within the context of these attempts to reduce civic friction and to increase the authority of the elites over their communities that the commissioners can be seen as trying to re-cement the unity of the local Catholic and Protestant elite. They set down new ground rules for their respective participation in local government and accorded them increased responsibility and powers over their communities.

2.2 The Commissions in Poitou-Aunis:

In the case of Poitou-Aunis, the full text of the commission hearings has never been found, however we do possess a 17th century legal text probably drawn up in 1643 when the Catholics initiated a series of challenges to Huguenot interpretations of the number of Temples allowed to them in the different ordinances and decrees issued by the Parabère-Langlois commission.[14] This document along with the work of François Garrisson permit us to reconstruct the order and approximate dates of the commissioners' visits.

---

12. See, among others, Bercé, Y-M (1976) *La fête et la révolte.* Paris: Hachette and Le Roy Ladurie, E. (1979) *Le Carnaval de Romans: De la Chandeleur au mercredi des Cendres, 1579-1580* Paris: Gallimard.
13. Hanlon, G. (1989) *l'Univers des gens de bien: Culture et comportements des élites urbaines en Agenais-Condomois au XVIIe siècle.* Bordeaux: Presses universitaires de Bordeaux , pp. 277-300. See also Luria, K. (1991) *Territories of Grace: Cultural Change in the 17th Century Diocese of Grenoble.* Berkeley: University of California Press, chap. 5.
14. Loride, P. (1643) *Observations sur le procès verbal de Monsieurs de Parabère et Langlois, commissaires exécuteurs pour l'Edit de Nantes, 1599.* Bibliothèque nationale, 4 Ld 176 294.

To go even further in analyzing the type of intervention carried out in the region, we possess the full minutes of the commissioners' visit to the key city of La Rochelle.

There are no signs that the Poitou Commission used other delegates than Parabère and Langlois to carry out its visits. According to François Garrisson, the visits began with the most difficult town, La Rochelle, where the town fathers received Parabère and Langlois on 25 July 1599.[15] The La Rochelle negotiations lasted until the final religious ceremonies on 6 August and Garrisson notes that the commissioners left the town on 8 August. Thereafter, the 1643 *factum* indicates that Parabère and Langlois stopped at Fontenay, Niort, Saint-Maixant and Lusignan to negotiate the designation of the two temples to be allowed in each *sénéchaussée*. As in Dauphiné, they tried to calm local tensions. Another of the 1643 *factums* informs us that in Lusignan the Protestants wanted to obtain rights to the use of the church bell to which they had contributed. However, the commissioners awarded the bell to the Catholics, asking them, in turn, to contribute to the purchase of a second bell for the Huguenots.[16] In contrast to Dauphiné, there appears to have been little money accorded by the commissioners to build new buildings or to resolve problems with bells or cemeteries. One exception to this was Fontenay, where they apparently agreed to finance the repairs on Notre-Dame church which was returned to the Catholics after having served as a Huguenot temple.[17] In total, the visits of Parabère and Langlois in Poitou-Aunis seem to have lasted from 25 July to about 20 August (See Map 2).

It was clearly La Rochelle which constituted the major challenge for the commissioners since it was the unique case of a large town where the commissioners were to be responsible for reintroducing Catholic worship. The difficulties foreseen with this mandate seem to have led the Sieur de la Force, himself a Rochellais, to refuse service as the Protestant commis-

---

15. Garrisson, p. 95. Although Garrisson seems to give the correct order of the visits, he is wrong in indicating that the commissioners entered La Rochelle on July 23. The minutes of the visit note that they entered the town on 25 July, see 'Procès verbal faict par messires Parabère et Langlois, commissaires nommés par sa majesté en l'année 1599 (juillet et août)', BM La Rochelle, ms. 163, f.1.

16. *Factum pour les habitants de Lusignan faisant profession de la RPR* in Lièvre, A (1856) *Histoire des protestants et des églises réformées du Poitou.* Paris: Grassart, I, 266.

17. Lièvre, I, 266.

sioner.[18] Within the city as well, there appears to have been considerable dissension between political leaders and the Huguenot congregations over the attitude to adopt in the face of the Commission. The town councillors, or *échevins*, a rather closed group whose elections were assured by co-optation from a cohort of 100 burghers, seem to have been ready to negotiate with the commissioners.[19] However, the burghers, for their part, were afraid that the councillors would give in too easily to the commissioners' demands. They met together and elected fifteen representatives, five from each parish, to be added to the city delegation. When they presented themselves before the councillors, the latter slammed the door in their faces contending that such a large delegation would make negotiation impossible. At that point the Calvinist clergy moderated the dispute, convincing the burghers that only two of their representatives would be sufficient.

The burghers accepted this compromise on the condition that the Council would not conclude any peace without first submitting the proposed pact to public scrutiny and approval. The *bourgeois-marchand*, Pierre Bernardeau was chosen to be one of the representatives, the other was the Sieur Courault.[20]

It was in this context of internal hostility and distrust that the commissioners arrived before La Rochelle. The resumé of their meetings with councilmen and with Catholics, visits to former Catholic churches, monasteries and convents is presented in fourteen folios and allows us to compare the operations of Parabière and Langlois with those of Lesdiguières, de Vic and Rabot in Dauphiné.[21] The scope of the apprehended dissidence in La Rochelle is seen in the fact that the Crown commissioners prefaced their visit to the town by a meeting in the bourg of Moray, outside the city walls, with two of the Councilmen, Sieurs Cholles and Beaupreau. The councilmen assured Parabière and Langlois that the Mayor, councillors, and *paires*

---

18. Garrisson, p. 94.
19. Trocmé, E. (1950) 'La Rochelle de 1560 à 1623. Tableau d'une société reformée au temps des guerres de religion', thèse de la Faculté de théologie protestant de Paris, pp. 181-183.
20. Merlin, J., pasteur, 'Diaire de Jacques Merlin ou Receuil des choses [les] plus mémorables qui se sont passées en ceste ville [de La Rochelle] de 1589 à 1620', Dangibeaud, C. (ed.) (1878) *Archives historiques de la Saintonge et de l'Aunis*, vol. 5. Paris: Champion, p. 86. On this question see also Robbins, K. (1997) *City on the Ocean Sea: La Rochelle, 1530-1650. Urban Society, Religion and Politics on the French Atlantic Frontier*. Leiden: Brill, pp. 247-248.
21. 'Procès-verbal faict par messieurs Parabière et Langlois', fos. 40-52.

were disposed to accept all the clauses of the King's edict, but that they intended to register several protests concerning the terms of the document. Under these conditions the Crown councillors entered La Rochelle on Sunday, 25 July, and immediately met with the Mayor, councillors and *paires* in the Hôtel de Ville. Just as in Dauphiné, the commissioners began their meeting by showing the assembled men the edict with the royal seal, reading them the relevant clauses of the document before proceeding to discuss the measures necessary for the execution of the text and the reestablishment of Catholic worship. For their part the town fathers protested that the royal edict had not yet been officially registered by all the Parlements and that Catholic services should not be reestablished in La Rochelle before all of the kingdom had accepted the edict. However, they signified that both they and the reformed church were ready to accept the edict if the Commission would add several of their complaints, protests and suggested modifications to the eventual text of their visit. The commissioners noted that they understood that their eventual decrees should take account of the fact that the majority of the town was protestant with the Catholics composing only a twentieth of the population. They noted as well that it was understood that Catholics should avoid provocative displays, like processions, that could threaten the calm and public order of the community.

The commissioners proceeded to carry out inspections of former Catholic buildings and sites which could be returned to the Catholics and restored to their former uses. Having visited these sites, they met again with city authorities and Catholics to discuss their final decisions. The commissioners were particularly concerned that their recommendations do nothing 'to stir up emotions, disputes or controversies which could trouble the religion and *tranquilité publique* of the town'.[22] Pastor Merlin, in his contemporary account of the city s history, tells us that the actions of the commissioners went well beyond the interventions noted in the minutes of their visit. On 27 July, for example, Parabère held a meeting with several of the elders of the Protestant community at Pastor Dumont's house and he pleaded with them to set an example of obedience to the King's orders. He reminded them that elsewhere in France, Catholics were being asked to accept the establishment of Huguenot churches and services and their resistance could affect the whole process of implementing the Edict.[23]

---

22. *Ibid.* fo. 46.
23. Merlin, p. 87.

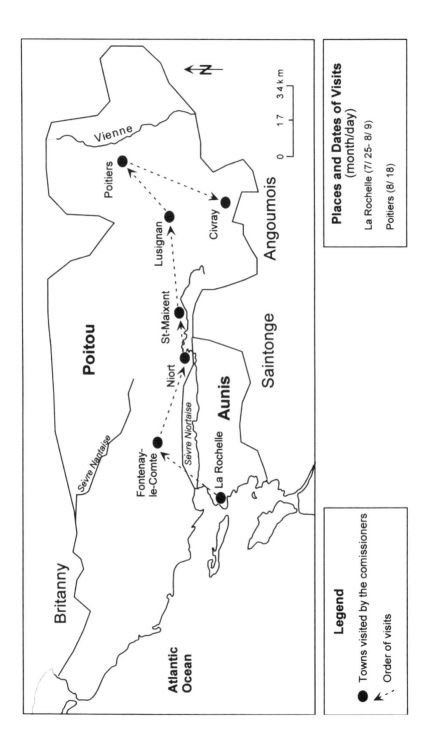

Map 2: Execution of the Edict of Nantes in the Provinces of Poitou and Aunis, 1599.

In the text of the commissioners' report on the subject of the Catholics, it was noted that they would accept what was 'reasonable' and 'in conformity with the King's edict'. However, the diary of Pastor Merlin noted the very determined resistance of the Huguenot community to the concessions demanded of them. At several points the community was close to rejecting the reestablishment of Catholic worship. The debate continued up to 3 August when, after the interventions of the mayor, Parabère and Langlois, the Huguenot community was finally satisfied when the commissioners agreed to attach certain conditions to their recommendations, like the permission accorded to the Huguenots of the town to hold public synods and *colloques* and that all these agreements were conditional upon the edict eventually being registered by the Parlement of Bordeaux.[24] These conditions having been accepted, the commissioners ordered M. Michel Bodeychles, spokesman for the Catholics, to contact the Bishop of Saintes, Nicolas Cornu de la Courbe, asking him to come to La Rochelle and preside over the ceremony reestablishing Catholic worship.

On 4 August, there were the preludes to the final ceremony. Early in the day the mayor annonced to the sound of trumpets that in conformity with the King's edict, the interdictions on masses, religious ceremonies and catechism were lifted. But, with the arrival of the bishop's delegation, new problems seem to have sprung up. The commissioners note that they held new meetings with the theologians, the bishop's representatives and with the Catholic community to try to persuade them 'of the difficulties' inherent in insisting on too many concessions.[25] Questions seem to have been posed relative to recovering more cemeteries and to the need for a long ceremonial procession through the town to mark the restoration of Catholic services. Even the question of churches seems to have resurfaced. On that issue the commissioners were forced into more precision: the ruined churches of Notre-Dame de Cougnes and of St Nicolas were to be left as they were and if any new cemetery space was needed it was to be found outside the walls. The other ruined parishes, St Sauveur, St Jean de Perot and St Bartholomé, could be recovered by the Catholics when the need was felt. It was stated clearly that St Marguerite's Chapel was to become the main Catholic church. The monastery of the Cordelliers was to be handed

---

24. *Ibid.*, pp. 88-98.
25. Among the Bishop's representatives were M. Joachim Roul, archdiacre, M. Johan Barentesaux, docteur en théologie, M. Jehan Mecorier, curé de St-Nicolas, 'Procès-verbal fait par messieurs Parabière et Langlois', fos. 47-48.

back to the monks, but this transfer was not to compromise the activities of the Huguenot College that had been set up in the monastery. As for the other convents and monasteries, it was reiterated that they were to be returned as soon as the leases on the property and buildings expired.

It was noted that the Catholic religion would be reestablished and that any inhabitant who 'touched' a Catholic or caused 'trouble' would be arrested and imprisoned. As for the Catholics, the commissioners asked that the 'faithful, curés, priests and religious show moderation (*modeseté*) and that preachers of all religions weigh their words' to avoid provoking problems. Finally, as to the cemeteries, it was ordered that the St Bartholomé cemetery be divided into two sections and that each religious group be attributed a section to bury their dead. Tensions remained high, however, and Pastor Merlin notes that even as the implementation of the edict was announced on 4 August, a group of women, children and young artisans broke into St Marguerite's from which the Huguenots were recovering their furnishings to make way for the Catholic takeover. The insurgents began to smash windows, break up the pulpit and rip off wall panels.[26] Immediately the Catholics demanded to know who was to pay for repairing the building and that issue was added to the last minute negotiations.

Within this highly charged atmosphere, the commissioners negotiated the final terms with the Catholic representatives and on Friday, 6 August, together with the mayor of the town, they followed the Bishop of Saintes to St Marguerite's church. He proceeded to consecrate the church then celebrate mass in his pontifical robes. The mass was followed by the singing of a *te deum*. The next day, the commissioners must have been very uneasy when the Bishop led a procession to the ruins of St Bartholomé's church accompanied by a number of faithful and, according to Pastor Merlin, he consecrated the ruins, taking possession of the site for the Catholics, after this he returned to St Marguerite's for the service.[27] This visit must have taken the form of the very type of procession that the commissioners had feared and it indicated clearly the insistence of the Catholic church on recuperating its former holdings.

Just as in Dauphiné, this resumé concerning the restitution of the Catholic religion to La Rochelle demonstrates the pivotal role of the local elite. From the very beginning they were seen as the ones responsible for

---

26. Merlin, p. 99.
27. *Ibid.*, p. 100.

their community as the commissioners in La Rochelle and in Dauphiné pressured them to adhere to the clauses dictated by the Crown. This process demonstrates the particularly difficult context under which the La Rochelle negotiations were carried out. On the side of Parabère and Langlois, the edict and royal decrees gave little room to manoeuvre. The Catholic religion had to be restored. However, they did not go to the extent of trying to work out political power sharing arrangements for the municipal councils either in La Rochelle or in the other towns of Poitou-Aunis and they did not try to avoid differences by paying for repairs to damaged Catholic or Protestant buildings. Their resumé shows that they did try to forbid provocative demonstrations as had the commissioners in Dauphiné. However, at the last minute, Parabère and Langlois were pushed even further than their initial arrangements when the Bishop's representatives arrived and obviously required that the commission decisions be more clearly articulated, specifying which churches were to be returned, under what conditions and when. The Archbishop of Saintes also held the very type of triumphalist procession that Parabère and Langlois had hoped to avoid.

As for the mayor and councillors of La Rochelle, they were under extreme pressure from the commissioners and the Crown to be accomodating at the same time that they were held responsible by the local population for protecting Huguenot interests and for not conceding too much. There was an evident distrust between the local population and their leaders from the very beginning of the process. The population would have liked a larger, more representative delegation to negotiate with the commission, but the town council refused, allowing the addition of two symbolic representatives and vainly promising to consult the general population. This distrust was also evident in the break-in which had led to the smashing of windows and the breaking up of wall panels in the Huguenot hall which was about to become St Marguerite's church. This whole climate of suspicion seems to have led Parabère to meet with the Huguenots on 28 July, a meeting not noted in the commissioners' report, to plead with them to be reasonable and he continued to meet with them even as they tried to obtain concessions from him to offset the demands of the Catholic representatives and clergy.

Kevin Robbins has underlined the fact that a climate of suspicion and mistrust dominated the La Rochelle political life from the time of the Reformation and culminated in a major town revolt in 1614.[28] The town

---

28. Robbins, Kevin (1995) 'The Social Mechanisms of Urban Rebellion: A Case Study of Leadership in the 1614 Revolt at La Rochelle', *French Historical Studies*, XIX, 2: 559-

council was selected by a process of cooptation that allowed little or no input from ordinary townspeople. The negotiations with the commissioners underline the difficulties that the town elite faced in conceding the points required by the Crown while receiving in return only the right to petition the king to convene public Huguenot synods and colloques and to require that the Edict of Nantes receive full approval, particularly from the Parlement of Bordeaux.

3. Conclusion

In both of the regions under study it becomes evident that these commissions represented a first step in trying to resolve local difficulties and that in the case of Dauphiné, the commissioners were able to put into place a certain framework for the resolution of problems between the two groups. However, in neither region did these interventions guarantee religious peace. In Dauphiné, where the local agreements appear substantial, there were still outbreaks of religious turmoil in 1625-26 under the direction of the Huguenot Captain de la Tour Montauban and when Lesdiguières died in 1626, he had just finished supervising the destruction of the Huguenot fortress at Pouzin.[29] In Poitou-Aunis, where hostility was even more evident in 1599, the possibility of recurring armed conflict remained present. This situation led the Crown to dispatch further commissions to the province. In 1611 the Crown sent the Sieur de St Germain de Clan, Huguenot and the ever-present Méry de Vic, *maître de requête*, to try to reconcile the two communities and in 1623 another pair, the Sieurs Amelot, Catholic, and Chalas, Huguenot, were to hear the grievances of each party to try to arrive at lasting solutions. [30] Nevertheless, the hostility led to open warfare between 1614 and 1616 when even Poitiers was almost taken by the Huguenot troops of the Duke of Rohan. Again from 1621, royal forces reentered the region beginning the long task of retaking the *places de sûreté* surrounding Poitiers and La Rochelle, all of which led up to the siege and eventual capture of La Rochelle in 1627-28. These continuing outbursts of hostility and warfare show the limits of both the commissioners' pacifica-

590.
29. Hickey, Daniel (1986) *The Coming of French Absolutism.* Toronto: University of Toronto Press, p. 166.
30. Lièvre, I, 281 and 303.

tion efforts and the accompanying conciliation dynamic especially in the context of Poitou-Aunis. The framework proposed in the Edict of Nantes was far easier to impose in some regions than in others and in the final analysis it depended upon the stability and credibility of the local elites who were responsible for selling the compromises to their town and village constituents.

Bibliography

Manuscripts:

'Procès-verbal faict par messires Parabère et Langlois, commissaires nommés par sa majesté en l'année 1599.' Bibliothèque Municipale de La-Rochelle, ms. 163.

Printed:

'Edit de Nantes avec les brevets et les articles secrets', pp. 294-334 in Mousnier, R. (1964) *L'assassinat d'Henri IV*. Paris: Gallimard.
Loride, P. (1643?) *Observations sur le procès-verbal de Monsieurs de Parabère et Langlois, commissaires exécuteurs pour l'Edit de Nantes, 1599*. N.P. Bibliothèque Nationale, 4Ld 176 294.
Merlin, J., pasteur, 'Diaire de Jacques Merlin ou recueil des choses [les] plus mémorables qui se sont passées dans ceste ville [de La Rochelle] de 1589 à 1620, Dangibeaud, C. (ed.) (1878) *Archives historiques de la Sain-tonge et de l'Aunis*, vol. 5. Paris: Champion.
Putod, J-A. 'Minute du proces verbal faict en Daulphiné sur l'exeqution de l'edict de Nantes par Messeigneurs les commissaires deputez par le roy a cest effect l'an 1599,' pp. 57-227 in Rabut, E. (1987) *Le Roi, l'église et le temple. L'execution de l'Edit de Nantes en Dauphiné*. Grenoble: La pensée sauvage.

DAVID J. B. TRIM

Edict of Nantes:
Product of Military Success or Failure?

The Edict of Nantes is often portrayed as the product of military failure. Henri IV was forced to convert because the Protestants could not win a final military victory, but even after reasserting royal power he was not strong enough to avoid making concessions to the Huguenots – and so, it is argued, some sort of religious compromise was inevitable if peace was to be obtained. This is the orthodoxy of historians, but it was also the view of contemporary or near-contemporary observers: one seventeenth-century *intendant* (Cardin Le Bret), for example, described the Edict of Nantes as 'cette ombre de loi que *la nécessité du temps a tiré par la force* de la piété de nos Rois'.[1]

If this interpretation were true, then the 'adventure of religious pluralism' was adventurous indeed, because it lacked the ultimate sanction of military force. 'Fanatics' had always believed that the conflict would be settled by the military victory of one or other of the parties; moderates from a very early stage sought (and kept seeking) a compromise.[2] Why, then, did a negotiated settlement succeed after 1598, yet not before? By the middle of the seventeenth century, the royal chancellor could describe the Nantes settlement as being the foundation 'de la tranquillité publique'.[3] By then, however, it had acquired moral force from the passage of time and through association with the legend of Henri 'le grand' (an important legend, as will be seen); attitudes in the late-sixteenth century were quite different. As a number of scholars have pointed out, the Edict of Nantes was neither the first edict issued by the

---

1. Bonney, R. J. (1978) *Political Change in France under Richelieu and Mazarin, 1624-1661*, Oxford: Oxford University Press, p. 384, quoting G. Picot, (1558-1655) *Cardin Le Bret et la doctrine de la souveraineté* (Nancy, 1948), p. 189, emphasis mine.
2. Vaissière, P. de (1925) *Henri IV*, Paris: Fayard, p. 488; and the references in note 4, *infra*.
3. 16 June 1656, British Library, Harleian MS 4489, fo. 2. (I owe this reference to Richard Bonney.)

crown in an attempt to end the wars of religion, nor the first peace settlement which provided for at least some degree of religious pluralism.[4]
Why was the pacification of 1598 able to survive for nine decades when
not one of the nine other edicts of the *guerres de religion* period was
able to last for even nine years?

This essay argues that the success of the Nantes settlement stemmed
from Henri IV's military success. An analysis of his conduct of war
during the 1590s sheds new light on the royal military position in 1598
and thus on the true nature of the 'adventure in religious pluralism' – it
was incompatible with military triumph as later events would prove; but
it was also incompatible with military failure. It was only made possible
by such military successes as Henri IV and his supporters enjoyed in the
decade before the Edict of Nantes; and by the image of the king, created
from these successes and from how he conducted not only the war, but
also himself.

There seems little doubt that Henri de Navarre did abjure the reformed faith largely because he could not become undisputed king of
France as a Protestant: the Huguenot minority could not coerce the
Catholic majority even with the aid of other Protestant powers and the
support of a few *politiques*. But having obtained the support of Catholics
did not mean that Henri would be able to suppress the Protestants, even
had he wanted to. The French monarchy had found from 1563 onwards
that the Huguenots could not be defeated even by an undisputed king.
Thus, it may seem that the reason for the Edict of Nantes is clear: the
inability of any party to achieve total victory on the battlefield and in the
trenches; an inability the participants recognised after thirty-five years of
trying and failing. However, while this may well be the reason for why
Henri IV issued the Edict of Nantes, it does not explain the pacification's lasting success. It does not explain why seventeenth-century
France was able to enjoy a relatively prolonged period of religious peace
and, if not perhaps an adventure in religious pluralism, then at least an
experiment in religious tolerance.

---

4.   See Roberts, P. (1998) 'The Most Crucial Battle of the Wars of Religion? The Con-
      flict over Sites for Reformed Worship in Sixteenth-Century France', *Archiv für
      Reformationsgeschichte* 89: 247-266; Potter, D. (ed.) (1997) and trans. *The French
      Wars of Religion: Selected Documents*, New York: St. Martin's Press, p. 242; see
      also the papers of Penny Roberts and Mark Greengrass elsewhere in this volume.
      For a chronological summary of the wars and the edicts of pacification, see Table 1.

After all, the kings of France had been Roman rather than Reformed from 1562 to 1589 and the Catholics' inability decisively to defeat their Protestant enemies had been identified at an early stage. Yet the previous edicts, despite the sincere intentions of many of those who were party to them, had lasted on average only two years, two months and one week by my calculations – and even if these are not exact, their trend is clear.

Table 1: – Edicts of Pacification and civil wars in France, 1562-1598.

CIVIL WAR	COMMENCED	CONCLUDED BY
(Prior to nominal outbreak of hostilities		Edict of St. Germain, January 1562[1]
First	March-April 1562	Peace of Amboise, March 1563
Second	September 1567	Edict of Longjumeau, March 1568
Third	August 1568	Peace of St. Germain, August 1570
Fourth	August 1572	Treaty of La Rochelle, June 1573
Fifth	February 1574	'Peace of Monsieur', May 1576
Sixth	March 1577	Peace of Bergerac, September 1577
Seventh	January 1580	Peace of Fleix, November 1580
Eighth[2]	Winter 1586-87	Edict of Nantes, April 1598

Notes:
1. The Edict of St. Germain, January 1562, was an attempt to *avert* war.
2. Not always known by this title; also called 'The War of the Three Henrys'. The nominal conclusion of a particular civil war did not necessarily mean the end of actual hostilities throughout the country.

After 1598, however, there was no outbreak of confessional conflict until the Rohan rising of 1612, which did not rend the kingdom asunder as had most of the earlier civil wars. I very much take the point of Mack Holt's description of the period 1610-1629 as being that of 'the last war of religion' – 1598 was not a clean break with the past; yet as Holt concedes, it *was* a clear watershed and it broke the cycle of civil war.[5]

---

5.   Holt, M. P. (1995) *The French Wars of Religion, 1562-1629*, Cambridge: Cambridge University Press, pp. 173, 214; Labrousse, E. (1985), 'Calvinism in France, 1598-1685', in M. Prestwich (ed.) (1985), *International Calvinism*, Oxford: Clarendon Press, p. 287. On the Rohan rising, see note 53, *infra*.

Again, however, the question must be asked why *then* and not before? I subscribe to David Potter's views that (*pace* Denis Crouzet) 'the
argument that a neo-stoic concept of tranquil obedience to the state was
spreading, in itself explains little beyond the realm of ideas'; and that the
rather more obvious answer of "'War weariness" is too simple an explanation'.[6] Or at least war-weariness in the simple way that it is generally
meant is too simple an explanation. Parties to ideological conflicts do
not make peace because of war-weariness alone. The Huguenots' Dutch
allies had been fighting for almost as long as the French in a war as, or
more, intense – and just as in France signs of war-weariness were apparent in the Dutch Republic (and in Spain, too) in the late 1590s. But,
because the Dutch and the Spanish would not compromise, they kept up
the struggle for another ten years, which saw the greatest campaigns of
the whole war. Simple weariness of war may well have motivated yet
another edict of pacification,[7] but it is unlikely to have caused lasting
peace – that is, to have prevented the resumption of hostilities which
must have seemed likely. After all, the edicts of pacification were generally not looked on kindly by contemporaries: the very first edict of the
guerres de religion period (that of January 1562), for example, was condemned (in retrospect) by the prominent Catholic general Gaspard de
Saulx-Tavannes, as being 'la porte par où les Huguenots sont entrez en
France'.[8] Edicts, despite their pacificatory intent, exacerbated rather than
eased tensions throughout the entire period of the wars of religion – and
this was also true of the terms of the Edict of Nantes, as Penny Roberts
points out. Catholics and Protestants alike were dissatisfied with its
terms and protested against its provisions.[9]

They did not, however, go back to war. War-weariness alone will
not suffice to make *ideologically*-motivated belligerents accept a compromise peace. They must have reason to believe that they cannot obtain
all their goals through war. If they still hope to do so, then, because they
are motivated by principle, they will be prepared to fight on in the hope

6.   Potter (1997), p. 242. Cf. Crouzet, D. (1990) *Les guerriers de Dieu: la violence au
     temps des troubles de religion vers 1525-1610*. Seyssel: Champ Vallon, 2 vols.
7.   The Parlement of Paris, for example, in 1593 urged the necessity of working 'as
     promptly as possible for the peace of the people, because of the extreme necessity
     they are in': decree on the succession, 28 July 1593, in Potter (1997), p. 230.
8.   *Mémoires de tres-noble et tres-illustre Gaspard de Saulx, Seigneur de Tavannes*, in
     J.-F. Michaud and J.-J.-F. Poujoulat (eds) (1838), *Nouvelle collection de mémoires
     pour servir à l'histoire de France*, 1st ser., 8, Paris: p. 247.
9.   Roberts (1998), pp. 247-248, 262, 265-266.

of somehow achieving victory – regardless of war-weariness. Modern conflicts in Palestine, the former Yugoslavia and Ireland are good examples of this. Parties to such ideological conflicts have to be sufficiently defeated to feel that war is not the best means of achieving their ends. They have, in fact, to have a military incentive for peace. In France around the year 1600, both parties had such an incentive to abide by the edict of pacification, because they did have reason to believe that the 1598 settlement was the best they could hope to achieve. Both Catholics and Protestants had achieved their primary objectives; they had preserved their core principles intact, as it were. Neither were happy with having to give up their secondary goals – but they had been persuaded by events in the 1590s that these could not be achieved by resorting to war again. Hence, war-weariness could take its full toll. This was where France after the Edict of Nantes differed from France after previous edicts: never before had the confessional rivals been convinced that war did not offer a better alternative to the compromise peace terms. By 1598, however, the adherents of both the Roman and the Reformed communions had been given good reason to think that any future campaigns would be for naught. It was then and only then that they became sufficiently weary of war to prefer peace.

What gave them reason to reach this conclusion? What convinced them that the provisions of Nantes would not be improved by a resumption of hostilities? It was the military success of Henri de Navarre and the image that this created. This, in turn, was due to a number of factors. Henri IV built on Henri III's reforms; he had greater financial and military aid from foreign allies than the Huguenots had previously enjoyed, support which continued after his abjuration of Calvinism; and, thanks not least to the talents of men such as Maximilien de Béthune, duc de Sully, he controlled a greater resource base than any of his royal predecessors during the wars of religion. But these factors alone were not enough; they were anonymous and while they had an undoubted impact on the conduct of war in the 1590s, they could not directly be capitalised on by royal propagandists – they would not impinge themselves directly on the consciousness of nobles or *bourgeois*. The military success of Henri IV and his cause, to which these factors greatly contributed, was embodied and personified in (and indeed owed much to) the leadership of the king and the image that was created of him as both monarch and great captain.[10]

Mark Greengrass has stressed that royal propaganda 'played on the simple desire for peace'.[11] However, the king's propagandists also emphasised his traditional, chivalric, martial virtues, such as his courage, his skill at arms and his military leadership. The 'definitive image of the king' from the 1590s is, as Greengrass himself notes, that of 'Henri IV on a leaping charger, baton in hand, a white scarf flowing behind him' – the cavalry general, charging upon his enemies (as he did at the great battles of 1588-90), or pursuing them from his kingdom.[12]

This image was an important and an enduring one,[13] but it was not *just* an image: Palma Cayet's perspective on Henri was that 'he was always on horseback, ready in pursuit'.[14] At Ivry in 1590 the king bade his cavaliers 'raliez vous à mon panache blanc' – and in the confusion of a cavalry melee, when his standard bearer was slain, this is precisely what they did.[15] The royal publicists were able successfully to propagate their potent image of the king because it was the *actualité* and this was crucially important. An honourable reputation could not be faked, even by the most efficient publicity machine. It could be obtained *only* by *demonstrating* that one possessed martial skill and great courage, by feats of arms in war. This is precisely what Henri de Navarre did from the War of the Three Henrys and onwards; providing an appropriate stage to demonstrate his *valeur* and *prouesse* was the point of many of his actions, at the strategic, tactical and personal levels.

---

10. See Potter, D. (1995) 'Kingship in the Wars of Religion: The Reputation of Henri III of France', *European History Quarterly* 25 (1): 485-528; Greengrass, M. (1989) 'Henri IV et Elisabeth: les dettes d'une amitié,' in *Henri IV: Le roi et la reconstruction du royaume*, Pau: Editions J. & D./Association Henri IV, pp. 353-370; *idem* (1995) *France in the Age of Henri IV*, 2nd. ed. London: Longman, pp. 124-134; and Buisseret, D. (1968) *Sully and the Growth of Centralized Government in France 1598-1610*, London: Eyre & Spottiswoode.
11. Greengrass (1995), p. 85.
12. *Ibid.*, 84.
13. Bibliothèque Nationale, fonds français 23335, fos. 100-13; Cornette, J. (1993) *Le Roi de Guerre: Essai sur la souveraineté dans la France du Grand Siècle*. Paris: Payot & Rivages, p. 266.
14. Greengrass (1995), p. 75.
15. Agrippa d'Aubigné (1620) *Histoire universelle*, vol. 3, Maillé: Jean Moussat, p. 231; see Oman, C. (1937), *A History of the Art of War in the Sixteenth Century*. London: Methuen, p. 502.

In the early days, Henri was king not of France but of an army – it was, as he admitted to Du Plessis Mornay, 'the sole basis' of his authority.[16] All early-modern armies were prone to desertion, so that it was essential that Navarre be popular with his soldiers. However, the character of this army made it a special challenge. Its hard core was made up of nobles and their retainers, mostly mounted.[17] The king's cause depended on these mostly volunteer aristocratic cavalry, who, as Davila reported, 'bore Arms only for Honour'.[18] Kirsten B. Neuschel and Arlette Jouanna have shown how the French nobility lived in a culture of honour that was performance oriented – it was necessary to do deeds of prowess and have them witnessed in order to win a great reputation. Further, noble culture also prized independence and individualism.[19] Because of their cultural values and because of the localised nature of the *guerres de religion*, Huguenots tended to go home and attend to local concerns, save when a truly great matter was in hand, or when inspired by results – or by a leader.[20] As contemporaries declared, 'the valour of the French is such a nature that unless it is employed at once it ebbs away.'[21] By seeking battle, the ultimate stage of honour, Henri ensured that his nobles were less likely to slip away because they felt their presence was not required, or because they suffered from *ennui*: when these cavaliers followed his white plumes (purchased for a hundred *écus*)[22] in a charge they would find themselves, as their king told them, 'au chemin

16. Greengrass (1995), p. 73.
17. Public Record Office, State Papers France, 23, fo. 28; *Calendar of State Papers and Manuscripts, Relating to English Affairs, Existing in the Archives and Collections of Venice and in Other Libraries of Northern Italy*, vol. 9, *1592-1603*, (ed.) H. F. Brown (London: HMSO, 1897), p. 9, no. 23.
18. Love, R. S. (1991) '"All the King's Horsemen": The Equestrian Army of Henri IV, 1585-1598', *Sixteenth Century Journal* 22 (3): 511-33 (quoting Davila at p. 513).
19. Neuschel, K. B. (1989) *Word of Honor: Interpreting Noble Culture in Sixteenth-Century France*, Ithaca & London: Cornell University Press; and Jouanna, A. (1992) 'La noblesse française et les valeurs guerrières au XVIe siècle', in G.-A. Pérouse, A. Thierry and A. Tournon (eds), *L'homme de guerre au XVIe siècle*. St. Etienne: Université de Saint-Etienne, pp. 205-217.
20. See Neuschel (1989) 39-59; and Palma Cayet, P.-V., *Chronologie novenaire*, in J.-F. Michaud and J.-J.-F. Poujoulat (eds) (1838)_ *Nouvelle collection de mémoires pour servir à l'histoire de France*, 1st ser., 12, Paris: p. 171.
21. Giovanni Mocenigo to the Doge and Senate, Chartres, 14 Apr. 1592, *Calendar of State Papers Venetian*, 9: 23, no. 55.
22. Russell of Liverpool, Lord (1969) *Henry of Navarre*. New York: Praeger Books, p. 95.

ɔire et de l'honneur.'[23] Further, because his reckless courage
combat was so inspiring, his heroics served a pragmatic pur-
ɪe Huguenots would not have served so faithfully a commander
ɹs less obviously imbued with all the virtues of the martial, chi-
culture to which they subscribed. The same is true of the Catholic
s who joined the king when his status was still questionable.[24]
Ƒhe need to inspire his own troops and to win over nobles and nota-
ɟ from outside his camp informed all, and influenced many, of Henri
's actions. This is not to say that his behaviour was entirely calcu-
ɭted. He probably was genial, open and impetuous by nature – but it
ɪlso suited his purposes to be that way.[25] Similarly, Henri's strategy, his
tactics and his apparently rash and imprudent behaviour while on campaign doubtless reflect his personality, but they also helped serve his
purposes.

Henri intentionally sought battles, for example, whereas the Duke of
Parma and his other opponents preferred to manoeuvre. In 1590, for example, he deliberately lured the duc de Mayenne into the battle of Ivry.[26]
The king was criticised at the time (by Queen Elizabeth) and has been
much criticised since by (English) historians, for attacking Noyon in the
summer of 1591, rather than going straight to Rouen to join the Earl of
Essex's English expeditionary force.[27] However, when the king captured
the town, it was, as Elizabeth's ambassador reported, 'a matter of great
consequence and credite to the Kinges partie, not so much in respecte of
the importance of the towne as for the dishonor which the enemie hathe
receaved in publicke opinion for not relievinge the same'.[28] In May
1592, during operations around Rouen, the Venetian ambassador observed that 'the obvious intention of the Duke of Parma to refuse a battle

23. Aubigné (1620), p. 231.
24. See D. Buisseret and B. Barbiche (eds), *Les Oeconomies royales de Sully*, 2 vols.
Paris: C. Klincksieck, 1970, 1988. 1: 307-308; Oman (1937), pp. 467, 483.
25. Lloyd, H. A. (1973) *The Rouen Campaign 1590-1592: Politics, Warfare and the
Early-Modern State*, Oxford: Clarendon Press, pp. 14-15, 159; Oman (1937), pp.
466-467; Slocombe, G. (1931) *Henry of Navarre: A Passionate History*. London:
Cayme Press, pp. 299-300.
26. Oman (1937), p. 496; Seward, D. (1971) *The First Bourbon: Henri IV, King of
France and Navarre*, London: Constable, p. 80.
27. See Lloyd (1973), pp. 105-106.
28. Sir Henry Unton to Lord Burghley, Dieppe, 15 Aug. 1591, in J. Stevenson (ed.)
(1847) *Correspondence of Sir Henry Unton, Knight, Ambassador from Queen
Elizabeth to Henry IV, King of France*, London: Roxburghe Club, p. 39, no. 21.

has caused the King to draw nearer to the enemy's camp, so that by a closer siege he may force the Spaniards to accept action'.[29] In 1596, the fall of Calais was a great blow to the royalist cause. As one contemporary observer put it: 'The kingdom is exhausted; no money can be raised by extraordinary measures. The nobility is worn out and weary, and many who are in duty bound to the King's service do not go'. War-weariness might have led to peace; but instead, Henri reacted with vigour, encouraging his supporters 'and promising to … wipe out this insult.'[30] He took to the field immediately and moved his army north, taking the town of La Fère en route. This action had no great strategic significance, but it was crucial because it served, as the Venetian ambassador reported, to 'encourage the French to change their resolutions', helping Henri to raise loans of 200,000 *écus*, and leaving the Spanish and their League allies cast down.[31]

Henri's strategy was thus to seek action; then, when battle was joined, Henri's tactics and personal conduct left no one in any doubt that he was a *preux chevalier*. At Coutras, Arques and Ivry, he led the main Huguenot cavalry charges and was caught up in the thick of the resulting mêlées. In the skirmishing around Rouen in 1591-92, Henri was to the forefront. Thus, in February 1592 near Aumale, Henri with a small force of cavalry 'found himself face to face with the vanguard of the enemy', as the Venetian ambassador noted. The king personally led the last squadron covering the retreat of the main body and was wounded.[32] Two weeks later, the duc de Guise (thinking Henri bedridden) occupied a strategic position near the royal camp; but the king, still leading from the front, fell on the enemy detachment and routed it.[33] He was in the front rank again at Fontaine-Française in June 1595, where, having scouted ahead of his own army's advance guard with a mere hundred or so horse, he became embroiled with the powerful Spanish vanguard. The king was fortunate to escape with his life in this 'périlleux' action, as he himself admitted. His way out was to launch a furious charge, then,

29. Giovanni Mocenigo to the Doge and Senate, Chartres, 14 May 1592, *Calendar of State Papers Venetian,* 9: 30, no. 69.
30. Piero Duodo to the Doge and Senate, Paris, 3 May 1596, *Calendar of State Papers Venetian,* 9: 197, no. 431.
31. *Oeconomies Royales de Sully,* 2: 26; Piero Duodo to the Doge and Senate, Paris, 11 and 25 May 1596, *Calendar of State Papers Venetian,* 9: 201, 205, nos. 435, 445.
32. Giovanni Mocenigo to the Doge and Senate, Chartres, 12 Feb. 1592, *Calendar of State Papers Venetian,* 9: 10, no. 25; *Oeconomies Royales de Sully,* 1: 301-306.
33. *Calendar of State Papers Venetian,* 9: 13, no. 33.

when the Spanish recoiled, personally to conduct a retreat in which he was one of the last to leave the field.[34]

In sieges, too, the king was foremost in the fight. At Rouen (where, in the siege of 1562, Henri's father had been shot dead while in the trenches) the king insisted on taking his turn, like every other gentleman at arms, in standing guard-duty in the trenches every fourth night; and he distinguished himself by his intemperate bravery in a (failed) assault on the walls.[35] At the critical siege of Amiens in 1597, it was reported that 'the king ... is perpetually exposed to dangers'; he wielded a pike himself when helping to drive a Spanish sortie from the royalist lines; and on another occasion in the trenches, a man with whom he was conversing was shot dead at his side.[36]

The king's behaviour caused comment even at the time. After the skirmish at Aumale the Duke of Parma allegedly dismissed Henri as 'only an officer of light cavalry', rather than a general.[37] After the assault on Rouen which followed soon after, Sully took the king to task for risking his life in such a fashion. Henri's answer is instructive. It could not be helped, he said, for he was fighting 'pour ma gloire et pour ma couronne' (note his order of precedence!). When Sully pressed him, Henri explained in more detail why he acted as he did. The majority of his army, all the Catholics, followed him not because they endorsed his faith or claim to the throne and would soon join the League if he did not impose upon their sense of honour.

> Pour toutes ces raisons endures-je d'eux tous mille choses qui me faschent bien fort, et hasardes-je ainsy tous les jours ma vie, *pour maintenir ma reputation* ... puisqu'il m'est beaucoup meilleur de mourir les armes à la main que de voir disperser mon royaume.[38]

De Thou, for one, understood why the king acted as he did, writing that the inspiration of Henri's courageous conduct was crucial in deciding the issue of the battle of Ivry. Venetian ambassadors likewise perceived the king's intentions: reporting after an action in 1591 that 'His Majesty

---

34. See *Oeconomies Royales de Sully*, 1: 13; *Mémoires de Tavannes*, p. 500; Oman (1937), p. 533; Slocombe (1931), p. 197; Russell (1969), p. 127.
35. *Oeconomies Royales de Sully*, 1: 284, 286-287.
36. *Calendar of State Papers Venetian*, 9: 279, 286, nos. 597, 613; Seward (1971), p. 117.
37. Quoted in Love (1991), p. 512.
38. *Oeconomies Royales de Sully*, 1: 288, 290.

ran some risk in his desire to set an example to the others who are backward at attacking unless his Majesty exposes himself to danger'; writing in 1592, after Henri had 'ordered a concentration of all his troops' against the Duke of Parma, that the presence of the king 'inspires them with the hope of victory'; and observing that, at the siege of Amiens in 1597 (where Henri was in the thick of things), 'it is incredible the way in which men rally to his Majesty'.[39]

Furthermore, Henri sought to prove himself a successful warrior king against the Spanish in particular. The Spanish had been the national enemy throughout the sixteenth century; moreover, as contemporaries knew (both Catholic and Protestant, both French and foreign), Spanish troops were the main prop of the League.[40] Professor Elliott has taught us that the Spanish in this period were concerned with *reputacion*,[41] but they were not alone. By seeking battle, and then by his actions whether on the field or in the trenches, Henri was showing that he was a better general, more courageous and more skilled at arms than the famous Spanish commanders such as the great Parma. He reduced their reputation, while enhancing his own. This was the way to detach the French, in particular the nobility, from their Hispanic alliance: not simply by inflicting reverses on the Spanish but showing them to be not worthy of being relied on. As the Queen of England put it in a letter to one of Henri's commanders in 1595, 'the need of the king [was] to to stifle the pride of his enemies'.[42]

The risks paid off. By his deeds of *prouesse*, he not only inspired his army – he also inspired the whole nation. Henri enjoyed success against the Spanish on the battlefield and in sieges and he broke French faith in Spanish arms by a combination of his generalship and his prowess. It is

---

39. *Histoire universelle de Jacques-Auguste de Thou*, French trans., vol. 11, Basle: Jean Louis Brandmuller, 1742, p. 146; Giovanni Mocenigo to the Doge and Senate of Venice, 30 Dec. 1591, *Calendar of State Papers Venetian*, vol. 8, *1581-1591* (London: HMSO, 1894), p. 570, no. 1138; same to same, 11 Feb. 1592, *ibid.*, 9: 9, no. 23; Pierre Duodo and Francesco Contarini to the Doge and the Senate, Paris, 20 Sept. 1597, *ibid.*, 9: 286, no. 613.
40. Note well Charles, duc de Guise to the Count de Mansfelt, (1593) Paris, 12 Aug., Koninklijke Bibliotheek (Den Haag), 121. A. 2., file 10.
41. Elliott, J. H. (1983) 'A Question of Reputation? Spanish Foreign Policy in the Seventeenth Century', *Journal of Modern History* 55 (3): 475-483.
42. Elizabeth to M. de Vidausan, Nonsuch, 25 Aug. 1595, Archives des Affaires Etrangères, Mémoires et Documents Angleterre 98, fo. 19.

no coincidence that the Edict of Nantes and the Treaty of Vervins (ending the war with Spain) were concluded within a month of each other.[43]

The king's war-effort depended, of course, on the efforts of many soldiers and administrators around him, so that this emphasis on his personal image may seem overstated, especially to modern eyes. Yet early-modern warfare was as much about reputation, about image, about perceptions, as about what we today would call strategic reality. This was why the king's first campaign following his accession to the throne was to besiege Paris in 1590. The city was, of course, strongly anti-Protestant and heavily defended, while the royal army was suffering from desertion and lack of supplies. However, to besiege the capital of the kingdom was important because it demonstrated Henri's intentions. It clearly showed that he meant to *be,* not just have the title of, king of France; it signalled in unequivocal fashion his determination to rule over the whole of his kingdom. Many of his followers had counselled him to retire beyond the Loire – retreating to his strongholds in the south was a ploy Navarre had used previously, but this was before he was king of France. Anne d'Anglure, seigneur de Givry, now posed his sovereign the crucial question: 'Qui vous croira roy de France, quand il verra vos ordonnances datées de Limoges?'[44] And Henri knew the answer.

By attacking Paris, Henri showed that he was a king. He did not take Paris on this occasion, to be sure; but by his campaigns throughout the 1590s he eventually created for himself the image of 'un Démon de batailles', as he was called after he recaptured Amiens in 1597. It was 'sa prouesse' that brought victory to his armies; and 'Toute l'Europe, tous les hommes, voz ennemis mesmes en rendent les tesmoignages deubz à vostre vertu'.[45] This was open flattery, but the qualities the writer chose to attribute to Henri are suggestive. All men knew of the king's qualities: what other veteran of Jarnac and Moncontour was still living and fighting? François de La Noüe and Henri de Guise were dead, but Henri de Navarre still lived; the best armies in France and Spain had been sent against him, but he had survived, despite 'les grandes et terribles dangers'.[46] He did not always win, but he could not be defeated, for

---

43. April and May 1598 respectively.

44. See Sully, 1: 142; Palma Cayet, p. 246; de Vaissière (1925), pp. 333-334 (quoting Givry at p. 334).

45. Séguier de Villiers to Henri IV, (1597), Archives des Affaires Etrangères, Mémoires et Documents France 372, fos. 102-104 (at fo. 102v).

46. *Ibid.*, fo. 102v.

his resistance continued at a level that left his enemies in despair. The duc de Mayenne blamed his utter defeat at Ivry on the king's 'desperate charge'.[47] Palma Cayet emphasised Henri's ability to endure the frequent journeys around the kingdom at the head of his army, and observed that it was this ubiquity and energetic commitment which was what the League most feared about him.[48] Within two hours of hearing the news of the fall of Amiens, the king was in the saddle, riding for Picardy, and de Thou's history emphasises the importance of the king's energy and personal example in regaining the city.[49] The 'vert galant' was indeed a 'démon de batailles'. Had they lived today, his enemies might have compared Henri to 'the Terminator': he'll come after you and he won't stop, you *can't* stop him, he'll keep on coming, that's what he does ...

To become king of France, Henri de Navarre had to be perceived as a king; and to be perceived as a king, he had to act like a king. It was because he was successful in so doing that he became king and was able, not to win the wars of religion, but at least to bring them to an end. Both Catholics and Protestants had no doubt that Henri was the most able and determined soldier of the wars, the most kingly monarch, too, since Henri II, perhaps since François 1er. Henri IV was seen as a generous and compassionate prince,[50] but even more his image was as a tireless and a victorious captain. Accordingly, when he issued an edict of pacification, there was a much greater willingness to accept it, despite some dissatisfaction with its compromises, because there was no reason to believe that continuing the war would bring better terms. De Thou, in his 'Ode à Henri IV', held up the king's image as indefatigable captain as a warning against those who might consider resuming hostilities:

Aussi quand des mutins la fureur inutile
Recommencent sans cesse une guerre civile
Te contraint de t'armer, & de les prévenir,
La victoire te suit, & ses faveurs nouvelles
Font voir à ces rebelles
Que tu sçais les punir.[51]

---

47. Quoted by Russell (1969), p. 95.
48. See his *Chronologie Novenaire*, p. 167; Greengrass (1995), p. 75.
49. *Calendar of State Papers Venetian*, 9: 260, no. 556; *Histoire universelle de Jacques-Auguste de Thou*, 11: 188.
50. Seward (1971), p. 81; Greengrass (1995), pp. 75, 85-86.
51. *Histoire universelle de Jacques-Auguste de Thou*, 11: 144.

The king, too, consciously played on his image, developed over the previous decade, when dealing with opponents of the Nantes pacification, such as the (briefly) recalcitrant *parlement* of Paris. He declared: 'Those which will not have my Edict to pass seek wars' but told the lawyers that 'I will not make the wars'. The ultra-Catholics would not have the king's energy and prowess at their disposal, so where was their hope of victory if conflict was renewed? Indeed, if the *parlementaires'* opposition went too far, as it had against Henri III, then they would be opposed by the king, who warned them: 'I have leapt upon the walls of cities ... I can leap over your barricades'.[52]

Of course, other conditions were also felicitous for a settlement by the end of the 1590s, as a number of the other papers in this volume indicate. However, had the zealots on either side believed that war might still have helped them to achieve their goals, they surely would have renewed the conflict after a short respite and the Edict of Nantes would have gone down with Bergerac, Saint Germain and the rest.[53] Had the king been totally victorious, of course, he could have imposed a settlement, *à la* Louis XIV; had he not been as victorious as he was, his compromise settlement could never have stuck. Henri IV was able to make the Edict of Nantes 'stick' because he had successfully reasserted the power and authority of the monarchy, but to a great extent it was because he had acted, waged war and personally fought like a king that he was able to do this.

---

52. Potter (1997), p. 250; Knecht, R. J. (1996) *The French Wars of Religion 1559-1598*, 2nd ed. London: Longman, p. 125.

53. There was no further Huguenot rebellion until after Henri's death. The Rohan revolt, being against a minor, was against a king who could have no record of military prowess; yet many Huguenots still preferred to present *cahiers* and work through negotiation. Thus, even without Henri IV's own dominant personality, his legend was still sufficiently influential to prevent the recurrence of war on a similar scale to that which began in 1562, during another regency.

Bibliography

Manuscript Sources:

Archives des Affaires Etrangères, Mémoires et Documents Angleterre 98.
Archives des Affaires Etrangères, Mémoires et Documents France 372.
Bibliothèque Nationale, fonds français 23335.
British Library, Harleian ms. 4489.
Koninklijke Bibliotheek (Den Haag), Handschriften, 121. A. 2.
Public Record Office, State Papers France, 23.

ALAN JAMES

Between 'Huguenot' and 'Royal': Naval Affairs during the Wars of Religion

In a memoir to King Henri III of 1588, the duc de Guise, leader of the powerful Catholic League and Admiral of the Levant, proposed the deployment of a royal fleet in the Atlantic as the only effective means of defeating the Calvinist Henri de Navarre.[1] Although such matters do not normally figure prominently in the historical writing on the French Wars of Religion, as the legally constituted Admiral of Guyenne, Navarre's naval strength was clearly seen as a serious threat. Guise claimed that by issuing passports to merchants in Bordeaux, and in other ports of his jurisdiction south of the Loire, Navarre was making at least 600,000 *écus* annually, and with armed ships of his own at sea policing commerce he made a further 200,000 *écus* directly from prizes on transgressors. Thus Navarre had made himself the real 'maistre de la mer' in France. As a consequence, traditional land-based warfare could not weaken him, and an organised naval response by the crown was required. For this reason, royal revenues would have to be awarded to Guise from commercial traffic in the estuaries of the Gironde and the Loire, as well as revenue from Normandy and Picardy. Of course, in a familiar story, the king not only refused to endorse Guise but under intense political pressure determined to be rid of his overweening influence by arranging his assassination in December that year. Yet this does not leave the proposal a mere curious detail in the history of the civil wars. Naval affairs were an integral feature of the confessional and political landscape of the time. The tensions that had been tearing at French society had affected maritime affairs deeply and by 1588 were particularly acute. This was so, not simply at the highest political level between the crown, Guise, and Navarre, but also between coastal communities. Moreover, this climactic year of internal civil strife converged with the dramatic international events of the

---

1. British Museum, Lansdowne Ms. 57, f. 76, 'Proposals of the Duke of Guise, for setting a navy to sea, with the means to defray the charge of the same, 1588'.

Spanish Armada and with an emerging Ibero-Dutch naval conflict. Indeed the weakness of the French monarchy, both at home and abroad, was reflected in its long-standing need to define and exercise a naval authority which could overcome, not just endemic regionalism in maritime government and competing noble interest, but entrenched confessional divisions.

Since the early 1560s, there was a *de facto* religious pluralism in the navy with the Huguenots providing most French maritime and overseas activity. In this light, it is hard to avoid the conclusion that the sea had an important place in the formation of Huguenot identity, accounting in some measure for the on-going place of the port city of La Rochelle at the heart of the movement.[2] The source of Huguenot naval strength was the city's direction of privateering, conducted, at least nominally, under the legal authority of the Admiral of Guyenne, the young Henri de Navarre. In this capacity, he controlled local maritime justice through the distribution of *congés pour armer en guerre* and the corresponding authority to judge any prizes that were captured as a result. At the outbreak of the third civil war (1568-70), when La Rochelle became the centre of the Huguenot leadership's military effort, this authority was embodied in the council of Jeanne d'Albret, mother of the young admiral. As the final, legal authority over local maritime affairs, this council was a clear expression of the city's spirit of independence from royal naval influence. Moreover, its control of local naval activity easily translated into remarkably well-organised forces for use against the crown.[3] Thus along with the support of their English co-religionists, who arrived in their defence at the royal siege of La Rochelle early in 1573, the Huguenots represented a serious naval challenge.[4]

Along with the crown's frustrations at the siege, the contrasting success of its Protestant minority and its own inability to impose its authority in the distant ports and harbours throughout France led to the elaboration of a long-term legislative project to invigorate the authority

---

2. Parker, D. (1980) *La Rochelle and the French Monarchy*. London: Royal Historical Society, pp. 62-63.
3. Dietz, B. (1952-58) 'The Huguenot and English Corsairs during the Third Civil War in France, 1568 to 1570', *Proceedings of the Huguenot Society* 19: 278-294; Pablo, J. de (1956) 'L'armée de mer huguenote pendant la troisième guerre de religion', *Archiv für Reformationsgeschichte* 47: 64-76.
4. English forces had also briefly occupied Le Havre. Tom Glasgow, Jr. (1968) 'The Navy in the Le Havre Expedition, 1562-1564', *Mariner's Mirror* 54: 281-296.

of the office of Admiral of France. Yet this effort was not focused on Guise but on Henri III's favourite, Anne de Joyeuse, who was named to the office in June 1582 in place of the duc de Mayenne, future leader of the League.[5] In typical fashion, Joyeuse's nomination was accompanied by royal letters clarifying his legal authority and privileges.[6] Due to the disruptive circumstances of the wars, Joyeuse was explicitly given extensive military authority over fortifications, ports, ships, and munitions along with the necessary financial independence to order associated payments from the royal treasury. To help direct local, private violence, the admiral was also given particular authority over maritime justice. He was guaranteed the freedom to continue the practice of naming vice-admirals who would hold equal authority in his absence (and who, it should be noted, in most cases were the truly active naval players involved in administration and in campaigns). Equally, in exchange for the suppression of the admiral's annual pension of 6,000 *livres* the crown dropped its claim, previously expressed in legislation of 1554, to the exclusive right to nominate officers of the local admiralty courts in favour of the admiral.[7] No longer just a fiscal office with limited responsibility and a set income, therefore, the admiralty was to become a more independent charge with potentially important military consequences. Of course, the admiral's effectiveness still depended upon the recognition of his personal legal privileges. For this reason, protecting the admiral's potentially lucrative rights from local encroachments and rationalising the collection of revenue was the focus of the crown's efforts, and letters to this effect soon followed.[8] These culminated in the extensive edict of March 1584 which was to elaborate, once and for all, the existing legal

---

5. Michel Vergé-Franceschi makes the important observation that the nobility had an interest in naval office in the sixteenth century. Yet he implies that there was royal indifference to the situation and concludes that the offices remained sterile, used only as pawns by competing noble families. Vergé-Franceschi, M. (1997) 'L'amirauté de France dans la deuxième moitié du XVIe siècle: un enjeu entre catholiques et protestants', in M. Acerra and G. Martinière (eds) *Coligny, les Protestants et la mer*. Paris: Presses de l'Université de Paris-Sorbonne, pp. 35-43; 'Les amiraux de France, 1492-1592: Treize terriens', in Masson and Vergé-Franceschi (eds) *La France et la Mer*, pp. 177-191.

6. AN Marine B[4]1, fos. 35-8, 'Lettres pour le sr de Joyeuse admiral de france et de bretagne', 24 June 1582.

7. Taillemite, E. (1993) 'Les Ordonnances de marine au XVIe siècle', in P. Masson and M. Vergé-Franceschi (eds) *La France et la mer au siècle des grandes découvertes*. Paris: Tallandier, pp. 55-68.

8. BN Fr. 17329, 'edit pour le fait de l'admirauté, 1582', 6 August 1582.

structure of French maritime government as well as the authority of the admiral as expressed through the local admiralty courts, the *tables de marbre de l'amirauté* as courts of appeal, and above them the parlements of Rouen and Paris.[9] In addition to a potentially lucrative source of personal income, this network of courts was theoretically the local expression of the authority of the admiral and, by extension, of the crown itself.

In practical terms, however, the French admiralty was weak and its jurisdiction was effectively reduced to Picardy and Normandy alone. In Brittany, for example, it would be nearly impossible to have Joyeuse's rights and the other terms of the edict of 1584 enforced, for the admiralty of France had never been recognised there. Traditionally, the governor acted as admiral, and maritime justice was the exclusive reserve of the Breton parlement administered locally by royal judges, not by admiralty courts in the name of the admiral of France. Thus a far clearer indication of the extent to which a coherent royal naval authority could plausibly be expected to function throughout France is found in a compromise that was reached between Joyeuse and the new provincial governor, the duc de Mercoeur, to share responsibilities for maritime affairs.[10] The short-lived agreement betrays not just competition between the two offices on a jurisdictional, or even personal, level but a difference in priority, with the governor concerned more with provincial affairs and commerce and the admiral with international and military matters. According to this agreement, royal courts would continue to hear maritime cases (though agreeing to keep a separate register). In times of peace, captains leaving Breton ports for trade within Europe and for the Barbary coast would receive their passports from the governor. Yet reflecting the over-riding military priority of the crown's legislation at this time, in times of war such passports would be issued by the admiral. Furthermore, the admiral's traditional right to issue *congés pour voyages en long cours* was to be respected as were his revenues from any prizes captured in the course of the voyage.

---

9. Isambert, Jourdan and Decrusy (eds) (1822-33) 'Edit sur la jurisdiction de l'amiral, le droit de prise, la pêche du hareng, l'entretien des navires, etc.', *Recueil général des anciennes lois françaises* 16: 556-590.

10. BN Dupuy 464, f. 5, 'Articles accordez entre Monsieur le duc de Mercoeur gouverneur et lieutenant général pour le roy en Bretagne et Monsieur le duc de Joyeuse admiral de france et de bretaigne sur l'administration de leurs charges', 5 April 1584.

The promotion, as far as possible, of a strong, loyal admiral of France with real personal military influence beyond the borders of Normandy and Picardy had three principal motivations. First, as Guise would imply, with the continued strength of Huguenot privateering in the Atlantic, the admiralty of Guyenne was potentially more militarily potent than that 'of France'. Motivating the crown also was its desire to begin to play a naval role on the international stage. Specifically, Joyeuse's nomination to the charge in 1582 coincided with a royal naval expedition to the Azores in support of Portuguese rebels against Spain. Although Joyeuse himself did not personally lead the disastrous campaign, the crown had clearly recognised the need to rationalise maritime government in order to facilitate the co-ordination of the many, dispersed resources needed for operations of this size (reportedly over sixty ships in this case).[11] More generally, from 1584 naval power simply assumed a greater place in European affairs. Spanish military successes that year led to the recapture of Antwerp in 1585, and with the resulting Dutch blockade of the Scheldt, it could be said that an era of commercial embargoes, economic warfare, and naval strength was emerging in northern Europe.

Finally, the need to define a strong, royal admiralty also reflected internal developments and was pursued to very specific political ends. The 1584 edict coincided with a dramatic shift in French politics following the death of the last Valois heir to the throne. This left the Calvinist Henri de Navarre as heir presumptive, heralding the rise of the Catholic League in opposition and the most destructive phase of the civil wars. For the crown, defending the legal rights of the admiral was a means of displacing countless local rival claimants, and so on a grander scale was also one potential avenue of opposition to League influence in coastal provinces. In Brittany, however, since the constitutional claims of the admiral were extremely tenuous, this opportunity began to crumble almost as soon as it presented itself. Presumably, it was to try to secure Mercoeur's loyalty and to keep him from the clutches of the League that royal policy concerning maritime government in Brittany took an abrupt shift in 1584. On 26 April, *lettres patentes* guaranteed that as long as Mercoeur remained governor no change to his original provisions would be allowed. In March the following year, Brittany won other minor concessions as well as guaranteeing the jurisdiction of its

---

11. Knecht, R. J. (1998) *Catherine de' Medici*. London: Longman.

courts. Then, following Joyeuse's death in battle in 1587, the pretence was dropped altogether. A royal declaration of 17 August 1588 declared that the agreement between the two was 'cassez ... comme chose n'ayant eu lieu'. Mercoeur's provincial admiralty rights were restored in full, and no future innovation in Brittany was to be attempted.[12]

In Normandy, however, the admiralty remained a much stronger political card in the royal hand. Yet even here and in Picardy, its effectiveness still depended upon guaranteeing the strictly personal authority of the admiral and his independence, for in practice neither the authority of the office nor of the admiralty courts was widely recognised.[13] Indeed the parlements of Rouen and Paris as sovereign courts for maritime affairs were deeply suspicious of the admiral's authority and of the role of the admiralty courts themselves. In practice, they often existed in name only and were displaced entirely by the ordinary courts, whilst the *table de marbre de l'amirauté* was frequently overlooked as an intermediate court of appeal. Thus the edict of 1584 also gave the admiral certain personal privileges associated with his military functions which lay beyond the competence of the courts altogether. Local communities near the coasts of France, for example, were subject to the *guet et garde*, that is to military duty either in local militias or simply by providing watches and warnings against the approach of raiders from the sea. The crucial point is that the levies that were raised on the local parishes for this protection were paid directly to the admiral. To this end, the edict reserved for him the appointment of the *capitaines et gardes des costes*, with any currently in the service of local governors or others requiring *lettres d'attache*. Formalising what was essentially a personal, fiscal and military jurisdiction in this way risked conflict with the administration of the ordinary courts, and for that matter with the admiralty courts themselves, for these *capitaines* were, in effect, personal agents of the admiral who were expected to defend his privileges and to collect money on his behalf.[14]

Protecting the independent, financial privileges associated with the charge of admiral in this way was essential to the crown's wider naval designs. As Admiral Henri de Montmorency later said to Louis XIII in

---

12. BN 500 Colbert 292, fos. 26, 29v-30, 30v.
13. Darsel, J. (1969-73) 'L'amirauté en Normandie', *Annales de Normandie* 19-22.
14. In a commission to a *capitaine* in Calais in 1623, Admiral Montmorency recognised this and had to forbid him to 'entremettre ... au fait de la justice et visitation (des vaisseaux)'. AN Z^{1}D 6, fo. 67.

defence of the use of personal agents to collect revenue from the *guet et garde*, 'l'admiral doit jouir du droit de guet.... Sy l'admiral perd ce droit ... le roy perd le droit, et en le perdant, la conservation des costes maritimes'.[15] For the same practical reasons, other revenue to which the admiral was entitled could also be collected directly or policed by personal *procureurs* and *receveurs* at each *siège*, specifically for the protection of his own rights. Although the ordinary admiralty officers retained considerable authority to inspect ships and cargoes, they could not deal with 'ce qui concerne nos droicts et perception d'iceux'.[16] Therefore, insofar as the crown could be said to be pursuing a naval programme in the 1580s, it was giving its legal backing to the independent pursuit of the admiral's personal rights with his own *commis* and *receveurs*. This, it must be assumed, was seen as a more effective means of exercising naval influence and dislodging regional rivals than the almost universally ignored constitutional system of admiralty courts.

Joyeuse's nomination as admiral also foreshadowed an even bolder move by the crown in February 1583 to unify the divided governorship of the province in his favour, which among other things wedded the largely theoretical legal privileges of 'admiral' to the practical authority of 'provincial governor'. Yet if Joyeuse was to exercise practical naval authority, he would still have to overcome both the resistance of individuals such as the vice-admiral, Jean de Moy, who dominated Norman maritime affairs and the equally worrying Protestant activity in the province.[17] For if Normandy was the traditional legal heart of the Admiral's authority, the two key ports of Dieppe and Le Havre were its soul, and both communities had been particularly receptive to Reformed teaching. Recognising the potential danger this represented and the practical value to the crown of the ports themselves, when the two governorships fell vacant they were filled with relations of Joyeuse, de Chatte and Branças-Villars respectively, and *lettres patentes* even at-

---

15. BN Fr. 17329, f. 279, 'Mémoire de monseigneur le duc de Montmorency pour monseigneur le chancellier pour garder les costes de la mer'.
16. Isambert, *Recueil général*, pp. 558, 581. These personal receivers were specifically restricted to collecting the rights of the admiral, not those belonging to the king: AN Marine C^4 225, fo. 170, article 2.
17. This consideration of the Guise in Normandy is based on Carroll, S. (1998) *Noble Power during the French Wars of Religion: The Guise Affinity and the Catholic Cause in Normandy*. Cambridge: Cambridge University Press, esp. pp. 149-159, 195.

tempted to make them permanent, automatic extensions of the office of admiral of France.[18] In the following years, de Chatte provided the bulk of the naval strength that was sent to defend the port of Brouage in Saintonge, the Catholic stronghold nestled within Navarre's power base. Given Breton reluctance to participate in any such venture, the small Norman squadron of eight ships armed at Dieppe constituted the entire royal fleet that Henri III ordered to the area in 1586.[19] Reinforcing the bond between the government of Normandy and an invigorated admiralty 'of France' for Joyeuse, therefore, was not a perfunctory legal exercise. It was necessary to attempt to pursue the inter-related processes of co-ordinating naval resources for royal service, of checking the rising political influence of the Guise in the province, and of blocking the maritime influence of the Huguenots.

Naval affairs assumed a particular political poignancy following Joyeuse's death in battle in 1587. Although Guise had been victorious over Navarre's German reinforcements in the north that year, he was overlooked for the now vacant governorship of the province and for the admiralty of France in favour of another of the king's *mignons*, the duc d'Epernon.[20] The significance of such a move goes beyond the sign of royal favour or the personal political antagonisms that it demonstrates, for there were also immediate, practical reasons to keep the admiralty beyond the reach of the League. Previously, installing Joyeuse as admiral had put paid to League plans to invade England in 1582-83. By 1588, of course, the Spanish Armada dominated the naval affairs of western Europe, and Spain's need for a friendly channel port made the security of Picardy, in particular, a matter of considerable diplomatic concern for Henri III. The *ligueur* duc d'Aumale had been openly conspiring with the Spanish and took a number of Picard towns in 1587. Yet due, in part, to English intervention, the League was unable to take the main prize of Boulogne from Epernon, its local governor and new Admiral of France. That Philip II, therefore, remained without his safe haven in the channel for his fleet is not insignificant, for as Martin and Parker suggest, had

---

18. Rosenweig, L. (1856) *Office de l'amiral en France du XIIIe au XVIIe siècle*. Vannes, p. 16.
19. La Roncière, C. de (1923) *Histoire de la marine française* 4: 210-213.
20. According to Carroll, the 'major issues of contention' in the impending conflict between the king and the League were 'Epernon's position and the control of two key provinces: Normandy and Picardy'. Carroll, *Noble Power*, pp. 202-203.

Boulogne fallen into League hands 'the Armada campaign might have taken a very different course'.[21]

Thus from an international naval perspective, in 1588 when Guise presented his naval proposal to the king, defending Boulogne from the League was actually the most important role the French crown could play. Indeed it seems the greatest naval challenge for the crown at the time was simply to maintain its neutrality in very difficult circumstances. Accordingly, Epernon's activity as admiral in 1588 involved, above all else, enforcing his authority in Norman and Picard ports. Specifically, he received news of ships being armed for action against England at Dieppe with *congés* issued by the Duke of Parma. This was an affront both to his authority and to royal naval policy, threatening an era of co-operation with England that was just emerging. At about the same time that he is-sued orders for the arrest of the Dieppois ships, however, Epernon also confirmed a standing *congé* previously issued by Joyeuse to a Breton captain to make war on Huguenot shipping from La Rochelle (which was closely linked to English privateering).[22] Thus, however well the news of the Armada's defeat was received by Henri III, he was not willing to condone unfettered Rochelais privateering on Spanish targets either. The office of admiral was still intended to be an expression of royal inde-pendence, from Guise and Navarre alike (and, by extension, from their respective foreign allies).

Nevertheless, with Joyeuse's recent death and the failure to extend the admiralty into Brittany, this rather limited policy of defending a fragile neutrality was a sign that the greater royal naval experiment was falling apart. Moreover, the wider political victory of the Guise in 1588 very soon made any sort of valuable independent political role for the admiralty a nonsense.[23] The only alternative to accepting Guise's domi-nation may well have seemed to be embracing Huguenot naval power, and indeed a window of opportunity seemed to be opening for them to

---

21. Martin, C. and Parker, G. (1988) *The Spanish Armada.* London: W.W. Norton, p. 124.

22. BN Fr. 5156, 'lettres du duc d'Epernon', fos. 9,11,14, 15. I am embarking on a full study of the organisation, size, and international support network of Huguenot pri-vateering and its relationship to the French crown in the sixteenth century.

23. When Epernon retired the office in favour of his brother La Valette in February 1589, the League-dominated Estates-General insisted, on the charge that he already held too many charges, that he immediately give it up in turn. That same month, Henri III recognised Antoine de Brichanteau, marquis de Nangis as admiral.

define more fully the emerging shape of French maritime government. Although we cannot quantify Huguenot naval strength at this point, or confirm Guise's assessment of it, in the years following the siege of the city, La Rochelle continued to operate as a centre of privateering, which remained an important source of revenue for the Huguenot movement.[24] And in contrast to the recent experience of the French crown, Henri de Navarre had been in a position to offer naval support, however limited, to Elizabeth I in 1588. From 1584, when Navarre had become heir presumptive, a feeling of confidence and anticipation of French maritime fortunes can be found in the works of some Huguenot writers. La Popelinière, for example, greeted Joyeuse's nomination with enthusiasm, defended his theoretical claim to universal authority, and called on the nation to greater naval glory.[25] Similarly, Duplessis-Mornay envisaged a powerful international league against Spain and urged the adoption of a far-reaching programme of maritime power.[26]

Unfortunately for those Huguenots who envisaged a global maritime strategy for France, however, the future was not so bright. Whereas for the Dutch, policing the Scheldt and imposing retaliatory commercial restrictions against the southern provinces and Spain in a combined commercial and military war at sea from 1584-85 meant that privateering, and its proper regulation locally, to some extent defined their identity, Huguenot naval power took a very different turn. Though maritime activity remained important, for some at La Rochelle, the promotion of local naval power now seemed less likely to offer the promise of independence and strength for the city that it once did but the decidedly less enticing prospect of being drawn into the costly struggles of the Protestant leadership. Merchants seemed more concerned with re-establishing trade and with protecting their privileges than with main-

24. Greengrass, M. (1999) 'Financing the Cause: Protestant Mobilization and Accountability in France (1562-1589)', in Benedict, Marnef, van Nierop, and Venard (eds) *Reformation, revolt and civil war in France and the Netherlands 1555-1585*. Amsterdam: Royal Netherlands Academy of Arts and Sciences, pp. 233-254.
25. La Popelinière (1585) *L'amiral de France et par occasion de celuy des autres nations*. Paris.
26. Duplessis-Mornay (1824) *Mémoires et correspondance* 2: 580-593; Poton, D. (1997) 'Philippe Duplessis-Mornay et la mer: Discours au roi Henri III sur les moyens de diminuer l'Espagnol (1584)', in Acerra and Martinière (eds) *Coligny, les Protestants et la Mer*, pp. 145-154.

taining military potential as such.[27] Indeed, even from the earliest days of the Huguenot movement in France under Admiral Coligny, there was a discernible tension between the interests of the merchants and privateers of La Rochelle and the Calvinist military leadership. To a large extent, for the Rochelais, naval strength was important primarily as a safeguard of their local commercial interests and privileges.

La Rochelle's independent maritime activity had always enjoyed a measure of legitimacy afforded by the admiralty of Guyenne. Yet as Navarre moved closer to the throne, the ambiguous relationship between 'Huguenot' and 'royal' naval power became more difficult for the city to sustain. Although naval matters remained important to the Huguenots, their unwillingness to compromise and to co-operate fully with outsiders made it difficult for Navarre to capitalise on his naval strength in his capacity as Henri IV. Initially, a Rochelais fleet was sent by the king to strike at Nantes, the heart of League influence in Brittany. Yet in preparation for the siege of Rouen of 1592, Henri IV had to gather sufficient naval forces to clear the Seine and to complete an effective blockade. In order to secure the necessary financial support, he ordered the collection of a *droit de convoi* on ships entering and leaving the ports of the admiralty of Guyenne. This, apparently, was a step too far for the merchants of La Rochelle and played into the hands of those elements of Rochelais politics who resisted co-operation with the king. Early in 1592, Henri IV commissioned two captains from nearby Marennes to collect the levy by force if necessary, and five or six ships were stationed in the roadstead to this end. In response, the city directed land-based artillery at the unwanted force, equipped a number of warships of its own, and in February forced it to retreat. In November, the crown stepped up the pressure with a small fleet sent from Brouage by the governor St Luc, and in March 1593 more ships arrived to enforce the collection of the levy.[28]

This picture of Henri IV using force against the city to solicit naval support is a far cry from the 'maître de la mer' described by Guise. Indeed, the situation for French naval power had become desperate. Not only was Huguenot naval support unreliable, but in Brittany, Mercoeur had aligned himself with the League and opened the port of Blavet to

27. Robbins, K. C. (1997) *City on the Ocean Sea: La Rochelle, 1530-1650*. Leiden: Brill, pp. 220-221.
28. Merlin (1878) *Archives historiques de la Saintonge et de l'Aunis* 5: 63-380, 405-407; Trocmé and Delafosse, *Commerce Rochelais*, pp. 24-25.

Spanish forces. Even the Norman foundation of the French admiralty was divided. Dieppe served as the conduit of English military support for the royalist effort, but Villars had joined the League, and from his base in Le Havre controlled the Seine and was instrumental in defending Rouen against the royal siege from November 1591. For practical naval support in Normandy, Henri IV could only count on de Chatte and on that of the Dutch and English. Despite the arrival of a Franco-Dutch fleet early in 1592 to complete the royal siege of Rouen, the navy could do nothing to turn the royalist fortunes around in the face of Spanish reinforcements, and the siege was lifted in April 1592.[29]

Since the siege of La Rochelle of 1572-73, the Huguenots had proven equally difficult to defeat militarily at sea, to control, or to assimilate, and this proved costly to the crown's on-going commitment to the development of a coherent naval authority. In February 1594, Henri IV offered the admiralty to the *ligueur* Villars to help secure his capitulation, but in doing so he also regained Rouen and Le Havre bringing some crucial stability to the recently divided Norman admiralty.[30] With the installation of Charles de Montmorency as admiral following Villars' death in 1595 the tenuous claim to universality in royal maritime government was revisited. Yet Huguenot naval strength still lingered on the legal edge of French maritime government, neither flourishing as an independent Protestant power nor fully integrating within a royal, catholic model. For all its international connections and support for Protestant privateers from other provinces, Rochelais naval strength was still regionally driven and correspondingly difficult to harness and control remotely. In this respect, it is typical of French maritime government in general which was exceptionally fragmented. Most ports, or coastal regions, whether with Catholic or Protestant majorities, were difficult to influence and operated under long-standing traditions of virtual independence.

---

29. For an account of the 'battle of the Seine', La Roncière, *Marine française* 4: 222-228. In October 1592, Henri IV had tried to put an end to the competing claims for the office by naming Biron, who had led the royalist army in Normandy, as admiral.
30. Benedict, P. (1981) *Rouen during the Wars of Religion.* Cambridge: Cambridge University Press, pp. 227-228.

Part 2

Religious Pluralism in Literature

LUC RACAUT

The Cultural Obstacles to Religious Pluralism in the Polemic of the French Wars of Religion

In his recent book on religious co-existence, *La paix de religion*, Olivier Christin argues that only the emergence of an *Etat impartial* put an end to the bloodshed of the French Wars of Religion.[1] The idea of a secular, autonomous political reason, he argues, saved the kingdom from the ruin born out of confessional division. The Edict of Nantes epitomizes this nascent political reason, promulgated by a State that vowed to protect all its subjects, regardless of their confessional orientation. The Edict of Nantes, as it was demonstrated elsewhere in this collection, was but the last of many edicts of pacification promulgated throughout the French Wars of Religion. The conciliatory spirit expressed in the Edict of Nantes had its roots in the ideas of Michel de L'Hôpital and the efforts of Catherine de Médicis to obtain religious peace. But the policy promoted by the Regent and the chancellor never represented the opinion of the majority, or those of the Gallican institutions. Indeed their conciliatory efforts provoked fierce opposition from the pillars of orthodoxy that were the *Parlement* of Paris and the Sorbonne. If the idea of religious pluralism made good political and philosophical sense, as Christin has shown, it faced formidable resistance, notably from the traditional upholders of orthodoxy.

The Edict of Nantes aimed to pacify two diametrically opposed cultures that had been pitched one against the other for nearly half a century. Throughout the Wars of Religion, Catholic polemic demonized Protestants and sought to mobilize the Catholic community against them. The Protestant apologists, by contrast, derived a sense of justification and vindication from persecution, principally through a comparison with Early Church Martyrs. The respective parties' perceptions and distrust of the other were difficult to overcome.

---

1. Christin, Olivier (1997) *La paix de religion: L'autonomisation de la raison politique au XVIe siècle.* Paris, Seuil, p. 16.

The printing press played a significant role in forging Catholics and Protestants' respective perceptions of the other. The central role of Geneva in disseminating the Calvinist message in France has been well demonstrated by Robert Kingdon and others since.[2] Catholic contributions to the Reformation debate, on the other hand, have not received as much attention. From the sending of Calvinist missions in France in 1555 until the outbreak of the civil wars, the Catholic community grew increasingly aware of the presence of a religious minority in its midst. The accidental death of Henri II in the summer of 1559 precipitated events and from the Conspiracy of Amboise (1560) onwards, the kingdom was irremediably divided. This attempt to free the young King François II from the influence of the Guise, which tragically backfired, was the origin of a flurry of polemical literature defending the respective sides' agenda. The Protestant party asked for the dismissal of the Guise from court while Guise apologists pointed to the Protestants as dangerous rebels and agitators. From this point onwards polemical literature, on both sides of the confessional divide, followed the development of events closely. Adversarial polemic, often vitriolic in its content, was therefore a considerable obstacle to religious pluralism.

Control of the printing press played an important part in the emergence of an autonomous political reason. Henri of Navarre could not promulgate his agenda for peace until he had wrested control of the Parisian printing presses from the hands of the League. The Edict of Nantes, like all other edicts of pacification, was printed in the royal printing houses that had been set up for that purpose by Michel de L'Hôpital in 1561.[3] The control of the printing medium is therefore crucial to the emergence of the idea of religious pluralism. It determined the ability of the emerging *Etat impartial*, described by Christin, to propagate these ideas in the kingdom. At the beginning of this initiative, during the reign of Charles IX, printing was still controlled by the traditional upholders of orthodoxy, the Sorbonne and the *Parlement* of Paris. These powers of censorship were used positively to promote the publication of Catholic tracts that were extremely adverse to pluralism and advocated persecution. This production has been largely overlooked in the historiography

---

2. Kingdon, Robert (1956) *Geneva and the coming of the Wars of Religion in France, 1555-1563* Geneva.
3. Pallier, Denis 'Les réponses catholiques', in Roger Chartier and Henri-Jean Martin (eds) (1983), *Histoire de l'Édition Française*. 3 vols, Paris, Promodis, I, p. 340.

of the French Wars of Religion, despite the insights that it provides into the *mentalité* of those opposed to religious toleration. Conflict over control of the printing press erupted on the eve of the Wars of Religion, with the publication of a book that had been approved by the *Parlement* and the Sorbonne but was offensive to the Crown.[4] In October 1561, this inflammatory anti-Protestant work provoked the reaction of the English ambassador in Paris, Throckmorton, who asked for it to be removed from circulation:

> Lately a lewd book came to his hands, printed at Paris, wherein the author speaks slanderously of Kings Henry VIII. and Edward VI. It is dedicated to the Constable, to whom he addressed his complaint to have reformation of the matter, who procured order to be addressed to his son, Marshal Montmorency, to have all the books suppressed, and the author is likely enough to be punished.[5]

In compliance with the ambassador's remonstrance, Montmorency publicized an order forbidding printing without the authorization of the King or his council, thus conflicting with the *Parlement* and the Sorbonne's prerogatives.[6] This order came in the wake of the refusal of the *Parlement* of Paris to ratify the edict of pacification of January 1562 that included unprecedented measures of conciliation. The King had authorized Montmorency to have the Edict of January immediately printed by Charles Langelier although the *Parlement* had refused to ratify it.[7] From 1562 onwards the Crown gradually wrested the censoring powers from the traditional censors, a trend which culminated with the Edict of Moulins in 1566.[8] Henceforth the Crown could turn its powers of censorship, originally designed to stem the flow of Protestant books, against

---

4. Gay, Jean (1561) *Histoire des scismes et heresies des Albigeois conforme à celle du present: par laquelle appert que plusieurs grands princes, & seigneurs sont tombez en extremes desolations & ruynes, pour avoir favorisé aux heretiques.* Paris, Pierre Gaultier.
5. Stevenson, Joseph (ed.) (1866), *Calendar of State Papers, Foreign series, of the reign of Elizabeth, 1561-1562.* London, Public Record Office, IV, no. 833, p. 503.
6. Guilleminot, Geneviève (1977) *Religion et politique à la veille des guerres civiles: Recherches sur les impressions françaises de l'année 1561.* 2 vols, unpublished thesis of the Ecole des Chartes, I, p. 11.
7. Droz, Eugénie (ed.) (1970-76), *Chemins de l'Hérésie.* 4 vols, Geneva, Droz, I, p. 375, III, p. 407; Pallier, 'Les réponses catholiques', p. 340.
8. Guilleminot-Chrétien, Geneviève 'Le contrôle de l'édition en France dans les années 1560: la genèse de l'édit de Moulins', in P. Aquilon and H.-J. Martin (eds) (1988), *Le Livre dans l'Europe de la Renaissance: Actes du XXVIIIe Colloque international d'Etudes humanistes de Tours.* Nantes, Promodis, 378-385, pp. 382-383.

disaffected Catholics who disapproved of the royal policy of conciliation. This became particularly relevant during the League when Henri III
attempted to use these prerogatives to quash the doubts that were raised
about his ability to reign.

*   *   *

James K. Farge has noted that the history of the Reformation in France
had too often been written from the point of view of the agents of
change, a point of view which has been adopted wholesale by the historical tradition born out of the Enlightenment.[9] This is also true of the
historiography of the French printed book that is dominated by Geneva
and the Protestant movement. I should like to challenge the premise, at
least as far as France is concerned, that the Protestants were better than
the 'forces of reaction' at harnessing the relatively new medium of
printing. French Catholic print in the vernacular has been understudied
and underestimated by many historians. Its quantity and impact was considerable and it enabled French Catholics to compete on an equal footing
with the Genevan Reformers.

The target audience of vernacular polemic was very clearly defined.
The Catholic authors who wrote in the vernacular all justified their
seemingly radical move from Latin by the need to reach *les simples*. The
argument ran that it was necessary to write in the vernacular so that the
simple who were most at risk from heretical conversion, would be instructed. Catholics clearly misunderstood and overestimated the impact
of the Protestant printed book on the 'masses'. It was the literate élite
that were most at risk of being converted to Protestantism through the
printed medium. Nonetheless, following the rhetoric which had been
employed in the Lutheran Reformation, French Catholics justified their
use of the vernacular, maintaining that they wished to appeal to 'the lay
common folk'. It is very difficult to gauge the impact that printed polemic had on 'the population at large'. By all accounts, printed books
had only a small audience predominantly composed of the urban élite.
Estimates of literacy and population given by Jeffrey Sawyer indicate
that by 1615, 'the most popular pamphlets might have reached the hands

---

9.   Farge, James K. (1992) *Le parti conservateur au XVIe siècle: université et Parle-
      ment de Paris à l'époque de la renaissance et de la réforme.* Paris, Les Belles
      Lettres, p. 25.

of 1% of France's urban population'.[10] But these ideas did not circulate exclusively within literate circles as they were also expounded from the pulpit.[11] Indeed many polemical authors were also celebrated preachers like Antoine de Mouchy, Robert Ceneau and René Benoist.[12] The boundary between avowed aims and hidden agendas was often thin, as many books appearing to be works of theology for the layman were in fact polemical tracts.[13]

The material found in these pamphlets at once reflected and influenced the perception of Catholics and Protestants of one another and confirmed their expectations. Catholic authors added credence to their words by resorting to the ubiquitous 'rumour', like Robert Ceneau who wrote: 'je n'en scay rien que par ouyr dire'.[14] The best example of the cross-fertilization between written polemic and the spread of rumours by word of mouth is provided by the account of the affair of the rue St Jacques. On the night of 4 September 1557, students of the Collège du Plessis stumbled upon a clandestine Protestant meeting in a house nearby where between three and four hundred people had gathered to celebrate the Lord's Supper. Many people were arrested, notably women, who were led through the assembled crowd. The Catholic polemicists used this event as the basis for accusing Protestants of conducting orgies and engaging in acts of sexual promiscuity including adultery, incest, and sodomy. Accusations of ritual murder, infanticide and cannibalism appeared in the course of the controversy as the persecutions emboldened Catholic preachers and polemicists. The affair of the rue St Jacques was earmarked as a significant event in the history of persecution by the

---

10. Sawyer, Jeffrey K. (1990) *Printed Poison: Pamphlet Propaganda, Faction Politics, and the Public Sphere in Early Seventeenth-Century France.* Oxford, Oxford University Press, p. 48.
11. Scribner, Robert (1981) *For the Sake of Simple Folk.* Cambridge, Cambridge University Press, pp. 2-3.
12. Taylor, Larissa J. (1999) *Heresy and Orthodoxy in Sixteenth-Century Paris: François Le Picart and the Beginnings of the Catholic Reformation.* Leiden, p. 2-5; Tallon, Alain (1997) *La France et le Concile de Trente, 1518-1563.* Rome, pp. 735, 741-742.
13. Higman, F. (1998) 'Les genres de la littérature polémique calviniste au XVIe siècle', *Travaux d'Humanisme et Renaissance*, 326, 437-448.
14. Ceneau, Robert (1562) *Response catholique contre les heretiques de ce temps.* Paris, Guillaume Julien, sig. E1ʳ.

Protestants, and described by Barbara Diefendorf as contributing to the 'intensification of religious hatreds'.[15]

In addition to these accusations, Catholic polemicists made comparisons between Protestants and medieval stereotypes of heretics to justify persecution at a time when the Court seemed to be in favour of conciliation.[16] For example, entire chapters of Antoine Du Val's *Mirouer des Calvinistes* (1562) are eloquently entitled 'qu'il fault brusler les Calvinistes' and 'que les rois doivent punir les heretiques'.[17] These accusations were used hand in hand with arguments that Protestantism threatened to take over the body politic like a disease and turn the moral order upside down. Inversion was readily used by Catholic polemicists who aimed to demonstrate that the Reformation was a manifestation that 'time was out of joint'. Antoine de Mouchy, for example, writes in the wake of the affair of the rue St Jacques in 1558: 'Maledictions sur ceulx qui disent le mal estre bien: & le bien estre mal. Qui mettent tenebres pour lumiere, & lumiere pour tenebres: qui mettent chose amere pour doulce, & chose doulce pour amere'.[18] Similar imagery was often used employing analogies which reflect social, political and religious disorder. In a similar way, Jean Gay, a member of the conservative *Parlement* of Toulouse, described Protestantism as a synonym for disunity and divisiveness:

> Et pour aultre plus grand signe d'atheisme, contre eulx ne faut sinon noter le desordre & confusion qui journellement est entre eux par continuelles sedition, scismes et diversité d'opinions de toutes anciennes heresies, & inventions d'aultres nouvelles.[19]

This opposition between order and chaos is only one aspect of the way Protestantism was seen to be turning the 'world upside down'. The opposition of health and disease was another metaphor for heresy that was used by the polemicists who likened heresy to a disease.

---

15. Diefendorf, Barbara B. (1991) *Beneath the Cross: Catholics and Huguenots in Sixteenth-Century Paris.* Oxford, Oxford University Press, p. 50.

16. Racaut, Luc (1999) 'The Polemical use of the Albigensian Crusade during the French Wars of Religion', *French History*, 13, no.3, 280-302.

17. Du Val, Antoine (1562) *Mirouer des Calvinistes et Armure des Chrestiens, pour rembarrer les Lutheriens & nouveaux Evangelistes de Genéve.* Paris, Nicolas Chesneau.

18. Mouchy, Antoine de (1558) *Responce a quelque apologie que les heretiques ces jours passés ont mis en avant sous ce titre: Apologie ou deffence des bons Chrestiens contre les ennemis de l'Eglise catholique.* Paris, Claude Frémy, sig. A4ᵛ.

19. Gay, *Histoire des scismes*, p. 39.

Catholics also used misogynistic arguments asserting that Protestant preachers were pandering to women (referred to as *femmelettes*) who were easily converted due to their 'natural' weakness. For Robert Ceneau, the Reformation turned the 'natural' authority of men over women upside down by allowing women access to Scripture, although they lacked the intellect and the moral fibre to understand its teachings.[20] Ceneau was sure to find a ready audience for these arguments as they drew on a long tradition of misogyny, found in the literary culture of the medieval period and the Renaissance.[21]

The authors of these pamphlets were often high-ranking members of the Gallican Church. Antoine de Mouchy (1494-1574), syndic of the Faculty of theology of the University of Paris, was instrumental in the purge of the *Parlement* and took part in the Colloquy of Poissy.[22] Robert Ceneau, bishop of Avranches, was chosen by the Cardinal of Lorraine, along with de Mouchy, to represent France at the Council of Trent.[23] René Benoist, the confessor of Mary Stuart and author of a vernacular translation of the Bible, was also a syndic of the Sorbonne.[24]

Catholic propagandists were successful in fostering an image of Protestants as dangerous and treacherous agitators, enemies of the kingdom and of true religion. They associated the Protestants with monstrous crimes, evoking medieval stereotypes such as the 'medieval Manichee'.[25] Despite the efforts of the Protestants to counteract these accusations, this image of Protestantism stuck until far into the seventeenth century. Catholicism was predominantly associated, in the minds of the illiterate majority, with unity and tradition summed up in the inscription found on the façade of the Hôtel de Ville: 'One king, one law, one faith'.[26] Protestants were portrayed as challenging both unity and tradition and were associated with the cultural themes of the 'world turned upside down' and rebellion.

---

20. Ceneau, *Response catholique*, sigs E4^{r-v}.
21. Matheson, Peter (1996) 'Breaking the Silence: Women, Censorship, and the Reformation', *Sixteenth Century Journal*, 27, 97-109.
22. Feret, P. (1900-09) *La Faculté de Théologie de Paris et ses Docteurs les plus célèbres: Epoque Moderne XVI - XVIIIème siècle*, 6 vols, Paris, II. pp. 51-55.
23. Tallon, *La France et le Concile de Trente*, p. 735.
24. Pasquier, Emile (1913) *René Benoist: Le Pape des Halles (1521-1608)*. Paris.
25. On the 'medieval Manichee' see R. I. Moore, (1985) *The Origins of European Dissent*. Oxford, Blackwell, pp. 9-20, 243-246.
26. Diefendorf, *Beneath the Cross*, p. 159.

To use the analogy of disease, so prized among Catholic authors, ideas spread like viruses.[27] Peter Matheson uses this analogy to describe the spread of the Reformation in print: 'universal access to public media can carry the bacilli through the body politic'.[28] The recurrence of certain themes in so many different sources suggests that they enjoyed a wide distribution not only in print, but also in the predominant medium of orality.

Protestants were aware of the power of propaganda and attempted to counteract the polemic of their opponents. This concern can be found among Protestant authors who wrote 'pour servir, en commun, à tout le peuple' to dispel the false image of the Protestants that the Catholics were disseminating.[29] For example, Nicolas des Gallars accused the Catholics of rousing the 'commun populaire' against the Protestants:

> Les suppots de Satan [...] s'attachent maintenant aux Rois, maintenant aux Evesques, maintenant aux Docteurs, puis au commun populaire, crians à l'aide & à l'arme, pour esmouvoir tout en rage, & enflammer les coeurs à l'effusion du sang des innocens.[30]

Similarly, the Protestant minister Antoine de la Roche Chandieu, accused the Catholics of encouraging outbreaks of violence through demagogy and the spreading of false accusations:

> Je laisse à parler de la cruauté dont & grans & petis ont usé depuis vingt cinq ou trente ans en çà contre les enfans de Dieu: mais n'aguere a on apperceu comme ceste rage s'emflamme de plus en plus: ainsi que le populaire a bien monstré en la fureur dont il a esté esmeu contre hommes & femmes craignans Dieu, & mesme contre Dames & Damoiselles d'estat & renom, lesquelles autrement il n'eust osé regarder qu'avec crainte & reverance.[31]

---

27. Rushkoff, Douglas (1991) *Media Virus! Hidden Agendas in Popular Culture.* New York, Ballantine Books, pp. 9-10.
28. Matheson, *The Rhetoric of the Reformation*, p. 28.
29. Roche Chandieu, Antoine de la (1563) *Histoire des persecutions, et martyrs de l'Eglise de Paris, depuis l'an 1557. Jusques au temps du Roy Charles neufviesme.* Lyon, [Senneton frères], sig. b1[r].
30. [Nicolas des Gallars], *Seconde apologie ou defense des vrais chrestiens, contre les calomnies impudentes des ennemis de l'Eglise catholique. Ou il est respondu aux diffames redoublez par un nommé Demochares docteur de la Sorbonne* (n.p., s.n., 1559), sigs A2[v], D6[v]-D7[r].
31. Chandieu, *Histoire des persecutions*, sig. b2[v].

Public opinion emerged during the Wars of Religion as a political force to be reckoned with and the failure to recognize its political significance contributed to the difficulties of Henri III's reign. Henri III had begun to acknowledge the importance of propaganda when he resorted to the printing press to celebrate his military successes at Jarnac and Moncontour. But he could do little to turn the table on his opponents after the day of the barricades when the League employed sympathetic Parisian printers to vilify him.[32] The League was remarkably successful in imposing its vision of Henri III on the public, to the extent that it has remained in the French collective memory to this day. The realization of the potential danger and usefulness of propaganda increased during the reign of Henri IV whose popular legend is even more notorious.[33] But, as Sawyer suggests, it seems that this lesson was not properly drawn until the beginning of the seventeenth century:

> Pamphlet authors and political leaders [...] worked hard to influence the general public's perceptions of the conflict [...]. Experienced tacticians [...] realized that the confrontation would actually be won in the sphere of public opinion before it was won on the battlefield [...]. Governments sought to control the printing press from the beginning. It is well known that this effort broke down in the sixteenth century, once pamphlets began to be used systematically as weapons in the arsenal of Protestant [and Catholic] reformers [...]. Effective control of the printing industry did not begin until the 1620s, when Richelieu was finally able to enforce the law.[34]

At the beginning of the French Wars of Religion, however, 'public opinion' was not wholly recognized as either a legitimate or desirable political force. Although its influence was acknowledged in passing, it was invariably described as a negative and dangerous entity. Words describing 'public opinion' were pejorative. 'Opinion' connoted an entrenched view closer to 'belief' or 'doctrine' than 'judgement' or 'opinion' in the modern sense. For the Catholics, 'opinion' was synonymous with heresy and discord:

> Voiez combien les heretiques sont fertiles à porter & produire tousjours de nouveaux monstres: car à peine trouverez vous un seul de ceux qui ont mis en avant quelque nouvelle heresie (ou bien qui en ont renouvellé quelque une des anciennes,

---

32. Pallier, 'Les réponses catholiques', p. 342.
33. Barbiche, Bernard 'Le régime de l'édition', in Chartier and Martin (eds), *Histoire de l'Édition Française*, I, 367-377, pp. 368-369.
34. Sawyer, *Printed Poison*, pp. 5, 25, 46.

& de celles qui de long temps ont esté condamnées) qui ne soi tousjours accompagné de plusieurs erreurs monstrueux, & plusieurs prodigieuses opinions.[35]

For the Protestants, on the other hand, it was synonymous with libel and defamation: 'Et m'esmerveille comment un Magistrat tant renommé, qu'est la Court du *Parlement* de Paris, permet, que si meschantes opinions soient publiées, voire avec privilege'.[36] On both sides of the confessional divide, there was no such thing as a 'good' opinion and diversity of opinion was actively discouraged. Nonetheless there was a reluctant realization among polemical authors that popular perceptions could be moulded and somehow mattered.

The polarisation and over-simplification of complex and ambiguous issues characteristic of propaganda pervades the material published throughout the Wars of Religion. As one of these authors, Robert Ceneau, put it: 'Il faut ou estre totalement calviniste ou estre entièrement fidelle, finablement ou tout blanc ou tout noir; car la foi nette et entière ne reçoit rien mixtionné'.[37] The polarization of issues was a leading characteristic of the Catholic reaction, and it was arguably the most formidable obstacle to the establishment of religious pluralism. Robert Ceneau and others abhorred the 'middle ground', specifically because it allowed for the development of self-determination and choice. By polarizing the issues in this way, these authors were hoping that their audience would stick to what they knew best, that is the old religion, and end the dangerous debate initiated by the Reformers. Anti-Protestant works were intended for Catholics and did not seek to convince the heretics of their errors. To use Cold War rhetoric, the aim of the authors of Catholic polemic was 'containment' rather than 'roll-back'. It was not until the end of the civil wars that Catholic writers pursued a more positive policy of conversion and Catholic regeneration. It should be added that this change of tone in Catholic writings was the result of pressure

---

35. Hozius, Stanislas (1561) *Des sectes et heresies de nostre temps: traicte composé premierement en Latin, par reverend Pere en Dieu monseigneur Stanislas Hozie, Evesque de Varme en Pouloigne, dedié au roy de Pouloigne, & nouvellement mis en François*. Paris, Vascosan, p. 48.
36. [Augustin Marlorat], (1561) *La Response aux lettres de Nicolas Durant, dict le Chevalier de Villegaignon, addressées à la Reyne mere du Roy. Ensemble la Confutation d'une heresie mise en avant par ledict Villegaignon, contre la souveraine puissance & authorité des Rois*. n.p., s.n., sig. E7[v].
37. Ceneau, *Response catholique*, sig. A7[r]. I owe this quote to Tallon, *La France et le Concile de Trente*, pp. 331, 432, 502-503.

from both the Court of the Bourbons, and the influence of the Council of Trent.

*   *   *

The anti-Protestant polemic of the French Wars of Religion fostered the development of two entrenched worldviews and although there is evidence of cross-fertilization between the two discourses there was no real dialogue. Only when an independent arbiter, the *Etat impartial* described by Christin, was able to enforce peace with the Edict of Nantes, could both parties agree to disagree. The polemic of the Wars of Religion was the product of a *mentalité* that rejected religious pluralism as an aberration at best. There is evidence that this view survived long after the Edict of Nantes and its revocation as it was still debated at the turn of the twentieth century in the context of the separation of Church and State:

> On sait que les ennemis de la République, coalisés sous le nom de *nationalistes*, et se couvrant du masque de la religion pour mieux tromper la foule, ont entrepris, sans motif avouable, une violente croisade contre les minorités religieuses, contre les protestants et les juifs.[38]

This example shows that the idea of religious pluralism, which emerged during the Wars of Religion, was still problematic for our near contemporaries. The resilience of this debate testifies to the formidable challenge facing those who advocated religious pluralism in the sixteenth century.

---

38. Rabaud, Camille (1901) *Ce que la France doit aux Protestants.* Paris, p. 5. It should be noted that the title page of this pamphlet bears a list of bulk prices: 'Prix: 50 Centimes, pour la propagande, Cinq exemplaires, 1 fr. 50; - dix, 2 fr. 50; - vingt, 4 fr.'.

Bibliography

Primary Sources:

[Gallars, Nicolas des] *Seconde apologie ou defense des vrais chrestiens, contre les calomnies impudentes des ennemis de l'Eglise catholique. Ou il est respondu aux diffames redoublez par un nommé Demochares docteur de la Sorbonne* (n.p., s.n., 1559).

[Marlorat, Augustin], *La Response aux lettres de Nicolas Durant, dict le Chevalier de Villegaignon, addressées à la Reyne mere du Roy. Ensemble la Confutation d'une heresie mise en avant par ledict Villegaignon, contre la souveraine puissance & authorité des Rois* (n.p., s.n., 1561).

An., *Advertissement a la Royne Mere du Roy, Touchant les miseres du Royaume au temps present, & de la conspiration des ennemis de sa Majesté* (Orleans, [Eloi Gibier], 1562).

Calendar of State Papers, Foreign series, of the reign of Elizabeth, 1561-1562 (London, Public Record Office, 1866), IV, no. 833.

Ceneau, Robert, *Response catholique contre les heretiques de ce temps* (Paris, Guillaume Julien, 1562).

Du Preau, Gabriel, *Des faux prophetes, seducteurs, & hypocrites, qui viennent à nous en habit de brebis: mais au dedans sont loups ravissans* (Paris, Jaques Macé, 1563).

Du Val, Antoine, *Mirouer des Calvinistes et Armure des Chrestiens, pour rembarrer les Lutheriens & nouveaux Evangelistes de Genéve* (Paris, Nicolas Chesneau, 1562).

Gay, Jean, *Histoire des scismes et heresies des Albigeois conforme à celle du present: par laquelle appert que plusieurs grands princes, & seigneurs sont tombez en extremes desolations & ruynes, pour avoir favorisé aux heretiques* (Paris, Pierre Gaultier, 1561).

Hozius, Stanislas, *Des sectes et heresies de nostre temps: traicte composé premierement en Latin, par reverend Pere en Dieu monseigneur Stanislas Hozie, Evesque de Varme en Pouloigne, dedié au roy de Pouloigne, & nouvellement mis en François* (Paris, Vascosan, 1561).

Mouchy, Antoine de, *Responce a quelque apologie que les heretiques ces jours passés ont mis en avant sous ce titre: Apologie ou deffence des bons Chrestiens contre les ennemis de l'Eglise catholique* (Paris, Claude Frémy, 1558)

Rabaud, Camille, *Ce que la France doit aux Protestants* (Paris, 1901).

Roche Chandieu, Antoine de la, *Histoire des persecutions, et martyrs de l'Eglise de Paris, depuis l'an 1557. Jusques au temps du Roy Charles neufviesme* (Lyon, [Senneton frères], 1563).

Sorbin, Arnaud, *Histoire des albigeois, et gestes de noble simon de monfort. Descrite par F. Pierre des Vallées Sernay, Moine de l'Ordre de Cisteaux* (Paris, Guillaume Chaudière, 1569).

LORIS PETRIS

Faith and Religious Policy in Michel de L'Hospital's Civic Evangelism

The boundaries between the emerging religious confessions remained unclear until the years 1559-1563, with the result that Christians often had difficulty in locating their religious identity with precision. If the broad avenues of the rival ecclesiologies are delineated, the religious sensibility of many individuals remains *terra incognita*. The religious stance of Michel de L'Hospital (1505?-1573) is one of these uncharted areas where misunderstanding has been frequent. Ideological interpretations have either elevated the Chancellor of France (1560-1573) onto a pedestal or hurled him into the mud. There have been legends of a crypto-Protestant Chancellor, a founder of the *Politiques*, a liberal thinker, an apostle of freedom of conscience and a humanist born tolerant. Myths of L'Hospital as a magistrate who was tolerant on principle and as a sceptic rationalist have recently been revived. Yet, the central question is not L'Hospital's confessional choice, but his personal attitude towards religion and his religious policy. These two areas were closely linked into a coherent evangelical sensibility that sought to work actively within the sphere of politics and society. Deploring that the *Icones* of Théodore de Bèze depicted L'Hospital with a candle behind him for not having declared himself 'ouvertement du party de ceux de la Religion', André Thévet concludes that there is

> une infinité de personnes, qui l'on veu vivre à la Catholique: si ce n'a esté de coeur on ne le sçauroit deviner, cela estant un secret, qui n'est revelé aux hommes.[1]

Yet, the *Carmina* and the speeches of L'Hospital provide evidence that 'cela a esté de coeur' and unambiguously deny the charge of nicodemism, hypocrisy or scepticism. Though they do not show any clear decision along the confessional divide, such as in his attitude to the Eucharist, they reveal L'Hospital's personal religious sensibility and his

---

1. Thévet, A. (1584) *Les Vrais Pourtraits [...]*, Paris, fo. 576v.

political attitude towards religious pluralism. Though some lacunae remain, these texts permit a fuller evaluation of the Chancellor's personal belief and religious policy.

The Humanist's Evangelical Commitment

The *Carmina* blend the humanist criticism of religious hypocrisy with the Gallican onslaught on Roman corruption.[2] Whereas the speeches will be more circumspect, L'Hospital's Latin poetry satirizes Rome, pontifical ambitions and the corruption of the Council of the Church. It is dismayed at this *Urbs* abandoned to astrology, nepotism, luxury and to the *libido dominandi*,[3] so that 'neither man nor horse ever came back better from Rome'.[4] More than conventional *topoi*, these attacks aim at the confusion between the secular and the religious spheres: 'it is sacrilegious for the people to meddle with sacred matters and for the priest with the profane'.[5] Through the inhuman priest who rides a horse, calls men to arms and points out the victims,[6] the Gallican magistrate harshly criticises the discrepancy between nomenclature and reality:

> But, however, the name of Christ is put forward as an excuse on every altar and we call our nation with Christ's name and furthermore we openly acknowledge our master and our God: we are interested only in names and in the mere appearances of things [...][7]

---

2. See Crouzet, D. (1998) La Sagesse et le Malheur. Michel de L'Hospital, chancelier de France. Seyssel: Champ Vallon, 1998, 60-77 and Petris, L. (1998) 'Michel de L'Hospital et les guerres d'Italie: *De postrema Gallorum in Italiam expeditione carmen* (1557)', *Bibliothèque d'Humanisme et Renaissance,* LX: 77-105. The present article, written before the publication of D. Crouzet's study, shares with it several conclusions.
3. See *Michaelis Hospitalii Carmina,* Amsterdam: Balthasarem Lakeman, 1732 (abbr. AMST), 37-38, 42-47 and 174-176; *Œuvres complètes,* P. J. S. Dufey (ed.) (1824-1826), Paris; Geneva: Slatkine, 1968, III, (abbr. DUFEY), 53-55, 60-66 and 268-270.
4. *'Nam Roma nec vir, nec equus melior redit unquam'* (AMST, 174; DUFEY, 269), a common proverb (Le Roux de Lincy, *Le Livre des proverbes français,* Paris, 1859, I, 296).
5. AMST, 316; DUFEY, 414.
6. AMST, 372; DUFEY, 505-506.
7. *'Attamen & Christi nomen praetexitur aris / Omnibus, & nostram Christi de nomine gentem / Dicimus, ac vulgo dominumque Deumque fatemur: / Nos rerum species & nomina sola tenemus [...]'* (AMST, 314-315; DUFEY, 411-412).

This acknowledgement of religious hypocrisy and moral decadence has two consequences: the further interiorization of L'Hospital's religious sensibility and the primacy of an evangelical *orthopraxis* over conventional orthodoxy. In other words, a simultaneous and synergetic emphasis both on piety and works.

L'Hospital always portrays social evil as the external symptom of ontological evil inherited from the original sin. The social satire wells up from his Augustinian consciousness of man's sinful nature. In a letter to Antonio Vacca,[8] he questions the link between salvation and works, 'because the question of annihilation or salvation of souls is neither a slight nor a joking matter'.[9] His *ruminatio mortis* faces the implacable question of retribution for the deeds of this life:

> After so many efforts, will there be, Vacca, any reward? [...] Nothing if, forgetting the ancient pact, we follow the things we have before rejected and discarded, as the dog goes back to his vomit and eats again the food once spewed.[10]

If piety does not motivate them, while works may in themselves be necessary they are insufficient. 'To Heaven, to Heaven, we must yet pray for the same Grace that, once granted, will blow instantly within our hearts and will ignite a holy fire'.[11] In contrast to the Protestant emphasis on predestination, for L'Hospital Grace is freely granted to everyone. Yet, only faith can help man deserve God's Grace in a spiritual synergy where man has a free initiative but God retains the authority. Human freedom must cooperate in Grace's gift: man must overcome worldly torments through prayer, trust in God and personal involvement to become, as Pantagruel put it, 'cooperateur avecques luy'.[12] This Grace accessible to all requires works. Far from discouraging human action, it entails human collaboration: 'all virtue rests on action; closed within, it is of no use to unfortunate mortals. Empty trust is put in vain in works; our hand must be kept busy night and day'.[13] Here we are at the heart of

---

8.   AMST, 344-349; DUFEY, 451-457.
9.   AMST, 344; DUFEY, 451.
10. *'Ecquid erit praemi post tantos, Vacca, labores? [...] Si nos immemores antiqui foederis illa / Missa prius sequimur rejectaque, non aliter quam / Quae redit ad vomitum canis, expulsumque resumit / Ore cibum [...]'* (AMST, 345; DUFEY, 452), reminiscence of Proverbs 26, 11 or II Peter 2, 22.
11. AMST, 346; DUFEY, 453.
12. Rabelais, *Quart Livre*, chap. XXIII. See AMST, 17-22; DUFEY, 28-33.
13. AMST, 346; DUFEY, 453-454.

a civic evangelism that reconciles the interiorization of faith with the requirements of a civic life: this was of critical importance for a magistrate imbued with Ciceronian and Senecan wisdom. Indeed, the *Carmina* and the speeches, pen and words, are different means for acting and revealing this evangelical faith centred on Grace and action:

> Nobody, however pious he may be, gains access to Heaven by personal merit, even after a blameless life. Nobody can be his own guide on the path leading beyond the stars. God's Grace leads us and drags us right to Heaven. This is entirely God's gift [...][14]

Grace and action collaborate in a strict hierarchy. *'Nemo Deum novit nisi cui concesserit ille'*:[15] the Augustinian awareness of divine election and of the human inability to pry into God's will implicitly criticises those who claim that knowledge of God could be attained through human wisdom and religious precepts. Yet, L'Hospital's initially negative anthropology does not lead to a pessimistic view of the human condition. Though man must not rely excessively on his own powers, he must nevertheless have trust in his own moral strength. Deeply imbued, but not overwhelmed, by a sense of human depravity, L'Hospital blames himself for his ignorance and his will to bargain salvation with his creator.[16] Yet, the consciousness of his own inner merits lays the foundations for his collaboration with the divine plan: immediately after complaining about his own sinfulness and lack of worth, L'Hospital tells Vacca that such success as they have achieved in life is due to their personal merit rather than family influence or nepotism.[17]

L'Hospital's christocentrism establishes a strict hierarchy between the pagan and the Christian spheres. Platonic and Stoic themes serve Christ, who remains the paradigm. Thus, in order to console his friends and to define Christian poetry, L'Hospital takes the priest as the exem-

---

14. *'Nemo suis meritis aditum sibi fecit olympo, / Quanvis ille pius, quanvis sine crimine vixit: / Nemo sibi dux ipse viae super astra ferentis: / Ipsa regitque trahitque Dei nos gratia caelo. / Donum hoc omne Dei est [...]'* (AMST, 368; DUFEY, 500), recollection of Ephesians 2, 8 or Romans 5, 15-16. To link to AMST, 341; DUFEY, 447.
15. AMST, 33; DUFEY, 47, inspired by Matthew 11, 27.
16. *'O caecas hominum mentes, ignaraque corda !'* (AMST, 70; DUFEY, 77), *variatio* on Lucretius, *De Rerum natura*, II, 14, also on the ceiling of Montaigne's library. Also in AMST, 440.
17. AMST, 346-347; DUFEY, 454-455.

plar and asserts that pagan works are no match for the Holy Scriptures.[18] The *res christianae* must prevail over the *verba profana*. In a letter to Corbinelli, he regrets having lost so much time studying only *verba* that are devoid of reality.[19] 'Therefore, let us not be deceived by the vain school of wise men or the passion of eloquence: worldly knowledge is inflated to no purpose; the true and lasting wisdom is in Heaven'.[20] In this context, L'Hospital accentuates the gulf between divine omnipotence and the vanity of human life, echoing his epistle to Achille Bocchi and his own verses that Montaigne later had copied onto the beams of his library:

> *[...] Nostra vagatur*
> *In tenebris, nec caeca potest mens cernere verum*[21]

To explore causation without God's help is to risk losing one's way: it is to risk the fate of Icarus, the embodiment of human presumption. His was a negative *curiositas* that sought to pry into God's will, instead of a positive *curiositas*, to know oneself.[22] One must be prepared to suffer exile, threats, discomfiture or even death for Christ, but never overconfident in one's strength or weak in one's resolve.[23] Here again, L'Hospital outlines an *aurea mediocritas* transposed into three areas: self-knowledge, profane versus Christian truth and poetry.[24]

God's vision is all-encompassing: 'the depths of our hearts are open to Him and nothing anywhere escapes Him or remains hidden to Him.'[25] This *Deus absconditus*, whose vision is superior to that of the legendary Argus, requires worship and profoundly simple human response. As God sounds out the depths of our heart, spiritual emotion prevails over its visible expression; Christian poetry must seek to emulate the simplicity

---

18. See AMST, 307, 318-319 and 12; DUFEY, 403, 416-417 and 22.
19. AMST, 338-343; DUFEY, 444-450, to link to Erasmus, *De rebus ac vocabulis*. The corruption of words is opposed to the royal verbal transparency. See R. Descimon (ed.) (1993) *Michel de L'Hospital, Discours pour la majorité de Charles IX et trois autres discours*. Paris: Imprimerie nationale, 121 (abbr. *Discours*).
20. AMST, 342; DUFEY, 449, reminiscence of I Corinthians 1, 20-21 and 3, 19.
21. AMST, 93; DUFEY, 120, verses located here for the first time. See Montaigne to L'Hospital, April 30, 1570.
22. AMST, 208-214; DUFEY, 281-288.
23. AMST, 341; DUFEY, 447.
24. AMST, 318-319 and 341; DUFEY, 416-417 and 448.
25. AMST, 29; DUFEY, 42. The king's sight is therefore also panoptical: 'L'œil de justice voit tout, le roy voit tout' (*Discours*, 110).

of God's word. A unified vision based on this concept of *simplicitas* links L'Hospital's views on poetry, morals, law and religion. In all these areas, this clarity of purpose enables men to employ poetic images, money, texts, sacred rites and so on, in God's service instead of being dependent on them. In a letter to Claude d'Espence, L'Hospital's view of God determines the Christian poetic style that is adopted:

> Let us worship, I say, this holy, unique and supreme God with a pure heart and with a bare and simple worship, just as He is Himself guileless and immutable. Let our style be unaffected, easy, unfussy, unadorned, yet full of gravity [...][26]

L'Hospital did not have to read Calvin's call for a 'clarté de parole' based on a 'simplicité rude, et quasi agreste'.[27] In 1563, he praised the early Christians, who 'worshipped the divine might with a plain form of service, in simple and unified rites' and reminded his readers that Christ's disciples were not scholars but ignorant fishermen.[28] Similarly, he contrasted the virtues of a simple life to the luxury that reigned at court and bred corruption and greed.[29] In matters of law, he condemned petty quibbles and disputes, arguing that truth and justice required simplicity and sensitivity rather than complexity.[30] Just as God can be approached only 'as an image, a shadow, as reflections of things in a mirror',[31] man should not pry into His will. The external rituals of the faith should be kept to a minimum. In L'Hospital's speeches, religious simplicity and oratorical atticism are inseparable and opposed to doctrinal quarrels and unending discussions:

---

26. '*[...] Illum inquam summum, sanctum veneremur, & unum / Pura mente Deum, nudoque ac* simplice cultu, / Ut simplex *ipse est, nec re mutabilis ulla. / Sit sermo incomptus, facilis, non anxius, omnem / Ornatum fugiens, plenus gravitatis [...]*' (AMST, 29; DUFEY, 43). See Petris, L. and Schneider, A. (1999) '*Nec enim est infans sapientia semper.* Définition et illustration d'une poétique chrétienne dans les *Carmina* de Michel de L'Hospital', in P. Henry and M. de Tribolet (ed.) *In Dubiis Libertas.* Mélanges d'histoire offerts au professeur R. Scheurer. Hauterive: Attinger, pp. 193-203.

27. Calvin (1541) *Institution de la religion chrestienne*, I, 8, 1.

28. AMST, 294; DUFEY, 396, reminiscence of Acts 2, 46 and AMST, 343; DUFEY, 449-450, recollection of Acts 4, 13.

29. See AMST, 214-228 and 189-195; DUFEY, 289-305 and 232-239.

30. See 7 September 1560 (AN, X^{1}A1595, fo. 200v°-203r°) and AMST, 84-89; DUFEY, 113-118. See *Discours*, 123-124.

31. AMST, 33; DUFEY, 48. See I Corinthians 13, 12.

[...] nostre religion ne gist poinct en dispute ny en fondement de doctrine, mais en *simplicité* et humilité, comme il appert par la remonstrance d'un personnage, vieillard non gueres savant, ny versé en dialectique, et ne sachant autre chose que Jesus-Christ et iceluy crucifié, comme il est escript en l'Histoire ecclesiastique. Lequel, par *simplicité de parolle* et confession de foy, convainquit de grandz dialecticiens qui n'auroyent par plusieurs jours esté convaincus ny confutez par les plus savans.[32]

Far from representing a negative philistinism, L'Hospital's rejection of abstruse dogmatic quarrels is a positive decision based on the primacy of the *simplicitas pietatis* in faith. 'Why should we declare ourselves Christ's disciples if no there is no real image of Him expressed in ourselves?'[33] The *imitatio Christi* demands an active and truthful expression of faith through works:

He who is learned in divine and human laws does not seem worthy to me, unless he has the additional attribute of zeal for equity and good, joined a love to piety, favouring the poor as much as the rich and sharing generously the revenues of churches to the needy.[34]

An evangelical orthopraxis thus prevails in L'Hospital over formal doctrinal orthodoxy, because the former is based on love (*caritas*), that is on faith and deeds, the latter on doctrinal discussion, that is on words alone and not deeds. The mystery of nativity holds for him more meaning than precise definitions of the Eucharist. Thus, his poem dedicated to Claude d'Espence does not digress into dogmatic discussed, but focuses on four essential elements of faith: the poverty endured by the Incarnate Christ, the revelation granted to gentiles as opposed to the arrogance of the Jews, the practical evangelical precepts and the spreading of the new faith through moderation and exemplary behaviour.[35]

---

32. *Harangue de Monsieur le Chancelier de France, faicte à l'assemblee de Poyssy [...]*, Lyon: B. Rigaud, 1561, 8, inspired by Sozomene, *Hist. eccl.*, I, 18. To oppose to AMST, 26; DUFEY, 38.

33. AMST, 262; DUFEY, 354. See Colossians 1, 15 and II Corinthians 4, 4.

34. '*Nec mihi dignus erit divina humanaque jura / Qui didicit, si non idem conjunxerit aequi / Atque boni studium, si non pietatis amorem: / Et nisi pauperibus faveat, locupletibus aeque, / Et nisi templorum reditus largitur egenis.*' (AMST, 263, v. 50-54; DUFEY, 355). See v. 287-323 and Repetti, R. (1990) *L'Educazione di un Re fanciullo: Michel de L'Hospital e la consacrazione di Francesco II (1559)*. Genova: ECIG.

35. AMST, 30-37; DUFEY, 44-52.

The Chancellor's Religious Policy

Foreshadowing the later words of Montaigne, the disgraced Chancellor reflected that 'there is no vice that idleness does not engender, whether you are slow or quick witted; weeds spread at will in uncultivated fields'.[36] This acknowledgement of the perils of idleness justified both his poetic writing and his commitment to civic life. Far from leading to a withdrawal into the self, the process of religious interiorization was expressed in the *Carmina* as faith made manifest through resolute *labores* committed into God's keeping. The speeches included the trust in the civilising power of words and the will to act in response to the real situation through the power of oratory and the enactment of laws and edicts.[37] Herein lies the underlying cohesion between the written and spoken word: deeds are as vital to an individual's life as piety is essential to social life. This link is illustrated by the motto of Charles IX which was chosen by L'Hospital, *Pietate et Iustitia*. The *Carmina* and the speeches are not two separate activities, *otium* as against *negotium*, but two expressions of the will to act upon reality in accordance with a christocentric ideal, the end-product being a unified civic evangelism.

L'Hospital's rejection of violence has long been mistaken with the defence of freedom of conscience. Yet, just as with Erasmus, his religious stance provides evidence for the viewpoint of an unambiguous advocacy of religious unity whilst simultaneously acknowledging the ineffectiveness of violence on consciences: this was an evangelical and Erasmian principle before it became a practical observation. Inspired by the Scriptures and the Church Fathers, the Chancellor condemned violence in the religious sphere as inhuman, useless and dangerous, leading only to hypocrisy or atheism. While the Duke of Guise attempted to curb heresy by force, L'Hospital exhorted Guise's brother, the Cardinal of Lorraine, to work for religious unity only through his eloquence and his piety, 'because it is stupid to think that this division of minds can be settled by the power of the sword and with gleaming armour. You will slaughter a few [heretics], but the earth, fertilised by such calamities and drenched with their blood, will throw up many more'.[38] Since Catholics

---

36. AMST, 353; DUFEY, 477, to link to AMST, 4-10; DUFEY, 12-18. See Montaigne, *De l'oisiveté* (I, 8).
37. See Petris, L. (1999) 'Guerre et paix dans les *Carmina* de Michel de L'Hospital', *Bibliothèque d'Humanisme et Renaissance* LXI : 95-108.
38. AMST, 290; DUFEY, 391, to oppose to AMST, 80-81; DUFEY, 89-90.

had plundered temples and Protestants had slaughtered priests, L'Hospital refrained from coming down in favour of one extreme or the other.[39] For him, Christ's life was sufficient example to condemn in advance any recourse to violence:

> The founder of our faith loved peace, and ordered us to abstain from armed violence; through His death, He taught us to endure violence, to withstand blows and even death; He did not want to compel and terrorise anybody through threats, nor to strike with a sword; but instead he sought to convert hardened souls and hearts through words.[40]

The sword cannot force consciences, which *'non ulla potest vis laedere ferri'*. Yet, this acknowledgement of an inalienable freedom does not lead to an unrestrained apology of freedom of conscience. Instead, the means of restoring religious unity are changed: the task is, only through love and persuasion, to 'instruire et endoctriner' those who are spiritually sick. Conscience may not be controlled through coercion, but is nevertheless not fully autonomous.

Is this criticism of violence against consciences a mere pragmatic consequence of the ineffectiveness of repression, or is it a more positive response, resulting from an *a priori* evangelical refusal to compel consciences? Reflection on the texts attributed to L'Hospital leads unambiguously to the second interpretation: the failure of coercion is simply an additional argument justifying the Chancellor's moderation. At the core of his political pragmatism stands a civic evangelism which determines his political choices. The extermination of heretics would be 'non seulement repugnante au nom de chrestien que nous portons, mais à toute humanité'.[41] As such it was to be abhorred by Christians: 'Violenter et persecuter à feu et à sang' the Protestants would be to 'faire la guerre à la nature et dechirer brutalement l'humanité'.[42] Even when the Chancellor advocated that legislative measures were required for politi-

---

39. AMST, 293; DUFEY, 394.
40. *'[...] hic pacem nostrae fundator amavit / Relligionis, abesse procul nos jussit ab armis: / Vim sufferre, patique suos & verbera, & ipsam / Mortem morte sua docuit: nec cogere quenquam, / Nec terrere minis voluit, nec caedere ferro: / Sed potius mollire animos & pectora dictis.'* (AMST, 291; DUFEY, 391-392).
41. *Mémoires de Condé*, Sécousse (ed.) (1743), London, 6 vol., II, 610.
42. *Discours sur la pacification des troubles*, in Taillandier, A. H. (1861) *Nouvelles recherches historiques sur la vie et les ouvrages du chancelier de L'Hospital*. Paris: Didot, 310; DUFEY, II, 194.

cal reasons, these were attuned to his own philosophical position. Humanist and evangelical arguments were adapted to political circumstances, but remained his central preoccupation. Similarly, L'Hospital often had to hide the *honneste* behind the *utile*: moderation and piety were both more honourable but also more effective in the correction of error.[43] L'Hospital argued that the history of Christianity provided irrefutable evidence that religion did not expand through violence and deception.[44] Christians in the first three centuries of the faith did not seek to

> extend their territorial borders by force, or guard their kingdoms with armed troops; instead, they were satisfied with humble abodes, they used their own hands to gain their food, and they approached God with tears and prayers for mercy [...][45]

They never converted with the sword: 'their distinctive feature was to persuade and to risk danger, but never to compel others. And they were not allowed to resist force, scarcely being allowed even to avoid it by flight'.[46] Heresy and dissension were not removed by force of arms, by guile or deceit, but 'by an exemplary life, by prayers, by genuine dialogue and in the early councils of the Church'.[47] L'Hospital thus attains the heart of his religious policy: 'Establish your code of conduct first and matters of doctrine will follow' (*Formandi primum mores, doctrina sequetur*).[48] Moral rectitude prevails over dogmatic demands; *pietas* expressed in the form of ethical conduct necessarily shapes dogma in a positive way. This was L'Hospital's fervent hope, yet in the circumstances of the mid-sixteenth century, it came close to postponing firm decisions in doctrinal matters.

Long before the 'ne forcez à coups d'espees nos consciences' of the *Exhortation aux Princes*, the refusal to compel consciences is best expressed in L'Hospital's speeches, where political choices embody Christian ideals. On 5 July 1560, in his first speech, L'Hospital argued that to take arms was exceedingly dangerous:

---

43. Petris, L. (1998), *art. cit.*, v. 139-141.
44. AMST, 36; DUFEY, 52.
45. AMST, 38; DUFEY, 54.
46. AMST, 372; DUFEY, 506.
47. AMST, 295; DUFEY, 397.
48. AMST, 296; DUFEY, 398.

les mallades de l'esperit ne se guarissent comme celles du corps [...] L'opinion se mue par oraisons à Dieu, parole et raison persuadee.[49]

False opinions must be amended, but not coerced. Some five months later, at the opening session of the General Estates in Orleans, he criticized coercion in matters of faith:

> Et si c'est religion chrestienne, ceux qui la veulent planter avec armes, espees et pistolets, font bien contre leur profession, qui est de souffrir la force, non la faire [...] Ne vaut l'argument dont ils s'aident, qu'ils prenent les armes pour la cause de Dieu, car la cause de Dieu ne veut estre defendue avec armes: *Mitte gladium tuum in vaginam*. Nostre religion n'a prins son commencement par armes, n'est retenue et conservee par armes.[50]

L'Hospital advised instead the use of 'armes de charité, prieres, persuasions, parolles de Dieu, qui sont propres à tel combat', because 'la bonne vie, comme dit le proverbe, persuade plus que l'oraison. Le cousteau vaut peu contre l'esprit, si ce n'est à perdre l'ame ensemble avec le corps'.[51] Similarly, on 3 January 1562, he argued that 'la diversité de religion', which dated back to 1517 or 1518, had increased 'quelque resistance que l'on y ait fait, par le feu ou par le glaive, qui ne sont pas les armes dont l'on a deu user en telles choses'.[52] Thus, although Michel de L'Hospital's political attitudes evolved, so that by the end of 1561 he had moved from a position supporting religious concord to one of support for provisional civil tolerance, there remained an essential continuity in his thought: this was the denial of the validity of coercion of conscience. Religious unity could not, in his view, be achieved at the expense of the humanity and the essential nature of free belief. This view had Pauline and Erasmian origins, but had never previously been asserted with such energy by such an influential politician.

This refusal of enforced indoctrination and exclusivist intransigence was not based upon a sceptical viewpoint but on a maturing evangelical sensibility endowed with additional political insights resulting from his high office and his humanist education. Well aware of the doctrinal disputes but refusing to enter into them, L'Hospital regretted that 'we fight

---

49. 5 July 1560, Parliament of Paris, AN, X[1A]1594, fo. 312v°.
50. 13 December 1560, Orléans, Pierre de La Place (1565) *Commentaires de l'Estat de la Religion et Republique [...]*, s.l., 129v; *Discours*, 82-83. Quotation of John 18, 11.
51. La Place, *op. cit.*, 131v-132r; *Discours*, 86.
52. 3 January 1562, *Mémoires de Condé, op. cit.*, II, 606.

with words and arms as to which view of the working of the Holy Spirit is the true one. Yet at the same time, we neglect the ten golden commandments delivered to Moses on the top of the high mountain, the Master's words and the decrees of the early Councils of the Church'.[53] L'Hospital's refusal to use names such as 'huguenots' and 'papistes',[54] is a consequence of his refusal to endorse the confessional divide. The *Carmina* reveal that interiorization of faith made it possible for him to go beyond the confessional choice. Neither Papalism nor Calvinism were sufficient but, instead, a civic evangelism within a Gallican Catholic framework, which avoided the label of 'heretic' and emphasised instead what both sides had in common: Christian baptism.[55]

What was L'Hospital's answer to the challenges of religious pluralism? Modern concepts of tolerance were almost inconceivable for a sixteenth-century mind because it entailed the acceptance of error and of the crime of *lèse-majesté*.[56] The confessional divide implied intransigence and therefore intolerance. In the west, the emphasis had been and remained the primacy of unity over diversity, of one single truth over errors. How did the Chancellor respond to the escalation of confessional antagonism? His first, indeed his only, long-term ideal remained the primacy of religious unity. From his appointment as Chancellor in mid-May 1560 to the failure of the Colloquy of Poissy, while distinguishing between social and religious issues,[57] he made it clear that toleration was inconceivable:

> C'est follie d'esperer paix, repos et amitié entre les personnes qui sont de diverses religions. Et n'y a oppinion qui tant perfonde dedans le coeur des hommes que l'oppinion de religion, ny qui tant les separe les uns des autres [...] Et est difficile que les hommes, estans en telle diversité et contrarieté d'opinions, se puissent contenir de venir aux armes.[58]

He temporised, arguing that the wheat must be left with the chaff until the Council of the Church had settled the issues.[59] At the opening of the

---

53. AMST, 227; DUFEY, 304.
54. 13 December 1560, La Place, *op. cit.*, 132r; *Discours*, 86-87, which anticipates the edict of 19 April 1561.
55. See *Harangue, op. cit.*, 9.
56. See the paper of Richard Bonney in this volume.
57. 7 September 1560, Parliament of Paris, AN, X[1A]1595, fo. 201r; *Discours*, 49.
58. 13 December 1560, Orléans, La Place, *op. cit.*, 130r-131r; *Discours*, 83.
59. 5 July 1560, AN, X[1A]1594, fo. 312v, to link to Matthew 13, 24-30. See Bainton, R.

Colloquy of Poissy, he still contended that religious diversity was the main cause of the troubles.[60] Yet the failure of the Colloquy forced the government to find new solutions. L'Hospital's speech of 3 January 1562 demonstrates that by the end of 1561 the desire for unity at all costs has been tempered because it was *now* seen as unrealistic: confessional unity temporarily ceded primacy to provisional civil tolerance. Already in his speech on 12 November 1561 at the *Parlement* of Paris,[61] when he distinguished between eternal laws and temporary remedies, the Chancellor had paved the way towards his speech at the assembly of Saint-Germain, where religious pluralism was regarded as possible within a single family (L'Hospital's daughter and wife were Protestants):

> Le roy ne veut point que vous entriez en dispute quelle opinion est la meilleure, car il n'est pas ici question de *constituenda Religione, sed de constituenda Republica.* Et plusieurs peuvent estre *Cives, qui non erunt Christiani.* Mesmes un excommunié ne laisse pas d'estre citoyen [...] comme l'on dit que *vitia uxoris aut sunt tollenda, aut toleranda.*[62]

Citizenship is thus no longer based on religious choice: this cataclysm virtually makes the distinction between the political sphere and the world of faith. However, this tolerance is just a 'lesser evil' strategy that accepts which cannot be eradicated, a stopgap imposed by the 'nécessité du temps', a *pis-aller* which selects one 'scandale pour en eviter un plus grand'.[63] As an apologist of the edict of Amboise (1563) puts it, 'permission n'est pas approbation'.[64] Therefore, beyond the temporary medicine, religious unity remains the long term ideal, even until 1568:

> Ainsy le coeur du Roy plein de charité et d'amour paternelle, ne doit souffrir une si sanglante et felonne obstination, que d'exterminer une si grande partie de ses subjects, s'il y a moyen de les ramener à leur devoir, et les reconcilier ensemble.[65]

(1932) 'The parable of the tares as the proof text for religious liberty at the end of the XVIth century', *Church History* I: 67-88.
60. '[...] la diversité des opinions estoit le principal fondement des troubles et seditions [...]' (La Place, *op. cit.*, 240r).
61. AN, X^{1A}1599, fo. 2v-4v.
62. *Mémoires de Condé, op. cit.*, II, 612.
63. E. Pasquier, *Lettres historiques*, D. Thickett (ed.) (1966), Geneva: Droz, 85.
64. *Mémoires de Condé, op. cit.*, IV, 426.
65. Taillandier, A.H., *op. cit.*, 311; DUFEY, II, 197. See Crouzet, D. (1994) *La Nuit de la Saint-Barthélémy. Un rêve perdu de la Renaissance.* Paris: Fayard, 205-213.

And nobody can ever be sure that there is no further avenue left to bring back the Protestants into the *Corpus christianum* by means of a lowering of the doctrinal demands made for their reintegration into the Catholic church.[66]

Despite the various shifts in royal policy between the Conspiracy of Amboise and the Saint-Barthomew Massacres, the personal synthesis within L'Hospital of religious commitment and practical policy, i.e. his civic evangelism, enabled him to instil a sense of moral and spiritual emphasis within the body politic. His religious viewpoint was more than a conventional Catholicism of its time or an opportunistic utilitarianism: it was founded on a deepening faith that sought to influence the reality of a confessionally divided society. Conscience, in his view, must neither be left to an autonomous existence nor coerced, forced by violence or fear. This double requirement of respect both towards man and truth justified a religious policy that refused coercion without sacrificing the objective of religious unity and the protection of the truth. From end of 1561, it resulted in the Chancellor simultaneously backing the idea of temporary civil tolerance while remaining a firm adherent to the long-term ideal of religious unity.

Did L'Hospital's political realism determine his religious standpoint or vice versa? The first hypothesis is tempting but is ultimately inconclusive. The Chancellor's political pragmatism occurred for only a few years in office, whereas the *Carmina* reveal an ever-deepening and coherent evangelical religious sensibility. It was not political pragmatism that directed L'Hospital's religious sensibility, but the opposite. In the political sphere, the king and the law conditioned the social expression of faith, but in L'Hospital's personal life, religious commitment determined his whole existence, his choices and above all his refusal to accept political compromise at the expense of his spiritual viewpoint.

---

66. For sources, see Turchetti, M. (1991) 'Une question mal posée: Erasme et la tolérance. L'idée de *sygkatabasis*', *Bibliothèque d'Humanisme et Renaissance* LIII: 379-395.

YVONNE ROBERTS

Jean-Antoine de Baïf and the Adventure of Pluralism

It may not seem an obvious choice to look for evidence on this extraordinary adventure into what must have seemed like dangerous plurality in the verse of the Pléiade poet, Jean-Antoine de Baïf. The last few years have seen a revival of interest in the work of this poet who for too long was dismissed as a pale imitator of Ronsard. Now at last his many talents as songwriter, dramatist, court poet and producer of some of the most magnificent court festivals of the late Renaissance are beginning to be acknowledged. As yet, however, the interest of his political verse has been largely ignored and the original and radical revision of the theory of monarchist government, based on the submission of the sovereign to the legal code, unexpectedly formulated by this devoutly Catholic courtier and faithful servant of Catherine de Médicis, has never received the attention it deserves. This is true even of *Les Mimes,* the satire composed with the original aim of providing firm support for royal absolutism and the policies of reconciliation of Henri III. Over fourteen years between 1574 and 1588, the work developed to contain an emerging concept of natural human rights, where the claims of conscience are recognised as paramount and where the advocacy of a consensual civil faith is based on grounds of religious toleration rather than political necessity. The criticism of Henri III that the poem now contains is both vivid and effective. Above all, *Les Mimes* showed Baïf to be a master of political propaganda. The appearance in this long poem of any topic guarantees that, in his expert estimation, it represented an emotive trend of opinion which could be utilised for the purposes of political persuasion. This is equally true of the militant Gallicanism, the sincere Tridentine views, the imported Protestant colour and the grim astrological foreboding. The period of writing of *Les Mimes* saw the penitential fervour encouraged by Henri III, the growing power of religious fanaticism in the form of the *Ligue* as well as the renewal of interest in Stoic thought and the growth of the Cult of Action.

The length of the writing career of Jean-Antoine de Baïf, stretching over nearly forty years, from 1549 to 1588, makes it possible to chart a clear development in his political and religious thought. From his first involvement in the Valois propaganda machine in 1565, he promoted Catherine de Médicis' familiar message of unity and reconciliation under the Catholic monarchy. In August 1572 the Saint-Barthélemy massacre – *le carnage d'ost'* (II, 460)[1] – was a pivotal event in the formation of Baïf's political thought. The hatred of intolerance, and the unambiguous refusal of involvement with religious fanaticism (*La rage*), continued to provide the passionate impetus for his lifelong involvement with the *Politique* cause.

> Qui sera mon amy, que jamais ne la sente,
> Mon amy ni les siens. (II, 381)

The powerful opening lines of the poem *A monseigneur de Lansac* make clear Baïf's distress at the atrocities.

> DEBONAIRE LANSAC, disons-nous mal-heureux
> D'estre nais en ce siecle! ô mille fois heureux
> Ceux qui sont morts devant, & ceux qui sont à naistre,
> Pour ne voir les mal-heurs qu'entre nous voyons estre!
> Nous, qui du sang de Christ nous vantons rachetez,
> Qui ne croyons qu'un Dieu: quelles mechancetez
> Ne se font entre-nous? Hé! le fils à son père
> Va machinant la mort, & le frere à son frere,
> Le voisin au voisin: il n'y a plus de foy:
> On ne creint plus un Dieu, lon foule aux piés sa loy. (II, 378)

It is no surprise to find that the eschatological current which was so influential in determining the collective consciousness in the second half of the sixteenth century was also present. Baïf was convinced that Divine punishment was fully deserved. The complete destruction of the human race would not be too harsh a penalty for the unutterable sins which have been committed.

---

1.   Marty-Laveaux, C. (1881-1890) – *Euvres en rime de Jan Antoine de Baïf, Secrétaire de la Chambre du Roy, avec une notice biographique et des notes.* Collection La Pléiade française, 5 vols, Paris: Alphonse Lemerre. All references to the work of Baïf, with the exception of *Les Mimes*, are to this edition where there are no line numbers.

Bien que la terre ouvrant les abysmes du monde,
Nous eust tous engloutis dans sa pance profonde;
Bien que les cieux déclos eussent plu dessus nous
Les foudres orageux de leur juste courroux;
Et de ses flots enflez la grand' mer effroyable
Eust noyé des humains la race miserable,
Encores n'eussions-nous à moitié satisfait
Au mal que meritoit nostre mechant forfait. (II, 379)

The conclusion reached by Baïf is both unexpected and of far reaching importance.

Pour nous perdre du tout, il ne l'a voulu faire,
Mais à la repentance a tasché nous attraire. (II, 379)

The time gained by the divine forbearance must be used to examine the causes of the evil and to take all necessary action to ensure that it can never be repeated. This is to be done not by recourse to the wisdom of the ancients but by deliberate concentration on the contemporary fact. (II, 379) Indeed a refusal to look back to an idealised past will continue to be an important component of Baïf's personal philosophy. Both the suspicion of the value of traditional wisdom when weighed against empirical evidence and the optimistic belief in a perfectible future, which reflects the pride in contemporary achievement evident in many other writers of the period, will be modified in new directions in *Les Mimes*.

There is no doubt that *Les Mimes* was deliberately planned as a vehicle of propaganda. For some years, possibly even during the time in Poland, those close to Henri III, Corbinelli and Pibrac in particular, had been preoccupied by the difficulty of ensuring that knowledge of the King's *politique* policies reached as wide a public as possible. As early as 1568 Corbinelli and his friends were studying the work of Rabelais, then a deeply unfashionable author. It would seem from the two epitaphs for Rabelais composed by Baïf at this time that he was a member of the group and certainly many of the strategies later employed in *Les Mimes* show the influence of these readings. From this same period dates the interest in the work of the historian Francesco Guicciardini. An introductory sonnet by Baïf appears in the 1568 translation by Jérome Chomedy of *L'Histoire d'Italie,* but it is the second edition of 1574 which provides the clearest evidence of the real interest of the work for Henri III and his advisors. Two significant copies of this printing survive – one destined for the personal use of the King, printed on high quality paper and bearing his arms, the other covered in notes in the hand of Corbinelli which are mainly concerned with differences in viewpoint between Guichardin and Machiavelli. But the advice on which Corbinelli wished his monarch to focus is contained in Chomedy's *Epitre au lecteur*. Here he emphasised Cicero's teaching that public opinion is the greatest weapon in the armoury of either advocate or ruler.[2] Within a very short period of his accession to the throne, Henri III began to take active steps to encourage the production of works defending the legitimist viewpoint. It is from this time onwards that Baïf is known to have received the generous funding which enabled him to subsidise the works of writers favourable to the *Politique* cause. These works were destined for a new public, designed above all to attract the positive adhesion of those considered by Henri and his advisors to form their natural supporters, the moderate Catholic majority of parliamentarians and the newly important class of lawyers and administrators created by the needs of the Valois regime.

It was towards this second group that Baïf directed his persuasive talents, a group whose tastes and education he shared and who, again like him, had much to lose from the breakdown of the central state and a return to feudal rule. As a result, while the polemic is reduced to its broad emotive lines, the tools of persuasion are rich in information on the aspirations and fears of the educated, middle class Parisian at the end of the sixteenth century. Baïf's contribution to the war of propaganda was the satirical work *Les Mimes*. In appearance, it is nothing more than a harmless collection of proverbs, interspersed with more organised epistles to friends. He made use of his unrivalled knowledge of the popular songs, street cries, proverbs and popular sayings of the 1570's, as well as trading in the manner of Rabelais on the contemporary love of enigma and hidden meaning, to fashion verses to attract those unlikely to read a formal work of political rhetoric. The reader is constantly urged on by the promise of a subversive message and made to feel one of a selected elite admitted to dangerous secrets.

---

2.   Fournel, J-L. (1992) 'Lectures françaises de Guichardin' in *La circulation des hommes et des œuvres entre la France et l'Italie à l'époque de la Renaissance*. Paris: C.N.R.S. 1992.

Je ne sçay que trop de nouvelles,
Tu es mort si tu les revelles. (126, ll. 1225-1226)[3]

On closer inspection, though, *Les Mimes* is less innocent. The names of those to whom the poems are addressed have their importance: many were in fact personal friends of Baïf but all were part of the inner circle of Henri III's council, all would be dismissed by him in his final bid to rule without Catherine, and indeed all would continue to serve Henri de Navarre. It is the development of Baïf's thought from a starting point of complete acceptance of the Valois message to an original and radical revision of the theory of monarchist government that forms the vital core of the work.

The forces and pressures which Baïf used for his manipulative ends are of two sorts, those which had their origin in the current worries and preoccupations of both the poet and his targeted audience and those, no less indicative of the prevailing climate, which reflected popular stylistic and literary tastes which were not always shared by the writer of the propaganda. In the first category, the main obsession was with the dread of mob rule, a fear which had a long history in Baïf's poetry. Even the pastoral poems, commenced during his student days, reflected the first troubles of the religious wars[4] and, by 1569-70 and *L'Hymne de la Paix,* Baïf was convinced that he was witnessing the disintegration of traditional society. (II, 223-29). In a powerful passage in the *Mimes* of 1576, he catalogues those vices which have caused the extinction upon this earth of what for Baïf never ceases to be the primordial Christian virtue, Charity. No vice is missing from this age where God is forgotten. The whole range is here from envy and slander to pillage and slaughter. The cumulative effect of the repetition and of the short abrupt phrases forcefully underlines the gravity of the situation as it appears to Baïf.

Rien plus ne se voit que feintise:
Rien que faulse opiniastrise:
Rien que larcin & cruauté:
Rien que toute audace rebelle:

---

3. All references to *Les Mimes* are to Vignes, J. (ed.) (1992) *Mimes, enseignemens et proverbes.* Geneva: Droz.
4. This appears to have been a common preoccupation amongst the group of young poets which included Jacques Bereau and Vauquelin de la Fresnaye.

Rien que debauche, & point de zele:
Rien qu'erreur & desloyauté. (68-69, ll. 85-90)

More evil than this climate of crime is the fact that, due to the blunting
of sensibilities by the atrocities of the religious wars, these outrages pass
without comment.

Mespris de Dieu, tout vilain vice,
Orgueil, insolence, avarice,
Tout parjure, nulle pitié,
Brutalité plus que brutale,
Brave en cet age desloyale. (68-69, ll. 91-95)

Society is in disarray, the tide of displaced persons has swept into the
towns, bringing with it the fear of mob violence as the already fragile
economy founders. All certainties of behaviour have vanished, the most
holy ties are broken and, and here Baïf mimics the concerns of his mid-
dle-aged readership, the youth of today are completely out of hand.

O l'horreur de tant de turies
De Citoyens à Citoyens! […]
Rien n'a valu le nom de Pere,
Ny de fils: rien le nom de Frere,
Pour garantir de la traison,
Où ne s'est elle débordee
Nostre jeunesse outrecuidee? (104, ll. 830-842)

By the date of writing of the final *Mimes* the obsessive fear of the consequences of mob rule, as keenly felt by the readers as by the poet,
provided both motive and justification for a strict public order policy to
cope with the climate of rapid social disintegration.

Baïf's final dissatisfaction with the weakness of Henri III led him to
envisage a form of contract between king and people. This in no way
implied support for democratic consultation. Baïf appears to have associated the experiment in democratic government of the Swiss cantons
with popular uprisings and to be fearful of the same situation arising in
France. Throughout the first two books of *Les Mimes,* the only two published during Baïf's lifetime, there is a clear message for the reader.
Only the monarchy can provide the strong leadership necessary for the
stability of the country. But in the final *mimes,* which can be dated to
1588, there is in Baïf's reading of the situation, an imminent and very

real risk of the collapse of the monarchy and the fragmentation of the central state. The return of power into the hands of the feudal lords would leave the people without the protection that it is the duty of the King to provide. Baïf concludes this book with an eloquent plea to those in positions of power to prevent the outbreak of another religious war.

O sang royal, doux & bons Princes,
Vous les Gouverneurs des provinces,
Qui des grans honneurs avez part,
Officiers de la Couronne:
Justiciers: Tous d'une ame bonne
A ces advis ayez esgard.
Voyez de la France les larmes.
N'esmouvez les iniques armes
Pour à nos maux remedier.
La France est assez ruinée. (369, ll. 619-628)

Jean Vignes finds in these lines, with the successive mention of the orders of the establishment, a resemblance to Ronsard's *Remonstrance au peuple de France*. There is, however, a vital shift of emphasis. Baïf appeals to the Gallican sympathies of his targeted audience, which he certainly shares, by including in his men of influence the powerful class of Royal administrators and lawyers. The Gallican theory of resistance held that it was the duty and right of the properly constituted officials of the central government to take control in the case of a tyrannical or impotent ruler. The method had the advantage of avoiding all recourse to democratic consultation and was also favoured by the Protestants who had already experienced the reality of mob involvement..

Baïf had in fact played on the Gallican sensibilities of his readers from the start of *Les Mimes*. A new preoccupation had surfaced in the limited first edition, written before the autumn of 1576, with verses expressing extreme distaste for the Holy League whose first meeting was held in the May of the same year.

La figue j'appelle la figue.
Pour entrer en la saincte ligue,
Faut vomir la poison d'enfer. (85, ll. 454-456)[5]

---

5. See Vignes' note on line 455 for his reasons for disagreeing with Augé-Chiquet who considered these lines an expression of sympathy with the league.

The joking references to papal elections were also assured of a good reception.

Les asnes s'affublent de chapes:
Dieu sçait comment se font les Papes. (87, ll. 493-494)

The suspicion of too close links with Rome and the fear of the treachery of the League will be exploited until the very last *mimes*. Baïf knew that his audience shared his anger at the signing on 9 September 1585 of the papal bull which ignored the rights and privileges of the French church. The Protestant leaders, Henri de Navarre and Henri de Condé, were declared heretics and banned from the succession to the throne. The bull had been obtained largely through the efforts of the Jesuit Claude Mathieu who had pleaded the cause of the *ligueurs*. A provision of the bull dispensed the followers of Navarre and Condé from all oaths of allegiance and made it lawful for their former vassals to take arms against them. For Baïf, this was a licence to kill. Any intending thief or assassin, or for that matter adulterer or traitor, troubled by lingering twinges of conscience, could seek reassurance from Père Mathieu! In the current religious context, the open reminder that the Papacy had never interfered in secular affairs without great risk to itself cannot be dismissed as mere rhetoric.

O Papauté donne toy garde
Que le feu justement ne t'arde,
Que tu commences d'alumer:
Tant que de Paix tu fus nourrice,
Dieu t'a esté doux & propice:
Dieu t'a faict sur tout estimer.
Mais tu n'émeus jamais la guerre
Entre les Princes de la terre
Que tu n'ais couru grand hazard. (385, ll. 1051-1059)

For his own proposals for a consensus religion Baïf drew on a code of belief common to Gallican and Protestant. In this he was greatly aided by his knowledge of contemporary tastes. In humanist circles, Stoic philosophy had been of interest for many years: Baïf himself had made use of many elements of the thought since 1559. (IV,385) Nevertheless the great vogue for works of popularisation of Stoic thought did not take place until shortly after the publication of *Les Mimes*.

By the 1581 edition of *Les Mimes,* Baïf is advising the application of the Stoic principle of abstention from involvement in matters of religion. The strongly Catholic tone of the first book had disappeared. Baïf now limited himself to precepts from the Gospels which were acceptable to Catholic and Protestant alike, or to developments of the ten commandments. Many passages of biblical reminiscences were cleverly tailored to appeal to the Protestant reader, particularly in the call for moral reform. There was at the same time a firm avoidance of sectarian debate. Religious speculation was pointless. God's purpose could never be understood by Man.

> Faut reverer Dieu, faut le creindre.
> L'esprit humain ne peut ateindre
> Au secret du conseil divin,
> Qui construit ordonne & dispose,
> Fait & conserve toute chose
> En sa propre & certaine fin. (247, ll. 2011-2016)

From the basis of this fideist principle Baïf proceeded to elaborate the deliberate policy of abstention from argument on religious dogma into a moral code which he hoped would be acceptable to both sides in the sectarian conflict.

He takes as his starting point the consensus which holds as axiomatic the worship of God. Trust in the Almighty provides the sole source of security in an ever changing world, where the lessons of the past have ceased to be of relevance. Above all religion is still valued as the only force capable of enforcing the observance of moral values. The teaching for the new consensus religion, valued mainly as a regulator of civic life, is to be based on a respect for prevailing habits and traditions. Finally there is to be a blunt refusal to countenance any form of sectarian conformity.

> Tant de mal pour un peu de pain!
> D'une forme tous pieds ne chausse. (338, ll. 1188-1189)

The allusion to the controversy over the Real Presence in the celebration of the mass, one on which there was and remains an irreconcilable difference between Catholic and Protestant, is unexpected. Baïf's own Catholic faith never faltered; he spent many years of his life on four meticulous translations of the psalms and wrote religious poetry of quality.

Few things could illustrate better than these two lines the strain of the horrors of the religious wars and the vital importance that Baïf attached to the attempts to find some form of modus vivendi, however fragile. Denis Crouzet has emphasised the importance of Stoic philosophy during the 1580s.[6] Although his own explanation for the final clearing of the climate of doom is based on different grounds, he believes that the Stoic cult of tranquillity of mind provided valuable protection against the pervading cult of astrological eschatology. Above all, the Stoic philosophy had an attraction for those who wished to retain a stance of human dignity, even in the face of events of which they were helpless spectators, thus providing comfortable common ground for those on either side of the religious divide.

In this climate of obsessive fears and actual suffering and hardship, the deeply rooted belief in an impending divine punishment is unlikely to be overlooked by a writer seeking a potent method of persuasion. Baïf makes several references to an impending conjunction of the planets Saturn and Jupiter in the sign of the Ram, Aries, which had since the XVth century been held to foretell the end of the world. In the main these would appear to be a deliberate borrowing of the colour of popular literature. But in one significant passage there is an unusual, positive use of the imagery. In the important mime addressed to Pomponne de Bellièvre, Baïf interprets the impending conjunction of the planets as a prediction of a major change of the existing world order.

Car ce n'est en vain que s'apreste
La grand' assemblee qui s'arreste
En l'astre du Mouton doré.
Quand les planettes s'y conjoignent
De toutes choses ils témoignent
Un ordre nouveau restoré. (238, ll. 1771-1776)

The rare event is welcome: the consequent upheaval will bring to power the long awaited Ideal King.

The king is never given a name, and indeed at the time of writing Henri III had a male heir in François d'Alençon and it was not yet impossible that he would have a son. It can be seen from this *mime,* however, that before 1581 Henri III's most trusted administrators were

---

6.   Crouzet, D. (1990) *Les Guerriers de Dieu,* 2 vols. Paris: Champ Vallon.

beginning to form the political theories which would eventually enable them to transfer their loyalties to a new king. There are now, Baïf tells Pomponne de Bellièvre, only two visions of the future. Either the warring sides will succeed in destroying the whole of society or God will appoint a New King.

> C'est, ou que la guerre cruelle
> D'une vengeance mutuelle
> Ce malin siecle abolira,
> Ou que par le destin celeste
> Un homme de Dieu cette peste
> D'un saint remede guerira. (238, ll. 1765-1770)

It is never questioned that the awaited saviour of the country will rule as a king. Above all, as a peace-keeping king, he will ensure that the laws are swiftly obeyed.

The arrival of the Ideal King is awaited with the willingness to experiment and the openness to change, both already present in the poem to Lansac, which have been evident throughout *Les Mimes*.

> Nostre France est tousjours la France:
> Mais des hommes la mesme engeance
> Change de façon et de meurs. (236, ll. 1711-1713)

It was inevitable in this climate that there should be much discussion of the qualities required of the Ideal King. The Cult of Action, which had its origins in the reforms of the Council of Trent, had a lasting influence on these debates. The Council of Trent had taken a stand against the Protestant doctrines which stressed the unworthiness of man and the impossibility of his doing any real good, which denied his free will, his co-operation with God, and his actual merit. The widespread acceptance of the Tridentine doctrine concerning the value of human effort provided common ground for all Baïf's readers, since the increasing interest in social structures on the Protestant side had by now led to the same effects. For Baïf, faith and good works are inextricably linked. Inward conviction is no more than hypocrisy unless it is accompanied by outward effect.

> Non pour en faire une parade,
> Ou quelque vaine mascarade,
> A piper les autres humains:

Non pour en abusant, la dire:
Mais pour dedans son cœur l'escrire,
Mais pour la mettre dans ses mains. (71, ll. 157-162)

This opinion is expressed even more succinctly in the second book.

Dieu en la bouche est peu de chose
Qui ne met les deux mains au fait. (182, ll. 497-498)

The insistence on active spirituality, and the belief that the Christian faith is best lived in the world, lie behind much of Baïf's criticism of Henri III. Baïf had admittedly good political reasons for criticising Henri III's lack of attention to the affairs of government.

Negliger ses grandes afferes,
Vaquer tout à choses legeres:
Sans lire, livres fueilleter:
Compter fueillets sans rien escrire:
Plorer pour rien: pour mal fait rire:
Au monde baille à caqueter. (368, ll. 601-606)

On an even more fundamental level, for Baïf and his targeted audience inactivity is the sign of a complete lack of moral worth.

Mais qui fétard en tout sommeille,
Ny de soymesme se conseille
Ny prend d'ailleurs enseignements,
N'est bon à rien, vit inutile:
Dedans sa chair son ame vile
Sert de saumure seulement. (367, ll. 577-582)

The cult of Action increased in importance as the century progressed. The clever handling by his propagandists of the perceived resemblance of Henri de Navarre to the popular portrait of the Ideal King certainly played a part in the formation of the climate of opinion which made possible his accession to the throne.

Much as he had recognised from its beginning the popular enthusiasm for the teachings of the Stoics, Baïf took advantage from 1574 of the changing literary tastes which would later be conveniently classified as baroque.. Baïf was, not for the first time, in the forefront of a new literary movement: every element of his style will survive to be used to very good effect by Agrippa d'Aubigné as well as by the collective writers of the *Satyre Ménippée* in the later polemic. Of these stylistic features the most revealing is the greatly increased use of concrete imagery. The effectiveness of the criticism of Henri III mentioned above, described as idly turning the pages of a book rather than accused of the generalised sin of idleness, can surely hardly be bettered. Similar examples of abstract concepts expressed in concrete imagery abound in the work. The dozen words of the striking image Baïf finds for an unworthy king do more damage than a lengthy tirade.

> Trop mieux sieroit une marote
> Qu'un sceptre au poing d'un Prince fat. (381, ll. 953-954)

In another example, he makes use of a personified metaphor, which also combines a theatrical sense and a feeling of movement, to express his deep-rooted feeling that all moral standards are now reversed.

> J'ay veu doubles vilains de race,
> Chevaliers panadez d'audace:
> J'ay veu les nobles avilis,
> Abaissez d'estat & courage,
> Estafiers, en piëtre équipage,
> Suivre les vilains anoblis. (245, ll. 1969-1974)

This again is a use of imagery, the imagery of the upside-down world, which went on to form an essential weapon in the *littérature de combat*. The prime justification of the *topos* of the *monde à l'envers* in the eyes of its users was the sins of Henri III and its purpose to proclaim the scandal of a universe where such sins were permitted. The idea that the essential rôle of the king was to provide moral leadership to his people was still deeply ingrained in monarchist theory, as one of the first poems addressed to Henri III by Baïf makes clear.

> Pour dresser à son exemplaire
> Son peuple, reduit à bien faire
> Sous la divine voulonté. (V, 267)

Everywhere the sheer pace of the writing, together with Baïf's love of verbs of movement, significantly increases both the energy of the expression and the desperation of the search for a solution to the problems facing society. The direct, pared down style of the verse, which differs so radically from what has come to be considered as the Pléiade norm, reflected the impatience with metaphysical and aesthetic preoccupations which had become common amongst a whole generation of writers. Baïf now condemns the thirst for abstract knowledge: it serves only to distract from the imperative need for action. For Jean-Antoine de Baïf this was a change in outlook which could not have been predicted from his Pléiade beginnings. This is the man jokingly referred to by his friend du Bellay as 'le docte, doctieur et doctime' Baïf. Du Bellay had expressed the hope that the first philosophical work to rival the Greek or Latin authorities would soon be written in the French language. By the end of his life, le docte Baïf questioned the real relevance to contemporary problems of any work of scholarship, modern or classical. Humanist learning had finally become an unacceptable luxury.

Baïf's personal religious faith had never altered. The intense hatred of all manifestations of religious intolerance, the fear of mob rule and the willingness to experiment with new structures of society, without seeking sanction from classical or religious authority had formed an essential part of his belief since the Saint-Barthélemy. *Les Mimes* had occupied Baïf intermittently for some fifteen years, from 1574 until shortly before his death, during this time his main concern had continued to be with the musical productions from which he gained the highest artistic satisfaction and public recognition. He had embarked on *Les Mimes* with enthusiasm, at times even with amusement. At first the message was strongly Catholic, with eloquent passages on the Real Presence of the Mass and on the outrages committed by Protestant iconoclasts. Then appeared the attempts to find common ground with the Protestant readers but it was only after a further ten years of war that Baïf outlined the principles of his consensus religion. He has finally reached the point where, in contrast to the firm policy of One Church, One King of the first mimes, he now acknowledges the vital necessity of the separation of State and Religion.

Since his early twenties Baïf's poetic productions had born the mark of his preoccupation with the social disorder caused by the religious conflict. The final disillusionment with the usefulness of humanist studies of a Pléiade poet, whose artistic credo was founded on classical learning, is a poignant proof of the war-weariness of an entire generation. The years of greatest hardship for the people of Paris were, of course, still to come. Without the philosophical common ground which Baïf had exploited in *Les Mimes,* the adventure of religious pluralism would have been impossible. Stoic teaching provided an intellectual framework which made it possible to retreat from the extreme positions on either side and, aided by skilful presentation, Henri de Navarre emerged as the Ideal King. Baïf died in the early autumn of 1589, only weeks after the assassination of Henri III – convinced, no doubt, that he had witnessed the event he had long feared, the extinction of the central state and the return to what he saw as the barbarism of feudal rule.

Part 3

Religious Pluralism in Towns

TIMOTHY WATSON

'When is a Huguenot not a Huguenot?' Lyon 1525-1575

Why is the notion of religious pluralism in early modern France such a problematic concept? Much of the problem is that, as a number of essays in this volume make clear, modern ideas of pluralism are foreign to the sixteenth century. Most contemporaries – even so-called moderates like Michel de L'Hospital – viewed the practical toleration of heterodoxy as at worst abhorrent, and at best only a *pis-aller*.[1] But there is a further, more subtle underlying problem, which is the artificiality of the rigid categories commonly proposed. Particularly in the early years of the French Reformation, before the coining of the term 'Huguenot' and its adoption as a convenient party label, the boundaries between 'true' and 'false' religion were fluid and permeable. The comforting illusion that 'Gaul has no monsters'[2] concealed a genuine plurality of religious understanding, bound in a web of traditional social and ideological attitudes, and persisting only as long as it was not called into question; but the starkly bipolar categories that replaced it were equally unsatisfactory.

In this essay I shall be exploring some ways in which Huguenots are not Huguenots: that is, ways in which definitions based purely and primarily on religious categories do not, in and of themselves, provide an adequate explanation for the conduct of believers either individually or corporately in this most confusing of periods. I shall be proposing two alternative sets of categories, each representing opposite sides of the same question, or – to adopt a metaphor suggested by Natalie Davis – opposite ends of an axis of measurement on the multi-dimensional chart which is required to reflect the complexity of early modern French society and culture.[3] This is not to deny the crucial importance of 'putting religion back into the Wars of Religion'. Rather, it is to suggest that it

---

1. Loris Petris in the present volume.
2. Alain Tallon in the present volume.
3. Davis, N. Z. (1975) *Society and Culture in Early Modern France.* Stanford University Press, p. xvii.

was the tension between different religious, social and ideological imperatives that made the Wars of Religion so complex; and that contemporaries, unable to come to terms with the reality of religious pluralism, tended to look for explanations on a less metaphysical level.

1.1 When he's 'popular' [4]

Much historical energy has been expended on the question of how far manifestations of heterodox belief were expressions of social discontent and class tension.[5] This seems at least partly to miss the point. Many of the available sources might be more productively used to explore what the opinion-formers of the day thought, rather than what was actually happening. If local elites initially conceptualised public displays of heterodoxy as a subset of popular revolt, rather than of religious reform, then this must have had implications for their role as policymakers.

One early Lyonnais commentator who articulated the connection between heterodox religious views and mob violence was the humanist doctor, city councillor and rampant self-publicist Symphorien Champier in his account of the notorious *Grand Rebeine* or grain riot of 1529.[6] This claim that the *Rebeine* involved activity by 'Vaudois', often misinterpreted, helps us to understand the assumptions of the consular elite in the early years of the French Reformation. Champier actually lays the blame on a range of stock characters including: Waldensians; drunken artillery officers; servants wanting to be equal to their masters; and 'vignerons' and 'taverniers' opposed to a new tax on wine. And the particular offence for which he blames the 'Vaudois' is the damage done to statues during the sacking of his house, for which misdeed a purely secular explanation might seem equally reasonable. Religious heterodoxy thus is presented not as assent to a set of heretical propositions, but as a caricatural feature of the *menu peuple* at their most troublesome: not in terms of a 'body of belief', but a 'body of believers' – and very much lower body at that.

---

4. The use of the masculine pronoun is deliberate: my Huguenots are almost without exception male, reflecting the social and political spheres under discussion.
5. See for example Heller, Henry (1986) *The Conquest of Poverty: the Calvinist Revolt in Sixteenth Century France*. Leiden.
6. Champier, Symphorien (1529) *Cy commence ung petit livre de lantiquite origine et noblesse de la tresantique cite de Lyon.* Lyon, fos. 14r-26v.

Similar attitudes are evident in the account of the first public demonstration of proto-Huguenot enthusiasm in Lyon in the summer of 1551, given by the diarist Jean Guéraud, a merchant who held a minor office in the city's customs bureau. Guéraud's account describes a rag-tag mob – 'un tas de menu peuple ... tant hommes que femmes ... tant grands que petits' – marching armed through the city singing the psalms of Clément Marot. He further specifies that the focus of their blasphemous critique is 'moquerye et opprobre des ministres et serviteurs [de l'Eglise]'.[7] Order is restored by the arrival in town of the royal lieutenant-governor; a number of arrests are made, and the rebellious mob disperses accordingly. There is a curious tension in Guéraud's presentation of these disturbances partly as a disturbing religious novelty (evident particularly in the use of vernacular psalms), but partly as a popular disturbance drawing on a long tradition of anti-clericalism largely independent of the movement for church reform. And the account of the repression, efficiently executed by a combination of city militia and royal troops, has striking parallels with the city's response to the *Rebeine* of 1529. Here we are not far from Champier's world of drunken soldiers and Waldensian bogeymen.

By the summer of 1560 events in Lyon – notably the execution of 'cinq écoliers de Lausanne' in May 1552 – had made it clear that adherents of Reformed ideas were to be found throughout society.[8] But it was not yet clear how much common ground there was between the turbulent artisans in their 'conventicules' and those members of the educated elite who might be drawn to the ideas of Reformed theologians. The first use of the word 'Huguenot' in the council minutes is particularly instructive. It occurs in a complaint addressed to the city council by a group of foreign merchants, concerned at rumours of trouble from a mysterious group 'par certains appellez huguenaulx', and from among the 'gens mecanicques'. The merchants offer to put on and to pay for an extra city watch. The councillors reject the offer, replying that 'la dieu grace le peuple de ceste [ville] vit aultant paisiblement qu'en ville du royaulme'.[9]

---

7. *La chronique lyonnaise de Jean Guéraud 1536-1562*, ed. by Jean Tricou (Lyon, 1929), no. 66; N. Z. Davis, 'The Protestant Printing Workers of Lyons in 1551', in *Aspects de la propagande religieuse*, by G. Berthoud and others (Geneva, 1957), pp. 247-257.

8. Gascon, Richard (1971) *Grand commerce et vie urbaine au XVIe siècle: Lyon et ses marchands.* Paris, II, p. 464.

9. A[rchives] M[unicipales de] L[yon] BB 81, fos. 304-305 (3 Sept 1560).

Conceptually this is clearly a step forward, with the embryonic use of a 'party label' for the reform-minded. But the word is clearly being used here in the specific context of popular disorder, and the *laissez-faire* response of the councillors indicates their assumption that 'Huguenot' activity could be safely contained within the normal structures of repression, reinforced by a comforting myth of civic harmony.

A comparison of two public order disturbances of 1560-1561 shows us that this policy, without the benefit of foresight, did make considerable sense. On 4 September 1560, within 24 hours of the merchants' offer, a Huguenot conspiracy was discovered at dead of night in the city, led by a young nobleman, Maligny, who had been involved in the Amboise plot earlier in the year. Maligny's attempted insurrection was successfully repressed according to the familiar pattern: a police action by the city's *arquebusiers*; reinforcements arriving in the shape of royal troops; gibbets on the Saône bridge. Indeed, the council's main priority after the event seems to have been persuading the lieutenant-governor, La Motte-Gondrin, to keep his men out of the town, on the understandable assumption that a royal army was likely to be more of a threat to public order than any number of Huguenot insurgents.[10] Then on 5 June 1561, a Protestant fanatic, a painter from Champagne named Denys de Vallois, tried to desecrate the host during the Corpus Christi procession. His arrest and execution did not placate the Catholic crowd, who broke into the nearby municipal college and murdered the principal Barthélemy Aneau, a respectable man suspected of Protestant leanings.[11] This demonstration that Catholic mobs could be at least as much of a threat to public order as Protestant ones can only have justified the council's reluctance to take sides.

It was not until the autumn of 1561 that the members of the Lyon city council began to face up to the fact that characterisations of the Reform movement as 'popular' were not merely inadequate but a serious distortion of the truth – and that in the event of a religious civil war there were those from among their own number who would be prepared, somewhat to their own surprise, to ally with their Huguenot coreligionists rather than with their consular colleagues.

---

10. AML BB 81, fos. 306 ff.
11. AML BB 82, fo. 45v.

1.2 When he's 'elite'

Why did Lyon's consular elite take so long to realise the potentially divisive nature of the Reform? One answer can be found in the attitude of benign tolerance which was a feature of Lyon's intellectual environment, one aspect of the cosmopolitanism famously identified by Lucien Romier.[12] The welcome extended to heterodox intellectuals such as Etienne Dolet is well-known. More specifically to our purposes, among the councillors and their immediate circle there were a number of men and women who were known to be at least sympathetic to the Reform: the Nuremberg financier Jean Cleberger who married the widow of a man burnt in Paris for heresy; or Hugues de La Porte who in the council meeting held to discuss the 1551 psalm-singing riots was prepared to stand up and voice his sympathy with the wider cause of church reform.[13] A number of the regents at the municipal Collège de la Trinité were also reform-minded, men such as Florent Wilson whose publications betray an interest in the works of Italian Reformers such as Ochino.[14]

Of course, an interest in 'progressive' intellectual trends did not imply that one was socially radical: these men shared their more religiously conservative colleagues' distrust of 'la foule'.[15] Champier himself had helped to set up the municipal college in 1527, and the regents were aware that they were working at an institution run by and for the city élite: they had to escort their students through the streets on their way to and from mass, and complaints of harassment by Rhône boatmen were commonplace.[16] A concern for social proprieties was also evident in the first Reformed church of Lyon. Claude Baduel, pastor in 1551, had himself run the municipal college in Nîmes; his comments on the psalm-singing artisans (in a letter to Calvin) are scathing. How horrible, he complains, to hear the praise of God coming from the mouths of Epi-

---

12. Romier, Lucien 'Lyons and Cosmopolitanism at the Beginning of the French Renaissance', in *French Humanism 1470-1600*, ed. by W. L. Gundersheimer Macmillan, 1969, pp. 90-109.

13. Davis, N. Z. 'Poor Relief, Humanism and Heresy', in *Society and Culture*, p. 35; AML BB 72, fo. 47v.

14. Christie, Richard Copley (1909) 'Volusene, Florence', in *Dictionary of National Biography.* London, XX, pp. 389-391.

15. Yvonne Roberts in the present volume.

16. Groër, Georgette de (1995) *Réforme et contre-réforme en France. Le collège de la Trinité au XVIe siècle à Lyon.* Paris, p. 40.

cureans; and he says that he has instructed his congregation not to become involved.[17] Baduel's main concern is clearly to keep his activities out of the public eye, but his contempt for the unruly and, more to the point, disobedient artisans is also marked.

This is the background against which we must view the council's changing response to the religious developments of 1559-1562. Even though it was becoming increasingly apparent that religious tensions were a more serious problem than had previously been supposed, it was far from clear that elite and popular sympathisers were likely to make common cause. The most striking example is that of the man who took the leading role in the suppression of Maligny's insurrection in September 1560: the city's lieutenant-captain, Georges Renoard. It was Renoard who led the city's *arquebusiers* in the operation to clear up the Huguenot safe-houses, discovering caches of mattresses and weapons, and Renoard who was on hand to arrest Le Vallois in June 1561.[18] From these two examples it is clear that he had the full confidence of his consular colleagues. Yet Renoard was attracted to the new religious ideas. In November of 1561 he was one of three councillors to support an appeal by four Huguenot merchants who asked the council for permission to hold public assemblies.[19] And in April 1562, when Lyon fell to the armies of the baron Des Adrets, Renoard chose to stay in the city and to serve the newly Huguenot city council.

Renoard's change of heart must be dated somewhere between the early autumn of 1561 and the spring of 1562. He is particularly noteworthy as an example of a 'gamekeeper turned poacher', but there were others – both current councillors (Pierre Sève, Henri de Gabiano) or former ones (Hugues de La Porte, Leonard Pournas) – who made the same journey at the same time. This evidence that by 1561 the council was split from top to bottom on religious matters helps us to understand why the tendency to treat religious disorder as purely a police matter was so marked. It was indeed the failure of the two religious factions on the council to broker a more creative solution (such as the cross-confessional watch proposed by the royal lieutenant-governor) which left the council

---

17. *Calvini Opera*, XIV, 147-149 (quoted by Davis, 'Protestant Printing Workers', pp. 247-248); M.-J. Gaufrès, (1880) *Claude Baduel et la réforme des études*. Paris, pp. 257-259, 273-276.
18. AML BB 81, fo. 305; AML BB 82, fo. 44.
19. *Guéraud*, no. 275.

gridlocked and the city fatally vulnerable to Protestant troops in the early days of the religious war.[20]

To what extent, if at all, then, did elite solidarity survive the disaster of 1562, and the four years of uneasy toleration that followed the pacification of 1563? One source gives us a fascinating insight into this question. The lists of 'Huguenots reduits et non reduits' drawn up by the militia captains (*penons*) in 1568-1569, after the Catholics had retaken control of the city at the outbreak of the second religious war, reveal a striking difference in attitudes between rich and poor areas.[21]

The lists for poorer *quartiers*, often drawn up by *penons* whose illiteracy places them fairly low on the social ladder, are remarkably detailed. The *penonage* of Jacques de Troillat produced two cahiers totaling 11 pages, listing both 'obstinate' and 'reduced' Huguenots. Among the 'obstinate': Jehan Colz, a Flemish ropemaker, has been living in Lyon for eighteen months; he might be disposed to make trouble, but has two small children and his wife is heavily pregnant. Among the 'reduced': Pierre Sachet, a goldsmith, is a local man of 28, single, but a weakling, incapable of making trouble 'par l'indisposition de sa personne'.[22] The lists for richer *quartiers* are very much less informative. That for the *penonage* under the command of the council secretary lists only twenty names, all of whom are Huguenots who have now recanted and (he claims) now regularly attend church.[23] That under the command of the eminent publisher Guillaume Rouillé contains a special category of 'converted Huguenots who have made a confession of faith since the beginning, and who have since lived, and still live, as Catholics and regularly attend church'. The first name on this list is Thibaud Payen, also a publisher.[24] One is tempted to surmise that Rouillé created this favoured category especially to safeguard the reputation of his business acquaintances.

The lists give us some indication that old alliances among the social elite might sometimes prove elastic enough to survive a remarkable amount of stress, and that while the poor would always be regarded with suspicion, there would often be more opportunity for elite Huguenots –

20. Gascon, II, pp. 477-478.
21. Gascon, II, p. 520 *et seq.*
22. AML GG 87, nos. 3 & 4.
23. AML GG 87, no. 9.
24. AML GG 87, no. 14.

suitably 'blushing and repentant' (as one Lyon author puts it)[25] – to slip back into their former place in society, keeping of course a low profile. When is a Huguenot not a Huguenot? When in happier times he was a neighbour or work colleague; when he was careless, or foolish, or carried away by a misguided youthful enthusiasm over which a veil can now be quietly drawn. It is not unreasonable to suppose that the same social alliances which made the fragmentation into religious parties so traumatic – and so unpredictable – should begin quietly to reassert themselves in the well-heeled sidestreets of the *quartier* Saint-Jean after a decent interval.

*   *   *

Our second axis of measurement runs initially parallel to the first, but the outbreak of the religious wars in this instance leads to a more radical crisis of the traditional interpretation, and the redrawing of the chart on very different lines.

2.1 When he's a 'patriot'

The word 'patriot' is not one used by the citizens of Lyon to describe themselves; they would probably have said something like 'servant of the *chose publique*'. In the specific context of civic patriotism, it does however suggest a certain gut level of prejudice which matches quite well the curious mix of municipal pride and small-minded provincialism which characterised the mindset of the consular elite. You could be a patriot by virtue of being born in Lyon, invoking your loyalty to 'la patrie où j'ai pris ma naissance' despite having moved away to Paris and joined the king's service.[26] Conversely, you could be a *Lyonnais d'adoption*, like the numerous intellectuals (the Savoyard Symphorien Champier among them) who moved to the city and played such an important part in its political and cultural life. Or indeed you could be a patriot while being a 'foreigner' in the modern sense, like the Italian Thomas Gadagne who became *sénéchal* in 1554, and whose loyalty to

---

25. *Les épigrammes latines de Guillaume Paradin*, ed. and tr. by J. Descroix (Villefranche, 1936), no. 86: 'Sur la ville de Lyon ramenée à la concorde'.
26. AML AA 33, no. 39 (1 July 1568): letter of Claude Le Juge to the council.

the city was duly praised by the public orator.[27] What mattered was not your place of origin so much as your willingness to put yourself at the service of the 'chose publique', often – particularly if the service involved consular office – sacrificing a considerable amount of time and money to do so.

Patriotism was not merely a question of loyalty to the 'republic' of Lyon; it also entailed the adoption of some traditional enemies. The consular institutions of Lyon had come into being in the early fourteenth century as the result of a power struggle between the inhabitants and their feudal seigneurs the archbishop and cathedral chapter which ended with the reunion of the city to the French crown in 1314. There was thus a long-standing tension between council and clergy as the former institution progressively usurped the latter's traditional rights and responsibilities; these tensions were still very much in evidence in the sixteenth century, particularly as the archbishop retained some secular authority in the form of the *justice ordinaire*. The tension between council and chapter was exacerbated in the 1540s and 1550s by the chapter's attempted interference in civic affairs ostensibly as a champion of the 'people' against increasing tax demands, and were not helped by attempts by the archbishop to persuade the council to hand their lay-controlled, municipal college over to the Jesuits. Patriots, then, were not particularly sympathetic to the demands – or the views – of the clergy.[28]

Relations with the king were also complex when viewed through a patriotic filter. Theoretically, the king was the source of the council's authority; historically, the guarantor of the city's charter. But patriots might also recall that Lyon had been the capital of Roman Gaul, and that its institutions had their own autonomous traditions traceable back (with the humanist sleight-of-hand that was such a feature of civic republicanism) to the Roman senate or the city council of Athens.[29] More daringly, the kingdom of France could be presented by civic orators in their speeches as a republic similar in kind to their own, with the king himself little more than a glorified *prévôt des marchands*, bound by custom to respect the rights and privileges of his people and dependent upon institutions such as their own to hold him to the traditional limits on royal

---

27. Girinet, Jean (1555) *Orationes duae, Lugduni comitiis consularibus habitae*. Lyon: de Tournes, p. 18.

28. *Histoire de Lyon*, ed. by A. Kleinclausz Lyon, 1939, I, pp. 220-242; Gascon, I, pp. 427-431.

29. Champier, fos. 8-9.

authority.[30] Patriotism thus provided a theoretical framework within which the council could resist the royal will.

More practically, there were a number of questions on which the council did not see eye to eye with the king and his representatives. Predictably, these were mostly to do with money: the councillors had even spent a week in a royal gaol in 1548 for their inability to pay the latest *solde des gens de guerre*, not something that was likely to make for continued good relations with the crown.[31] But the councillors also had a distinctively local perspective on military matters such as fortifications, with a particular hostility to the presence of royal troops, both on theoretical grounds – the city was a 'ville frontière' with nominal responsibility for its own defence – and on the basis of a number of bad experiences with passing armies.[32] We have already seen this reluctance in evidence in September 1560, when the council did all it could to avoid the stationing of a royal garrison in the town.

What happened to these traditional policy aims after 1560, when the 'Huguenot question' begins to be asked with increasing frequency? The short answer is that patriots became confused as to where the city's true interests lie, reluctant to come to any firm conclusion on matters of religion, but seeking above all to safeguard the local traditions of independence from royal or clerical interference, and falling back on a policy of containment which they hope will keep things more or less under control. These were the men who welcomed the news of the colloquy of Poissy sent to them by the city's agent at court, praying with him: 'dieu veuille le tout conduire en bonne paix'.[33] Seen from their point of view, this is not vacillation but a sensible conservatism in the face of a developing religious situation that they were not equipped to understand or to deal with. It is one of the tragedies of 1562 that the outbreak of armed conflict made such a position increasingly untenable.

The fall of Lyon to the Protestants in April 1562 led inevitably to a bifurcation of this tradition of civic patriotism. The Catholic Jean

---

30. Marnaz, Antoine (1574) *Paraenesis ad cives Lugdunensis.* Lyon: Rigaud, p. 11; Masso, Antoine de (1556) *Orationes duae, comitiis consularibus Lugduni habitae.* Lyon: Rouillé, p. 37.
31. Doucet, Roger (1937) *Finances municipales et crédit public à Lyon au XVIe siècle.* Paris, p. 41.
32. AML BB 47, fo. 86v: payment to *capitaine* Lorges to ensure good conduct of his men 'affin d'obvier aux insultes et a tous juronnemens'.
33. AML AA 32 no. 84 (21 August 1561).

Guéraud, in a diary reference made on 8 May 1562, excoriates the twelve councillors 'pour avoir mis un si peu d'ordre à la conservation et tuition de cette tant noble et tant estimée ville'.[34] For their part, the Huguenot councillors clung to the tradition as a key weapon in their attempts to emphasise the continuities (both real and imagined) between their own and previous administrations. Their position is most clearly set out in a manifesto entitled *La juste et saincte defense de la ville de Lyon*, published in 1563. The title is self-explanatory: its authors claim that their action in taking over the administration of the city was necessary to protect themselves from the murderous designs of Catholic extremists, reinforcing their case with reference to traditional anti-clerical arguments, particularly the corruption of the clerical courts and the clergy's self-indulgent love of Lyonnais cuisine. They are also careful to reiterate at every stage their loyalty to the king, and to demonstrate their religious and social conservatism by calling for the punishment of Anabaptists.

The ever-widening gap between these two interpretations was to prove a serious problem in the late summer of 1563, during the negotiations for the return of Lyon to royal control after fifteen months of Protestant rule. The official Huguenot position regarding the Catholic councillors who had fled the city during the religious wars was that they had abandoned their offices and had no right to return. And indeed the Huguenots had not removed them from office upon coming to power; they had simply elected twelve additional councillors, which allied with their sympathisers on the original council gave them a clear majority, and it was some months before the last of the Catholic councillors finally abandoned any effort to co-exist under the new arrangements and left the city.[35] For their part, of course, the Catholics claimed to be the true patriots, seeing the Huguenots as traitorous usurpers, and demanding to be reinstated.

A discussion of this matter at a Protestant assembly of notables on 19 August 1563 is illuminating.[36] The assembly concluded that the forms for the council elections had been followed in the election of replacements, and that to disregard the new election would be to contravene the 'ancient statutes of the city'. The majority view was clearly that the old councillors should not be allowed back because of their dereliction of

---

34. *Guéraud*, no. 312.
35. Gascon, II, pp. 478-481.
36. AML BB 83, fos. 133r-133v.

their duty: 'if they had been true citizens, they would have remained in the city'. But there was a minority view which eventually won some support: that 'pour paciffier la ville en paix il fault chercher tous les moyens'. And throughout this discussion, there is no use of religious party labels: the Catholics are referred to simply as 'les vieulx conseillers', as if the question of constitutional propriety was genuinely the only issue.

Eventually the deadlock could only be broken by the royal nomination of six councillors from the Huguenot camp, and six from the Catholic, with peace between the factions guaranteed by royal troops answerable to the lieutenant-governor.[37] Accepting this outside intervention in the internal affairs of the council must have been a bitter pill for all concerned, illustrating the extent to which the pre-war notion of patriotism and civic autonomy had completely broken down.

2.2 When he's an 'estranger'

The Reformation, as every schoolchild knows, began in Wittenberg in 1517. The consequent temptation in the French context to link religious heterodoxy with foreign influence was as attractive to contemporaries as it has often been to historians. Lyon's business links with Southern Germany (particularly in the printing industry) and its lack of agents of control such as a *parlement* or university theology faculty made it likely that the city would be a seed-bed for the new religious ideas. However, these same factors also made it easier to underestimate the seriousness of the problem by treating heterodoxy as essentially a 'foreign' phenomenon.

The initial attitude of the city council to foreign 'Lutherans' is apparent in their handling of the case of Baudichon de La Maisonneuve, a Bernese merchant whose indiscretions in a tavern led to his arrest by the *justice ordinaire de l'archévêque* on suspicion of breaking the Lenten fast. The councillors' priority, encouraged by vigorous representations from Berne, seems to have been to get Baudichon out of the city before any more embarrassment was caused to their profitable business relationships with the Swiss cantons, and when Baudichon was convicted

---

37. Gascon, II, p. 503.

and handed over to the secular arm, he was promptly set free.[38] Lyon depended for its prosperity on maintaining the privileges accorded to foreign merchants during the fairs, including the right to commercial secrecy and the right to immunity from prosecution for crimes not committed on French soil. These privileges were jealously guarded and well-publicised: the 1560 edition of the privileges was even printed in a pocket format for distribution free of charge to four hundred French and foreign merchants.[39]

By the 1550s the situation had hardened, and a small number of Protestants were burned in Lyon, for the most part foreign intellectuals (and the occasional artisan) who served if anything to perpetuate the myth of heterodoxy as 'other'.[40] Meanwhile, rumours abounded of contacts with heterodox publishing houses in Geneva, and of an illicit trade in heretical books entering the kingdom through Lyon buried in bales of cloth and other bulky merchandise. That this trade was public knowledge is apparent in a despairing series of letters written by the cathedral chapter around 1560 to the archbishop and the officers of the *sénéchaussée*.[41] But the city's commercial interests still took precedence, and calls for bales to be searched went unheeded. Furthermore, a number of councillors had business interests in Geneva, and at least one, Antoine Vincent, was in the process of setting up a printing press there.[42] Such associations were clearly not regarded as problematic at this stage.

The persistence of this identification of Huguenots as in some sense external, despite growing evidence to the contrary, was made easier by the fact that a number of those who were implicated in insurgency during the crucial period 1559-1562 had indeed come from outside the town. To take the two notorious cases discussed above, both Maligny and Denys de Vallois were 'estrangers', the latter executed, the former fleeing the city: both therefore 'out of sight, out of mind'. It was clearly in the council's interest to maintain at least the patriotic fiction that the inhabitants of Lyon continued to live as peacefully together as any city in the king-

---

38. Naphy, W. G. (1995) 'Catholic Perceptions of French Protestantism: the Heresy Trial of Baudichon de La Maisonneuve in Lyon, 1534', in *French History*, 9, pp. 451-477.
39. AML BB 82 fo. 10v.
40. Kleinclausz, I, pp. 398-408.
41. Archives Départementales du Rhône BP 3993, nos 1 & 2.
42. Droz, E. 'Antoine Vincent: la propagande par le psautier', in *Aspects de la propagande religieuse*, pp. 337-367.

dom; and perhaps there were some who believed their own propaganda. It was once more not until the late autumn of 1561 that more conservative councillors noted with surprise and alarm the number of local notables attending Protestant services, by which time the rapidly developing national situation had made a crisis almost inevitable.[43]

In the newly xenophobic atmosphere ushered in by the crisis of 1562-1563, this perception that Huguenots were in some way 'foreign' – which had allowed an indigenous Reformed church the space to develop more or less undetected – was to became something of an Achilles heel for the Reformed community. The Catholic faction on the city council, now working with the clergy and royal governor, were no longer prepared to put the privileges of foreigners ahead of the security needs of the city. The dependence, both real and imagined, of the Huguenots of Lyon on foreign support was thus easily adapted by Catholic zealots after 1563 into a rhetoric of exclusion which was to prove notably effective.

This rhetoric is most strikingly exemplified in a speech made by Claude de Rubys in December 1567, on the occasion of the first consular election held after the collapse of the bipartisan council on the outbreak of the second religious war. Rubys opens the speech with a patriotic appeal to the assembled company:

> Aussi estime je, qu'il n'y a nul qui ne s'employe, ou du moins, ne se doive employer volontiers en ce en quoy il cognoit povoir (tant peu soit il) proufiter à sa patrie.[44]

The criticism of the Huguenots which follows is a fully-developed statement of the perceived linkage between heresy and sedition. He describes the Protestant councillors as 'ces faux imposteurs' who, in taking up arms against the king, have revealed themselves as rebels and traitors for whom religion is no more than a pretext. The proof of these allegations is to be found in Germany where 'souz mesme couverture' the princes have tried to remove themselves from obedience to their rightful emperor, and above all in Geneva – 'Genève, dy-je, par trop voisine de nous' – where religion was merely an excuse for what is in fact a revolutionary movement directed against the rightful seigneurs, the bishop and

---

43. Gascon, II, pp. 472-473.
44. Rubys, Claude de (1568) *Oraison prononcee a Lyon a la creation des conseilliers et eschevins*. Lyon: Jove, fos. 2-5.

the duke of Savoy. Fortunately, the French have been able to learn from 'ces examples estrangiers' and can now purge the foreign bodies from the body politic by exiling all known Huguenots from the city.

The most striking feature of Rubys' presentation is his refusal – just like the Huguenot councillors in August 1563 – to take the religious pretentions of his opponents seriously. The 'Religion Prétendue Réformee' is precisely that: a mask for atheism, traitorousness and sedition. Picking up a Cold War analogy suggested by Donald Kelley: seen from Lyon, Geneva is not so much 'Mecca and Moscow'[45] as Havana, not a centre of ideological or religious propaganda so much as a hotbed of rebellion, and disturbingly close at that. When is a Huguenot not a Huguenot? When he's an 'estranger'; a traitor; loyal to a foreign power; seeking to turn Lyon into a Swiss canton – and if he is not one yet then let us, by expelling him, make him so.

Conclusion

The prudent historian must acknowledge that the writing of religious history is a complex, often contentious process. To borrow another methodological analogy, often we are obliged to proceed rather like particle physicists, faced with the inscrutable Black Box of personal religious belief, and often lacking the secondary evidence we would need to make properly informed judgements. Firing in particles along the two trajectories I have suggested – popular/elite, patriot/*estranger* – is at least one way of getting some useable results out of our Black Box, in order to trace the rise and fall of certain ideological languages, while paying particularly close attention to the precise chronology of religious and political change. But the results are bound to be confused and partial, for history is not an exact science.

The problems of definition we have been considering are of course by no means specific to the Reformation period. Sociological analyses of religious change can be enriched by analogies from different times and places. One striking contemporary example is the current debate in the Anglican Communion over homosexuality, a contentious question which has led to a break-up of old alliances and the formation of improbable

---

45. Quoted by Elizabeth Eisenstein (1979), *The Printing Press as an Agent of Change.* Cambridge University Press, II, p. 402 note 334.

new ones (in this case, between Anglo-Catholic traditionalists and conservative Evangelicals), and has left a goodly percentage of moderates wringing their hands as the middle ground they occupy becomes narrower and narrower. Would it be too far-fetched to draw parallels between the Colloquy of Poissy and the 1998 Lambeth Conference, at which a number of 'liberal' American bishops were loudly confronted by their African colleagues with accusations of 'racism' and 'imperialism'? Particularly in a situation where contending factions are reluctant to concede the good faith of their opponents, the languages of elitism and patriotism, it is clear, still have their uses.

Bibliography

Archival sources:

Archives Départementales du Rhône BP 3993.
Archives Municipales de Lyon AA 32, 33.
Archives Municipales de Lyon BB 47, 72, 81, 82, 83.
Archives Municipales de Lyon GG 87.

Printed sources:

Champier, Symphorien, *Cy commence ung petit livre de lantiquite origine et noblesse de la tresantique cite de Lyon* (Lyon, 1529).
Descroix, J. (ed. & tr.), *Les épigrammes latines de Guillaume Paradin* (Villefranche, 1936).
Girinet, Jean, *Orationes duae, Lugduni comitiis consularibus habitae* (Lyon: de Tournes, 1555).
Marnaz, Antoine, *Paraenesis ad cives Lugdunensis* (Lyon: Rigaud, 1574).
Masso, Antoine de, *Orationes duae, comitiis consularibus Lugduni habitae* (Lyon: Rouillé, 1556).
Rubys, Claude de, *Oraison prononcee a Lyon a la creation des conseilliers et eschevins* (Lyon: Jove, 1568).
Tricou, Jean (ed.), *La chronique lyonnaise de Jean Guéraud 1536-1562* (Lyon, 1929)

PHILIP CONNER

Peace in the provinces. Peace-making in the Protestant South during the Later Wars of Religion

Confessional conflict characterised the period of the Wars of Religion in France. Polemic, disputation, sacrilege, murder and massacre all provoked wild emotional responses. But to what extent did these outrages influence inter-confessional relationships on a more daily basis? Gregory Hanlon's illuminating study of Layrac suggests a rather different picture.[1] By the seventeenth century, Hanlon argues, toleration in southwest France was not only common but it was normal. Interaction on a daily basis between the Catholic majority and Calvinist minority was a pragmatic response to the daily challenges of living: neighbours associated with one another, traded with one another, entertained one another, attended one another's weddings, even intermarried.[2] But what is by no means clear is how regions of France moved from a situation of deep and mutual hatred to this more enlightened co-existence.

---

1. Hanlon, G. (1993) *Confession and community in seventeenth-century France. Catholic and Protestant co-existence in Aquitaine.* Philadelphia: University of Pennsylvania Press, especially pp. 97-119. See also, Benedict, P. (1996) 'Un roi, une loi, deux fois: parameters for the history of Catholic-Reformed co-existence in France, 1555-1685', in Ole Peter Grell & Bob Scribner (ed.) *Tolerance and Intolerance in the European Reformation.* Cambridge: Cambridge University Press, p. 84 and Benedict, P. (1994) *The Huguenot population of France, 1600-1685: the demographic fate and customs of a religious minority.* Philadelphia: American Philosophical Society, pp. 69-70.
2. For examples in Montauban of Protestants participating in Catholic sacramental life, see Archives Départementales de Tarn-et-Garonne (hereafter cited as ADTG) I 1, fo. 123r, 202r; intermarrying, see ADTG, I 1, fo. 330r-v, 351v; entertaining one another, see ADTG, I 1, fo. 133r, 189r, 193r-v, 242v, 276r. This is a picture confirmed by other recent studies on consistorial records. See especially Chareyre, P. (1987) 'Le consistoire de Nîmes, 1561-1685', Thèse de doctorat (Université Paul Valery, Montpellier), II. 562-594; Mentzer, R. (1991) 'Ecclesiastical Discipline and communal reorganisation among the Protestants of southern France', *European History Quarterly* 21: 163-183.

In France, peace-making was not merely a question of how to inte-
grate the Protestant minority. From a provincial perspective, it is
possible to identify localities in which the Protestant population comprised the confessional majority. This study focuses upon the Huguenot
heartland of Montauban which was located upon the boundaries of Guyenne and Languedoc in south-west France.[3] Throughout the period of the
Wars of Religion, Montauban remained militarily undefeated. Moreover,
through both periods of war and peace, the town was governed almost
entirely by Protestant magistrates. Montauban, to all intents and purposes, was a Protestant town. This was a pattern which was replicated in
the towns, villages and seigneurial lands around Montauban. Pacifying
localities such as this was essential if peace across the kingdom was to
prevail. This contribution will examine both the challenges that faced
those implementing peace and the inventive means that the crown
adopted to secure the region's loyalty. In particular, it will follow the
career of Guichard de Scorbiac, a Protestant member of the local Montauban elite who strove against considerable odds to effect a peace-
making process.

Montauban stood at the centre of a cluster of Protestant satellite
towns but the bulk of the countryside between these urban communities
remained Catholic. In addition the Catholic strongholds of Toulouse,
Albi and Agen were uncomfortably close. This patchwork of confessional loyalties induced deep fears and reinforced a sense of isolation
among Protestants, a sense that the enemy was close at hand.[4] The ebb
and flow of armies, militia and roguish bands over a protracted period of
time dislocated town, and in particular, country life. While strongholds
such as Montauban could protect themselves behind their fortifications,
rural areas fared less well. The billeting of troops upon villagers was accompanied by demands for staples such as bread, livestock, wood and
wine which were paid alongside the impositions extorted by the occu-

---

3. Montauban is currently forming the focus of my doctoral thesis, 'Strength in Adver-
    sity: the Huguenot Heartland of Montauban during the Wars of Religion'
    (University of St Andrews, forthcoming).
4. Estèbe, J. (1974) 'Les Saint-Barthélemy des villes du Midi' in *Actes du colloque
    l'Admiral de Coligny et son temps*. Paris: SHPF, p. 720; See also Cabié, E. (ed.)
    (1906) *Guerres de Religion dans le sud-ouest de la France et principalement dans
    le Quercy d'après les papiers des Seigneurs de Saint-Sulpice de 1561 à 1590*. Albi,
    pp. 198-200, 761.

pying forces.[5] These oppressive demands came up against the relative inelasticity of local economies. Even before the coming of the wars, many villagers existed on the margins of subsistence and could easily be pushed beyond that margin when asked to support troops. The sense of insecurity that these afflictions brought to rural locations meant that land often remained untilled, leaving country folk facing the prospect of starvation.[6] This atmosphere of despair prompted villagers to flee the countryside and seek relative safety behind city walls. Particularly during times of war Montauban became a magnet for the dispossessed. Each year of unrest brought yet greater pressures to bear on the already unstable economic base of the region.[7]

In these disrupted times, one of the greatest difficulties confronting the authorities was in implementing agreements at the local level which had been made on the national level. These difficulties were intensified during times of civil war for it was the local pattern of conflict and the local balance of power that dictated the extent to which royal edicts were implemented.[8] For example, Protestant strongholds such as Montauban simply did not heed legislation issued by the king during times of war which forbade them from worshipping in their *temples* and prohibited Protestants from holding royal offices. The point is clear: in order to

5.   ADTG, 1 BB 25, fo. 52r-54v, 111v-113v (no. 5); Archives Communales de Saint Antonin (hereafter cited as ACSA), BB 1, fo. 313r; ACSA, BB 2, fo. 47v, 55r; ACSA, EE 2, 'Etat du département des vivres et munitions de guerre' (1575). See also Cabié (ed.) *Guerres de Religion dans le sud-ouest*: pp. 733-734, 770-771, 779; Serr, G. (1941) *Documents et souvenirs du XVIe siècle sur les Protestants Montalbanais*. Toulouse, pp. 24-27, 68-69, 116-118; Greengrass, M. (1985) 'The later Wars of Religion in the French Midi', in Peter Clark (ed.) *The European crisis of the 1590s*. London: George Allen & Unwin, pp. 108, 111, 116.
6.   'Proces-verbal aux excès des calvinistes' in Canet, L. (ed.) (1925-31) *Lectures d'histoire locale sur le Tarn-et-Garonne*. Montauban: Forestié, II. 251-254; Cabié (ed.) *Guerres de Religion dans le sud-ouest*, pp. 770-771; Mentzer, R. (1987) 'Bipartisan justice and the pacification of late sixteenth-century Languedoc', in Jerome Friedman (ed.) *Regnum, religio et ratio*. Kirksville: Sixteenth Century Essays & Studies, p. 129.
7.   ADTG, 1 BB 26, fo. 94r and ADTG, 1 BB 28, fo. 23v. There are strong parallels in the impact of the religious wars in Languedoc and those of the Thirty Years War in Germany. In this regard I have greatly profited from Theibault, J. (1995) *German villages in crisis. Rural life in Hesse-Kassel and the Thirty Years War, 1580-1720*. New Jersey: Humanities Press, especially pp. 135-157.
8.   Benedict, 'Un roi, une loi, deux fois', pp. 75-76; Benedict, P. (1998) 'Les vicissitudes des églises réformées de France jusqu'en 1598', in Michel Grandjean & Bernard Roussel (ed.) *Coexister dans l'intolérance*. Geneva: Labor & Fides, p. 63.

have any practical effect, there had to be some correspondence between the law and the local situation. The attempt to balance these considerations was the goal of the peace-making process.

The Edict of Nantes brought an end to direct fighting between religious parties, but the edict was not the beginning of the process of peacemaking. Rather it was the latest in a series of settlements which sought to resolve confessional conflict. Towards the end of each religious war, there came a point at which formal hostilities were drawn to a close. On a local level, peace was borne from a sense of powerlessness, an inability to overcome one's opponents by force of arms.[9] But while mediation could provide the broader juridical framework for peace, immediate sources of conflict often remained unresolved. That this was so is expressed by the way in which an 'informal' war continued after the edicts of pacification, a conflict whose tensions were harder to assuage. Some of these tensions may have been the result of lingering sectarian scores which had yet to be settled. Indeed there were those within the Huguenot movement who viewed the terms agreed upon in the edicts of pacification with deep suspicion.[10] This unsettled situation was also perpetuated by those who sought to use the disorders as a front for their own banditry and brigandage. Through the early 1580s, a time of 'formal' peace, the Catholic Estates of Languedoc, the Protestant provincial assemblies, and town magistrates of both Catholic and Protestant persuasion complained repeatedly about those from both sides of the confessional divide who continued with their predatory activities.[11]

Against this background of continuing disorder, peace brought with it enormous tensions. In Montauban, Catholics who had fled during the wars, returned to find that their churches had been ransacked and destroyed.[12] They came back to find that their homes had been

---

9.   Hoffman, M. (1992) 'Third-party mediation and conflict resolution in the post-Cold War world', in John Baylis & N. J. Rengger (ed.) *Dilemmas of world politics. International issues in a changing world*. Oxford: Clarendon Press, p. 267.

10. Henry of Navarre singled out those ministers who 'ne marchent pas de mesme pied et font beaucoup d'effectz touts contrayres'. See *Lettres missives originales et instructions officielles reçues par Guichard de Scorbiac (1573-1601)* (Private archives of the Scorbiac family): no. 65.

11. Cabié (ed.) *Guerres de Religion dans le sud-ouest*, p. 723; Garrisson, J. (1980) *Protestants du Midi 1559-1598*. Toulouse: Privat, pp. 216-219 and p. 224, n. 34, n. 39.

12. Garrisson, *Protestants du Midi*, p. 164; Lestrade, J. (1939) *Les Huguenots dans les paroisses rurales du diocèse de Toulouse*. Toulouse; Passeret, G. (1975) 'Les pa-

requisitioned and their furnishings and goods had been auctioned off to pay for the costs of war. Those Catholics who had remained within the town had been burdened by discriminatory taxation and received a disproportionate amount of attention from the town judiciary.[13] Furthermore, although Catholic worship was restored following the pacification treaties, the bishop of Montauban was unable to reside in the town for fear of the people. This was hardly surprising given that the bishop's role as a local military commander.[14] The clergy of Montauban bewailed the deep-seated prejudice against them. They claimed that they were harassed on a daily basis; their attempts to collect their dues and reclaim their benefices were met with contempt. The impoverishment of the clergy at this time of peace left them with no option than to leave the town, 'to the great scandal of all the Catholic people of Montauban'.[15]

Similar complaints resonate through the period. Almost a decade after the Edict of Nantes, investigations revealed that the Catholic clergy

---

roisses rurales de l'actuel canton de Verdun-sur-Garonne au lendemain des guerres de religion (1597-1617)', *Bulletin de la Société Archéologique de Tarn-et-Garonne* 100: 81-92; Prouzet, J. (1976) 'Inventaire des villes et villages du département de l'Aude occupés, assiégés ou détruits lors des guerres de religion (1560-1596)', *Bulletin de la Société d'Etudes Scientifiques de l'Aude* 76: 233-255.

13. For taxation levelled against Catholics in Montauban, see ADTG, G 1213, no. 27 (1567-1569); ADTG, 7 CC 12, fo. 111r (1577); ADTG, 1 BB 25, fo. 111v-113v (no. 2, 3) (1586); ADTG, 1 BB 26, fo. 85r (1586); 'Dons des fruictz des biens catholiques absents de la ville de Montauban' in ADTG, Archives communales, AA 5, fo. 31v (1586) and fo. 32r-32v (1587) which lists the 'don des fruictz des biens catholiques absents de la ville...aux reparations et fortifications... pour la seureté et conservation de lad. ville', and 'Estat de la recette des deniers provenue des affermes des biens et héritaiges des catholiques absents dudit Montauban' in ADTG, 9 CC 4, fo. 1v-2r, 6v, 8r (1587). For taxation against Catholics in the neighbouring town of Saint Antoinin, see ACSA, BB 1, fo. 199v (1569), 282v, 293v, 295v, 311r (1572); ACSA, BB 2, fo. 268r (1580). With regard to the judicial treatment of Catholics, it is interesting to note that in the civic criminal records of Montauban, ten cases of adultery ended in convictions of which seven were referred to the Parlement of Toulouse, the final court of appeal for Catholics, a proportion which far outweighed the size of the Catholic population resident in Montauban. See ADTG, Archives communales 5 FF 2, fo. 27r, 34r, 39r-v, 40v, 41v-42r.

14. ADTG, GG 226, fo. 24bis; Benoit, D. (1910), *Les origines de la Réforme à Montauban*. Montauban: Forestié, p. 94; Moulenq, F. (1991) *Histoire du Tarn-et-Garonne*. Paris, I. 49.

15. 'Coppie des mémoires envoyés en court par le clergé de Montauban, 1578' in ADTG, G 1213, no. 37; Cabié (ed.) *Guerres de Religion dans le sud-ouest*, p. 864. For a wider discussion of the disruption of ecclesiastical taxation in the dioceses of Languedoc, see Michaud, C. (1981) 'Finances et guerres de religion en France', *Revue d'Histoire Moderne et Contemporaine* 28: 572-596.

could not sustain themselves either within Montauban or in its neighbouring towns and villages. The bishop and the cathedral chapter lamented a situation in which several articles of the Edict of Nantes had yet to be implemented by the town magistrates.[16] What particularly upset the clergy was the ambivalent attitude of the town's magistrates to the acts of sectarian aggression which punctuated the period: instances in which the Catholic dead were disinterred, clergy beaten up, and their congregations scorned.[17] The magistrates appeared in no hurry to repair and restore the town church which had been appropriated as an artillery warehouse.[18] In this tense atmosphere, one can only imagine the magistrates' apprehension when the bishop announced that in 1606 he would lead a solemn procession through the town to celebrate the feast of Corpus Christi, the first such procession since the outbreak of the first religious war.[19]

Implementing peace was not a straightforward process. The impact of war through the latter part of the sixteenth century upon a region in which Catholic and Protestant communities stood side by side made the implementation of peace difficult.[20] The peasants who lived beyond the walls of Montauban but within the town's jurisdiction, for example, were overwhelmingly Catholic. Yet, a vocal Protestant minority sought to dominate and govern peasant life and even intimidate the Catholic majority so as to ensure that that same Protestant minority represented the

---

16. ADTG, 1 BB 35, fo. 95r-97v (1606).
17. 'Complainte par le syndic de clergé du diocèse de Montauban, 1607' in ADTG, G 1213, no. 26. For similar problems of maintaining peace between Catholics and Protestants in Castres in 1613, see ADTG, Archives Communales, 21 GG 3, liasse 84.
18. ADTG, Archives Communales, 19 GG 1, liasse 36, no. 82, 83 (1607).
19. ADTG, 1 BB 34, fo. 75r-76v; ADTG, 1 BB 35, fo. 81v-85r. The re-institution of Catholic processions in Montauban came unusually late. In Castres and Nérac, Corpus Christi processions had already been held in 1596 and 1601 respectively. For the disruptions that processions could provoke, see Benedict, P. (1981) *Rouen during the French Wars of Religion*. Cambridge: Cambridge University Press, pp. 61-62 and Crouzet, D. (1990) *Les Guerriers de Dieu. La violence au temps des troubles de Religion, vers 1525-vers 1610*. Paris: Champ Vallon, I. 595.
20. Sauzet, R. (1985) 'Le refus de la Réforme protestante. La fidélité catholique en Bas-Languedoc calviniste' in *Les Réformes. Enracinement socio-culturel*, Actes du XXVe colloque international du Centre d'Etudes Supérieures de la Renaissance. Paris, pp. 355-361.

peasants' wider interests on the town council.[21] Such rivalries fed ongoing conflicts which disregarded formal truces and treaties.

Given the simmering tension between Catholics and Protestants throughout the period of the Wars of Religion it is difficult to differentiate times of peace from times of war. But there was a difference borne out by the way in which both the Catholic *and* Protestant political establishment sought to extinguish sources of disorder during times of formal peace. By the mid 1570s, Protestants had consolidated their strength in several towns and localities across southern France and this prompted a shift in the way in which peace-making was conducted. No longer could it be a question of Catholic sources of authority in the provinces imposing peace upon the Huguenots. In Montauban and its surrounding region, the late 1570s saw the Catholic crown turning to the Huguenot leadership for assistance in peace-making, endowing them with authority to maintain peace and order within those areas that they dominated. By investing the Huguenot political establishment with the responsibility of peace-making, the crown was able to work with the Huguenot movement to instil order.[22]

The role of Huguenot leaders in the peace process enabled the crown to tap into the deep sources of loyalty that many of the provincial nobles and town elites continued to feel for the crown. Raymond Mentzer's study of the Lacger family of Castres communicates very effectively how this Huguenot family pinned its hopes and ambitions upon its service to the crown. Mentzer demonstrates how royal office-holding conveyed status and public power which in turn generated a growing sense of dependency on the part of the officeholder towards the crown.

---

21. ADTG, Archives Communales, 19 GG 1, liasse 84 (1599): the minutes of a meeting in the seneschal court reveal that 'la plus grande partie des paysans habitantz de ladite jurisdiction de Montauban sont de la religion Catholique Romaine et font profession d'icelle et que le nombre des paysans qui font profession de la Religion Reformée dans ladite jurisdiction est fort petit. Neanmoings lesd. paysans de la Religion Reformée de ladite jurisdiction veulent dominer et suppediter tous les autres paysans Catholiques d'icelle juridiction qui sont à la campagne'. It was confirmed by several other witnesses that the number of 'paysans' that made profession of the Reformed faith in the jurisdiction was 'fort petit en esgard aux autres Catholiques' and that the former wanted to 'dominer et avoir l'authorité et gouverner sur toutz les autres paysans Catholiques de lad. jursidction, singullièrement lorsqu'il est question du consulat'.

22. It has been argued that the crown had little choice in this policy given the situation of near anarchy in the Midi. See Knecht, R. (1998) *Catherine de' Medici*. London and New York: Longman, pp. 193-196, 201.

In Catholic France, being a 'Protestant loyalist' was not a contradiction in terms and, indeed, the Lacger family's 'politique' acceptance of royal authority and emphasis upon political unity rather than confessional uniformity assured the Lacgers a crucial role in easing the tensions between the crown and the local Protestant community in Castres.[23] The way in which the public face of the Huguenot cause could transform itself into the public face of order is again demonstrated in Montauban by Guichard de Scorbiac.

Guichard de Scorbiac was a central figure in the municipal elite of Montauban, elected as first consul of the town in 1563 and 1573. He was subsequently appointed to the seneschal court, the Parlement of Toulouse and its *Chambre de l'Edit* while also developing links with the court of Henry of Navarre. In 1579, he was selected as one of Navarre's *Maître des Requêtes* and at the outbreak of war in 1588, he became Navarre's *Surintendant Général* for finances in the *généralité* of Montauban.[24] Research into the private archives of the Scorbiac family reveals a man who, as an established member of the local political elite, found himself at the interface between the Protestant community of Montauban and Henry of Navarre. Guichard de Scorbiac articulated Navarre's voice in the province, liaising with his regional war council, the local nobles and the magistrates of Montauban and those of other neighbouring towns. Scorbiac informed Navarre of the state of munitions within Montauban and the progress of work on the town's fortifications.[25] Navarre delivered instructions to Scorbiac with regard to raising the requisite sums for the war effort, paying the troops, overseeing his patrimonial lands, resolving administrative deadlocks, organising political assemblies and publishing propaganda for the cause.[26] In short, Scorbiac came to be the lynchpin of Navarre's control over the parts of Upper Languedoc and Guyenne around Montauban, overseeing Hugue-

23. Mentzer, R. (1994) *Blood and belief. Family survival and confessional identity among the provincial Huguenot nobility*. Indiana: Purdue University Press, pp. 12-14, 42-45, 60-61, 166.
24. Documents familiaux (Private archives of the Scorbiac family), liasse 1, no. 6, 11.
25. For example, *Lettres missives*, no. 5, 30 and 44 respectively. See also, ADTG, 1 BB 25, fo. 6r-8r, 26r-27r, 32r, 82r-83r, 145r.
26. *Lettres missives*, no. 83-86, 89, 97-98, 115, 117, 120, 123 and 137. For documents relating to the publication of propaganda, see *Lettres missives*, no. 15, 16, 39a and 39b (1579-1582) and ADTG, 1 Mi 1, no. 27 and 'Bibliographie Montalbanaise' in Forestié, E. (1898) *Histoire de l'imprimerie et de la librairie à Montauban*. Montauban: Forestié, no. 14-16, 32.

not administration, finances and justice. As Mark Greengrass has argued, such relationships had the ability to sustain 'the channels of communication between locality and centre in a way that no bureaucratic arrangement, no intelligence system, no network of *intendants* could match because it grew out of and matched local patterns of thought and behaviour'.[27]

Scorbiac was a power-broker. Particularly interesting is the manner in which Scorbiac was able to sustain his career in an almost seamless fashion through both periods of war and peace in the latter part of the sixteenth century. This situation is less perplexing if one takes into account that the protector of the Huguenot cause, Henry of Navarre, had been appointed by the crown as the royal governor of Guyenne. The transformation of 'rebel-leader' to peace-keeper was experienced at every level of Huguenot direction. It was a reality which many of the more zealous Protestants viewed with suspicion, if not outright hostility.

Following the Conference at Nérac in 1579, Scorbiac met with Catherine de Medici and delegates from the Parlements of Paris and Toulouse in a bid to develop guidelines with which to implement peace across the locality.[28] Later that year a commission, comprising two Protestants, Scorbiac and the Vicomte de Gourdon, and two Catholics, Saint-Sulpice and the sieur de Vezins (the seneschal of Quercy), was established by Catherine de Medici to tour local towns and temper frictions and to address their findings to the royal authorities in Bordeaux.[29] Before the commission set out, Henry of Navarre forwarded to the Protestant members of the delegation petitions and letters from a number of Reformed communities that felt particularly aggrieved.[30] By developing a regional picture of confessional tensions, Scorbiac, as the Protestant representative responsible for implementing peace, found himself in a better position to resolve the challenges facing Reformed communities across the region.

---

27. Greengrass, M. (1996), 'Functions and limits of political clientelism in France before Cardinal Richelieu' in Neithard Bulst, Robert Descimon *et al.*, (ed.) *L'Etat ou le Roi, les fondations de la modernité monarchique en France (XIVe – XVIIe siècles)*. Paris: MSH, pp. 72-73.

28. 'Mémoires de Guichard de Scorbiac' in *Livre de Famille* (Private archives of the Scorbiac family), fo. 11v.

29. *Lettres missives*, no. 14.

30. *Lettres missives*, no. 15, 18; ADTG, Ms. 12, p. 257.

The emergence of a bi-confessional stance against disorders had become a new feature of the peace-making process. One of the first problems addressed by the 1579 commission was to defuse a situation in which a fort belonging to the bishop of Cahors had been commandeered by Huguenots. Saint Sulpice had brought this to the attention of the Huguenot commander in the region, the Duc de Turenne, who had promised the Queen Mother and Henry of Navarre that he would enforce the provisions for peace. But neither he, nor the Protestant delegates of the commission, were able to persuade the Huguenot rebels to withdraw and it was agreed that troops and artillery would be mustered to dislodge the renegades.[31] Again in 1582, Henry of Navarre wrote to Scorbiac and the Vicomte de Gourdon asking them to resolve the sectarian tensions in the town of Varen. One year earlier, the Huguenots of the neighbouring town of Verfeil had committed 'one thousand insolences' against the Catholic community, sacking their church and casting down their reliquaries. Henry of Navarre instructed Scorbiac and Gourdon to act with common resolve in punishing the troublemakers. Furthermore, if the problems in Varen proved intractable, Henry of Navarre warned that he and his Catholic counterpart had agreed that they would both sanction the use of force.[32] These examples are instructive for they show how Huguenot lines of command in the province were allowed to remain intact throughout periods of peace although they were now being employed towards a different goal, namely the shoring up of the king's edicts.

The Catholic and Protestant political elite faced a common challenge of disorder. Henry of Navarre played an active part in the pursuit of peace, instructing the magistrates of Montauban to maintain order and forbid all persons from carrying arms for war or faction. In particular, he exhorted Scorbiac to ensure that the town understood the value of peace, of 'casting aside all commotion and disagreements which were contrary to the well-being and service of His Majesty'.[33] In an impassioned plea to the consuls of Montauban in 1582, Navarre ordered the town authorities to exact exemplary punishment against those who acted as rebels and reprobates and failed to observe the terms of pacification. And to facilitate this process, Navarre called for a collaborative approach between

---

31. 'Mémoires de Scorbiac', fo. 14r; Cabié (ed.) *Guerres de Religion dans le sud-ouest*: pp. 481-485. See also Greengrass, 'The later Wars of Religion', pp. 113, 130 n. 49.
32. *Lettres missives*, no. 42.
33. *Lettres missives*, no. 76.

Catholic and Protestant nobles against troublemakers and pleaded with the towns to communicate with one another and oppose the sources of disorder collectively.[34] In being able to obey the dictates of both the crown and Huguenot leadership, Protestant figures such as Scorbiac were offered the opportunity to prove themselves as loyal servants of the crown.

The Wars of Religion, or the 'troubles' as contemporaries called them, were not bounded by the strictures of formal periods of war and peace. While the edicts of pacification could often provide the framework for peace, rarely did they lead automatically to a workable solution. The pacification process was a reflection of the local situation. It required local initiatives and personalities, from both sides of the confessional divide, to interpret and implement provisions for co-existence. Accepting this reality meant embracing the 'other', however painful that may have been. This enabled the Catholic and Protestant political establishment to shape a political process which bestowed concrete concessions upon the Huguenots while keeping open the long-term goal of religious unity. In the short-term, the career of Guichard de Scorbiac is illustrative of the attempt to focus Huguenot sources of authority within a region upon the crown. By giving the Huguenot political elite a stake in the peace, by involving them in the process, the crown discovered an effective means to enlist the support of dissident elements that it could not control. By engaging with, rather than reacting against the Huguenot elite, the return of order and the promise of peace could be gradually and more effectively advanced. Reconciliation was an altogether different challenge.[35]

---

34. ADTG, 1 BB 23, fo. 79v-80r (1582): 'Les consulz ayant faicte assembler le conseil général pour traicter et resoldre des affaires concernans l'execution et entretenement de l'édit de pacification, suyvant le mandement du sieur Roy de Navarre... Et pour mieux faciliter ce dessus, les gentilhommes tant catholiques que de la religion seroient admonstés, comme aussi toutes lesdictes villes et communautés, d'avoir entre eulx une bonne correspondence, afin de s'oposer et empescher par toutz moyens telles entreprinses et faire obeyr le Roy, suyvant le voloir et intention que sa Majesté à l'entretenement de son édit de paix'.

35. See here, Benedict, 'Un roi, une loi, deux fois', pp. 91-93; Pettegree, A. (1996) 'The politics of toleration in the Free Netherlands, 1572-1620', in Grell & Scribner (ed.), *Tolerance and intolerance*, p. 198.

Bibliography

Primary Material

1. Archives Départmentales de Tarn-et-Garonne

1 BB 23-35: Registres des déliberations consulaires de Montauban (1581-1606)
GG 226 & G 1213: Fonds de l'Evêché de Montauban (1562-1602)
7 CC 12: Livres des comptes consulaires (1577-1578)
9 CC 4: Comptes spéciaux divers (1587)
I 1: Régistres du consistoire de Montauban (1595-1598)
    Archives communales, AA 5: Livre noir de l'hôtel de ville de Montauban (1559-1614)
Archives communales, 5 FF 2: Régistre des sentences criminelles (1534-1606)
Archives communales, 21 GG 3, liasse 84: Articles sur l'église Catholique à Montauban (1599-1613)
Archives communales, 19 GG 1, liasse 36, no. 82, 83, 84: Articles sur la restauration de l'église Catholique à Montauban (1607)

2. Archives Communales de Saint Antonin

BB 1-3: Registres des déliberations consulaires de Saint-Antonin (1561-1589)
EE 2, 'Etat du département des vivres et munitions de guerre ordonné et sauf remboursement' (1575)

3. Archives privées de la famille Scorbiac

'Mémoires de Guichard de Scorbiac' in *Livre de Famille.*
    Lettres missives originales et instructions officielles reçues par Guichard de Scorbiac (1573-1601)

4. Printed primary material

Cabié, E. (ed.) (1906) *Guerres de Religion dans le sud-ouest de la France et principalement dans le Quercy d'après les papiers des Seigneurs de Saint-Sulpice de 1561 à 1590.* Albi.

Canet, L. (ed.) (1925-31) *Lectures d'histoire locale sur le Tarn-et-Garonne.* 3 vols., Montauban: Forestié.

ELIZABETH C. TINGLE

The Intolerant City? Nantes and the Origins of the Catholic League 1580-1589

During the night of 6-7 April 1589, Marie de Luxembourg, duchesse de Mercœur, had 80 leading citizens of Nantes arrested and imprisoned in the royal château. The detained men were from the municipal government and the city's law courts, the *Chambre des Comptes*, *présidial* and *prévôté*. The town government was secured by a *Conseil de l'Union*, with members from the clergy, garrison, law courts and municipality. Such was the Nantes 'coup' of the Catholic League. Nantes became the capital of Leaguer Brittany under the command of the royal governor, the duc de Mercœur. Not until 1598 did the town surrender to the king.

The traditional explanation of the League coup in Nantes emphasises religion as the primary cause: a proud Catholic culture strengthened by the city's strong Spanish affinities and trading links, made militant by the threat of a heretic king in 1589.[1] Guy Saupin has argued for a combination of religious factors and social cleavage within the Nantes elites, between Leaguer merchants and royalist *officiers*, with differing views of the role of the state in municipal affairs, while Robert Harding has seen the origins of the League in a religious-political movement against corruption in the royal state.[2] In this paper, the primacy of religion as a reason for rebellion against the Crown will be explored. How was it that a city and province so little touched by Protestantism could have adhered for so long to the Catholic League? Secondly, was the province's Catholicism a manifestation of secessionist aspirations? Thirdly, how united were the Nantes elites in the League movement? Particular focus will be on two issues, religious intolerance and political motivation among the city elite.

1. Collins, J. B. (1994) *Classes, Estates and Order in Early Modern Brittany*, Cambridge, p. 129.
2. Saupin, G. (1998) *Nantes au temps de l'Edit*, La Crèche, p. 204; Harding, R. (1981) 'Revolution and Reform in the Holy League: Angers, Rennes, Nantes', *Journal of Modern History*, 53, pp. 379-416.

I.

Religion was an important stimulus to Nantais adherence to the Catholic League: the defence of the 'true' faith against 'heresy' was a concern of the city government after 1560 and a central motive in 1589. During the reigns of François II and Charles IX, the city government showed little toleration of Protestantism, favouring firm measures against heresy. These mirror those found in other northern cities such as Rouen and Troyes.[3] In December 1560, the city council urged the lieutenant-governor Bouillé to expel Calvinists from Nantes; in May 1561 a council of 12 notables was formed to prevent illicit assemblies and in August 1561, the *procureur* Jehan du Luc was dismissed because of suspected Reformed sympathies.[4] The municipality consistently opposed royal edicts of toleration: in March 1562 the council commissioned 12 *procureurs* to oppose the registration of the Edict of Saint-Germain and remained implacably against the provision of a site for public Protestant worship after the Edict of Amboise of 1563, even in the suburb of La Fosse.[5] In particular the mercantile elite feared the impact of a policy of toleration on their trade with Spain, on which both the rich and large numbers of the poor depended for their livelihoods.[6] Following the Edict of Saint-Germain of 1570, the council obtained an interdiction on Protestant worship in its jurisdiction, forcing the community to travel to seigneurial sites a league from Nantes. Finally, the Treaty of Nemours of 1585 saw the outlawing of Protestantism and Mercœur took the opportunity to expel heretics from the city.[7]

---

3. For Troyes see Roberts, P. (1996) *A City in Conflict. Troyes during the French Wars of Religion* Manchester, chapters 5 and 6; Benedict, P. (1981) *Rouen during the Wars of Religion* Cambridge, pp. 118-122.

4. Saupin, *Nantes*, p. 111.

5. Archives Municipales de Nantes (hereafter A.M.N.) BB 4 f.347v. Assemblée du conseil des bourgeois. Penny Roberts has written in detail about the negotiations between Nantes' city council, its Protestant minority and the Crown over the siting of a place for worship in the 1560s. See Roberts, P. (1998) 'The Most Crucial Battle of the Wars of Religion? The Conflict over Sites for Reformed Worship in Sixteenth-Century France', *Archiv für Reformationgeschichte*, 89, pp. 247-267.

6. Saupin, *Nantes*, pp. 169-170.

7. Pocquet, Barthélemy (1913) *Histoire de la Bretagne*, Tome V, Rennes, p. 88.

But while official city policy was uniformity of religion and eradication of heresy, in practice there was relatively little formal persecution of Protestants. A Reformed Church was founded in Nantes in the autumn of 1560 and Antoine Bachelard, a pastor from Geneva, founded a consistory in the city in September 1561 and appeal was made (unsuccessfully) to the lieutenant-governor to allow the community to conduct services in the local Catholic churches of Notre Dame and Saint-Jean-de-Jerusalem.[8] The 1560s did witness tensions between Calvinists and Catholics: for example, in August 1561 a prayer meeting at the home of the bookseller Papollin ended with the sacking of his house and in December a building used for *prêches* in nearby Le Pressoir was burnt down. In retaliation, Mass at the Cathedral was disrupted by armed horsemen and artisans throwing missiles at the altars.[9]

Calvinists were few in number in the city: in the early 1560s, less than five per cent of the population, half that of other French towns.[10] They were rarely harshly treated by the authorities: Papollin appealed, although unsuccessfully, to the municipality for compensation for the rioters' damage to his property. After 1562, the small community of Protestants survived, quietly, without enforceable rights but little persecuted except during periods of open warfare, when the community was expelled from the city. François Oyseau acted as pastor in Nantes between 1563 and 1585, although worship was relegated to sites outside of the city walls. There was no Saint Bartholomew's day-inspired massacre. Foreign Protestants were resident throughout the wars: in 1598 the Dutchman Jehan Heinrich obtained letters of naturalisation indicating that he had been resident in the city for 19 years.[11] Roberts observes that Protestants in Nantes presented themselves as living harmoniously with all but a few vindictive local Catholics, as stipulated in repeated royal decrees.[12] As Konnert observes for Châlons-sur-Marne, the city council had a policy of official hostility to Calvinism while allowing Huguenots tacit toleration in practice, or at least freedom of conscience, providing

---

8.   Roberts, P. 'The Most Crucial Battle', p. 254.
9.   A history of Protestantism in southern Brittany during the 1560s is summarised in Pocquet, *Histoire de la Bretagne*, V, pp. 52-58.
10. Saupin, *Nantes*, p. 87.
11. Saupin, *Idem*, p. 40.
12. Roberts, P. 'The Most Crucial Battle', p. 261.

that they did not disturb the peace or threaten the public culture of Catholicism.[13]

The religious climate of the 1580s which coloured the choices made in 1589 were thus not caused by long-standing antipathy towards Huguenots based on inter-communal tensions. Rather than increasing sectarian hatred of Protestants, the period saw a rapid growth of militant Catholicism, with broader religious and social objectives than the extirpation of heresy alone, although this was certainly an outwardly-expressed sentiment. The expansion of Catholic piety is a nationally-observed phenomenon in France in the second half of the sixteenth century, shown in a number of recent urban studies and by the work of Denis Crouzet.[14] Begun in the early 1560s as part of a reaction against the religious and cultural threat of Protestantism, the pious upsurge was renewed in the 1580s, with new moral themes and devotional practices, and reached its height during the League years. The characterisics of the new spirituality were lay bequests, endowments and confraternity membership; clerical initiatives in preaching and sacred processions; new devotions such as that of the *oratoire* and the foundation of new religious orders, and secular politicisation of devotion in the form of Catholic leagues, as described by Benedict for Rouen and Diefendorf for Paris.[15]

Enhanced Catholic piety amongst the elites of Nantes, clerical and lay, is shown by a number of indicators. Firstly, from the 1570s, at least one group of the Cathedral clergy of Nantes was promoting a message of clerical and moral reform, in sermons, published works and by acting as a 'moral' pressure group on the city council's *assemblée générale*, which included representatives of the cathedral chapter. Bishop Philippe du Bec had been present at the final session of the Council of Trent in 1562 and was amongst the clergy urging adoption of the Council's rulings at the general assembly of the French clergy in 1579. The *théologal* of Nantes cathedral after 1574, Jean Christi, was a student and editor of the sermons of the Parisian preacher Simon Vigor; he preached and represented the canons in the municipal assembly. Secondly, there were pious foundations of masses and church improvements; for example, the chapel

---

13. Konnert, M. (1989) 'Urban Values Versus Religious Passion: Châlons-sur-Marne During the Wars of Religion', *Sixteenth-Century Journal*, XX, 3, p. 388.
14. Crouzet, Denis (1990) *Les Guerriers de Dieu*, 2 vols, Paris.
15. See Roberts, *A City in Conflict*, pp. 163-5; Benedict, *Rouen*, pp. 192-194; and the upsurge of Catholic piety is a major theme of the study of B. B. Diefendorf, (1991) *Beneath the Cross. Catholics and Huguenots in Sixteenth-Century Paris,* Oxford.

dedicated to Saint Catherine built on the quay of La Fosse by the Ruiz family. Thirdly, at parish level, increased attention was paid to sexual morality; the parish records of Saint-Nicolas include a separate baptismal register for illegitimate children in the 1580s.

What is interesting about the Catholic revival in Nantes of the 1580s is that it had its origins, not in the Wars of Religion, although these lent a new immediacy to pious activity, but to a longer-term reformist movement, often associated with the Tridentine reformers but seen in Brittany from the later fifteenth century. It is not the forms, but rather the longer-term origins of pious activity, that mark Nantes out from other northern French cities. Episcopal visitations of Breton dioceses were carried out, although irregularly, from at least the 1480s; religious education of children was a concern and a form of catechism drawn up in the Nantais in the early sixteenth century; parish registers for baptisms were begun in Nantes in 1405 and much of the rest of the province thereafter, showing a deep concern for morality and the use of the proper rites of the church. In Brittany in general, and in Nantes in particular, the concerns of Trent were already rooted in the ecclesiastical culture of the province.[16] This longer-term interest in church and moral reform provided a fertile background for adoption of new national concerns and practices of the 1580s although Harding's argument that by the 1580s a cultural revolution was impacting on city elites, activist in mentality, severe in morality and committed to instilling these ethics into civil society, is over-stated.[17] For much of the decade, pious concerns were expressed in traditional devotions: it was not until the later 1580s that we see features of the 'new' piety, penitential processions and new foundations, such as the Minimes in 1589.[18] Old and new themes converged in the rhetoric of public preachers such as Christi and Le Bossu, who called for the internal and spiritual renewal of the earthly city.[19] Much work remains to be done on the Catholic culture of Nantes, but at this stage it appears that while the city was not exceptional in its religious passions – and certainly did not experience the emotions of Paris – it was amongst the more devout of the northern French urban communities.

---

16. Devailly, Guy (ed.) (1980) *Histoire religieuse de la Bretagne,* Chambray.
17. Harding, 'Revolution and Reform', pp. 397-398.
18. This is also seen in Rouen. See Benedict, *Rouen,* p. 195.
19. Harding, *Idem,* p. 399.

While national influences were important, it was the secular concerns of the city that strengthened the religious convictions of its inhabitants, above all the advent of new external threats after 1580. War moved closer, with Rochelais pirates preventing trade in the Bay of Biscay and with military conflict in the marches of southern Brittany against Navarre and Condé. Here the horrors of military depredations were heightened by fears of Protestant occupation of the city, a menace exacerbated after 1584 with the advent of the possibility of Navarre as heir to the French throne. Thirdly, Catholic militancy may also have been stirred by the advent of a new alien group within the walls of Nantes after *c*.1585, Portuguese refugees from the Spanish annexation of 1580.[20] Outwardly Catholic, they were suspected of secret Jewish practices; tolerated because of trading links and royal orders, violence towards the community was to flare up at several points in the early seventeenth century.[21] These experiences heightened a fear of heresy but the Catholicism underpinning the League was much more than a crusade against Protestantism. Further research may show Nantes to be like Amiens, where violence towards Protestants declined during the League, a testimony to the success of the municipality in maintaining public order during these difficult years.[22]

The heightened pious sensibilities of the 1580s had an important impact on perceptions of secular problems and their remedy. As in the past, secular ills were understood in spiritual terms: explanation of calamity lay with God's displeasure with individual sin and vices in the kingdom at large. But the solution to such ills was increasingly seen in radical assuagements of the divine, by a new morality and piety in personal and public affairs. The Nantes Leaguers of 1589 had two, inter-related, religious objectives. Firstly, the defence of the monarchy against heresy through Navarre's disinheritance, an end to the royal policy of toleration, with the restoration of all French subjects to the Catholic church, and a restitution of a unified, Catholic public culture. Secondly, reform of the Catholic church itself through the restoration of spiritual values and the elimination of abuses amongst clergy and laity. But God would not be

---

20. Croix, A. (1970) 'Deux notes sur Nantes', *Annales de Démographie Historique*, p. 147.
21. In 1603 the *bureau de ville* sought to expel the community, which was saved by royal protection. Saupin, *Nantes*, p. 40.
22. Pelus-Kaplan, M.-L. (1996) 'Amiens, ville ligueuse: le sens d'une rébellion', *Revue du Nord*, LXXVIII, 315, p. 297.

placated by 'national' reforms alone: the efforts of all individuals, at city and at state level, were essential. The city in particular had to reassert itself as a unified moral and physical entity; to this end, increased devotional practices, processions, penitences and prayers were undertaken, such as Lenten processions with barefoot girls, in 1589.[23] The League coup of Spring 1589 was a mission to restore the body physical by healing the body spiritual, in an urban context.

II.

While the defence of religion was one motive for the coup of 1589, politics were an important source of discontent in Nantes. The political message of preachers criticising the royal state struck a chord with many Nantais, for whom reform of the body spiritual through the moral reform of the state was indistinct from material defence of the city.[24] Chevalier has argued that the Catholic League had its origins, in part at least, in mid-century changes in the relationship between the royal government and the cities of France, when the crown began to encroach on the functions of urban administrations.[25] Relations between Nantes and the Crown were strained after 1560 in four areas: religious policy, defence, taxation and venality. As shown above, the municipality opposed official policies of toleration of heresy in all its guises. Tensions with the military governors of the province and of the château of Nantes increased after 1562. The city government strove to limit the interference of military men in its affairs and to keep garrisons outside the town walls, stressing its right to self-defence with its own fortifications and citizen militia. In 1560, the *conseil des bourgeois* refused the château commander's orders for civilians to hand over their weapons to the garrison, for arms were needed for the night watch and guard duty by the militia.[26] There were conflicts over the financing of troops in 1568-70; the mu-

---

23. Harding finds, however, little evidence for Crouzet's eschatological anxiety in the sermon literature of Nantes, nor is there any in the municipal registers. The cure of the physical world, not the immanence of the next, was the great issue. Harding, 'Revolution and Reform', p. 410.
24. Harding, 'Revolution and Reform', p. 401.
25. Chevalier, B. (1982) *Les Bonnes Villes de France du XIVe au XVIe siècle,* Paris, pp. 1, 14.
26. A.M.N. BB 4 f.253v. Assemblée du conseil des bourgeois.

nicipality equipped 100 mounted arquebusiers to defend the town and *pays*, while refusing to pay for 200 foot soldiers demanded by the city's governor.[27] The fiscal demands of the Crown, allied to its practice of venality, also irritated: royal taxation on the province of Brittany rose to 2 million *livres* by 1576, largely raised by wine taxes, such that the cities paid the greater part.[28] Also, in 1575, 15,000 *livres* were levied on Nantes for a *solde des gens de guerre* and in 1582, a share of 37,000 *livres* plus a new consumption tax on wine were imposed.[29] Fiscal expedients, particularly the sale of judicial offices, were also pernicious. Alan James shows in his essay in this volume how the king tried to force (unsuccessfully) the Breton parlement to accept Joyeuse as admiral in the province in 1581, with the powers and sinecures that would allow. Harding shows that one of the main themes of radical preaching after 1588 was the corruption of the judicial system through venality.[30]

Yet despite grievances the Nantes city government was loyal to the Crown up to March 1589. Brittany was one of five *gouvernements* which opted for peace at the Estates-General of Blois of 1576 and on 12 January 1577, representatives of the three estates of Nantes, bishop du Bec, lieutenant-general la Hunaudaye and the mayor, Michel Loriot, signed a treaty of association with the Catholic League promulgated by Henri III in December 1576.[31] Throughout the 1580s the town's politics were studiedly neutral, seeking to avoid taxation and the quartering of troops. There is no evidence for Nantes' association with the Paris-led urban Catholic League promulgated in 1585. The Day of Barricades of Paris in May 1588 had no equal in the city and in February 1589, at Mercœur's instigation, an *assemblée générale* swore to obey the king and set up an extraordinary council of clergy, municipality and judiciary to oversee the maintenance of order.[32] The decision to rebel was taken quickly. It was the treaty between Henri III and Navarre of 3 April 1589 that forced an important section of the city council into opposition, led by Madame de Mercœur.

Loyalty to the Crown was deeply engrained among the Nantes municipal elite but dissatisfaction with royal policies was deep-rooted by

27. Saupin, *Nantes*, p. 120.
28. Collins, *Classes, Estates and Order*, p. 126.
29. A.M.N. EE 150 Fortifications; Collins, *Classes, Estates and Order*, p. 163.
30. Harding, 'Revolution and Reform', p. 403.
31. Pocquet, *Histoire de la Bretagne*, V, p. 71; A.M.N. EE 210 Ligue.
32. A.M.N. BB 21 f.177v-179r. Registres des délibérations de la municipalité.

1589. The principal cause was not encroaching state powers as suggested by Chevalier, but a collapse of government authority in the west after 1580. From the seventh religious war Nantes was increasingly concerned with maritime defence and drawn into the land conflict. 1579-80 saw the siege of Montaigu, on the Breton-Poitou border, with raids into the Nantais ravaging rural properties of the city's elites. By 1588 Huguenots based at Montaigu were a permanent threat to Clisson and Machecoul, less than 40 kilometres from Nantes. In October, Navarre's troops reached Vertou before laying siege to Beauvoir on the bay of Bourgneuf.[33] Much of the initiative and finance for the maritime and terrestrial defence of southern Brittany lay with the Nantais themselves. By the late 1580s the city employed 100 mounted troops on a seasonal basis, to protect the town and its *pays* from raids, particularly during harvest time.[34] In addition to defensive measures, the city council was subject to increasingly difficult negotiations and harsh fiscal demands from royal governors in the marches, virtually autonomous warlords acting in the royal name but over whom the king had increasingly less control. Governors and their agents posed as great, if not more of, a threat to the city's physical integrity and privileges than conflict with the Huguenots, and yet they were the only defence from the Protestant enemy.[35] There was constant tension between the governor and the municipality. Mercœur's siege of Blain was financed by a loan of 3000 *écus* and for the destruction of Montaigu, the city lent the duke 2250 *écus*, raised from 15 or so of its leading citizens.[36] In the Autumn of 1588, the city was faced with quartering or victualling troops; supplies of bread, wine and munitions were organised – by December 240,000 loaves had been commissioned.[37] The city felt abandoned and considered that it faced the problems alone in the province. In October, the *assem-*

---

33. A.M.N. BB 21 f.34r. Registres des délibérations de la municipalité.
34. Saupin, *Nantes*, p. 148.
35. P. Roberts has shown that in Troyes, the Guises as governors of Champagne, came increasingly to dominate the city government through their clients in the city council. See P. Roberts, (1992) 'Religious Conflict and the Urban Setting: Troyes during the French Wars of Religion', *French History*, 6, 3, pp. 260-261. In Nantes, the governor and his client, the commander of the château garrison, had more limited influence over municipal decisions and the town council modified or defied the governor's fiscal requests as late as 1588.
36. A.M.N. EE 211. Ligue.
37. A.M.N. BB 21 f.126r. Registres des délibérations de la municipalité.

blée générale opposed a royal levy of 30,000 *écus* on the bishopric and asked the king to suppress all taxation on the region for 20 years.[38]

The city government did not seek to augment its powers at the expense of the crown but was forced to fill the vacuum left by the retreating powers of Henri III's administration. The inability of the king to defend Nantes against Huguenot enemies and against exploitation by its own quasi-autonomous agents such as Mercœur, caused discontent. Religion and politics intersected for the fundamental causes of decayed authority and rising disorder were explained in divine terms: the visitation of God's ire on the subjects of the French king because of declining morality at court and toleration of a confessional rift in the realm. The solution was likewise expressed in religio-political terms, as in the League Manifesto of 1585: the restoration of religious unity and reform by the royal state, a combination of institutional and moral reforms. Yet in Nantes, there was no apparent revolutionary platform, as Harding has shown: the League was 'a revolt, not against the constitutional form of the state, but against the corruption of state institutions'.[39] The message of League sermons was the purification of political society through moral reform of personnel, but not the restructuring of the state itself.[40]

Traditionally, the actions of the Nantes elites have been interpreted as an attempt to restore provincial independence under a duke of Brittany, led by Mercœur who dominated the town and who had hereditary claims, through his wife, to the title. Yet neither Mercœur nor the city voiced overtly particularist sentiments at any time; even at the League Estates of 1591 no mention was made of the defence of provincial liberties.[41] Rather, rapid decisions had to be made as to the best methods of defending the city's physical integrity, its fiscal basis and its spiritual welfare, upon which the former were seen to rest. By 1589, in the short term, support for the Crown against Mercœur would threaten the physical and spiritual community of Nantes. Mercœur's army was quartered in the suburbs of the city. Defiance of the governor could lead to the sack of the town. Moreover, Mercœur was greatly in debt to the city: to repudiate his political and military leadership was to forfeit large loans with no hope of restitution. He also had important clients in the urban elite.

---

38. A.M.N. BB 21 f.32 r. & v. Registres des déliberations de la municipalité.
39. Harding, 'Revolution and Reform', p. 405.
40. Harding, *Idem*, p. 414.
41. Saupin, *Nantes*, p. 147.

Conversely, after the truce of April 1589, support for the king might bring a Huguenot army into the city and even a Huguenot successor, by legitimate means. The threat to the religious and cultural basis of the town that this posed was unacceptable. In the longer term, the restitution of a Catholic municipal culture in a moderate but effective monarchy, with a relationship governed by contract, was the prime objective. Common cause with other cities and provinces in a Catholic League was the best way of putting pressure on the monarchy to achieve these aims.

III.

The economic interests of the mercantile elite of Nantes are traditionally held to have influenced the decision to opt for the League in 1589. A central plank of the city's economy was overseas commerce, particularly trade with Spain. A colony of Spanish merchants had been present in Nantes since at least the fifteenth century; parish registers of mid-century show c.130 such families, several of whom were amongst Nantes' elite, such as the Ruiz, who acted as consuls from Spain and lent money to the French Crown.[42] Pirates from La Rochelle threatened this activity throughout the 1570s and 1580s, and it was constantly feared that enforcement of royal policies of toleration of heresy would lead to economic reprisals by Spain. Saupin argues that protection of trade and the image of the Spanish king as the epitome of Catholicism were vital factors in the decision of the Catholic League and in 1590 the League in Brittany was supplied by Spanish troops.[43] But sentiment is impossible to quantify. A number of hispanic Nantais opposed the League: André Ruiz the younger was imprisoned as a royalist suspect in 1589. Released by the good offices of his sister with the duchess of Mercœur, he passed the League years quietly in his Nantes house, and welcomed Henri IV in 1598.

The broader economic and social context of the 1580s was more important than Spanish interests, not in forcing a decision to opt for the League but as further evidence of divine displeasure with the kingdom at large and the community of Nantes in particular. Severe harvest failure

---

42. Croix, 'Deux notes sur Nantes', pp. 144-147; Lapeyre, H. (1955) *Une famille de marchands: les Ruiz*, Paris, p. 55.
43. Saupin, *Nantes*, p. 38.

affected the *pays* Nantais twice in the 1580s, while war continually dev-astated the surrounding countryside. Subsistence crises provoked recession in manufacturing industry in the city and conflict disrupted riverine and maritime trade.[44] The city filled with refugees, creating se-vere problems of poor relief and epidemic control for the authorities. The islands of the Loire near Nantes filled with peasant families and their animals.[45] The municipality went to extraordinary lengths in the 1580s to relieve starving peasants who were flooding into the city. In 1584 and 1586, to keep the starving and their diseases at bay, the authorities pur-chased large quantities of grain and supplied it to parishes in the southern Nantes hinterland: in 1586, 50 parishes were supplied for 7 weeks.[46] Public work schemes were established in February 1587, March 1588 and throughout 1589, digging fortifications and repairing the city walls.[47] To finance such projects, collections were made in the city's parishes and in 1586, a loan of 800 *écus* was taken from eight of the city's wealthiest inhabitants. To pay for such schemes, taxes upon the whole city, irrespective of privilege, were ordered. When *officiers* and nobles refused, as in 1584, an edict from the *Parlement* was obtained to constrain them to pay.[48]

Militia service also expanded in scope. As well as constant defence of the city walls at night and the gates by day the militia increased its role as maintainer of public order. Surveys of households, for arms, pro-visions and household membership, and for 'foreigners' had been carried out periodically since 1560 and increased after 1580, when la Hunaudaye ordered each captain to visit all houses in their canton and to expel all strangers without reason for their visit, at least two or three times a week, under penalty of a fine.[49] By 1589, the militia was organised to survey the population of Nantes and had an increasingly professional conception of its civic function and duties. It would become an important agent of the maintenance of control of the city after 1589.

---

44. The letters of André Ruiz the younger show the disastrous effect of war on commerce, Lapeyre, *Une famille de marchands*, p. 586.
45. Poquet, *Histoire de la Bretagne*, V, p. 90.
46. A.M.N. GG 744 Assistance aux pauvres 1580-88.
47. Fardet, M. (1972) 'L'assistance aux pauvres à Nantes à la fin du XVIe siècle (1582-1598)', *Actes du 97e Congrès National des Sociétés Savantes*, Philosophie et Histoire, Nantes, p. 409.
48. A.M.N. GG 744 Assistance aux pauvres 1580-88.
49. A.M.N. EE 60 Milice bourgeoise.

Economic and social difficulties caused by war and harvest failure did not cause the Nantes elite to adhere to the Catholic League, but they provided support for theories of divine punishment for sin and stimulated policies which made easier the control of the city after 1589. A growth in city authority was rationalised and understood by theories of civic unity and Godly community in the face of enemies on many fronts. Civic duties were extended in volume and scope, to social groups which had previously considered themselves exempt.

IV.

It remains to be asked: who were the Leaguers in Nantes? The militants seem to have been a small group. The coup of 1589 was the work of a few, led by the duchesse de Mercœur, but one in which the majority of the Nantes municipal elite were, at least tacitly, in favour. This was no radical movement: all participants were moderates who sought to uphold the social order. The continuity of membership of the city administration is striking.[50] In the *bureau de ville*, the deputy mayor, Fourché de la Courosserie (who seems to have been a Mercœur client) remained in place, as did the six *échevins*. The *assemblée générale* was superseded for three months by a *Conseil de l'Union*, but the latter included many members of the former. By July, *bureau* and *assemblée* were in charge of city affairs once again. The fourteen captains of the city militia present in February 1589 were still in post in July; the only leader to be purged was the colonel, the mayor de Harouys, who was replaced by a loyal Mercœur man, Michel Loriot. There was less continuity among the staff of the judicial courts. As in many cities, *officiers* preferred to support the king. The leading royal officiers fled, mostly to Rennes: the *prévôt*, the *sénéschal*, the *premier président* of the *Chambre des Comptes* and the treasurer of the estates of Brittany, Gabriel Hus, for example. But 18 of the *officiers* of the *Chambre des Comptes* stayed in the city and 25 per cent of the magistrates of the Rennes *parlement* joined the League.[51] Individual motive is difficult to ascribe. Collins argues that the families

---

50. The statistical information for this section is taken from A.M.N. BB 21, using lists of names from all of the recorded *assemblées générales* and the meetings of the Conseil de l'Union.
51. Harding, 'Revolution and Reform, p. 388.

with close ties to the city chose to stay or return there, while those with less direct ties chose to flee.[52] Above all the League was a movement of defence of the city by its patricians as the best means of preserving the integrity of the town and of their own position within it.

V.

The main purpose of this essay has been to argue that the League in Nantes did not grow out of intolerance of heresy alone, nor was it solely a product of a Catholic militancy, with which the city and province became identified after 1598. Rather, it was a defensive movement born out of an ideology of Christian community as a means of restoring secular and spiritual order. There was a resurgence of the ideology of the 'bonne ville', reinvigorated by the experience of war in the 1580s, where active citizenship and autonomous communal government were the means of combatting military threats, food shortages and social dislocation. The decline of effective monarchy forced the city to attend to the defence of its own citizens, with its own material and moral resources.

But the Nantais remained loyal to the Crown until April 1589 when Henri III's treaty with Navarre forced the Mercœurs into the League camp. A majority of the city's elite opted to support Mercœur and thus to defend the city against the duke and the Huguenots at the same time. The motives of the Leaguers have to be seen from both a religious and cultural *and* a secular and political perspective, however, for the Nantais inhabited a sacramental universe. The troubles of the city stemmed from the disruption of war and the decline in royal authority. The roots of these disorders lay in divine wrath. Resolutions lay in the assuaging of God's ire. A Godly city could bring order to the lives of at least its own citizens. Mark Greengrass points out that the pamphlet of the *Manant* justifying the rule of the Sixteen in Paris shows the League to be a confraternity for the protection of the city in a Catholic commonwealth of God, Church and people.[53] Similar sentiments appear in Nantes. The League was also a means of exerting physical and moral pressure on the

---

52. Collins, *Estates, Classes and Order*, p. 129.
53. Greengrass, M. (1984) 'The Sixteen, Radical Politics in Paris During the League', *History*, 69, p. 434.

Crown to reform itself. Secular conflict and disorder would cease when the moral community of the kingdom and the city were restored. For this the Nantais had to wait until 1598.

Bibliography

Manuscript Sources.

Archives Municipales de Nantes (hereafter A.M.N.).

A.M.N. BB 4 Assemblée du conseil des bourgeois
A.M.N. BB 21 Registres des déliberations de la municipalité.
A.M.N. EE 60 Milice bourgeoise
A.M.N. EE 150 Fortifications
A.M.N. EE 210 Ligue.
A.M.N. EE 211 Ligue.
A.M.N. GG 744 Assistance aux pauvres 1580-88.

Part 4

Religious Pluralism after the Edict of Nantes:
Further Dimensions

·

RICHARD BONNEY

The Obstacles to Pluralism in Early Modern France

The study of the interaction of religion and politics, and the assessment
of the obstacles to pluralism in early modern France, has been hampered
by a lack of methodological clarity.[1] The aim of this chapter is to provide
a more sophisticated interpretation of the theoretical and practical limitations on religious pluralism in early modern France, with particular
emphasis on the obstacles to its acceptance. Firstly, the main arguments
for and against religious pluralism will be summarized. Secondly, drawing upon recent work by theologians and sociologists of multicul-
turalism,[2] a working model of the levels of pluralism in a society will be
proposed and tested in the subsequent discussion. Historical purists, who
reject any borrowing from the methodologies of the social sciences, may
object that to attempt to apply such a model to the complex conflicts of
early modern France is to risk anachronism. The justification for this
approach is to be found, simply and perhaps suprisingly, in the events of
a few weeks in January-February 1562, when the link between church
and state (as manifested in the traditional adage 'one law, one faith, one
king')[3] was challenged by the legislation proposed by the Chancellor of
France, Michel de L'Hospital.

---

1. An important article by Philip Benedict has identified some of the issues: Benedict,
    P. (1996), '*Un roi, une loi, deux fois*: parameters for the history of Catholic-
    Reformed co-existence in France, 1555-1685', *Tolerance and Intolerance in the
    European Reformation*, ed. O. P. Grell and R. W. Scribner, Cambridge: CUP, pp.
    65-93.
2. Blommaert, J. and Verschueren, J. (1996), 'European concepts of nation-building',
    The Politics of Difference. Ethnic Premises in a World of Power, ed. E. N. Wilmsen
    and P. McAllister. Chicago and London: University of Chicago Press, pp. 104-123.
    The scheme proposed here is a modification of that proposed in a letter from Lord
    Habgood, the former Archbishop of York, to *The Times,* published on 11 Oct. 1997.
3. A modification of Ephesians 4: 5 ('one Lord, one faith, one baptism'), which justi-
    fied the *jus reformandi*. The 'old proverb' *une foi, une loi, un roi* was cited by de
    L'Hospital in his speech on 13 Dec. 1560: Lecler, J. (1960) *Toleration and the Ref-
    ormation*, trans. T. L. Westow. New York and London: Association Press and
    Longmans, i. 71; ii. 45. Lecler suggests an origin for the adage (*ibid.*, i. 68) as far
    back as Hincmar's commentary on the treaty of Verdun (843).

There were two main attitudes towards religious pluralism in early modern Europe. The first position was a minority one, promulgated first by the German humanist and radical reformer Sebastian Franck, and subsequently developed more systematically by the Savoyard classical scholar and theologian, Sebastian Castellio. Castellio published his collection of opinions of learned men *Concerning heretics, whether they are to be persecuted and how they are to be treated...* (*De haereticis an sint persequendi*) at Basle in March 1554, in the aftermath of the execution of Servetus at Geneva the previous October.[4] Four years later, he pleaded that tolerance required the acceptance of the idea of *discordia* and the renunciation of false attempts to reach consensus (*concordia*): 'Grant me the liberty of my faith and the liberty to confess it, just as you wish that I grant you your own liberty.'[5] Directing his *Advice to a Desolate France...* in the autumn of 1562, after the outbreak of the first war of religion, Castellio argued that the essence of belief lay in the exercise of free choice by the believer.[6] God wants voluntary disciples: 'thy people shall be willing in the day of thy power, in the beauties of holiness' (Ps. 110: 3). True soldiers of Christ were volunteers, not forced conscripts.[7] The danger of violent persecution was that it brought about the very evil which it sought to avoid, for tyranny engenders sedition. There were countless sects who regarded themselves as Christian. To seek to coerce

---

4. Guggisberg, H. (1996) 'The secular state of the Reformation period and the beginnings of the debate on religious toleration', *The Individual in Political Theory and Practice*, ed. J. Coleman. Oxford: European Science Foundation and Oxford University Press, p. 89.
5. Guggisberg, H. (1994) 'Tolerance and intolerance in sixteenth-century Basle', *Calvinism in Europe, 1540-1620*, ed. A. Pettegree, A. C. Duke, G. Lewis. Cambridge: Cambridge University Press, p. 157. More generally, *ibid.* 149-160 on Castellio's career at Basle and disputes with Calvin, Beza and others. Calvin had disagreed with Castellio as early as 1543-1544: Wendel, F. (1963) *Calvin. The Origins and Development of His Religious Thought.* London and New York: Collins, pp. 82-83. There are useful discussion of Castellio's thought in both Lecler, *Toleration and the Reformation*, i. 336-347 and Skinner, Q. (1978) *The Foundations of Modern Political Thought. II. The Reformation.* Cambridge: Cambridge University Press, pp. 245-250.
6. Lecler, *Toleration and the Reformation*, i. 74-77, summarizes the arguments. More detail in Buisson, F. (1892) *Sébastien Castellion: sa vie et son oeuvre, 1515-1563. Étude sur les origines du Protestantisme libéral français* 2 vols. Paris: Hachette, ii. 225-237. For Castellio, the principal cause of civil war in France was 'forcement de consciences'.
7. Mullan, D. G. (ed.) (1998) *Religious Pluralism in the West.* Oxford: Blackwell, pp. 109-110.

them all was to embark upon 'a war such as the Midianites had' (Judges 6-7).[8]

Thus Castellio arrived at the minimalist position for toleration: you should not force people's consciences, but allow those 'who believe in Christ and who accept the Old and New Testament, to serve God in your country, not in accordance with the beliefs of others, but in accordance with their own'.[9] Within Castellio's theory of toleration, monotheism was the basic belief. This might allow some place within the body politic for Jews and Muslims: 'if anyone denies the Lord God, this one is an infidel and atheist and is deservedly to be abhorred in the eyes of all.' Disagreements between the three main monotheistic faiths paralleled the disagreements between Christians over matters of doctrine: 'if these matters were so obvious and evident as that there is but one God, all Christians would agree among themselves on these points as readily as all nations confess that God is one.'[10] Castellio argued that Calvin wanted 'all those who grievously err to be killed unless they endorse the opinion of Calvin... If this were done, all who bear the Christian name would be killed, except Calvinists...'[11] Yet Christ had taught his follow-ers to pardon not seven times but seventy times seven (Matt. 18: 22).[12] A correct interpretation of the parable of the tares (Matt. 13: 28-30) would suggest that it was preferable that bad men live rather than one good man should be destroyed before the harvest at the Second Coming of Christ.[13] Persecution had always accompanied religious revival and, as Gamaliel had predicted (Acts 5: 33-9),[14] a belief system sanctioned by God could not be reversed by the actions of men. 'Who ever thought that he held a false religion? The Jews erred in persecuting Christ and the apostles. The gentiles erred who persecuted the Christians...'[15] The argument of reci-procity was fundamental in Castellio's system. Christ had used the argument when confronted for an opinion about the guilt of the woman caught in the act of adultery: 'he that is without sin among you, let him

---

8. *Ibid.*, p. 114.
9. *Ibid.*, p. 115.
10. Bainton, R. H. (trans.) (1935) *Concerning Heretics. Whether they are to be perse-cuted and how they are to be treated. A collection of the opinions of learned men, both ancient and modern.* New York: Columbia University Press, p. 132.
11. *Ibid.*, p. 265.
12. *Ibid.*, p. 125.
13. *Ibid.*, p. 277.
14. *Ibid.*, pp. 127, 279.
15. *Ibid.*, p. 278.

first cast a stone' (John 8:7). The logic of this moral argument was 'to say to those who force the consciences of others: "Would you like your own to be forced?" And their own conscience, which is worth more than a thousand witnesses, would then suddenly convince them so thoroughly, that they would be quite ashamed.'[16]

Whatever the validity and modernity of Castellio's arguments, there can be no doubt that in the 1550s and 1560s they represented a minority viewpoint. Though Chancellor Michel de L'Hospital may have read his works, there is no evidence that his own viewpoint was directly influenced by Castellio.[17] Nor is there any evidence that Castellio's arguments were taken seriously by the majority of French Catholics or Protestants. The *Exhortation aux Princes*, published at the end of 1561, was of greater contemporary importance, because it campaigned for freedom of conscience and may have influenced de L'Hospital after the failure of the Colloquy of Poissy. The *Exhortation aux Princes* did not justify two religions in a state in principle, but argued that Frenchmen should live 'in peace of conscience, without threatening other people's lives, and in the religion to which we have been called'. Gamaliel's agument in Acts 5: 34-40 was taken as Biblical justification, while the freedom of Jews within the Papal States was taken as the European precedent:

> For God's sake do not force our consciences to the point of a sword. All of us, Romans and Protestants, are united in one body through the holy sacrament of baptism. All of us adore the same God, not in the same way, perhaps, but with equal fervour.[18]

---

16. Mullan, *Religious Pluralism in the West*, p. 101.
17. Although his statement on 9 September 1561 against the coercion of conscience echoed Castellio: 'la conscience est de telle nature qu'elle ne peut estre forcée... la foy si elle est contraincte, elle n'est plus la foy.' Wanegffelen, T. (1997), *Ni Rome ni Genève. Des fidèles entre deux chaires en France au XVIe siècle*. Paris: Champion, p. 216.
18. Lecler, *Toleration and the Reformation*, i. 49-55. Smith, M. C. (1991), *Montaigne and Religious Freedom. The Dawn of Pluralism*. Geneva: Droz, pp. 37, 196. This text was for a long time attributed erroneously to Pasquier (e.g. by Ferdinand Buisson). Castellio claimed that it argued the same case as his *Advice to a Desolate France...*: Valkoff, M. F. (ed.) (1967), [Sebastian Castellio] *Conseil à la France désolée*. Geneva: Droz, p. 53: 'Mais devant que venir à ce poinct, je veux faire mencion d'un petit livre imprimé l'an passé en françois, dont le tiltre est *Exhortacion aux princes et seigneurs du conseil privé du Roy*, auquel livre est donné le mesme conseil que je veux donner, c'est de permettre en France deux Eglises'. The author thanks Loris Petris for this reference.

The spokesman for the opposing viewpoint was a Frenchman, Theodore Beza, who in September 1554 published at Geneva his *De haereticis a civili magistratu puniendis*...: this specifically refuted Castellio's work, justified the execution of Servetus and provided a traditional Augustinian defence of religious persecution by the civil power. The arguments in favour of toleration were tantamount to a 'charité diabolique et non pas chrétienne'. 'Le Seigneur', he contended, 'ne requiert pas seulement que nous ayons quelque conscience, mais bonne conscience.' The argument that 'chacun est sauvé en sa religion' was dismissed as 'un article de la doctrine de Mahomet'.[19] Beza drew upon the Magdeburg Confession (*Bekenntnis*), drafted by Nicolas von Amsdorf, which had opposed Charles V's imposition of the Interim of Augsburg.[20] The *jus reformandi*, in Beza's view, rested with the lesser magistrate, but his duty was to ensure conformity:

> [...] le devoir du Magistrat inferieur est de maintenir, tant qu'il luy est possible, en son pays et sous sa jurisdiction la pureté de la religion; en quoy il faut qu'il procede avec grande prudence et bonne moderation, mais si faut-il qu'il y ait aussi de la constance et magnanimité. Et de ceci la ville de Magdebourg a monstré de nostre temps un exemple bien notable [...] Ainsi donc, combien que plusieurs Princes abusent de leur office, je di [*sic*] toutesfois que quiconque estime qu'il se faille deporter d'user de l'aide des Magistrats Chrestiens que Dieu presente, à l'encontre de la violence externe des infideles ou des heretiques, cestuy-la despouille l'Eglise de Dieu d'un secours merveilleusement utile et mesme necessaire, toutes fois et quantes qu'ainsi il plaist au Seigneur.[21]

---

19. Dating from Guggisberg, 'Tolerance and intolerance in sixteenth-century Basle', p. 154. Discussion of the text in Lecler, *Toleration and the Reformation*, i. 347-350; Skinner, *The Foundations of Modern Political Thought*, ii. 209, 212-213, 216. Kingdon, R. M. (1955), 'The first expression of Theodore Beza's political ideas', *Archiv für Reformationsgeschichte*, 46 (1955), 88-100, reprinted in Kingdon, R. M. (1985) *Church and Society in Reformation Europe*. London: Variorum, ch. X. Kingdon, R. M (1960), 'Les idées politiques de Bèze d'après son *Traitté de l'authorité du magistrat en la punition des hérétiques*', *Bibliothèque d'Humanisme et Renaissance*, 22 (1960), 566-569. For the specific refutation of Bellius [= Castellio]: Buisson, *Sébastien Castellion*, ii. 23-25.

20. This is discussed in Skinner, *The Foundations of Modern Political Thought*, ii. 207-209. Lecler, *Toleration and the Reformation*, i. 253-260 documents examples of the Lutheran prince as defender of religious unity before the Peace of Augsburg.

21. Kingdon, R. M. (1970) T de Bèze, *Du Droit des Magistrats*. Geneva: Droz, pp. 69-70. English translation in Kingdon, 'The first expression of Theodore Beza's political ideas', p. 92.

Calvin seems to have approved of Beza's argument: the translation into French of a further edition in 1560 was achieved by one of his former secretaries, approved by the Genevan censorship authorities and published in the aftermath of the Conspiracy of Amboise. In April 1561, the Synod of Montauban specifically approved the argument that one of the duties of government was to suppress heresy: it sent a copy of its minute to this effect to the Geneva Company of Pastors.[22] For Calvin, the task of 'constituting religion aright' was attributed to human polity (*Institutes*, ed. 1559-60, 4.20.3). For Catholics and Protestants alike, intolerance was the norm; the acceptance of heresy was equated with heresy itself.[23] Few indeed were prepared to go as far as the apologist of the edict of Amboise (1563) who made the essential link in the modern argument for pluralism that acceptance of another viewpoint is not necessarily endorsement of it ('permission n'est pas approbation').[24] We may not agree with someone else's views: but our disapproval does not necessarily have to be malevolent, because our endorsement of the other viewpoint cannot be assumed. This modern form of reasoning was alien to sixteenth-century attitudes. Thus Calvin dismissed the arguments of Gamaliel in Acts 5: 34-40 as those of 'un sceptique [...;] son advis [...] est pour dissiper tout ordre de police et pour casser la discipline de l'Eglise'.[25] Instead, he preferred to cite Deuteronomy 13: 6-9 ('If thy brother [...] entice thee secretly, saying, Let us go and serve other gods [...] thou shalt surely kill him')[26] and Matthew 10: 34 ('I came not to send peace but a sword'),[27] arguing (*Institutes*, ed. 1559-60, 4.12.4) that churches could not 'long stand without this bond of discipline... which the Lord foresaw would be necessary'.

Whereas the Protestant acceptance of *de facto* toleration was a product of political expediency (the Reformed faith was the beneficiary of the concessions) and its position was riddled with inconsistency,[28] for

---

22. Kingdon, 'The first expression of Theodore Beza's political ideas', p. 98.
23. Tallon A.(1998) 'Rome et les premiers édits de tolérance d'après la correspondance du nonce Santa Croce', Grandjean M. and Roussel, B. (eds.) *Coexister dans l'intolérance. L'édit de Nantes (1598)*. Geneva: Labor et Fides, p. 342.
24. *Mémoires de Condé*, iv. 426, cited above in Loris Petris's chapter.
25. Buisson, *Sébastien Castellion*, ii. 46.
26. *Ibid.*, ii. 48.
27. Higman, F. M. (1998) *Lire et découvrir. La circulation des idées du temps de la Réforme*. Geneva: Droz, pp. 419-433.
28. Garnett, G. (ed.) (1994), [Stephanus Junius Brutus, the Celt], *Vindiciae, Contra Tyrannos: or, concerning the legitimate poiwer of a prince over the people, and of*

Catholics the text *Compelle intrare* ('Compel them to come in': Luke 14: 23)[29] seemed to provide a justification for religious orthodoxy being secured by the institutions of the church and state acting in collaboration. Other texts, such as Titus 3: 10 and 1 Corinthians 5: 9-13 provided an arsenal of theological arguments,[30] while the political reality was that it was of the nature of religions that the new tended to drive out the old.[31] Force might be needed to prevent this from happening, to preserve a unified body politic. 'Salvation by coercion' as it has been called,[32] if not the predominant viewpoint in Europe in the sixteenth century was common currency; and it remained so even late into the seventeenth century.[33] The complete eradication of heresy by force was reaffirmed by Pope Gregory XIII as a legitimate objective of French royal policy in the aftermath of the St Bartholomew Massacres.[34] Those advocates of toleration who noted that the Ottoman State harboured 'several religions and various sects in its borders' were said to injure the reputation of Christian princes: 'they want to measure their empires according to the tyranny of the Turks and dispose Christian customs in accordance with the monstrousness of the laws of the Turks'.[35] Islamic pluralism ought to set no precedent for Christians.

---

the people over a prince Cambridge: Cambridge University Press, pp. xlviii-xlix, who notes the 'disjuncture between people and church', the definition of the church which is 'hard to square with the author's own argument' and the 'existence of two churches in one people'. Smith, *Montaigne and Religious Freedom*, pp. 43, 199-200.

29. The text was not cited in the 1536 Edition of the *Institutes*: Battles, F. L. (ed. and trans.) (repr. 1995) [Calvin, J.] *Institutes of the Christian Religion. 1536 Edition.* Grand Rapids, Michigan: Eerdmans. The only reference to it in the 1559-60 edition was oblique: McNeill, J. T. (ed.) and Battles, F. L. (trans.) (1961) [Calvin, J.] *The Institutes of the Christian Religion.* Philadelphia: Westminster Press, 2 vols., ii. 1355 (4.16.31, para. 5).

30. Smith, *Montaigne and Religious Freedom*, pp. 65, 208.

31. *Ibid.*, p. 65, citing La Boëtie.

32. Duke, A. C. (1990) *Reformation and Revolt in the Low Countries.* London and Ronceverte: The Hambledon Press, ch. 7.

33. Repgen, K. (1987), 'What is a "Religious War"?', *Politics and Society in Reformation Europe. Essays for Sir Geoffrey Elton...*, ed. E. I. Kouri and Tom Scott. Basingstoke: Macmillan, pp. 311-328 at p. 311. Bluche, F. (1990) *Louis XIV*, trans. M. Greengrass. Oxford: Blackwell, p. 631.

34. Kingdon, R. M. (1975) 'Reactions to the St Bartholomew Massacres in Geneva and Rome', *The Massacre of St Bartholomew: Reappraisals and Documents*, ed. A. Soman. The Hague: Martinus Nijhoff, pp. 42-43, repr. in Kingdon, *Church and Society in Reformation Europe*, ch. xiv.

35. Mullan, *Religious Pluralism in the West*, p. 124.

'Toleration' was used by the majority of Frenchmen in the sixteenth and seventeenth centuries in the traditional sense, of acquiescing in a fault which had not been corrected; it was a restraint on one's hatred.[36] Calvin's used the expression *par tolérance* to describe an evil that was accepted.[37] Whereas liberty was a permanent state of affairs and just, tolerance implied a *de facto* recognition of an unjust state of affairs.[38] Even Chancellor de L'Hospital used the word 'tolerate' in this sense: 'We can live in peace with those who do not observe the same ceremonies... and apply what is said about the defects of wives... they must either be corrected or tolerated.'[39] In such a society, the best that could be hoped for was coexistence in a prevailing state of intolerance: *coexister dans l'intolérance.*[40] Nevertheless, to leave the argument there is to emphasise only the prevailing theoretical position and to go no further. To assert that the era of De L'Hospital and Montaigne[41] was not yet the era of Voltaire,[42] and that the modern argument for a neutrality of the law in matters of faith[43] was unthinkable for contemporaries, is to do no

36. Guggisberg, 'The secular state of the Reformation period and the beginnings of the debate on religious toleration', p. 87. Bejczy, I. (1997) *'Tolerantia*: a Medieval concept', *Journal of the History of Ideas*, 58, pp. 365-384, at p. 372.
37. Wanegffelen, *Ni Rome ni Genève*, p. 245.
38. Smith, *Montaigne and religious freedom*, pp. 47, 49, 202.
39. Quoted in the chapter by Loris Petris in this volume. Petris notes that de l'Hospital's wife and daughter were both Protestant. Lecler, *Toleration and the Reformation*, ii. 69.
40. The title of an important collection of articles on the regime of the edict of Nantes: Grandjean, M. and Roussel, B. (eds) (1998) *Coexister dans l'intolérance. L'édit de Nantes (1598).* Geneva: Labor et Fides.
41. The short study by Smith, *Montaigne and religious freedom*, is central to the issues raised by this chapter; the much longer study by Schaefer, D. L. (1990) *The Political Philosophy of Montaigne*. Ithaca and London: Cornell University Press, is less focused on the issue. Of particular interest, however, is Montaigne's comment (*ibid.*, p. 146) that French kings 'having been unable to do what they would, they have pretended to will what they could'. That is, concessions to Protestants were exacted under duress.
42. For Voltaire, in his *Traité sur la Tolérance* of 1764, written after the Calas affair of two years earlier, the test of a religion is its effect on society. Only if its social influence is pernicious may it be suppressed: 'That which gives no offence to society does not fall within the realm of justice.' McManners, J. (1998) *Church and Society in Eighteenth-Century France.* 2 vols. Oxford: Oxford University Press, i. 79; ii. 619-620.
43. On the grounds that if all religions are treated with equal disadvantage none can claim overt or inadvertent discrimination: Bradney, A. (1993) *Religions, Rights and Laws.* Leicester: Leicester University Press, p. 160.

more than state the obvious. Perhaps instead historians can usefully seek to establish a working model of the levels of pluralism in a society to test the practical limits of intolerance.

For De L'Hospital, what was at stake in 1562 was not a 'a religious constitution (*de constituenda religione*), but a civic constitution (*de constituenda republica*)'.[44] The edict of July 1561 had not succeeded; a new measure was needed, for laws should be fitted to circumstances 'as shoes to feet'. There was no case for a declaration by the king on one side of the religious dispute or the other. Such a declaration would imply that the king was prepared to assemble an army; any resulting victory would be equally damaging to the victor as to the vanquished. De L'Hospital's principal assertion astonished conventional Catholic opinion: he stated that that the king did not want a disputation on which truth claim was correct ('le Roy ne veut point que vous entriez en dispute quelle opinion est la meilleure').[45] There was ferocious opposition to the idea. The *Parlement* of Paris objected that the crown seemed to 'approve diversity of religion in this kingdom, which has never been the case from king Clovis I to this day'.[46] The breakdown of law and order was blamed on 'tolerance and impunity'; one religion recognized seven sacraments and was true; the other recognized two sacraments only and was false and heretical.[47] A royal interpretative declaration was issued on 14 February 1562, which met some of the objections of the *Parlement* of Paris and stated clearly that the wording of the January edict had not intended to 'approve two religions in our kingdom, but rather one only, which is that of the Holy Church, in which the kings our predecessors have ever lived'.[48]

The assertion of De L'Hospital was thus formally disavowed. Leaving aside the concessions made to heretical opinions, the principal

---

44. Wanegffelen, *Ni Rome ni Genève*, p. 215.
45. It is known that it did in Catholic Europe: Tallon, A. (1997) *La France et le Concile de Trente, 1518-1563*. Rome: École Française de Rome, p. 324. Telle, E.-V. (ed.) (1987) [Hotman, F.,] *La vie de Messire Gaspar de Colligny, Admiral de France*. Geneva: Droz, pp. 34-35.
46. Roelker, N. L. (1996) *One King, One Faith. The Parlement of Paris and the Religious Reformations of the Sixteenth Century*. Berkeley and Los Angeles: University of California Press, pp. 251-254.
47. Roelker, *One King, One Faith*, p. 266. Telle (ed.) [Hotman], *La vie de Messire Gaspar de Colligny*, pp. 29-30.
48. Potter, D. (1997) *The French Wars of Religion. Selected Documents*. Basingstoke: Macmillan, p. 33. Roelker, *One King, One Faith*, p. 253.

criticism of the policy of the Regent and her Chancellor was that the edict of 17 January 1562, rather than improving the situation, exacerbated local tensions.[49] The policy of the Chancellor had failed to work and had made everything worse.[50] This reputation for failure survived into the seventeenth century. Michel de L'Hospital was said not to have foreseen, nor to have taken adequate measures, to prevent the civil war which would inevitably result from the recognition of two religions in a single state: would that Chancellor Olivier had not died in 1560.[51] True or not, the January edict was vilified as the *casus belli*: 'Voilà... ce fameux Édit de janvier', wrote the Dauphin Louis and Bossuet in their *Règne de Charles IX* in the 1670s and 1680s, 'qui causa tant de troubles dans le royaume...'.[52] The fiction that a future general council of the Church would restore unity was used as pretext for continued 'provisional' edicts of pacification in subsequent decades.[53] The ultimate aim, on the Catholic side, remained 'concord' (and therefore the theological reunion of Protestants within a Gallican church), not pluralism (that is, the equality of two confessions).[54] Once there were massacres and counter-massacres, then the rival pamphlets drew upon existing stereotypes and helped create rival collective memories of oppression.[55]

This opposition in 1562 suggests that the vital factor in hindering any development from level one to a higher level of pluralism is the prevalence of fear and distrust within the majority community and the

---

49. For local tensions in the conflict over sites for Reformed worship: Roberts, P. (1998), 'The most crucial battle of the wars of religion? The conflict over sites for Reformed worship in sixteenth-century France', *Archiv für Reformationsgeschichte* 89, pp. 247-267.

50. Wanegffelen, *Ni Rome ni Genève*, p. 198 n. 1. Cf. Pasquier's conclusion on the Colloquy of Poissy, that it was 'un acheminement à nouveaux troubles'.

51. Cornette, J. (1998) *La mélancolie du pouvoir. Omer Talon et le procès de la raison d'État*. Paris: Fayard, p. 107.

52. Pouzet, R. (ed.) (1993), *Charles IX. Récit d'histoire par Louis Dauphin et Bossuet*. Clermont-Ferrand: Adosa, p. 81.

53. Smith, *Montaigne and Religious Freedom*, p. 49. For Postel, on the contrary, the Council was the reason no Gallican settlement had been attained: Tallon, A. (1997) *La France et le Concile de Trente, 1518-1563*. Rome: École Française de Rome, pp. 510-515.

54. Smith, *Montaigne and Religious Freedom*, pp. 68-69. Wanegffelen, *Ni Rome ni Genève*, pp. 175. *Ibid.*, p. 447: 'c'est l'egalité des Eglises et des opinions [...] qui maintient et conserve l'Estat' (Philippe Canaye, 1609).

55. Greengrass, M. (1999) 'Hidden transcripts: secret histories and personal testimonies of religious violence in the French wars of religion', *The Massacre in History*, ed. M. Levene and P. Roberts. New York and Oxford: Berghahn, pp. 69-88.

belief that the new religion does not seek coexistence but confessional exclusivism.[56] One of the achievements of Denis Crouzet's researches has been to demonstrate the traumatic effect of religious disunity on Catholic opinion in a body politic ruled by sacral monarchy, where the king was in effect simultaneously king, quasi-priest and judge.[57] The maxim *cuius regio, eius religio* in the Holy Roman Empire was a later formulation of the legist Joachim Stephani in 1582;[58] but there is not much doubt that it was the practice in the Empire from the earliest princely conversions to the Reformation in the late 1520s and early 1530s into the early seventeenth century.[59] The case of Brandenburg after 1613 was wholly exceptional: in this principality, where there was a strong representative institution and powerful cities, a compromise emerged under which a Calvinist elector ruled over a largely Lutheran population.[60] Elsewhere, if a prince converted to Lutheranism, or later, to Calvinism, then his subjects were expected to conform gradually. Of immediate relevance to the French context, Béarn became a Calvinist confessional state after 1571 until its reconquest by Louis XIII in 1620.[61]

---

56. For the distinction between exclusivism, inclusivism and pluralism: Race, A. (1993) *Christians and Religious Pluralism. Patterns in the Christian Theology of Religions.* 2nd edn. London: SCM Press.

57. Roelker, *One King, One Faith*, foreword by B. B. Diefendorf, xi. Cf. Jonathan Powis in *TLS* 11 Oct. 1996. Crouzet, D. (1990) *Les guerriers de Dieu. La violence au temps des troubles de religion, vers 1525-vers 1610.* 2 vols. Paris: Champ Vallon. Crouzet, D. (1994) *La nuit de la Saint-Barthélemy: un rêve perdu de la Renaissance.* Paris: Fayard..

58. Spitz, L. W. (1975), 'Imperialism, Particularism and Toleration in the Holy Roman Empire', *The Massacre of St Bartholomew: Reappraisals and Documents*, ed. A. Soman. The Hague: Martinus Nijhoff, p. 72. Ozment, S. (1980) *The Age of Reform, 1250–1550. An Intellectual and Religious History of Late Medieval and Reformation Europe.* New Haven and London: Yale University Press, p. 259 n. 13.

59. Lecler, *Toleration and the Reformation*, i. 277-286. Cohn, H. J. (1985) 'The territorial princes in Germany's Second Reformation, 1559-1622', *International Calvinism, 1541-1715*, ed. M. Prestwich. Oxford: Oxford University Press, pp. 135-165.

60. Though Johann Sigismund had wanted to reserve his right to impose the *jus reformandi*: Lecler, *Toleration and the Reformation*, i. 279. He also had to allow freedom of worship for Catholics in the Polish fief of the duchy of Prussia.

61. Greengrass, M. (1994), 'The Calvinist experiment in Béarn', *Calvinism in Europe, 1540-1620*, ed. A. Pettegree, A. C. Duke and G. Lewis. Cambridge: Cambridge University Press, p. 129.

The model of pluralism suggested here proposes four levels.[62] The first level is where there is no pluralism at all, a situation where there is no acceptance or coexistence with religious minorities. This might be termed 'confessional exclusivism'.[63] The outsider is stigmatized as the enemy; when the conflict is religious, the enemy is demonized and the conflict is therefore sanctified.[64] Insurrection to secure religious freedom or 'rights' may become a form of religious war in such circumstances and the forcible elimination of heretics become a process of sanctified violence or holy war.[65] A second level is where the majority culture merely coexists with minorities *de facto* (this might be termed 'confessional coexistence'): hostility to the minority cultures remains and the legitimacy of their existence is challenged. This state of affairs may contain the feature of 'culture wars' between cultures within the same state which remain totally separate.[66] A third level is where there is a reasonable welcome or even encouragement to other minorities so that a culture of citizenship for all faiths and cultures begins to emerge (this might be termed 'civic toleration'). Finally, a fourth level is where there is a mixture of religions and cultures existing side by side, with none predominating (the completeness of such pluralism depends on prevailing attitudes as to whether this is a desirable, harmonious and permanent state of affairs).

The prevailing viewpoint in France was one of confessional uniformity, summed up by the traditional maxim 'one faith, one law, one king'. If a Protestant leader became influential at court, as did Coligny in 1571-1572, the expectation was that this influence would be used insidiously to entice the ruling dynasty away from Catholicism. The failed

62. In contrast, Philip Benedict suggests essentially two stages, 'neither so generous as to provoke massive Catholic resistance, nor so restrictive as to prompt the same from the Reformed': Benedict, 'Catholic-Reformed co-existence', p. 83.
63. Sociologists might call this state 'homogeneism', with 'rehomogenization' the 'natural solution to problems caused by diversity': Blommaert and Verschueren, 'European concepts of nation-building'.
64. Ryan, S. (1996) '"The voice of sanity getting hoarse?": destructive processes in violent ethnic conflict', *The Politics of Difference. Ethnic Premises in a World of Power*, ed. E. N. Wilmsen and P. McAllister. Chicago and London: University of Chicago Press, pp. 150, 152.
65. Housley, N. J. (1999), 'Insurrection as Religious War, 1400-1536', *Journal of Medieval History*, 25 no. 2 pp. 141-154. Crouzet, *Les guerriers de Dieu*; Crouzet, *La nuit de la Saint-Barthélemy*.
66. Brooks, R. L. (1996) *Integration or Separation? A Strategy for Racial Equality*. Cambridge, Mass.: Harvard University Press, pp. 117, 249.

Protestant *coup d'état* at Meaux in 1567 was never forgiven by Catherine de Médicis and others because it was seen as an attempt to achieve this by force. With hindsight, we know that the Valois dynasty remained loyal to the Catholic faith, indeed that the last ruler of the dynasty excelled all his predecessors in terms of his religiosity. Yet contemporaries remained convinced of the threat of subversion of the dynasty, which deepened as the years passed and Henri III failed to lead a campaign against the Protestants. Guise, the public was assured, would never compromise; but the suspicion remained that, in the end, Henri III would make a treaty with Henri of Navarre, as he finally did in April 1589. No one really expected Navarre, once he became Henri IV of France, to act in any other way than favourably towards his co-religionists. The abjuration itself was a bolt from the blue; the acceptance of the abjuration among Catholics was slow in coming; and the Protestants were left bitterly divided on what course of action to follow once their leader – protector of the Reformed Churches, defender of the 'true religion'[67] and king in the years between 1589 and 1593 – had abandoned their cause.

In the years before 1562, the years between 1585 and 1598, and the years after 1685, it may be contended that France experienced level one, the level of confessional exclusivism. Level two, confessional coexistence, was attained, to a greater or lesser extent, in the years when edicts of pacification operated during the wars of religion and during the regime of the secret articles of Nantes until 1629. If, by the end of the wars of religion, many Catholics had come to acquiesce in confessional coexistence, this was not because they had become reconciled to Protestantism as a separate and 'genuine' faith in its own right. The desire for harmony and order rather than discord and division now operated in favour of peace, sometimes with a dose of neostoicism on the model of Justus Lipsius's *Of Constancy in Evil Times* (1584): better to 'endure any kind of punishment' meted out even by a tyrant than to precipitate civil war.[68] Jean Bodin was not exempt from these views.[69] Such acqui-

---

67. Commission of Henri de Navarre to Clervant and de Beauvoir, Nov. 1586, quoted in Raitt, J. (1993) *The Colloquy of Montbéliard. Religion and Politics in the Sixteenth Century*. New York and Oxford: Oxford University Press, p. 188.
68. Oestreich, G. (1982) *Neostoicism and the Early Modern State*, ed. B. Oestreich and H. G. Koenigsberger, trans. D. McLintock. Cambridge: Cambridge University Press, pp. 43-44. Bireley, R. (1990) *The Counter-Reformation Prince. Anti-Machiavellianism or Catholic Statecraft in Early Modern Europe*. Chapel Hill and London: University of North Carolina Press, p. 74. *Ibid.*, p. 90: Lipsius's distinctions in *On One Religion* between private belief and overt religious opposition and

escence was a civic ethic of withdrawal from violence rather than a civic ethic of pluralism. Hostility to Protestantism remained on the part of the Catholic majority; the Huguenots themselves were profoundly distrustful of the attitude of the crown and its advisers and sought to retain their political and military organization for self-defence. A case can be made for some degree of confessional coexistence in the years between 1661 and 1685, the years of attrition of Huguenot rights, simply because for part of the period (notably the years between 1669 and 1679) there was a lull in the legislative offensive by the crown. Nevertheless, these years are marked by a fierce sustained theological debate between Catholics and Protestants. Instead of a war of the sword, there was a war of the pen. The polemical war between 1598 and 1685 deepened, rather than bridged, the gulf between the two confessions. Separate Catholic and Protestant French Bibles continued to be produced;[70] Richard Simon's idea of a Bible acceptable to both Catholics and Protestants remained a chimera.[71] In terms of the practical, day-to-day, decisions of Catholics and Protestants (whether to intermarry or not), there seems to have been if anything a decline in inter-confessional co-operation in these years.[72]

---

his emphasis on the overwhelming need to prevent religious civil war are highly pertinent. However, vigorous measures were to be taken against active dissidents who threatened to disrupt the unity of the state.

69. Rose, P. L. (1987) 'Bodin's Universe and its paradoxes: some problems in the intellectual biography of Jean Bodin', *Politics and Society in Reformation Europe. Essays for Sir Geoffrey Elton...*, ed. E. I. Kouri and Tom Scott. Basingstoke: Macmillan, p. 281.

70. For Protestant Bibles: Delforge, F. (1989) 'Les éditions protestantes de la Bible en langue française', *Le Grand Siècle et la Bible*, ed. Armogathe, J-R. Paris: Beauchesne, pp. 325-340. For Catholic Bibles: Chédozeau, B. (1989) 'Les grandes étapes de la publication de la Bible catholique en français du Concile de Trente au XVIIIe siècle' in *Le Grand Siècle et la Bible*, ed. Armogathe, J-R. Paris: Beauchesne, pp. 341-360.

71. Solé, J. (1985) *Le débat entre Protestants et Catholiques français de 1598 à 1685*. 4 vols. Paris: Aux Amateurs de Livres, iii. 1769. *Ibid.* ii. 1009: 40 Protestant refutations of Richard Simon's *Histoire critique du Vieux Testament* (1678). Simon argued that the Protestant Biblical understanding was deficient: Steinmann, J. (1960) *Richard Simon et les origines de l'exégèse biblique*. Bruges: Desclée de Brouwer, p. 111. However, Bossuet was suspicious of Simon's links with the Protestants (resulting from his wish for a Bible translation acceptable to all): Woodbridge, J. D. (1989), 'Richard Simon le "père de la critique biblique", in *Le Grand Siècle et la Bible*, ed. Armogathe, J-R. Paris: Beauchesne, p. 198.

72. Though the evidence is still rather limited on this subject: Benedict, 'Catholic–Reformed co-existence in France, 1555-1685', pp. 89-90. Cf. Hanlon, G. (1993) *Confession and community in seventeenth-century France: Catholic and Protestant*

Level three, 'civic toleration', was attempted in the years between 1630 and 1661. The Huguenots could no longer defend their rights by their own political and military organization, because the secret articles of Nantes had been revoked in 1629. Yet many of their rights remained, and after 1648 they were, for some years, extended. However, this period fell far short of that 'reasonable welcome or even encouragement to other minorities' which permits 'a culture of citizenship for all faiths and cultures' to emerge. Instead, the prevailing attitude from that of Richelieu downwards was that of inclusivism. There was no recognition of Protestantism as a genuine faith in its own right, let alone genuinely reformed: the Reformed Churches of France were not called the ERF (*Églises Réformées de France*) by the government;[73] instead, their members were the RPR, those of the 'so-called Reformed faith'. There could be no question of placing the RPR on a par with Catholics. The issue of reintegration of those 'in error' into the 'true' Church was therefore a matter of timing rather than principle. If there was no offensive against the Huguenots under Richelieu and Mazarin, it was not necessarily that the chief ministers were more tolerant and far-sighted than Louis XIV and Chancellor Le Tellier in 1685, though as Cardinals of the Church they were certainly hostile to forcing consciences: it was that they had different priorities, above all winning the war against Catholic Spain.

Within the scheme outlined above, with the possible exception of Guillaume Postel,[74] only Castellio (mentioned above) and Jean Bodin

---

Coexistence in Aquitaine. Philadelphia: University of Pennsylvania Press, p. 109. Too much should not be read into the experience of one community (Layrac), although after the 1620s there was an abrupt change in the numbers and percentages of Protestant husbands partnering Catholic brides (as compared to the mixed marriages entered into by Catholic husbands).

73. This term was used by the Protestants themselves in their confessions of faith: Sunshine, G. (1990), 'French Protestantism on the Eve of St-Bartholomew: The Ecclesiastical Discipline of the French Reformed Churches, 1571-1572', *French History*, 4 (3), p. 352. Provincial Synods were still calling themeslves 'Synode provincial des Eglises Réformées de Dauphiné' etc. in 1657 and thereafter: Bolle (ed.), *Le Protestant Dauphinois*, p. 31. The term is also used by historians writing from a Protestant viewpoint: Labrousse, E. (1985) *Une foi, une loi, un roi? La Révocation de l'Édit de Nantes.* Geneva: Labor et Fides. Paris: Payot, p. 30.

74. Bodin, J. (1975) *Colloquium of the Seven about Secrets of the Sublime. Colloquium Heptaplomeres de Rerum Sublimium Arcanis Abditis*, ed. and trans. M. L. D. Kuntz. Princeton NJ.: Princeton University Press, p. xlii n. 81. Kuntz, M. L. D. (1981) *Guillaume Postel: prophet of the restitution of all things, his life and thought.* The Hague and London: Nijhoff.

towards the end of the wars of religion could envisage the fourth level, that mixture of religions and cultures existing side by side, with none predominating. The evidence for Bodin's unorthodox views is provided by the *Colloquium of the Seven about Secrets of the Sublime* (*Colloquium Heptaplomeres de Rerum Sublimium Arcanis Abditis*, c.1588). Such a long and complex work defies easy categorization and has been subjected to controversial interpretation.[75] The seven faith representatives[76] in an imagined dialogue discuss many issues and allude to the failure of earlier attempts at religious compromise, such as the Book of Regensburg of 1541.[77] To protect publicly the authority of different religions in the same city is recognized as 'the most difficult matter of all... the common people have been accustomed to claim power for themselves, and it is not even safe for princes to resist them.'[78] The limited Venetian liberty of religious practice is noted, as is the 'harmony' under Islamic rule in the Ottoman and Safavid states.[79] Polish liberty would perhaps have been an equally pertinent example, and was one with which Bodin was familiar.[80] The expulsion of the Jews by Ferdi-

---

75. Rose, P. L. (1980) *Bodin and the Great God of Nature. The Moral and Religious Universe of a Judaiser*. Geneva: Droz. The work is controversial because Rose assigns to Bodin a specific religious viewpoint within the discourses of the *Colloquium*, which would undermine his 'neutrality' as an observer. Cf. Rabb, T. K. (1994), 'Religious Toleration during the Age of Reformation', *Politics, Religion and Diplomacy in Early Modern Europe. Essays in Honor of De Lamar Jensen*, ed. Thorp, M. R., and Slavin, A. J. Kirksville, Missouri: Sixteenth Century Essays and Studies, 27, pp. 313, 318. The author takes Erasmus, Castellio, Milton, Williams and Locke as reformers and Bodin and Bayle as revolutionaries, 'the first of the moderns'. In his view (*ibid.*, p. 316), the touchstone was 'the attitude towards Judaism'. Compare Erasmus's virulent anti-Judaism: Margolin, J-C. (1993), 'Brièves réflexions sur l'antijudaïsme de Jean Chrysostome et sur celui d'Érasme d'après les Homélies *Adversus Judaeos'*, in *Les Pères de l'Église au XVIIe siècle. Actes du colloque de Lyon, 2-5 octobre 1991*, ed. Bury, E., and Meunier, B. Paris: Cerf, pp. 33-50.

76. These were Coronaeus (Catholic); Salomon (Jew); Octavius (convert from Catholicism to Islam); Curtius (Calvinist); Fridericus (Lutheran); Senamus (sceptic); and Toralba (naturalist). Kuntz pp. xliv-xlv. The names, but not the religious designations, given in Skinner, Q. (1978) *The Foundations of Modern Political Thought. II. The Reformation*. Cambridge: Cambridge University Press, p. 246, are slightly different.

77. Bodin ed. Kuntz, *Colloquium of the Seven*, p. 423.

78. *Ibid.*, pp. 466-467.

79. *Ibid.*, p. 467.

80. Bodin quoted by Bonney, R. J. (1989), *L'absolutisme*. Paris: PUF, p. 23. Cf. Müller, M. G. (1996) 'Protestant confessionalisation in the towns of Royal Prussia and the

nand the Catholic and the Koran burnings and forced conversions under Cardinal Cisneros are mentioned following upon a quotation of Tertullian's words: 'it is not for religion to compel, which ought to be undertaken for one's own accord, not by force.'[81] At the end, these seven early modern dialogists part company, holding no further conversation about religions, 'although each one defended his own religion with the supreme sanctity of his life'. They did so after extolling the precedents of Ancient Rome, especially the civil power's intervention on religious matters. The historical interpretation given to the Henoticon, the union of 482 ordered by the Emperor Zeno, is deficient: but the right of the ruler to propose an edict of union, to enforce restraint and to prevent seditious gatherings, is approved by all present.[82]

With Bodin, therefore, we have already almost arrived in the intellectual world of William Chillingworth in England in the 1630s.[83] In this world, there ought to be a separation of religion and politics. The state was allowed to coerce for political reasons. It should not coerce for religious reasons and in any case could not so effectively. As Bodin put it, 'it is possible for each man to enjoy liberty provided he does not disturb the tranquillity of the state, and no one is forced to attend religious services or prevented from attending.'[84] Yet matters could not be separated

---

practice of religious toleration in Poland-Lithuania', *Tolerance and Intolerance in the European Reformation*, Grell, O. P. and Scribner, R. W. (eds) Cambridge: CUP, p. 268. This situation arose from the fact that Henri III was a potential dual monarch: Filipczak-Kocur, A. (1997) 'Heinrich von Valois. Der polnische König (1573-1574)', *Der Herrscher in der Doppelpflicht. Europäische Fürsten und ihre Beiden Throne*, ed. H. Duchhardt. Mainz: Veroffentlichungen des Instituts für Europaische Geschichte Mainz. Abteilung Universalgeschichte. Beiheft; 43; pp. 53-76.

81. Bodin ed. Kuntz, *Colloquium of the Seven*, p. 468.

82. *Ibid.*, p. 471. Cross, F. L. and Livingstone, E. A. (eds.) (1997) *The Oxford Dictionary of the Christian Church.* 3rd edn. Oxford: Oxford University Press, p. 750, point out that the Henoticon formula did not secure civil peace.

83. Chillingworth, W. (repr. 1972) *The Religion of Protestants, 1638*. Menston: Scolar Press, p. 198: 'The Deifying our own Interpretations and Tryannous inforcing [*sic*] them upon others... is, and hath been the only fountaine of all the Schisms of the Church...'. Orr, R. R. (1967) *Reason and Authority: the Thought of William Chillingworth*. Oxford: Clarendon Press, p. 49. The author owes this point to discussions with Dr Andrew Lacey.

84. Bodin ed. Kuntz, *Colloquium of the Seven*, p. 467. But this was not the English understanding in 1640, nor was it Hobbes's view. Hobbes's definition of heresy is pertinent: 'For heresy is nothing else but a private opinion obstinately maintained, contrary to the opinion which the public person, that is to say, the representant of the commonwealth, hath commanded to be taught': Martinich, A. P. (1992) *The Two*

so easily in early modern Europe. The duty of the civil power was to take decisive action against heresy and not to appear indecisive or vacillating, which might make matters worse: this was the charge subsequently levelled against Michel de L'Hospital, a relatively late convert to the cause of toleration in 1561-1562. Almost uniquely among European statesmen of the time, L'Hospital was prepared to view the heretic as a Christian simply because of his baptism; thus his conscience should not be forced, although in the longer term there was an expectation that he would return to the flock of the faithful.[85]

The question was how long the civil power could be expected to wait and refrain from using its political authority to coerce obedience. The legislation from the edict of Fontainebleau of 1 June 1540 onwards equated heresy with a crime of treason.[86] Military action against heretics could be equated with action against rebels. The first war of religion in sixteenth-century Europe, the war of the League of Schmalkalden, was a war against rebels, at least in the interpretation of Charles V.[87] The Hu-

---

Gods of Leviathan. Thomas Hobbes on Religion and Politics. Cambridge: Cambridge University Press, pp. 59-60.

85. Tallon, A. (1998) 'Division de la chrétienté et invention de la diplomatie. La politique française face au Concile de Trente', *L'invention de la diplomatie. Moyen-Age–Temps Modernes*, ed. L. Bély. Paris: PUF, p. 43. Petris, L. (1998) 'Michel de l'Hospital et les Guerres d'Italie: *De Postrema Gallorum in Italiam Expeditione Carmen* (1557)', *Bibliothèque d'Humanisme et Renaissance*, 60 (1), p. 83: 'la dissolution de nostre eglise a este cause des heresies et la reformation pourra estre cause de les esteindre.' Such views were close to those of Charles IX (= Catherine de Médicis) and the Cardinal of Lorraine in 1562-1563: Tallon, A. (1997) 'Le Cardinal de Lorraine au Concile de Trente', *Le mécénat et l'influence des Guises. Actes du colloque tenu à Joinville du 31 mai au 4 juin 1994*, ed. Y. Bellenger. Paris: Champion., pp. 332-333.

86. Sutherland, N. M. (1980) *The Huguenot Struggle for Recognition*. New Haven and London: Yale University Press, pp. 34, 338. *Ibid.*, pp. 349-350, on the edict of Romorantin of May 1560, which did not 'distinguish between heresy and sedition' as has often been alleged. Cf. the situation in the Low Countries: Duke, A. C. (1990) *Reformation and Revolt in the Low Countries*. London and Ronceverte: The Hambledon Press. pp. 163-164.

87. Repgen, K. (1987) 'What is a "Religious War"?', *Politics and Society in Reformation Europe. Essays for Sir Geoffrey Elton...*, ed. E. I. Kouri and Tom Scott. Basingstoke: Macmillan, pp. 311-328. Some leading Lutherans argued that the original pretext for the war, the Schmalkaldic League's retention of Brunswick-Wolfenbüttel for religious reasons, was an insufficient reason for provoking Charles V ('it is none of our affair, what religion is established in such a land'): Brady, T. A. Jnr. (1994), 'Jacob Sturm and the seizure of Brunswick-Wolfenbüttel by the Schmalkaldic League, 1542-1545', *Politics, Religion and Diplomacy in Early Mod-*

guenots were depicted as rebels in the aftermath of the events of 1562, 1567, 1597, 1615, 1620, 1625 and 1627; and not infrequently as rebels in alliance with a foreign power or serving the interests of a foreign power:[88] the refusal of the Huguenots to assist in the recapture of Amiens in 1597 and the alliance of Philip IV with Rohan[89] in May 1629 were never forgotten. 'It is certain that as long as the Huguenot party subsists in France', Richelieu had written in November 1625, 'the king will not be absolute in his kingdom, and he will not be able to establish the order and rule to which his conscience obliges him and which the necessity of his people requires.' Pacification of the kingdom, however, would permit 'the ruin of the Huguenot party by peaceful means'.[90]

In his theoretical position as well Richelieu was a confessional absolutist. The peaceful conversion of Protestants was the objective of royal policy.[91] Attempts would be made to secure the conversion of prominent leaders of the faith, such as Claude Saumaise (later the author of the *Apologie royale pour Charles Ier, roi d'Angleterre*), who met Richelieu on 15 November 1640 but rejected his blandishments, preferring residence in the Low Countries and employment at the University of Leiden. The attempt to secure the conversion of Saumaise was blatant: if he were to join 'la vraye religion' it must seem to come 'de [s]a discretion'; if he resisted and returned to the Low Countries, this would be 'une honte et un déshonneur à la France'. Clearly Saumaise was perceived as invaluable because of his 'grande connoissance' and 'grandes

---

ern Europe. Essays in Honor of De Lamar Jensen, ed. Thorp, M. R. and Slavin, A. J. Kirksville, Missouri: Sixteenth Century Essays and Studies, 27, p. 41. There is a case for arguing that the war of Kappel of 1531, in which Zwingli was killed, was the first war of religion.

88. That the Huguenots were indeed supported by Elizabeth I after 1562 is demonstrated by Trim, D. (1999) 'The "secret war" of Elizabeth I: England and the Huguenots during the early wars of religion, 1562-1577', *Proceedings of the Huguenot Society*, 27 (2), pp. 189-199.

89. Rohan refused to consider that national interest might dictate the reduction of a privileged and independent power within the state, especially if it impeded the conduct of foreign relations (the situation with the Huguenots prior to the Peace of Alais): Salmon, J. H. M. (1987) *Renaissance and Revolt. Essays in the intellectual and social history of early modern France*. Cambridge: Cambridge University Press, p. 104.

90. Bonney, R. J. (1988) *Society and Government in France under Richelieu and Mazarin, 1624-1661*. Basingstoke: Macmillan, pp. 7-8.

91. Blet, P. (1967) 'Le plan de Richelieu pour la réunion des Protestants', *Gregorianum*, 48: 100-129.

lumières'.[92] How far was Richelieu prepared to go to secure the reunion of the churches (or as Laubardemont, one of his subordinates, expressed it, 'la conversion de tous les hérétiques du Royaume...')?[93] In his *Principaux points de la foy catholique*, written in six weeks in October-November 1617 and published the following year, Richelieu had replied to Huguenot retorts against Père Arnoux's polemics, alleging that the Huguenots were doing real damage within his own province of Poitou. The Huguenots had reason to be thankful to their monarchs, he claimed. The king should 'do good to them, working with all his power to eradicate the error that has taken root in their hearts and to secure their conversion...' Catholics did not hate the Protestants, he contended. On the contrary, they loved them; hence their wish to see them return to the truth.[94] Richelieu drafted a much more extensive treatment of the same subject, the *Traitté qui contient la méthode la plus facile et la plus assurée pour convertir ceux qui se sont séparés de l'Église*, in the years after 1636. (It was published posthumously under Mazarin, in editions of 1651 and 1657.) The interest of the doctrinal statement lies in its equation of error against truth with rebellion against legitimate power:[95]

> Comme l'hérésie qui attaque l'Église incessamment employe contre elle deux sortes d'armes: l'erreur pour combattre ses véritez, et la rébellion pour résister à la puissance légitime qu'elle trouve contraire a ses desseins [...] le Cardinal de Richelieu [...] arrachait ces deux sortes d'armes à l'hérésie.

The pluralist possibilities of early modern France had been most coherently identified in de L'Hospital's recognition in January 1562 that the state has no role in determining the validity of truth claims. The limits of pluralism in early modern France lay in Richelieu's reassertion in 1636 of the traditional equation of heresy with rebellion against the civil authority: though not intended by the Cardinal, the revocation of the edict of Nantes and the return to confessional exclusivism after 1685

92. Leroy, P. (1983) *Le dernier voyage à Paris et en Bourgogne, 1640-1643, du réformé Claude Saumaise. Libre érudition et contrainte politique sous Richelieu.* Amsterdam and Maarssen: APA, Holland University Press, pp. 82-83, 131, 203.
93. Stankiewicz, W. J. (1960) *Politics and religion in Seventeenth-Century France. A Study of Political Ideas from the Monarchomachs to Bayle, as Reflected in the Toleration Controversy.* Berkeley and Los Angeles: University of California Press, p. 116 n 63.
94. Bergin, J. A. (1991) *The Rise of Richelieu.* New Haven and London: Yale University Press, pp. 105-106, 170.
95. Stankiewicz, *Politics and religion*, pp. 127-128.

seem no more than the logical outcome of this argument. 'Salvation by coercion' could therefore be applied with the greatest severity on the orders of Louis XIV and Louvois. When Pope Innocent XI eventually condemned the coercion of conscience on 19 July 1688 ('we do not approve in any manner of these sort of forced conversions which, usually, are not sincere'),[96] it was too little and too late: the full implementation of royal authority by means of the intendants and the *dragonnades* had already achieved an apparent enforcement of conformity throughout the kingdom.

---

96. McManners, *Church and Society in Eighteenth-Century France*, ii. 584. McManners comments: 'cruelty had remained uncondemned until its work was done.'

KATE CURREY

Degrees of Toleration: The Conjuncture of the Edict of Nantes and Dynastic Relations between Lorraine and France 1598-1610

Introduction

In 1598, the year of the settlement known as the Edict of Nantes, the kingdom of France and the duchy of Lorraine were associated through a dynastic union. This was the marriage of Catherine de Bourbon, the Protestant sister of King Henri IV, and Henri, marquis du Pont, the Catholic son of Charles III, duke of Lorraine. This essay explores the complex conjuncture between the passing of the Edict of Nantes and this dynastic marriage. The first section considers the state of diplomatic relations between France and Lorraine during the later sixteenth century. The second explores the specifics of the marriage negotiations brokered between France and Lorraine in 1598. A third section then considers how the outcome of the marriage influenced France's attitude towards the duchy until Henri IV's assassination in 1610 and its eventual annexation by France in 1633.

Such is the synchronicity between the two events that, superficially at least, the Franco-Lorraine marriage could be seen as a positive analogy with the Edict, reflecting its pluralistic intentions and fostering amicable relations between France and one of its satellite territories. However, this essay rejects any assumptions that the marriage was conceived as a political 'happy ending' that echoed the efforts of Nantes to create a bi-confessional society within France.

The marriage was simply Henri IV's cynical effort to buy off his troublesome neighbour, Charles III. The state of war which had existed between the two states before 1598 (with Charles III taking the side of Henri IV's Catholic opponents, the so-called 'League') had focused upon their rival candidature for the French throne after the Valois dynasty died out. By offering him 500,000 crowns and his sister as a wife for his son, Henri IV was attempting to divert Charles III's sights from the French throne which he had coveted.[1]

Before I examine the events themselves in the light of these negative assertions, I should at least make some effort to present them in a more positive fashion. For example, is there any evidence to suggest that France could have influenced Lorraine to follow its model of confessional pluralism? If we were to accept Perry Anderson's model of state centralisation, ducal Lorraine should simply have been 'culturally 'assimilated'' by France and adopted a bi-confessional stance.[2] Mark Greengrass, however, argues that the reality of such situations was more complicated.[3]

Certainly, Charles III's duchy remained resolutely Catholic and he, with his pro-Counter-Reformation policies, was a veritable *soldat de dieu*.[4] Protestantism had only a limited force within ducal Lorraine. It was restricted exclusively to an urban environment, finding only sporadic support in such towns as St Mihiel and St-Nicolas-de-Port.[5] Thus, in French eyes, Charles III's Lorraine undoubtedly had a reputation for Catholic intransigence which took no account of France's concessions to the Protestant faction.

It is also necessary to disabuse the notion that the marriage of Catherine de Bourbon and Henri, marquis du Pont, was a match made in heaven. If one were to believe the propagandistic intentions of contemporary placards commemorating the event, this was undoubtedly the case.[6] These placards combine images with text. The first puns on the groom's title, the 'Marquis du Pont' with its depiction of a bridge, into

---

1. For a discussion of the late sixteenth century rivalry for the French throne, see Anderson, M. S. (1998) *The Origins of the Modern European State System 1494-1618*, Longman, London and New York, pp. 188-89.
2. For the centralised model of state growth, see Anderson, Perry (1979) *Lineages of the Absolutist State*, London.
3. For an analysis of this oversimplified model, see Greengrass, Mark (1991) *Conquest and Coalescence. The Shaping of the State in Early Modern Europe*, Sevenoaks, p. 6.
4. See Taveneaux, René (1986) 'L'esprit de croisade en Lorraine aux XVIe et XVIIe siècles', in *L'Europe, l'Alsace et la France*, Strasbourg, pp. 257-263.
5. Taveneaux, René (1991) 'La Lorraine au XVIIe siècle', in *Claude Gellée et les peintres lorrains au XVIIe siècle*, Paris and Rome, pp. 47-57, p. 53.
6. *Sur le bien et desiré mariage...*(Jean le Clerc, Paris, 1599), Paris, Bibliothèque Nationale, Collection Hennin, Serial No: G1514991139; *Sur le mariage de Monseigneur Henri...* (Matthew Becker, Frankfurt-am-Main, 1599), Paris, Bibliothèque Nationale, Collection Hennin, Serial No: G1514991137.

which Cupid is hammering nails. King Henri IV of France, in the costume of Caesar, stands on the right bank of the river. The couple, on the opposite bank, are united in marriage by Hymen. The accompanying verses compare the King's engineering of this marriage to Caesar's conquest of the Rhine.[7]

The other placard also shows a bridge, upon which the couple are standing. On either bank grows a palm tree, whose fronds have formed the arch of a bridge, another punning reference to the groom's title.[8] The deployment of the symbol of the palm contains yet another nuptial reference, this time procreation. Thus the hoped-for outcome of this union will be the birth of an heir to unite France and Lorraine.[9] In reality, this was neither a politically successful nor a fruitful union. However, the presence of these placards reminds us that at least, the occasion fitted into the conventional typologies used to celebrate dynastic marriages. M. S. Anderson is correct in describing dynastic marriages as 'visionary schemes' which were undermined by the reality of events.[10]

Neighbours at War: France and Lorraine 1559-1598

Let us look more closely at the state of political relations which prevailed between France and Lorraine from the mid-sixteenth century onwards. It would seem that France made concerted efforts to keep Lorraine under close supervision, especially after the death of duke François in 1545. This meant that the duchy was without an heir until the young Charles III came of age. In the meantime his mother, Christine de Denmark, was regent. However, her policies were distrusted by her

7.   'Ce Caesar qui premier pour Caesar se feit creindre,
      Brave establit un pont sur les vagues du Rhein,
      Pour faire avec le vol de son brave dessein
      Les Lauriers triomphans, & les aigles atteindre', see *Sur le bien* in note 6 above.
8.   An accompanying verse reads:
      'Ces amoureux palmiers de leur embrassement
      Font un pont continu, & continu passage.
      Et qui nous fait durer perpetuellement?
      N'est ce pas le bonheur du sacré mariage?', see *Sur le mariage* in note 6 above.
9.   On the imagery of the palm-tree in dynastic nuptials, see Watkin, David (1991) 'Iungit Amor: Royal Marriage Imagery in France 1550-1750', *Journal of the Warburg and Courtauld Institutes*, 54, pp. 256-261.
10. Anderson, *Origins*, p. 189

brother-in-law, Nicolas de Vaudémont, who feared she might form an alliance with the Empire and alienate France. So he sought French intervention and was made regent instead, whilst the ducal heir was sent to the French court for safekeeping.

This uncertain period for the duchy coincided with an important phase of French territorial expansion, where as part of its expedition to the Empire in 1552, it occupied the bishoprics of Metz, Toul and Verdun, which had formerly been in the possession of Lorraine.[11] To look at a map of Lorraine in the sixteenth century reveals a significant French presence within the duchy. In simple terms, using the river Meuse as a demarcation line, full ducal authority extended only to the portion of Lorraine which occupied its right bank (the 'Barrois non-mouvant'). France, however, controlled the left bank (the 'Barrois mouvant'). In effect, the duke of Lorraine was assiduous in controlling the portion of territory which was his.

It is evident that both parties were aware of the fragile unity which existed between them. If one agrees with Mark Greengrass's assessment of the attitudes of larger states to their satellites, in the case of Lorraine, France was 'aware... of the importance of sustaining local identities'.[12] Nonetheless, it seems significant that France made sustained efforts to shape the identity of the young Charles III in as French a mould as possible, which included his 1559 marriage to Claude de France, daughter of King Henri II and Catherine de Medici.[13]

Due to this marriage, the courts of France and Lorraine maintained friendly relations at a familial and a political level throughout the later sixteenth century. A round of seasonal and family celebrations connected Paris and Nancy, such as the 1564 christening celebrations of Henri, marquis du Pont, Charles III and Claude de France's heir at Bar-le-Duc. This event was attended by the French court as part of Charles IX and Catherine de Medici's propagandistic royal tour of 1564-1566.[14]

So how are we to explain the development which was to undermine relations between France and Lorraine, namely Charles III's designs upon the French throne, with the fragmentation of the Valois dynasty?

---

11. *Ibid.*, pp. 74-75.
12. Greengrass, *Conquest and Coalescence*, p. 6.
13. Choné, Paulette (1991) *Emblèmes et pensée symbolique en Lorraine, 1525-1633*, Paris, p. 132, n. 12.
14. See Boutier, J., Dewerpe A. and Nordman, D. (1984) *Un tour de France royal. Le voyage de Charles IX (1564-1566)*, Paris, for an account of this visit.

Historians of Lorraine have argued that Charles III's exposure to the French court fostered his latent political ambition.[15] It is also more than likely that his intermarriage with the Valois dynasty led Charles III to consider his son's candidature for the French throne as valid, based on his descent from the royal line. Evidence also suggests that such sixteenth-century French chroniclers as l'Estoile or Ossat raised the possibility that Catherine de Medici thought that Charles III's heir should inherit the French throne.[16]

Whatever the case, Charles III was determined in pursuit of his desired objective. Although King Henri III had inherited the French throne in 1574 on the death of his brother Charles IX and was to reign until 1589, Charles III was already scheming against France, as witnessed by his involvement with the aforementioned League, a group dedicated to ousting King Henri III and replacing him with the Protestant Henri of Navarre. Charles III's precise motives are hard to guess. It is likely he wanted to play an active part in determining the course of the succession so as to further his own chances.

King Henri III was surely aware of Charles III's political machinations, but does not seem to have taken direct action against him. During a royal visit to Nancy in 1583 he suggested the marriages of his favourites, Anne de Joyeuse and the duc d'Epernon to Charles III's daughters Christine and Antoinette. There is some evidence that Henri III raised the possibility of this dynastic marriage to assert closer control over the errant Charles III.[17] However, the plan was rejected by the duke, who argued that the posited matches were unworthy of his status.[18]

Charles III's doubtful loyalty to France was questioned further in 1582 when Salcède published a deposition implicating Charles III in the League's plot to overthrow Henri III. 1583 saw the arrest of the ducal historiographer François de Rosières. Rosières was the author of the Lorraine genealogy, the *Stemmatum Lotharingiae*, published in Paris in 1580.[19] Lorraine's ducal dynasty deployed artfully engineered genealogies to compete with royal dynasties, such as Champier's *Recueil des Chroniques* (1510), Boullay's *Genealogies* (1549) and Aucy's manu-

15. Choné, *Emblèmes*, p.132, n.12.
16. Davillé, Louis (1909) *Les Prétentions de Charles III*, Paris, pp. 16-17.
17. *Ibid.*, p. 44.
18. *Ibid.*, pp. 44-45.
19. For more on Rosières, see Choné, *Emblèmes*, pp. 46-47.

script *Epitome de l'origine et succession du duché de Lorraine* (1556).[20]
Rosières's book was accused of undermining the King's authority by
fostering Charles III's Carolingian descent. Charles III travelled to Paris
and secured Rosières' release.

Both the Salcède affair and the Rosières trial put Charles III's poli-
cies in jeopardy. With the death in 1584 of the final Valois heir, the duc
d'Anjou, Charles III went on the offensive yet again. The League met at
Nancy, in response to Guise pressure to use the disorder amongst French
Protestants to take control of the French throne. However, between them,
Henri III and Henri de Navarre attacked Lorraine and blocked Charles
III's access to France. A final meeting of the League in 1588 marked
Charles III's renewed efforts to strike back at France, but he was
thwarted at this point by the alliance of Henri III and Henri de Navarre.

Had King Henri III not died in August 1589, it is possible to argue
that Charles III was almost resigned to his lack of success. He was putting more effort into marital diplomacy, securing alliances with Florence
through the 1589 marriage of his daughter Christine de Lorraine to Ferdinand de Medici, and those of her sisters Elisabeth and Antoinette to
Maximilian of Bavaria (1595) and Wilhelm of Jülich, Cleves and Berg
(1599).[21] It is possible that Charles III was attempting to form a wider
network of alliances, from which he could either secure his claim to the
French throne, or attack it if necessary.

Immediately after the death of Henri III, Charles III's League forces
and Henri IV began a bout of fighting which lasted until the early 1590s.
Charles III was determined to overturn the French King and replace him
with his son. In response to Charles III's offensive, Henri IV mounted an
attack on Alsace which forced Charles III to defend the eastern borders
of Lorraine. Here Henri IV had the advantage, attacking the Lorraine
towns of Pont-à-Mousson and Nomény in the early spring of 1590.

Whilst the period between 1593 and 1598 witnessed a series of pacification treaties between the opponents, Charles III continued in his
unsuccessful efforts to get his son recognised as the heir to France.[22]'He
had hoped that his union with the League would gain him popularity in
France, but nobody took the marquis du Pont's candidature seriously.
However, the crowning of Henri IV at Chartres in 1594 led to peace

---

20. See Choné, *Emblèmes*, pp. 46-56.
21. On the motivations behind Charles III's marital policies, see *ibid.*, p. 181.
22. On these negotiations, see Davillé, 'Les relations d'Henri IV', p. 441.

between Charles III and Henri IV, although this would not be fully realised until Charles III received his 500,000 crown pay off in 1598.

Marital Diplomacy and the Franco-Lorraine Union

Let us now look more closely at the circumstances which led to the
marital alliance between France and Lorraine in 1599. It has already
been stated that Charles III had begun to expand his nexus of connections through marital diplomacy to compensate for the failure of his
military efforts to secure the French throne. Perhaps he hoped that a
marital alliance with France would bring him closer to his desired objective. In the case of Henri IV contracting a union with Lorraine, this could
well have been a motivating factor similar to those which had led to
other Franco-Lorraine unions, the desire to keep the duchy under French
surveillance.

Contemporary chroniclers had their own views on what had led to
this union, about which rumours had abounded since the 1580s. For example, as early as 1583, Du Plessis Mornay had regarded Charles III's
son as a possible marriage candidate for rhe King's sister, 'par le moyen
duquel on s'obligerait la Maison de Lorraine, qui seule semble faire obstacle à la grandeur qui se prépare au roi de Navarre'.[23] At this time,
Bernardo de Mendoza, the Spanish ambassador at the French court ,was
also spreading rumours that this union was to be negotiated.

A different version of this alliance was also debated by the duke of
Tuscany's Paris ambassador.[24] This would be the ultimate family union,
where Henri IV would marry a Lorraine princess, whilst his sister would
marry the marqus du Pont. However, it would seem that the proposed
union between the marquis du Pont and Catherine de Bourbon had its
merits, not the least that it would lead to better relations between France
and Lorraine, as implied by a 1587 letter written by Cavaillac to one of
the duke's emissaries; 'faire encore le mariage de Mme la Princesse de
Navarre avec M. le Marquis du Pont, pour plus étroitement lier d'amitié
ledit roi de Navarre et le Seigneur de Lorraine'.[25]

---

23. As cited in Ritter, Raymond (1985) *La soeur d'Henri IV, Catherine de Bourbon,*
     1559-1604, Paris, t.I, p. 265.
24. For both the Spanish and Tuscan speculations, see *ibid.*, pp. 304-306.
25. *Ibid.*

Not that the process of marital negotiation between France and Lorraine was entirely smooth. In September 1596, Henri IV wrote to Catherine de Bourbon, asking her to accept the suit of either Monsieur de Montpensier or the marquis du Pont, but she rejected both of them. It seems that at this time Henri IV was actually entertaining doubts about a union with Lorraine, because he feared that it would give Charles III too much leverage in his efforts to gain control of France. Instead, he asked his sister to accept Monsieur de Montpensier as a less controversial choice.

Nonetheless, despite Henri IV's evident misgivings, negotiations between France and Lorraine began in February 1597, through the mediation of Charles III's envoy, ducal Grand-Maître, Monsieur de Melay.[26] The key problem of these negotiations, as it was to remain throughout the brief marriage, was whether Catherine would renounce her Protestant faith, a condition which was set by her future husband. The possibility of her marriage to a member of a family 'maudite par tous les huguenots' must surely have been anathema to the Protestant Catherine.[27]

A meeting between the couple was engineered in Paris in May, 1597. On first impression, Henri, marquis du Pont, then aged 33, seemed elderly and unhealthy.[28] His view of Catherine was a little more positive in tone. Aside from the issue of Catherine's religion, negotiations were also confronting another obstacle, that of the couple's consanguinity in the 7th degree, which could only be surmounted by a waiver from the Pope. It is even possible that Henri IV welcomed this problem as a way of avoiding a potentially awkward union. Henri, marquis du Pont returned to Lorraine at the end of May and the negotiations rumbled on. Catherine de Bourbon still refused to renounce her Protestant faith.

The marquis du Pont returned to Paris at the end of July 1597. Back in Catholic Lorraine, the union provoked unease amongst the Jesuits at the university of Pont-à-Mousson. This institution, co-founded by Charles III in 1574, was a bastion of Catholicism in the duchy. The Jesuits argued that the union should only go ahead if the bride converted to Ca-

---

26. On the composition of the ducal household under Charles III, see Kate Currey, 'The Political and Social Significance of Court Festivals in Lorraine, 1563-1624', Unpublished D. Phil Dissertation, University of Sussex, 1996, Appendix D, 'Household Offices at the Court of Lorraine', pp. 311-312.
27. Ritter, *Catherine de Bourbon*, t. II, p. 176
28. Ritter devotes an entire paragraph to his physical description, see *ibid.*, t. II, p. 189.

tholicism.[29] Whilst Catherine refused to convert, she did initially agree to accept instruction in the Catholic faith, but did not keep her promise. In early August, the marquis du Pont again left for Lorraine, whilst Monsieur de Melay stayed in Paris to represent him. As might be expected, like the Jesuits of Pont-à-Mousson, the Pope was not enthusiastic about the proposed union.

At Toul in September, Charles III and his statesmen assembled to draw up his son's marriage contract. Ducal envoys were then sent to Paris in December but Catherine de Bourbon still would not renounce her faith. By May 1598, both sides were growing impatient with the delay.[30] In early June, Catherine announced that she would go ahead with the marriage. The presence of the marquis du Pont in Paris was still awaited. Nor had the Pope expressed his approval of the union. On 15 July, the marquis du Pont arrived in Paris, only to leave for Montceaux to settle a territorial dispute with the duke of Wurtemburg. He returned to Paris at the end of July, where his suit was finally accepted and the dowry settled.

Religion remained the only sticking point in the negotiations. The marquis du Pont attempted to impose conditions regarding the composition of his future wife's entourage as he did not wish to have Protestants in his household. The contract was witnessed on the 5th of August, Catherine brought a dowry of 300,000 *écus* and a further 200,000 *écus* were settled upon her by her husband. If her husband died, Catherine would get the use of his castle at Bar-le-Duc and two thirds of her dowry settlement. Charles III ratified this settlement on August 24th.[31]

Charles III and his son, Charles, cardinal of Lorraine, arrived in Paris in mid-September, to inform Henri IV of the Pope's displeasure that the union was to go ahead. A November wedding date was settled and gifts were exchanged. Meanwhile, Charles III entered into his own negotiations with Clement VIII. He was determined to gain acceptance for the union which he had sanctioned. However, the envoy Charles III dispatched to plead his case was arrested and imprisoned.[32] Although the marquis du Pont was supposed to be at the French court over the Christ-

---

29. On Pont-à-Mousson and its role in ducal Lorraine see *L'université de Pont-à-Mousson et les problèmes de son temps*, Nancy, 1974.
30. See Ritter, *Catherine de Bourbon*, t. II, p. 228.
31. For more details of this settlement, see *ibid.*, t. II, pp. 224-225.
32. *Ibid.*, t. II, p. 257.

mas period of 1598, he delayed his attendance there until the 5th of January, 1599.

At this point it is possible to observe how closely the marriage negotiations were bound up with those of the Edict of Nantes. Indeed, the two were concurrent. It seems as if all parties were anxious to get the wedding out of the way before the Edict was passed.[33] Charles III's chief concern was avoiding any problems resulting from bringing a Protestant bride to his duchy. He wanted to install her in the ducal castle at Bar-le-Duc rather than at Nancy.

Henri IV decided (for similar reasons, perhaps in the light of rumours of a St-Bartholomew's style massacre of Huguenots, heightened by the negotiations surrounding Nantes) to hold the wedding outside Paris, at St Germain-en-Laye.[34] The couple were betrothed there on the 30th January, 1599 and married the next day by the archbishop of Rouen, who all along had been anxious at incurring papal displeasure. Contemporary observers noted that despite the appropriate celebrations, the wedding was a subdued affair.[35]

Plans were made for the couple to leave for Nancy towards the end of February, just after the planned enregistration of the Edict. Charles III waited to receive the couple at Bar-le-Duc on the 4th of March, but due to Catherine's illness en-route, they did not arrive until five days later. Problems began almost immediately, again over the issue of Catherine's retinue. On the advice of Henri IV, her husband had removed all her Protestant servants. Catherine protested bitterly at this, because she thought her husband and her brother had colluded over the issue.

In mid-April, the couple went to Nancy, hosting visits from Archduke Albert of Austria and his wife, Isabella Clara Eugenia, first cousin to Charles III's children. Her journal gives an eye-witness account of Catherine at the court of Nancy. One entry recounts how Catherine excused herself early from the celebrations, having suffered a recent miscarriage.[36] It would seem that fertility was indeed a problem, as Catherine was soon to go to take the spa waters at Plombières to assist her in conceiving.[37]

---

33. *Ibid.*, pp. 269-270.
34. *Ibid.*, p. 271.
35. Ritter calls them 'ces noces furtives', see *ibid.*, p. 272.
36. See Duvernoy, E. (1914-15) 'Une Infante d'Espagne à la cour de Lorraine', *Mémoires de l'Académie de Stanislas*, pp. 66-85, p. 80.
37. Ritter, *Catherine de Bourbon*, t. II, pp. 303-305.

Despite a contemporary verse exhorting Catherine, 'vous vivez en la foi de l'église romaine', her Protestantism caused increasing problems for her husband's family.[38] Pope Clement VIII expressed his displeasure by severing papal relations with the bishopric of Toul and barred the marquis du Pont from attending mass. He attempted to get Catherine converted by the so-called 'pillar of catholicism', the Jesuit father Commolet.[39] But Catherine refused these repeated efforts to make her convert. In November 1599, she was addressed in her apartment in Nancy's ducal palace by what might be called a conversion team, consisting of her husband, Charles III and the cardinal of Lorraine. But this, too, was unsuccessful.

In evident desperation, Henri went to Rome for an audience with Pope Clement VIII in April 1600, where he hoped to plead his case, whilst Catherine remained in Lorraine. Henri met with the Pope on the 26th of May. According to Clement VIII, the only possible option for Henri was to leave his wife, which he was reluctant to do. In December, Catherine and her husband were reunited at Nancy. Throughout 1601, efforts were made to convert Catherine, who was present a the French court throughout the summer and early autumn. Her husband joined her there in late September. Catherine's continued repudiation of Catholicism frustrated her husband and brother. At one point Henri IV even threatened to put her to death if she did not convert.

In March 1602, the marquis du Pont wrote to the Pope to apologise for his wife's intransigence. He then heard (via an intermediary) that the Pope would shortly issue a dispensation allowing the marriage. In the event, this did not occur. The conversion stalemate lasted into 1603, when a royal visit to Metz that March led to renewed attempts to convert Catherine. More negotiations in Rome raised the issue of a dispensation allowing the marriage. Catherine was in Paris for the summer of 1603. During her absence, Charles III, perhaps acting in exasperation, or out of fear from papal reprisal, expelled all the Protestants from Bar-le-Duc.[40] Such punitive action against Protestants had not hitherto been undertaken by Charles III and is evidence of the gravity with which he regarded the situation.

---

38. *Ibid.*, p. 317.
39. *Ibid.*, p. 319.
40. *Ibid.*, p. 464.

More favourable conditions were issued by Clement VIII in December 1603. The marriage should be re-celebrated, any children would be Catholics and Catherine should be converted as soon as possible. In the event, the terms of this dispensation were never tested. After joining in with New Year celebrations at Nancy, Catherine (possibly pregnant) contracted a fever and died in February 1604. Her body was taken back to France for burial and not accorded the funeral rites which might have been expected for a duchess of Lorraine.[41]

Diplomatic Relations between France and Lorraine 1608-1633

The period between 1608 and 1610 brought a pivotal change to relations between France and Lorraine. Problems still existed over Charles III's desire to create a bishopric under his control which would rival France's presence in Metz, Toul and Verdun. The death of Charles III in 1610 lost Henri IV a formidable adversary. His heir, duke Henri II (1608-1624) lacked his father's political drive. At this point, the French King, Henri IV, decided that it would be a good moment to absorb the duchy into France. His plans were, however, halted by his assassination in 1610. The French take-over of Lorraine in the 1630s was not a foregone conclusion. Nonetheless, Charles III's political intransigence had taught France to distrust its ducal neighbour more than ever.

However, Henri II fostered good relations with France, if only because he lacked his father's political drive. He deliberately avoided involvement with the Frondes. Nonetheless, his brother, the Count of Vaudémont rapidly became involved in the Thirty Years' War, joining the Catholic League headed by his brother-in-law, duke Maximilian of Bavaria in 1619. Thus Lorraine could not avoid participation in a European theatre of war. After Henri II's death in 1624, the duchy was inherited by his nephew, duke Charles IV.

Franco-Lorraine relations deteriorated rapidly from this point onwards. Duke Charles IV feared the prospect of French invasion, but did nothing to moderate his policies. The French minister Richelieu, on the other hand, applied constant pressure to the duke's weak points, undermining his territorial control and his sovereign status. Throughout the

41. On the female funerals of the House of Lorraine, see Currey, 'Political Significance', pp. 62-63.

late 1620s France increased its political stranglehold upon the contested bishoprics of Metz, Toul and Verdun. At the same time, France refused to acknowledge Charles IV as the rightful ruler of Lorraine or to accept his feudal oath of allegiance for the portion of his territory that belonged to France. This was a reference to the fact that he had usurped his wife Nicole's rightful claim to the duchy in 1624. Nicole was the daughter of Henri II. However, Charles IV, whom she married in 1624, invoked Salic Law (which precludes female succession) to adopt the ducal title.

Duke Charles IV also earned French displeasure because of his connections with France's political malcontents, Gaston d'Orléans, King Louis XIII's disaffected brother and the Duchess of Chevreuse, both of whom were welcomed to the court of Nancy in the late 1620s.The final straw for the French was the marriage of Gaston d'Orléans to duke Charles IV's sister, Marguerite. However, it was doubtless Charles IV's decision to enter the Thirty Years War in 1633 to defend his uncle, Maximilian of Bavaria from attack by the Swedes which sealed his fate. Sweden, a French (1632) signed over important territory to France and prompted the French invasion of Lorraine in 1633.

Conclusion

This essay has examined whether the 1599 marriage of the Protestant sister of King Henri IV with the Catholic heir to the duchy of Lorraine can be construed as a political success. It has considered the close contextual connection between the Edict of Nantes and the finalising of this marriage to see if the union reflected the Edict's pluralist intentions. The resulting analysis of both France and Lorraine's political relationship between 1545 and 1633, besides the marriage negotiations themselves, lead me to back to the point I made at the beginning. Here I argued that the Nantes settlement had no chance of impacting upon a Catholic territory like Lorraine and that Henri IV simply used the marriage as a device to contain Charles III.

It emerges that both parties felt threatened by the existence and political ambitions of the other. Lorraine's pivotal position between France and the Empire gave it particular strategic importance in French eyes. It is possible to see that both sides pursued policies for their own benefit. In the case of France, this meant the containment of Lorraine, whilst the latter was concerned with maintaining its independence in relation to

France. We should also remember that policies owe much to the needs of their instigators. For example, Charles III of Lorraine was much more politically ambitious than his son Duke Henri II. Consequently, Duke Charles III was a much greater nuisance to France.

Overall, the political exchange between France and Lorraine during the period under discussion accords with Perry Anderson's description of France's 'convulsive progression' to absolutist rule, where long periods of inertia were interspersed by sudden decisive acts, of which the 1599 marriage was an important example.[42] This marriage was important in fostering this progression in that it attempted to bring Lorraine, always an intransigent neighbour, under closer French control. In the final analysis, it represents yet another stage in the process by which France's disenchantment with Lorraine brought about its eventual annexation in 1633.

---

42. Anderson, *Lineages*, p. 86.

ANDREW SPICER

Huguenots, Jesuits and French Religious Architecture in Early Seventeenth Century France

In the early seventeenth century two polemical engravings were published of the 'True Image of a Papal Church' and the 'True Image of the Apostolic Church'. The first illustrates the interior of a substantial Gothic church, elaborately decorated with statues, stained glass and altar paintings. It depicts aspects of Catholic theology and practice: the seven sacraments; low masses at the numerous side altars; the catafalque and coffin representing the round of services for the dead. The main focus of the church is the High Altar, concealed behind the rood screen, and a sense of spectacle is created by a cleric, dressed in rich vestments with a canopy held above him, wending his way in procession towards the east end of the church. The image is of a somewhat chaotic church interior; the sermon being delivered from the pulpit in the nave, is lost amongst myriad other activities. The 'True Image of the Apostolic Church' is radically different; the architecture is much simpler, with clear glass at the windows and the only decoration being the table of the Ten Commandments. In this church, there are just two accessible altars where communion is being administered in both kinds by a minister wearing a surplice. However the focus is the preaching of the Word of God, from the prominent pulpit in the nave. The congregation mainly ranged round the pulpit listening to the sermon.

These two engravings provide a striking contrast between a Protestant, in this case Lutheran, church and a post-Tridentine Catholic church. In the Catholic church the High Altar, albeit somewhat obscured, is the focal point of worship, whereas in the Lutheran church the preaching of the Word of God provides an alternative focus.

True Image of the Papal Church (cliché Bibliothèque nationale de France, Paris)

True Image of the Apostolic Church (cliché Bibliothèque nationale de France, Paris)

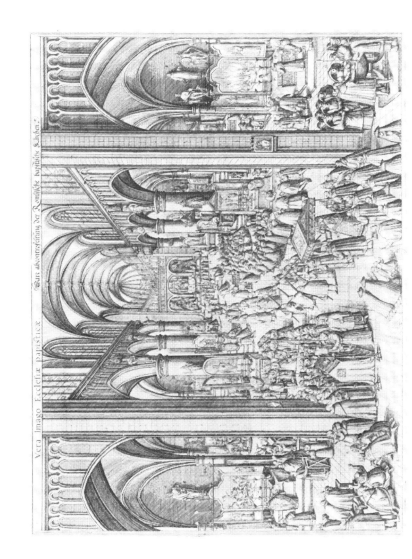

Vera Imago Ecclesiæ Papisticæ. Sanc abcontrafeteung der Romiische bapstice Sanben.

These images serve to confirm the view that from 'the religious controversies of the sixteenth century, Protestants got the pulpit and Catholics the altar'.[1] This essay will explore this view with a broad and introductory survey of the religious architecture of the late sixteenth and early seventeenth centuries in France.

During the 1560s, a new form of religious architecture emerged in France, the architecture of Calvinism. Initially the Huguenots met secretly in private houses but as the movement gathered momentum, they held open air assemblies. In the heady years of 1561-62, the Reformed movement began to assert itself and attempted to establish its own places of worship. Some communities met in the courtyards of private houses or in barns, elsewhere the Reformed requested and were granted permission to worship in little-used churches.[2] At Nantes, the Huguenots asked for the collegiate church of Notre Dame to be partitioned, the choir would be retained by the canons while the Huguenots would worship in the nave. The church of the Cordeliers at Condom was similarly divided.[3] Elsewhere, the Reformed took over churches which had been formerly occupied by the mendicant orders. In Nérac, the Queen of Navarre assigned a Franciscan church to the Reformed. Franciscan houses were also occupied at Orléans, Tours and Lyon, at Agen a Dominican house and at Blois, a Carmelite house.[4]

With such increasingly public demonstrations of the Reformed faith, the Crown attempted to establish a modus vivendi with the Huguenots culminating in the Edict of St. Germain which allowed them the right of assembly outside the walled towns. The Huguenots seized the opportunity to worship openly; in Rouen they met in the municipal market and at Toulouse they began to build their own meeting place, an elaborate wooden structure which resembled a covered market place.[5] However the massacre of a congregation worshipping in a barn at Vassy brought to an

---

1. O'Malley, J. W. (1993) *The First Jesuits.* Cambridge, Mass.: Harvard University Press, p. 91.
2. Roberts, P. (1998) 'The Most Crucial Battle of the Wars of Religion? The Conflict over sites of Reformed Worship', *Archiv für Reformationsgeschichte* 89: 255.
3. Roberts, (1998), p. 254; Baum, G., Cunitz, E., Reuss, R. (eds) (1883-89), *Histoire ecclésiastique des églises réformées*, 3 vols. Paris: Librairie Fischbacher, I, p. 878.
4. Baum, (1883-89), I, pp. 824, 877-878;
5. Baum, (1883-89), III, p. 2; Greengrass, M. (1983) 'The Anatomy of a Religious Riot in Toulouse', *Journal of Ecclesiastical History* 34: 372.

end this burgeoning Protestant freedom and precipitated the First Religious War. The Huguenots were initially remarkably successful in this
war, seizing a third of the sixty largest cities in France including Lyon,
Orléans and Rouen. In these towns, the mass was outlawed and the
churches were taken over for Reformed worship.[6]

Where the Catholic churches were seized by the Huguenots, they had
to be adapted for Reformed worship. The liturgy and architecture of the
churches was intended to foster belief in the sanctity and mystery of the
Mass; the high-point of the service was conducted apart from the congregation behind the rood screen. They also contained all the furniture of
Catholicism: numerous altars; statues, wall paintings and altar retables
depicting saints and Biblical themes; holy water stoups, and so on.
Therefore, in many cases the seizure of the churches was linked to outbursts of iconoclasm, destroying these images and trappings of
Catholicism, as the churches were adapted for preaching. The idea of
partitioning a church, separating off the choir and leaving the nave for
the Reformed worship reflects the significant change of emphasis. However attempts to remodel such buildings could never be entirely
satisfactory.

The Huguenot occupation of the Catholic churches was transitory.
The Crown soon recovered and began to recapture the towns that the
Huguenots had seized. In March 1563 the First Religious War came to
an end with the Peace of Amboise. Although not as generous as the Edict
of St Germain the agreement permitted Reformed worship in certain restricted areas but the Huguenots were also required to return church
property that they had seized.[7] The edict meant that unlike their co-
religionists in Geneva, Scotland and later in the Northern Netherlands,
who took over the existing ecclesiastical buildings and adapted them, the
Huguenots were obliged to construct their own places of worship and in
so doing provided structural evidence of the religious diversity in France.

Probably the most well-known image of a Huguenot temple is the
painting of Le Paradis in Lyon painted by Jean Perrissin. This was one of
four temples built in Lyon in 1564 after the Huguenots were obliged to

---

6. Benedict, P. (1996) '*Un roi, une loi, deux fois*: parameters for the history of Catho-
    lic-Reformed co-existence in France' in O. P. Grell & R. Scribner (eds) *Tolerance
    and Intolerance in the European Reformation.* Cambridge: Cambridge University
    Press, pp. 77-78.
7. Stegmann, A. (1979) *Edits des Guerres de Religion.* Paris: Librairie Philosophique
    J. Vrin, pp. 34-35.

leave the Franciscan church which they had been occupying. The building had an oval ground plan with a plain exterior. The focal point of the interior is the pulpit with segregated seating arranged before it; covered benches for the consistory and the catechising bench are beside the pulpit. Around the building is a gallery which is reached by an external staircase. The polygonal ground plan was a key element in the architecture of a number of Huguenot temples and recurs in the temples built in the Southern Netherlands during 1566.

The Reformed temples surprised contemporaries, as they provided such a contrast with traditional ecclesiastical designs, and so they sought precedents for these buildings. In Dieppe they commented that the temple 'c'estoit ung fort edifice, ressemblant au theatre de Rome, qu'on appelle Collysée ou arrenes de Nysmes'. Le Paradis was described as 'sembloit un vray théâtre pour jouer moralitez ou comédies'.[8] The situation was the same in the Southern Netherlands, the round temples erected in Antwerp in 1566 were described by one observer as resembling the Temple of Solomon and another commented that they were also like the church of St John Lateran in Rome. At Ghent one observer commented 'Looked at from both the outside and inside, the temple resembled a lantern or riding school, only much larger'.[9]

While the allusions to the Temple of Solomon lack foundation,[10] the interior of Le Paradis and other Huguenot temples certainly did resemble a theatre. This is perhaps not surprising because these buildings reflect the demands of Reformed worship. For Calvin a true church was a place where the Word of God was preached and the sacraments, baptism and the Lord's Supper, properly administered. Calvin valued the importance of the Lord's Supper and wanted it to be held frequently but the enforcement of discipline, to maintain the sanctity of the service, meant that this was impossible. Initially communion was held monthly but this had to be reduced to quarterly by the Genevan authorities. As a result preaching, which took place on Sundays and during the week, meant that sermons became the main focus of Reformed worship.

---

8. Baum, (1883-89), I, p. 348; Gigue, G. (1891) 'Jean Perrissin', *Réunion des Sociétés des Beaux-Arts des Départements* 15: 435.
9. Duke, A., Lewis, G. & Pettegree, A. (eds) (1992) *Calvinism in Europe 1540-1610*. Manchester: Manchester University Press, p. 153.
10. Spicer, A. 'Rebuilding Solomon's Temple? The Architecture of Calvinism', *Studies in Church History* forthcoming.

In the pre-reformation parish churches, the sermon had largely disappeared from the Mass during the Middle Ages but to an extent, the extraordinary and popular preaching of the mendicant orders had obviated this need. There was something of a revival of the mass sermon under the influence of Humanist reformers such as Guillaume Briçonnet who emphasised the importance of preaching in his diocese.[11] However, such sermons were only a part of the Mass and not the central part of the service. Generally preaching was an activity which took place outside the parish church; the mendicant orders could only preach in a church, other than their own, at the invitation of the priest or with the permission of the bishop. For the popular preachers, the churches were inadequate anyway as they could not accommodate the large audiences. As a result open air preaching in market places, open fields and the cemeteries became popular and continued during the fifteenth century.[12] Open air preaching was obviously dependent upon the weather but the mendicant orders also had their own churches that were designed specifically for preaching and to hold large audiences. In general, the choir and nave formed one open unit in these churches.[13] It is therefore not surprising that the Reformed were keen to occupy such buildings during the early 1560s.

Preaching took on a greater significance in the Reformed Church, as the means by which the Word of God as revealed in Scripture was communicated to the people. Calvin wrote: 'If our Lord gives us this blessing of His Gospel being preached to us, we have a sure and infallible mark that he is near us ... and that he calls us to Him as if he had His mouth open and we saw Him there in person'.[14] The congregation, as recipients of the Word of God, should receive it soberly, attentively and with reverence.[15] As a consequence the minister had to be audible and visible to the whole congregation, while also able to observe them. Seating was provided for the congregation to encourage a more attentive audience.

---

11. Taylor, L. (1992) *Soldiers of Christ. Preaching in Late Medieval and Reformation France.* New York: Oxford University Press, pp. 16-17.
12. Taylor, (1992), pp. 28-29; Moorman, J. (1968) *A History of the Franciscan Order.* Oxford: Oxford University Press, p. 363.
13. Moorman (1968), p. 363; Roth, F. (1966) *The English Austin Friars.* New York: Augustinian Historical Institute, I, p. 233.
14. Parker, T. H. L. (1992) *Calvin's Preaching.* Edinburgh: T&T Clark, pp. 1-4, 17, 35-47.
15. Parker, (1992), pp. 48-53.

Previously they may have sat on the floor or lounged against pillars and walls during the sermons, although women brought small stools and benches were provided for the magistrates.[16] Consequently Huguenot architecture was typified by the centrally placed pulpit with the seating ranged around it, akin to an auditorium.

The confidence of the Huguenots in the religious pluralism offered by the Edict of Nantes was clearly expressed through architecture. The polygonal ground plan of Le Paradis recurs in a number of Reformed temples constructed after 1598: Quévilly near Rouen (1599), Dieppe (1600), Caen (1611) and Montauban (1615).[17] Some of the temples erected in early seventeenth century were high status buildings, reflecting the latest architectural style. The Temple Neuf built at Montauban in 1615 reflected the importance with which the building was viewed by the consuls and the community. In a town where stone was rarely used, the brick built temple included significant classical stone detailing: pilasters, capitals, architraves, friezes, cornices. The main entrance was marked by two monumental columns and a plaque of black marble inscribed with gold lettering, the arms of the town and date of construction.[18]

The most important temple was built at Charenton for Huguenots at Court and in Paris. The first temple was designed by the royal architect and Huguenot, Jacques II du Cerceau in 1607, although his design seems to have been relatively simple. It was a rectangular building with a wooden roof and galleries. Inside there was a central open space and galleries supported by timber joists. One row of windows lit the main hall and there were rows of smaller windows to light the galleries. However this temple was destroyed by the Paris mob in 1621; its replacement was designed by du Cerceau's nephew, Salomon de Brosse, a Huguenot and the architect of the Luxembourg Palace. De Brosse's design reflected the importance of classical influences in French architecture and was based on a Vitruvian basilica. The temple was innovative as instead of small windows for the galleries, there was one row of tall windows that extended through the cornice and was cut across inside by the galleries to create a very light interior. The double

---

16. Taylor, (1992), p. 28.
17. Thomson, D. (1995) 'Protestant *Temples* in France c. 1566-1623', in J. Guillaume (ed.) *L'Eglise dans l'Architecture de la Renaissance.* Paris: Picard, pp. 245, 252-253.
18. Guicharnaud, H. (1991) *Montauban au XVIIe.* Paris: Picard, p. 95.

galleries with the pillars rising through two storeys and the inclusion of a new side-entrance, again closely reflected a basilica.[19] Charenton was very different from the polygonal temples and more homespun rectangular temples, such as Nanteuil-les-Meaux and Bègles.[20] However the building still reflected the importance of preaching with the centrally placed pulpit and provision of seating for the congregation. The well lit interior was important for the visibility of the preaching minister. The design was extremely influential not only for Protestant church architecture in general but also in the design of synagogues, particularly in the Netherlands during the later seventeenth century.[21]

Huguenot temples were only one aspect of the upsurge in religious building at the beginning of the seventeenth century. The end of the religious wars meant it was also a period of rebuilding and repairing the havoc wrought on ecclesiastical buildings; Catholic churches had proved to be an easy target for the Huguenots' iconoclastic attacks.[22] The damage done to the cathedrals was in some cases particularly serious;[23] at Orléans, the cathedral had been almost entirely destroyed in 1568 by the Huguenots in an explosion. Although de Brosse was initially consulted over the restoration in 1618, the cathedral was ultimately rebuilt in the Gothic style by the Jesuit architect Etienne Martellange.[24] This willingness to patronise Huguenot architects indicates that religious affiliation was not even an obstacle when it came to ecclesiastical design in the early seventeenth century.[25]

19. Coope, R. (1972) *Salomon de Brosse and the Development of the Classical Style.* Oxford: Zwemmer, pp. 183-186.
20. Dubief, H. & Poujol, J. (eds) (1992) *La France Protestante.* Paris: Max Chaleil, pp. 230, 368, 369.
21. Coope (1972), p. 197.
22. Davis, N. Z. (1987) *Society and Culture in Early Modern France.* Cambridge: Polity Press, pp. 173-74; Phillips, H. (1997) *Church and Culture in seventeenth-century France.* Cambridge: Cambridge University Press, p. 45.
23. Pérouse de Montclos, J-M. (1989) *Histoire de l'Architecture Française. De la Renaissance à la Révolution.* Paris: Mengès/CNHMS, pp. 170-171; Bergin, J. (1996) *The Making of the French Episcopate.* New Haven: Yale University Press, p. 135.
24. Coope (1972), p. 236; Montclos (1989), pp. 171, 172.
25. See Prestwich, M. (1985) 'Patronage and the Protestants in France, 1598-1661' in R. Mousnier & J. Mesnard (eds) *L'Âge d'Or du Mécénat.* Paris: Editions du CNRS, pp. 77-88.

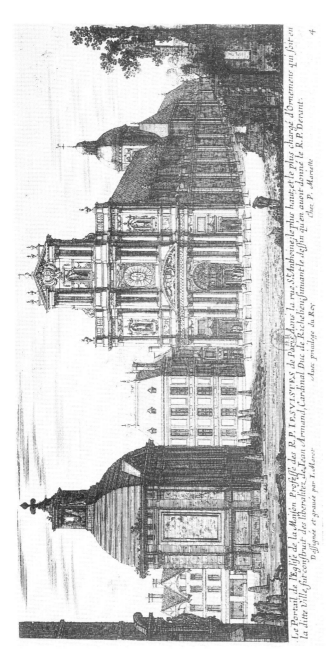

Le Portail, le l'Eglise de la Maijon Profeßé des R.P. IESVISTES de Paris dans la rue St Anthoine le plus haut et le plus chargé d'Ornemens qui foit en la ditte Ville, fut conſtruit des liberalitez, de Jean Armand, Cardinal Duc de Richelieu ſuivant le deſſin qu'en avoit donné le R.P. Derant.

Deſſigné et gravé par I. Marot.   chez P. Mariette.

Avec privilege du Roy   4

St Paul-St Louis (cliché Bibliothèque nationale de France, Paris)

Charenton (clich

Further impetus for Catholic building came from the religious changes of the Counter Reformation and the emergence of new religious orders. The Jesuits were recalled by Henri IV in 1603 and during his reign other religious orders settled in France: the reformed Augustinians, the Barnabites, the Brothers of Charity, the Capuchins and Capuchin sisters, the Feuillants, the Minimes and the Thérésiennes (Carmelites).[26] This reflected the significant religious revival and upsurge of lay piety and devotion in late sixteenth and early-seventeenth century France.[27] This revival was evidenced in stone with the construction of new places of worship for these communities. The Jesuits had begun to establish colleges and churches in France before the outbreak of the religious wars, their earliest being at Billom (1556), and by 1610 they had 45 houses in France. New churches were built for religious communities in many French cities. In Paris, churches were built by the Feuillants in 1601, the Minimes (1611), the Discalced Carmelites (1613), the Oratorians (1621), the Professed Jesuits (1627) and the Discalced Augustinians (1629).[28] These churches represent a significant break from the Gothic medieval tradition in France and reflect a new architectural style which was motivated by the reform of the Catholic Church.

The decrees of the Council of Trent reasserted the doctrines of transubstantiation, the seven sacraments, purgatory, the invocation of saints etc. One significant area of discussion for the Council was the proclamation of the faith by preaching.[29] In November 1563 the Council decreed:

> ... the office of preaching, which particularly belongs to bishops, should be exercised as often as possible for the salvation of the people ... Bishops are to announce the sacred scripture and the law of God in their own church either personally or, if they are legitimately prevented through others whom they appoint to the office of preaching; in other churches this is to be done by the parish priest ... this is to be done in the city or in any parts of the diocese that the bishop considers expedient, at least on every Sunday and solemn feast, and daily or at least three times a week during seasons of fasting, namely Lent and Advent ... and as often at other times as they judge appropriate. And the bishop should carefully instruct the people that each

26. Buisseret, D. (1984) *Henry IV.* London: Unwin Hyman, pp. 121-123.
27. Cruickshank, J. (1996) 'A Note on Lay Piety in the Early Seventeenth Century' in K. Cameron & E. Woodrough (eds) *Ethics & Politics in Seventeenth-Century France.* Exeter: University of Exeter Press, pp. 31-40; Ranum, O. (1968) *Paris in the Age of Absolutism.* New York: John Wiley & Sons Inc., pp. 109-131.
28. Montclos (1989), p. 179.
29. Jedin, H. (1961) *A History of the Council of Trent.* 2 vols. London: Thomas Nelson & Sons Ltd., II, pp. 122-123.

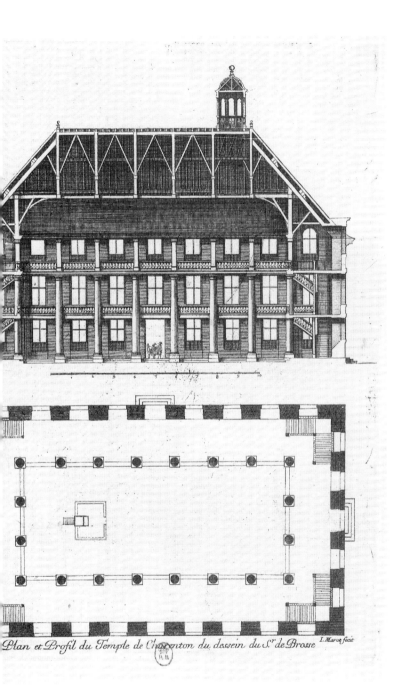

Plan et Profil du Temple de Charenton du dessein du S.ʳ de Brosse.   J. Marot fecit

of them is under an obligation to attend their parish church, when they can reasonably do so, to hear the word of God.[30]

The decree also stipulated that preaching by the mendicant orders was to be under the control of the bishops, even in their own churches. Although the Tridentine decrees were not promulgated in France for almost fifty years after the Council, nevertheless polemical preaching was important in meeting the challenge of Protestantism. The Catholic Church had quickly reacted against the heretical preaching of the Huguenots and launched their own counter-offensive.[31] The Jesuit Order in particular saw preaching as foremost in their three-fold mission. Initially the Jesuits imitated the practices of the mendicant orders but they went further with the frequency and length of their sermons. Junior members of the Order trained and practised delivering sermons; it was important that they should teach, move and please their audience. Preaching was a religious act in itself, the Word of God was being delivered by the preacher and as such he was an instrument of God's divine grace.[32] The parallels between the thinking of the Jesuits and Calvin in the significance of preaching are striking.

The Jesuits met with considerable success with their preaching in France. Emond Auger preached to large congregations in Lyon, Toulouse, Paris and elsewhere during the 1560s; Anthoine Possevin prepared the way for the Jesuits in Rouen, debated in print with Viret and in 1570 after five days of preaching in Dieppe, a third of the six thousand Huguenots in the town were said to have been miraculously converted.[33] The Jesuits were particularly active in securing conversions in the wake of the St Bartholomew's Day Massacre and one observer in Lyon commented at the end of December 1572: 'Our church has been very well attended during these feast days … So many come to the preaching of Father Possevino that sometimes the church with the new chapel can not hold the multitude. May God be blessed! No longer do people in Lyon say "Let's go to the synagogue of the Huguenots", but throughout the

30. Tanner, N. P. (1990) (ed.) *Decrees of the Ecumenical Councils*, 2 vols. London: Georgetown University Press, II, p. 763.
31. Taylor (1992), pp. 209-225.
32. O'Malley (1993), pp. 91-104.
33. Fouqueray, H. (1910-25) *Histoire de la Compagnie de Jésus en France.* 5 vols. Paris: Librairie Alphonse Picard I, pp. 532-540.

city they say "Let's go to the Jesuits".[34] Although the Jesuits have a
particularly high profile, they were only one of the religious orders at
work in France. Preaching was also the prerogative of other religious
orders which had an impact during the early seventeenth century such as
the Capuchins and the Oratorians founded by Pierre de Bérulle in 1611.
Furthermore, as we have seen, the Tridentine decrees indicated preaching was also the responsibility for the Bishop and the parish priest.

The importance of preaching, the emphasis on regular communion
and the reaffirmation of the sacraments had significant ramifications for
the design of Counter Reformation churches. These churches were characterised by the prominent high altar and a series of subordinate side
altars dedicated to saints which encouraged the celebration of private
masses and the cult of saints.[35] No less important was the need to accommodate the demand for regular preaching in these churches. The
main influence for this ecclesiastical building in France came from Italy.
In 1577 St Charles Borromeo published his *Instructionum fabricae et
suppellectilis ecclesiasticae libri II* which served as a guide to ecclesiastical architecture and furnishings.[36] His book was in fact a codification of
what had become ecclesiastical practice in Northern Italy in the years
since the sack of Rome in 1527.[37] The book made important statements
about the interior organisation and design of the church; the following
extract concerned the pulpit:

> In every parochial church ... a pulpit should be erected on the Gospel side to serve
> for the purpose of reading the Gospel and for religious preaching. It should be en-
> tirely made of strong wood and be of good form and construction. Finally, it should
> be observed that the ambones and the pulpit are suitably located in the body of the
> church in a prominent place where either the preacher or the reader can be seen and
> heard by all. [38]

---

34. Lynn Martin, A. (1974) 'Jesuits and the Massacre of St. Bartholomew's Day', *Ar-
    chivum Historicum Societatis Iesu* 43: 107.
35. Wright, A. D. (1982) *The Counter Reformation*. London: Weidenfeld & Nicolson,
    pp. 44, 226.
36. Summarised in Voelker, E. C. (1988) 'Borromeo's Influence on Sacred Art and
    Architecture' in J. M. Headley & J. B. Tomaro (eds) *San Carlo Borromeo*. Wash-
    ington: Folger Books, pp. 172-187.
37. Ackerman, J. S. (1972),'The Gesù in the Light of Contemporary Church Design', in
    R. Wittkower & I.B. Jaffe (eds) *Baroque Art: The Jesuit Contribution*. New York:
    Fordham University Press, pp. 20-21.
38. Voelker, E. C. (1977) 'Charles Borromeo's *Instructiones Fabricae et Supellectilis
    Ecclesiasticae*, 1577', unpublished Ph.D. thesis: Syracuse University, pp. 292-293.

This reflects how important preaching had become in Catholic churches and although the High Altar remained the principal focus in the church, it became essential for the pulpit to be located in a place where the congregation could hear and see the preacher. The concern for audibility was reflected in the directions given for the design of the church of San Francesco della Vigna in Venice in 1535:

> I recommend that all the chapels and the choir be vaulted because the word or song of the minister echoes better from the vault than it would from rafters. But in the nave of the church, where there will be sermons, I recommend a ceiling (so that the voice of the preacher may not escape, nor re-echo from the vaults).[39]

Such concerns about acoustics and the visibility of the preacher have a clear parallel in the architectural concerns of the Reformed.

The Jesuits were perhaps the most important church builders of the Counter Reformation but the notion of a Jesuit style *per se* has been dismissed, except in the most general terms. The most important Jesuit church and one of the most important churches of the second half of the sixteenth century was the Gesù built in Rome between 1568 and 1575. The Jesuits themselves had relatively little control over the design and construction of the building as it was underwritten by Cardinal Alessandro Farnese. The church was designed by his architect Giacomo Barozzi da Vignola; the Cardinal, rather than the Jesuits, made the architectural decisions in spite of their reservations about the suitability of the building for preaching.[40] (It is interesting in the light of the architectural forms chosen by the Huguenots, that Vignola initially considered an oval ground plan for the church.)[41] The resultant church had a large wide nave which allowed the Jesuits to preach to sizeable congregations, an unimpeded view of the High Altar with its elaborate tabernacle and a series of side chapels. This model was one which was utilised not only by the Jesuits in the design of their churches but by other orders such as the Theatines and the Oratorians.[42]

As has been seen there was a spate of religious building in Paris and the provinces with the conclusion of the religious wars. These churches

39. Ackerman (1972), p. 19.
40. Robertson, C. (1992) '*Il Gran Cardinale'. Alessandro Farnese.* New Haven: Yale University Press, pp. 184-189.
41. Robertson (1992), p. 187; Ackerman (1972), p. 24.
42. Robertson (1992), p. 181; Wright (1982), p. 226.

were inspired by the Italian models and in particular the Gesù. The church of the Feuillants provides a typical example; construction began in 1601 and it was consecrated in 1608. The church had a central nave, to each side of the nave were a row of six separate side chapels; the sanctuary was divided from the transepts by three steps before the High Altar. The design of this church was developed from the Gesù, reflecting the requirement of the Feuillants to meet together as a community for worship, which was not shared by the Jesuits.[43] Slightly later is the Jesuit church of St Paul-St Louis, begun in 1627 by Martellange which, perhaps not surprisingly, followed the model of the Gesù more closely but on a larger scale. It was the first church in Paris to achieve successfully a lantern dome and was the one of the most important churches in the development of classicism in France.

The religious pluralism of early modern France was therefore marked structurally by significant Catholic and, to a lesser degree, Huguenot building. However, in spite of their opposing theological perspectives, the influence of preaching in the design of Huguenot temples and Catholic churches is striking. Clearly the Catholic churches continued to have the High Altar as the focal point of their buildings, but like the Huguenots they were concerned to provide a prominent pulpit and a central unimpeded space which was acoustically sound for the delivery of sermons to a large audience. The cluttered interior represented by the artist of the polemical 'The True Image of a Papal Church' was an anathema to orders like the Jesuits. However there was a significant difference between the polygonal temples in Lyon and Montauban and the cruciform churches of St. Paul-St Louis and the Feuillants in Paris. In the most important and architecturally advanced Huguenot temple at Charenton, the similarity between the two architectural approaches to preaching is apparent. Perhaps such similarities should not be surprising for, in an age of religious co-existence, Catholics were prepared to employ Huguenot architects and they in turn were prepared to draw upon Catholic architectural models. De Brosse in his design of the Salle de Pas Perdus for the Palais de Justice in 1619, attempted to recreate the image of a Roman basilica and in so doing drew upon the interpretation of Vignola, Martellange and the churches being built in Paris at that time. He had also demonstrated his

43. Ciprut, E.J. (1957) 'L'Eglise du Couvent des Feuillants', *Gazette des Beaux-Arts*, 50: 39-40, 42.

familiarity with Vignola's design of the Gesù in his facade of the Parisian church of Saint Gervais.[44] It would be interesting to speculate that at Charenton, de Brosse was drawn not merely by his pursuit of the classical ideal to recreate Vitruvius's basilica but, imbued with the religious diversity of Paris, was also drawing upon the Counter Reformation's architectural response to the need to preach the Word of God.

---

44. Coope (1972), pp. 141-146, 151-152.

Daniella J. Kostroun

The Nuns of Port Royal:
A Case of Reasonable Disobedience?

One of the defining features of Louis XIV's absolutism was its invasion of religious conscience. Before Louis came to power, France tolerated religious pluralism under laws such as the Edict of Nantes, which allowed Huguenots freedom of worship and the right to fortify their own towns. Such tolerance, however, did not endure under Louis XIV, who made it his personal goal to unify France under the old medieval phrase 'one faith, one law, one king'.[1] While Louis attacked the broad doctrinal differences between Protestants and Catholics, he also targeted the less pronounced differences in emphasis and style that were a hallmark of Catholic reform vitality. This paper examines religious differences among Catholics through the case of the Port Royal nuns from 1609, when Abbess Angélique Arnauld reformed the convent, to 1661, when Louis began persecuting the nuns for Jansenism. By focusing on the nuns, this essay reveals how the struggles over religious conformity between king and Jansenists in the 1660s had a gendered component which originated in Angélique's experiences as a reforming abbess in the early part of the century. At that time, it was a common belief that, while all good Christians were obedient, women were naturally more obedient than men because of their sex. When Angélique reformed Port Royal, she developed a strategy through which she manœuvred her prescribed identity as an obedient woman – an identity that usually restricted women – to assert her own choices in reform. Her strategy was later adopted by nuns in the 1660s to resist the king when he persecuted them for Jansenism. It was also incorporated into the polemical pamphlets circulated by male Jansenists, who drew upon the nuns' practical experience of manipulating patriarchy to argue that the king's persecu-

---

1. For a recent analysis of the complex political, intellectual and institutional factors guiding Louis XIV's religious policies see Van Kley, D. (1996) *The Religious Origins of the French Revolution.* New Haven: Yale University Press.

tion of Jansenists was an abuse of power as well as a violation of God's natural order.

When Angélique decided to reform her convent in 1609, France tolerated not only the existence of Protestants, but also a wide diversity within the Catholic Church. This period – following the Wars of Religion – was one of intense religious renewal for Catholics, and France was flooded with new institutions and orders such as Bérulle's Oratory, Francis de Sales' Nuns of the Visitation, Vincent de Paul's Daughters of Charity, the Jesuits, the Capuchins, *et al.* Because the temporal authority in France never officially incorporated the decrees of the Council of Trent into French law, reform was not a centralised movement, but rather a spontaneous and haphazard affair. It happened only because individuals such as Angélique took the initiative.

Because individual reformers had different visions of how best to reform France, there was a de facto tolerance of diversity in these early years. For example, Francis de Sales once advised Angélique not to worry about the differences she detected among reformers. He wrote: 'It is difficult, my dear sister, to find a universal spirit ... and there is nothing wrong, it seems to me, to gather from several flowers the honey that we cannot find in just one'.[2] Such acceptance of difference, however, did not last into the second half of the century. When Louis XIV began tightening his control over political institutions, he did the same with the Church and no longer tolerated religious debate.

Angélique's story of reform illustrates the problems that religious diversity posed for women in the first decades of the seventeenth century. Although Francis de Sales saw nothing wrong with Angélique borrowing ideas from different reformers, he was unique in his positive attitude towards women. Most clerics regarded women as weak, ignorant and in need of tight supervision in spiritual matters.[3] Such misogyny was also reflected in civil laws, which placed women under the control of their husbands and fathers. Women who sought greater autonomy under these circumstances had to develop strategies to manipulate the system to their own advantage. In Angélique's case, she credited the overwhelming power of her 'natural' feminine obedience for the choices she made regarding her family and her reform.

2. Cognet, L. (1951) *La Mère Angélique et Saint François de Sales.* Paris: Editions Sulliver. p. 60.
3. Timmermans, L. (1993) *L'accès des femmes à la culture, (1598-1715).* Paris: Honoré Champion. pp. 478-479.

Angélique entered the Cistercian convent of Port Royal at the age of seven. By the age of fifteen she disliked being a nun to the point that she considered escaping to La Rochelle to live with her Protestant aunts.[4] These aunts explained to her that her vows were invalid because she was not yet sixteen and offered to take her in if she left the convent. According to her autobiography, her plan to run away was thwarted by a malarial fever, which left her bed-ridden for several weeks. Soon after her recovery, she forgot about becoming a Protestant, when a wandering Capuchin monk filled her with a passionate desire to reform her convent. Although it would have been more scandalous had she become a Protestant, Angélique's parents were nonetheless outraged when she decided to reform Port Royal. This was because reform signified a transfer of her obedience, as was evident in a meeting with her father in September of 1609. On that day, M. Arnauld stood outside the locked doors of Port Royal and ordered Angélique to open the convent door. Although he pounded at the door with his fists and yelled at her, she remained firm. She told him that she obeyed God, not her father, and that she could not open the door because this would be a mortal sin.[5]

Angélique was one of many of her generation to experience religious renewal under the influence of the Capuchin monks. In a study of seventeenth century religious vocations, Barbara Diefendorf finds that many young men and women abandoned their families to join the new religious orders and to devote their lives to Catholic reform. These adolescents often came from families that were recently ennobled through service to the king in finance and law. Their decision to join religious orders such as the Jesuits and Capuchins caused tremendous upheaval within their families since this meant a rejection of all that their parents had arranged for them in terms of securing the family name and fortune. In several cases, parents turned to the secular courts to obtain orders for the Church to annul the vows and return them their children.[6] The courts usually ruled in favor of the parents since they were filled

---

4. For more on the Protestant side of the Arnauld family, see Sedgwick, A. (1998) *The Travails of Conscience: The Arnauld Family and the Ancien Regime.* Cambridge, MA: Harvard University Press.
5. Cognet, L. (1950) *La réforme de Port Royal, 1591-1618.* Paris: Editions Sulliver. P115.
6. Diefendorf, B. (1996) 'Give us Back Our Children: Patriarchal Authority and Parental Consent to Religious Vocations in Early Counter-Reformation France', *Journal of Modern History* (68): 265-307.

with gallican judges who opposed the ultramontanism of the Jesuit and Capuchin orders. When compared with the adolescents studied by Diefendorf, Angélique's case was typical. For example, she was the daughter of a recently ennobled family within the judicial elite. She rejected her parent's authority because of her zeal for Catholic reform. This zeal was fostered by Capuchin monks whose influence over her outraged her father who was an anti-ultramontane gallican laywer in the Parisian Parlement. Although Port Royal would later be singled out as a Jansenist convent, there was nothing about Angélique's early reform to warrant such exceptionalism.

Once Angélique dedicated herself to reform, she faced the problem of finding a good confessor. Angélique found the Cistercian monks who were Port Royal's traditional directors to be completely unsatisfactory and wrote, '[they] preached so poorly that the sermons were no more than occasions to sin because of the way we made fun of them'.[7] The temptation for sin went both ways apparently, as she observed that the monks competed with one another for the nuns' attention and became 'envious and jealous of other monks who were better than them'.[8] These problems led Angélique to invite many confessors to Port Royal, including three Capuchins, one Jesuit, a Bernardin and a doctor from the Sorbonne.[9] Her problem, however, was that she was never able to place total confidence in any one of these men. Some 'split hairs too much' in matters of conscience and did not appeal to the side of her that 'loved sincerity and frankness'. Others, she claimed, were 'so limited in their knowledge that I conducted myself with much circumspection and restraint, consulting them only on those things where they seemed capable of giving me good advice'.[10]

Angélique worried that she 'conducted herself' too much and wrote Francis de Sales to ask if she had failed in her vow of obedience:

I have always operated by taking advice and direction from those who attended us as far as I could see that they advocated that which I wanted, … [and from] those who I believed favoured my thoughts and desires – this caused me considerable worry since in effect, it was me directing myself.[11]

---

7. Arnauld, A. (1949) *Relation écrite par la Mère Angélique Arnauld sur Port Royal.* L. Cognet (ed.) Paris: Grasset.
8. Cognet, *La Réforme*, p. 140.
9. Cognet, *La Réforme*, p. 191.
10. Cognet, *La Réforme*, p. 191.
11. Cognet, *La Mère Angélique,* p. 59.

Francis de Sales' response (cited above) was to 'gather honey' from 'different flowers' and not to worry as long as these directors were all men of the Church. He further expressed his concern for her exacting approach to piety and his fear that her reform was too rigorous for most nuns. He wrote: 'My daughter, would it not be better not to catch such big fish and to catch more?'[12] In diplomatic fashion, Angélique defended her reform – by replying that she wanted no more than to obey Port Royal's rule – while simultaneously agreeing with him by saying that had she created the rule, she would have made it softer.

Angélique corresponded with Francis de Sales until his death in 1622. The openness with which he discussed Church politics with her was one of the qualities that attracted Angélique to him. For instance, he complained about the king's practice of appointing abbesses. He described this as 'nothing other than pure usurpation, and an enterprise against the right of election which was never removed from female abbeys by the Concordat [of Francis I]'.[13] With regard to the debate between the regular and secular clergy, he explained to her why bishops should control reform. Angélique enjoyed discussing ecclesiastical matters with Francis de Sales because she needed to understand these for her own reform.

The question of who should control reform, for example, became an urgent one for Angélique in the 1620s. At this time, the abbot general, who had supported the strict observance of the Benedictine rule at Port Royal, was about to be replaced by a new abbot who advocated a more moderate reform.[14] Angélique's reform was in danger, and friends advised her to transfer Port Royal's jurisdiction over to the archbishop of Paris. She made this transfer in 1627 with the help of Sebastien Zamet, the bishop of Langres. Zamet had heard about Angélique's predicament and approached her with an offer to found a new religious institute for women, one that was dedicated to the perpetual adoration of the holy sacrament. Angélique accepted Zamet's offer, and together they transferred Port Royal's jurisdiction, bought a new house, and founded the Institute of the Holy Sacrament.

Soon after they began collaborating, Angélique realised that she had misjudged Zamet, and that his vision of reform did not match her own.

---

12. Cognet, *La Mère Angélique*, p. 67.
13. Cognet, *La Mère Angélique*, p. 77.
14. Cognet, *La Mère Angélique*, pp. 211-212.

For example, he brought Oratorian priests to the Institute to instruct the nuns in the mystical practices of the French Carmelites. Angélique had always admired St. Teresa of Avila's writings, and had a deep respect for the Spanish Carmelites, whom she believed to be genuine in their spirit of humility and poverty. However, she found the French Carmelites 'too witty and impassioned' for her taste.[15] Zamet also wanted the Institute to attract daughters of the high nobility and forbade Angélique to accept poor women without dowries into the convent.[16] He cultivated aristocratic values by introducing elements such as flowers, perfumes and luxurious fabrics into the Church ceremonies. He educated the nuns to be 'of good spirit' and 'capable of entertaining princesses'.[17] As for their piety, Zamet placed desks in each of their cells so that they could write down the 'pleasant thoughts that the Holy Spirit sent to them'.[18] All of this upset Angélique, who had struggled to install a spirit of poverty and humility among her nuns. There was little that was 'pleasant' about the reform she had initiated at Port Royal through personal acts of humility such as scrubbing down the kitchen, caring for the sick, and giving up her abbatial quarters to sleep in a hallway.[19]

Angélique dealt with her frustration by adopting a stance of ultra-obedience. Whereas initially, she spoke fervently with Zamet about reform, she now remained silent. She refused to participate in decisions, and merely followed his directions. Through this exaggerated display of submission and obedience, Angélique expressed to Zamet her desire to be rid of him. Her strategy worked when one day, Zamet told her that she 'disrupted [his work] here'. When she answered that she had done nothing against him, he responded, 'your shadow disrupts us.' To this she replied, 'send me wherever you want then, I will go there'.[20] In this way, Angélique told Zamet how she felt without ever transgressing her identity as a 'naturally' obedient woman.

Tensions between Angélique and Zamet remained until 1633, when Zamet was called away for business in his diocese. In his absence, he asked the abbot of Saint Cyran to supervise the Institute of the Holy Sac-

---

15. Adam, A. (1968) *Du mysticisme à la révolte: les jansénistes du XVIIe siècle.* Paris: Fayard. p. 125.
16. Arnauld, 125.
17. Adam, 110.
18. Adam, 110.
19. Cognet, *La Réforme,* pp. 101-110.
20. Arnauld, 127.

rament.[21] Although not authorised to preach at the Institute, Saint Cyran held conferences in the parlour where he outlined his system of penance based on the writings of the Flemish theologian, Cornelius Jansen. Saint Cyran called for the practice of 'renewals' whereby people abstained from Holy Communion until they felt genuine contrition for their sins. He also insisted on the inherent corruptness of the world and called upon Christians to 'moan silently' [*un silence de gémissement*] in their wretchedness. He argued that people could not change the world, but that God would hear and answer the silent cry of the truly devout.[22] When Angélique heard Saint Cyran speak, she wrote that she had finally found a man 'in whom the force of the spirit of truth overwhelmed me'.[23] She saw him as the confessor she had always sought since obeying him came without effort. In her words, he was 'the death of my will, my judgement and my own senses'.[24]

Many of the nuns were similarly overcome by Saint Cyran and began asking him for general confessions in order to begin their 'renewals'. While the other nuns confessed to Saint Cyran, Angélique waited. She explained in her autobiography that this was because she felt completely unworthy of him. When Saint Cyran asked her if she wanted to confess, she became 'tongue-tied' and could only ask him to pray for her.[25] Once again, the strategy of becoming extra-obedient worked for Angélique. As time passed, Saint Cyran realised that something was wrong, and that Angélique was engaged in her own 'silent moaning'. When he finally commanded her to tell him what was the matter, she 'opened her heart' and explained her problems with Zamet. She told Saint Cyran that many of her nuns wanted to follow him, and that they were prepared to abandon the Institute of the Holy Sacrament to return to Port Royal with him as their director.[26] Saint Cyran decided to help Angélique and, in 1636, she and several nuns returned to Port Royal. Saint Cyran was there for

---

21. Saint Cyran became Zamet's friend after he helped him in the *querelle du Chapelet Secret*. Orcibal, J. (1947) *Jean Duvergier de Hauranne, Abbé de Saint-Cyran et son temps (1581-1638)*. Louvain: Editions J. Duclot. pp. 305-334.
22. Adam, 122.
23. Arnauld, 142.
24. Arnauld, 141.
25. Arnauld, 144.
26. Arnauld, 145.

only two years however, because Richelieu imprisoned him in 1638 for publishing a polemical anti-Jesuit pamphlet.[27]

Angélique's autobiography ends with Saint Cyran's arrest in 1638 even though she did not die until 1661. By ending her life story at this point, she emphasised how he marked the culmination of her quest for spiritual fulfillment. Her saintly portrayal of Saint Cyran is significant because she wrote the autobiography in 1654-55, shortly after the publication of Innocent X's Constitution Cum Occasione (1653) which condemned five propositions drawn from Jansen's Augustinus. Although the bull never mentioned Port Royal, the convent was denounced in pamphlets at the time for harbouring the Jansenist heresy. Thus, Angélique's autobiography was ultimately a defence of Jansenism written during a time of persecution. However, her life story also serves as a useful entry into the religious climate of the early seventeenth century. The opportunities provided by religious reform, combined with the restrictions placed upon her as a woman, led her to develop strategies to determine her own future. In her case, she had the choice of obeying her father, becoming a Protestant, or of becoming an extra-obedient Catholic, accountable only to God. She chose the latter, and continued to use this strategy throughout her reform to determine her way within the confines of the Church.

Angélique's strategy of undermining male authority by adopting a stance of extra-obedience later became central to the nuns' resistance to Louis XIV's religious policies. For example, when a hostile bishop interrogated them for Jansenism, the nuns avoided answering direct questions about their spiritual beliefs by insisting upon their 'natural' ignorance as women. This strategy, developed by women to manipulate the restrictions placed upon their sex, was also adopted by male Jansenists who incorporated the nuns' gendered arguments into their polemical pamphlets.[28] These pamphleteers combined their theological arguments with the nuns' 'natural' ignorance to appeal for Christians to oppose Louis' religious policies in the name of the higher principle of the sanctity of individual conscience.

---

27. Upon Saint Cyran's arrest Richelieu was quoted as saying 'We would have avoided much disaster and disorder if somebody had arrested Luther and Calvin as soon as they began to dogmatise'. Adam, 140.

28. For background on pamphlet literature see Martin, H-J. (1993) *Print, Power, and People in 17th-Century France*. Trans. David Gerard. Metuchen, NJ: The Scarecrow Press. pp. 169-173.

The persecution of Port Royal began in 1661, when Louis XIV required all members of the French Church to sign a formula stating that they condemned with "heart and mouth" the five propositions condemned by Cum Occasione.[29] Although this formula attacked Jansenism, Louis' demand for a signature from everybody was part of his larger effort to unify the Church and ensure that it always supported, and never challenged, the authority of the monarchy. Jansenists had a variety of responses to the formula. While some refused to sign, others signed by making a distinction between doctrine and fact. This distinction was developed by Antoine Arnauld (Angélique's brother) and Pierre Nicole. They claimed that the doctrine condemned by the bull was heretical, but that it did not in fact appear in Jansen's *Augustinus*. When they signed, they added a clause stating that they maintained a respectful silence on the question of fact because this was knowledge based on human reason, not revealed truth. The king however, refused to accept respectful silence as an adequate sign of conformity, and began punishing the Jansenists for disobedience. The nuns were among those punished since they had signed with the doctrine/fact distinction. They argued that they could not sign on the matter of fact because they had not read the *Augustinus*. In addition, the nuns argued, any request for them to sign would be asking them to transgress God's natural order since Church law prohibited women from reading theological texts. When their archbishop ordered them to sign without distinction out of obedience to him, they replied that they had to obey their consciences first. Their consciences would not allow them to obey his command because they understood that other Church officials, equal in his rank and stature, had made the distinction.[30]

This response outraged the archbishop, who, between 1661 and 1669, repeatedly interrogated the nuns, refused them the sacraments and exiled them into other convents. The nuns called these punishments 'persecutions' and kept detailed records of them in journals. A report by Sister Madeleine Gertrude Dupré illustrates how the nuns resisted the archbishop, and by extension, the king. Her account of an interview with

---

29. Sedgwick, A. (1977) *Jansenism in Seventeenth-Century France: Voices from the Wilderness*. Charlottesville: University Press of Virginia. p. 108.
30. See the discourse given to the community of nuns by their abbess on November 19, 1661. Reproduced in [no author] (1724) *Relation de ce que c'est passé à Port Royal depuis le commencement d'Avril 1661 jusqu'au 27 du même mois de l'année suivante 1663* [No Place of Publication].

the archbishop in 1661 reveals how the conflict between the nuns and the archbishop hinged upon differing definitions of feminine obedience. Both agreed that as a woman, she was naturally ignorant and inherently obedient. To the archbishop, this ignorance meant she should obey his will without question. To the nun, her ignorance meant she should obey her conscience first.

Sister Gertrude's account also reveals the archbishop's hostile and aggressive interview style with the nuns. By drawing our attention to the way he silenced her with forceful interruptions, Gertrude underscores her identity as a helpless nun. Her interview began with the archbishop saying: 'Why, my sister, can you not sign? ... One would not stubbornly resist ... unless one has one's reasons'.[31] She responded: 'You are right, Monsignor, it would not be just to resist your wishes without reason, and if my conscience would allow me ...'. Here, she did not finish because the archbishop interrupted: 'My conscience, my conscience! Is it your conscience that prohibits you from obeying your archbishop?'. Gertrude struggled to answer him but was again interrupted (she mentions in a parenthetical note that he interrupted her more than six times during the interview). Finally, she explained that she could not sign the formula because it would be a false testimony. To this the archbishop responded: "I understand you well, and it is what I expected; to the degree that I, your archbishop, ask you to make a false witness, I would have you commit a sin'. Once again, Gertrude struggled to clarify her position without offending him: 'I see that I have not made myself well understood, and it is because I am a poor, ignorant...' And again, he cut her off, 'Ignorant, ignorant! It is true that you are quite ignorant, because you do not know how to obey'. He added, 'Do you not know that I have the right to command you, and that you must obey me?' She replied 'Yes, Monsignor, as far as God and my conscience will allow me'. She explained finally: 'I cannot sign the formula ... and condemn a book that I have never read and that I am incapable of understanding'. The key word to this response was 'incapable'. Gertrude argued that she could not obey him because natural and canon law made her incompetent to do what he asked of her. According to her logic, the injustice was not her resistance, but the archbishop's demand that she sign the formula in the first place.

These arguments had larger political implications for both parties. On one hand, the archbishop demanded that the nun follow his command

---

31. The interview is reprinted in the *Relation de ce que c'est passé...*

as God's representative, because it was her duty to be obedient. Obedient to him, that is, and by extension to Louis XIV. The nun, on the other hand, maintained that her obedience to God was conditioned by her gender – that is, by her ignorance and incompetence as a woman – and that she was therefore unqualified to obey Louis' request as passed on by the archbishop. While these political implications remained implicit in the nuns' writings,[32] male Jansenists stated them clearly in polemical pamphlets. These authors incorporated the nuns' experiences into broader theological arguments to present Louis' encroachment upon individual conscience as a violation of God's natural order.

The most important of these pamphlets was the *Apologie pour les religieuses de Port Royal* (1665) by Antoine Arnauld and Pierre Nicole.[33] The goal of this work was to uphold the right of all Christians to remain respectfully silent on questions of fact. The authors stressed that it was excessive for a king to demand signatures as a sign of interior belief because the interior realm of the human heart belonged to God, not men. Only God, they claimed, need concern himself with the inner soul since the soul is accountable only to God. Kings, in contrast, should satisfy themselves with external demonstrations of obedience and submission only. Any attempt by a king to control more than one's exterior behaviour was a vain transgression into God's sacrosanct territory.[34] The *Apologie* cited patristic texts to demonstrate that the Church had never demanded more than external signs of submission because it recognised that internal doubt in human affairs was necessary. In war, for example, soldiers must have doubt or they might never fight. If kings required soldiers personally to testify upon the legitimacy of a war every time they fought, soldiers would rarely do battle because they would not be able to say with certainty the reasons for war. This is because soldiers do not have the same knowledge as kings. Kings, however, allow soldiers to fight with doubt in their hearts, and are satisfied as long as soldiers follow the command to take up arms.

The *Apologie*, therefore, argued that all Christians harboured an interior space, which gave room for doubt in human affairs. In addition, the

---

32. Persecution journals such as sister Gertrude's circulated in manuscript form at the time.
33. Arnauld, A. and Nicole, P. (1665) *Apologie pour les religieuses de Port-Royal du Saint Sacrement contre les injustices et les violences du procedé dont on a usé envers ce monastère*. [No Place of Publication].
34. Arnauld and Nicole, 10.

Apologie presented the nuns as exemplary Christians who needed room for doubt. Unlike most humans, who were 'completely carnal and touched only by sensual and perceptible things',[35] the nuns were living embodiments of the highly cherished values of chastity, innocence and pure loyalty to God. While worldly people remained content as long as one '[did] not touch their goods, their body or their honor', the nuns in comparison, '[had] experience of the soul being in a state in which it knows no love for earthly things'.[36] For these women, making the distinction between doctrine and fact was an imperative because they feared displeasing God more than anything else in the world.

In addition to upholding the nuns as exemplary Christians, the *Apologie* used them to discredit the authority of the Jansenist persecutors. For example, in contrast to the nuns, who had only their consciences to sustain them, the archbishop had troops and *lettres de cachet* to back his will. Referring to the archbishop, the *Apologie* stated: 'One must swear that never has a Prelate been more dreadful, nor has one so visibly taken advantage of his secular might. He always has troops at his disposal which he sends wherever it pleases him...'.[37] Given this situation, 'no sex, no estate and no condition is exempt'.[38] Thus, by comparing the nuns' delicate consciences to the archbishop's recourse to force, the *Apologie* argued that the secular arm behind the archbishop was not there to uphold God's laws, but rather to violate them.

For the authors of the *Apologie*, the nuns were more than female martyrs who evoked sympathy and outrage. They were proof that the doctrine/fact distinction reflected God's natural order because not all humans had equal access to all knowledge. For example, in comparing theologians to nuns, the *Apologie* admitted that there were some 'theologians, most convinced of Jansen's innocence, who believe that they can sign [the formula] and that this will not harm the truth'.[39] The *Apologie* explained that these theologians signed because they knew enough about doctrine and Church affairs to weigh all of the factors. They justified their signatures by claiming that these were made in the higher interest of peace. Nuns on the other hand, did not have the wisdom of theologi-

---

35. Arnauld and Nicole, 12.
36. Arnauld and Nicole, 12.
37. Arnauld and Nicole, 75.
38. Arnauld and Nicole, 75.
39. Arnauld and Nicole, 11.

ans, nor should they. Because of their natural limitations, the nuns had to settle upon the one thing they knew for sure when asked to sign: the fact that they had not read Jansen's *Augustinus*. They needed the distinction according to the *Apologie*, because 'when those who are subordinate question whether or not they violate the natural law in obeying their superior, they must take greater precautions.'[40] Signing with the distinction therefore, protected the nuns from making a false testimony of faith out of ignorance.

We cannot know how many people read the persecution journals and the *Apologie*, nor can we know the effect these texts had on their readers. We do know however, that Louis was forced to compromise. By 1669, a group of powerful bishops had come together to protest his policy towards the Jansenists. They did so not because they sympathised with Jansenist theology, but because they believed that Louis was using the Jansenist crisis to encroach upon other areas of ecclesiastical jurisdiction.[41] Under pressure from these bishops, Louis and Pope Clement IX forged a peace which tacitly allowed the Jansenists to remain respectfully silent on the question of fact.

Although Clement IX pardoned the nuns, Louis XIV neither forgave nor forgot them. In the following years, he continued his efforts to eradicate religious pluralism with policies such as the Revocation of the Edict of Nantes. Finally, on October 29, 1709 he sent his lieutenant of police and several armed men to shut down the convent and exile the nuns. While he meant this to be the final blow to Jansenism, it backfired and helped to rekindle the movement. Eighteenth-century Jansenists pointed to Louis' treatment of the nuns as the quintessential act of royal tyranny, and once again upheld Port Royal as their banner in opposition to the king. Many historians of the eighteenth century, including Dale Van Kley, David Bell, Catherine Maire and Arlette Farge now argue that these Jansenists fostered a culture of partisanship, resistance and personal engagement in political affairs that helped to pave the way to Revolution.[42]

---

40. Arnauld and Nicole, 65.
41. Sedgwick, 138.
42. Van Kley, *The Religious Origins*. Bell, D. (1994) *Lawyers and Citizens: The Making of a Political Elite in Old Regime France*. Oxford: Oxford University Press. Maire, C. (1998) *De la cause de dieu à la cause de la nation: le jansénisme au XVIIIe siècle*. Paris: Gallimard. Farge, A. (1994) *Subversive Words: Public Opinion*

Thus, Port Royal had an enduring legacy in the eighteenth century that began a century earlier with its reform. This legacy had its roots in a mixture of Jansenist piety and female strategies of resisting patriarchy. Both developed out of Angélique Arnauld's experiences with the open religious climate in the years following the Wars of Religion. Although this period of religious pluralism provided Angélique with choices regarding her religious vocation, she still had to manipulate the restrictions placed upon women to assert her own will; first, against her father and later, against an unwanted confessor. Her strategy of adopting a stance of ultra-obedience was later adopted by other nuns to resist Louis XIV in the 1660s. In addition, male Jansenists incorporated the nuns' techniques into their polemical pamphlets successfully to oppose the king's religious policies. They were successful because they paired individual conscience with the 'natural' feminine characteristics of ignorance and obedience. Throughout his reign, Louis found ways – usually coercive ones – to overwhelm individual consciences. When he attacked the nuns, however, he was at a loss to overcome their resistance as forceful action against them only undermined his claims to legitimate authority. Thus, when he finally did resort to violence in 1709, his victory was a pyrrhic one. Port Royal was destroyed, but the memory of the nuns' persecution provided royal opponents with a powerful symbol of tyranny in action, which they were only too willing to use.

in Eighteenth-Century France. University Park: Pennsylvania State University Press.

Gillian Weiss

Commerce, Conversion and French Religious Identity in the Early Modern Mediterranean

Trading in the Mediterranean was a dangerous proposition during the latter part of the seventeenth century. When French merchants loaded their vessels with wine and cloth in Marseille, or tobacco and flour in La Rochelle, and set sail for North Africa, they risked their goods, their bodies and their faith. The lucky ones reached the French trading ports, or *échelles*, without incident but then lived uncertainly in Catholic enclaves on the edge of vast Muslim territory. The unlucky ones encountered pirates en route and simultaneously lost their merchandise and their liberty. Enslaved and held for ransom in Barbary, an area comprised of nations we now know as Libya, Tunisia, Algeria and Morocco, thousands of French captives spent months to decades awaiting deliverance. That these vulnerable Catholics would be lured or forced into Islam, that they would 'turn Turk' during their sojourn or captivity, was a terrifying possibility that the king, families and especially religious institutions tried to prevent at some cost. Yet even as French authorities worked to protect the Catholic identities of traders and slaves in the North African *échelles*, they bought and seized Muslim captives to row on the royal galleys and permitted a Muslim population of merchants to reside in French coastal cities. While guarding against apostasy among French subjects abroad, administrators did not promote and in fact largely discouraged Catholic conversion among Muslims in France. Why fight for Catholicism across the Mediterranean but suffer the presence of Muslims and practice of Islam within the kingdom? By exploring such a seeming paradox, this paper will reconsider both the locus of religious identity and the importance of religious homogeneity in early modern France. It will also point up the need to modify assumptions about the period before and after the revocation of the Edict of Nantes as one when royal policies towards religious minorities inexorably hardened and France's adventure of religious pluralism came to an abrupt halt.

Expressed anxiety about French subjects who 'prennent le turban aussi facilement qu'un bonnet de nuit',[1] as one French consul put it, fills both administrative correspondence, as well as published accounts about Barbary commerce and captivity by former slaves and their rescuers. During the seventeenth century, particularly from mid-century onwards, French royal and religious authorities employed four primary methods to avoid this eventuality. They inserted relevant clauses in their peace treaties with the Barbary powers;[2] they maintained Catholic institutions in North Africa; they controlled access to the *échelles* and they tried to repatriate subjects at the greatest risk – women, children and slaves. Although the king occasionally dispatched warships to compel, or emissaries to negotiate, the release of captives, and relatives sometimes managed to raise the necessary money to buy them back, more often the work of redemption fell to one of two religious orders, *Frères de la Sainte Trinité* (Trinitarians) and *Pères de la Merci* (Mercedarians). These two orders both established by Frenchmen at the end of the twelfth and beginning of the thirteenth century, had as their vocation the liberation of Catholics from the grip of the infidel. Between their founding in the Middle Ages until 1785, the date of their last rescue mission, French redemptive fathers attained the release of somewhere between 90,000 and 900,000 captives from Barbary.[3]

Consuls in the *échelles*, who presided over satellite French 'nations', also played an important role in surveying the religious allegiances of French subjects in North Africa. In fact, the first generation of Algerian consuls belonged to the order of Saint Lazare and used their posts to proselytise to French residents. Consuls maintained Catholic chapels and sponsored mass, investigated cases of apostasy, which they reported back to the Marseille Chamber of Commerce and the Ministry of the Ma-

1. Attributed to a consul during time of Colbert, cited in Hiély, Philippe (1996) 'XVIIe siècle age d'or de la piraterie en Méditerranée', *Cahiers du comité du vieux Marseille,* 2nd trimester, 70: 79.

2. The 1628 and 1689 treaties with Algeria and the 1682 treaty with Morocco, among others, contained clauses forbidding forced apostasy, stipulating that the French consul be informed of voluntary renegades or imposing waiting periods before conversion to Islam. See Turbet-Delof, Guy (1973) *L'Afrique barbaresque dans la littérature française au XVIe et XVIIe siècles.* Geneva: Droz, 151.

3. Figures fluctuate wildly, with members of the redemptive orders almost certainly inflating the numbers they claim to have rescued. S. Moreau-Rendu (1974) compares the various assertions in *Les captifs libérés et le couvent Saint-Mathurin de Paris.* Paris: Editions latines.

rine.[4] Consuls selectively redeemed captives, too.[5] Beginning in the final decades of the seventeenth century, the king also sought to impose Catholic adherence among his subjects residing in the *échelles* by issuing a series of royal ordinances. On October 21, 1685, for example, four days after the revocation of the Edict of Nantes made Catholicism a requirement for living in France, the promulgation of another edict made it a condition for participating in Mediterranean trade. Any merchant wishing to live or trade in North Africa needed to obtain a permit from the Chamber of Commerce, whose conditions for granting and renewing authorization, which included proof of Catholicism, became more stringent in the decades that followed. Later edicts stipulated that French merchants in Barbary be at least 25 years of age, stay no longer than ten years, leave their wives and daughters at home and keep away from 'femmes indigènes'. Merchants who contracted marriages with local women lost their rights as members of the French nation and their ability to pass on French citizenship to their children.[6] The underlying assumption of these increasingly strict regulations seems to have been that French subjects, especially members of vulnerable groups like women and children, who lingered too long in Barbary or interacted on intimate terms with Muslims, risked betraying their God and their king.

Somehow these concerns about the pernicious effect of contact with Muslims appeared more urgent in Barbary than on French soil. French

---

4. Consuls reported home about apostasies and made sure they were voluntary, as a 1744 form attests: 'Nous ... soussignés Drogmans du Consulat de France en cette Echelle de ... certifions & attestons à tous qu'il apartiendra, que le ... du mois de ... de l'année ... ayant été apellés par le Cady au ... *Mekemé* ... pour, suivant l'usage établi en cette Echelle, assister à l'apostasie du nommé ... *Matelot* ... François, au bord de Capitaine ...'; reproduced in Jean-Baptiste Germain, *Recueil de formules pour les consuls et les chanceliers des échelles du Levant et de Barbarie* (s.e., s.l., 1744), 56 (Thanks to Mitra Brewer, a graduate student at Georgetown University, for this reference).

5. In 1675 the France nation in Algiers lent Alexis Fougasse of La Ciotat 'cent vingt piastres de huict reaux sevillanes mexicaines pour le tirer des mains de son susd Patron, et luy conserver sa liberté avec sa religion qu'il estoit en danger de perdre s'il l'on avoit reffusé'. Promisary note from Alexis Fougasse issued by Chancellery of Algiers, 4 March 1675, Archives de la chambre de commerce de Marseille (ACCM), G40.

6. See Pellegrin, Nicole 'La Presence des Français dans les échelles du Levant et de Barbarie (de 1685 à 1793)', Mémoire de maîtrise d'histoire économique, Université de Provence, 1970-1971 for an analysis of the settlement permits and Debbasch, Yvan (1957) *La Nation française en Tunisie (1577-1835)*. Paris: Editions Sirey, 442-447 for the texts of some of these royal ordinances.

kings may have preferred to rule over a homogenous Catholic population, but in port cities, at least, they followed a long tradition of
swapping religious priorities for perceived commercial and strategic
benefits. On several occasions during the seventeenth century French
leaders invited Muslims into the kingdom or gave them conditional asy-
lum. Out of self-interest, if not pity, royal authorities allowed France to
serve as a temporary sanctuary for Muslims mistreated by other European powers. Before his death in 1610, for example, Henri IV granted
permission to 50,000 destitute Moriscos banished from Spain to traverse
the Pyrenées into France and either make their way to North Africa or
remain in selected southern regions, provided that they gave up Islam
and embraced the apostolic faith. Over protests from town councils and
local residents, who feared that these Muslim refugees would bring with
them poverty and disease, not to mention disturbing religious mores,
small numbers of Moriscos did stay behind in Bayonne, Toulouse, Marseille and Toulon. The first article of the 1628 peace treaty between
France and Algiers was written in the same spirit of accommodation. It
declared 'qu'à tous les esclaves musulmans réfugiés des païs de ses [the
Dey's] ennemies, abordant dans la France, sera donné libre passage pour
venir à Alger et défense sera faite aux gouverneurs des villes et des ports
du royaume de France et à toutes autres personnes de rendre ny vendre
les dits Muslulmans à ses ennemis'.[7] This practice of providing refuge to
Algerian slaves continued at least through the first half of the eighteenth
century.[8]

---

7. For more details about the Morisco exodus from Spain to France between 1610 and
    1613, see Santoni, Pierre (1996) 'Le passage des Morisques en Provence (1610-
    1613)', *Provence historique* 46, no. 185: 333-383; Cardaillac, Louis (1971) 'Le pas-
    sage des Morisques en Languedoc', in *Annales du Midi: Revue archéologique,
    historique et philologique de la France Méridionale.* Toulouse: Edouard Privat,
    259-298 and Michel, Francisque (1847) *Histoire des races maudites de la France et
    de l'Espagne.* Paris: A. Franck.
8. Article 1 of the peace treaty signed in Algiers on 19 September 1628 is reprinted in
    Belhamissi, Mouluy (1988) *Les captifs algériens et l'Europe chrétienne, 1518-1836.*
    Algiers: Enterprise Nationale du Livre, 104. See ACCM, GG34 and GG51 for ex-
    amples of Marseille as a temporary haven for Muslim galley slaves. When four
    Algerians who escaped from Malta in 1728 by boarding a French boat were sold, the
    French consul in Algiers protested the violation, writing that respecting the liberty
    of escaped Muslim captives was 'un droit et un usage constamment observés'. Ar-
    chives nationales (AN), Affaires Etrangères, B11124, f. 30 v., May 1729; cited in
    Belhamissi, *Les captifs algériens*, 106.

Throughout the seventeenth century, particularly during the reign of Louis XIV, and in contradiction to the 'there are no slaves in France'[9] maxim, French leaders aggressively searched for Muslims, or 'Turks,' as they were known regardless of geographic origin, to serve on the Mediterranean galleys. Captured at sea by merchants, purchased at slave markets on the island of Malta or in the *échelles* by consuls, Turks had reputations as the best and hardiest rowers; and the king and his ministers deemed their labour crucial to the strength of the royal galleys, which in turn reflected the eminence of France. In 1695, at the height of the galley system, when the French fleet boasted twenty-five ships of 5,000 men, 24% of them were Muslims.[10] During the winter months when the galleys remained at port, Muslim slaves were a familiar presence in Marseille and Toulon. They worked in manufacturing and set up shops along the waterfront. As trading centres that at least theoretically welcomed foreigners for the purposes of commerce, Marseille and Toulon also hosted significant numbers of Muslim merchants and sailors. From approximately 1691 on, Muslims buried their dead and said prayers in their own cemeteries.[11] As with the arrival of Moriscos earlier in the century, the presence of North African traders and so-called Turkish slaves met with a degree of resistance from the local population. After Barbary pirates attacked a French ship in 1620, a mob in Marseille massacred 48 Muslims, including two ship captains and two Algerian ambassadors.[12] Repeated opposition to the Muslim burial grounds in

---

9.   Louis XIV explained this exception accordingly: 'Tout homme qui a une fois touché les terres du royaume est libre, et on ne se dispense de suivre cette loi que pour les Turcs et les Mores qui sont envoyés à Marseille pour le service des galères, parce que, avant d'y arriver, ils sont achetés dans des païs étrangers où cette espèce de commerce est establie.' AN, Marine B626, f. 431; cited in Nékrouf, Younès (1987) *Une amitié orageuse: Moulay Ismaïl et Louis XIV*. Paris: Albin Michel, 431.

10.   Belhamissi, *Les captifs algériens*, 38.

11.   For photographs by Arnaud Bizalion of what purports to be the 'Ancienne Mosquée des Galères. Le Prado. Marseille', see Ecole d'art et d'architecture, Marseille-Luminy, ed., (1983) *Influences de l'Orient sur l'architecture en Provence*. Cavaillon: Imprimerie Rimbaud, 30. In 1777 the Marseille notaire Grosson affirmed in his *Almanach historique de Marseille*, 211-214, that at the end of the Muslim cemetery at the *Champs major* stood a small mosque in which Muslim galley slaves and merchants passing through Marseille prayed on Fridays. Cited in Masson, Paul (1938) *Les galères de France, 1481-1781: Marseille, port de guerre*. Paris: Librarie Hachette, 451.

12.   'Histoire du massacre des Turcs à Marseille en 1620', in *Documents de l'Histoire de Provence*, ed. Edouard Baratier (Toulouse: Privat, 1971), 191-193. Originally published Lyon: Chez Cl. Armand, 1620, reprinted by Henri Delmas de Grammont

Provence lasted into the 1780s.[13] Nevertheless, the crown stuck by its policy of accepting and even protecting Muslims in France throughout the early modern period.

The discrepancy in attention to the threat posed by Islam in Barbary and France raises the question: how much and why did the French fear for the souls of captives in North Africa? As representatives of the Church, Trinitarians and Mercedarians most likely were truly afraid that Catholic slaves in Barbary would convert to Islam, though exciting emotion and exaggerating the dangers of apostasy also worked to the religious fathers' advantage in raising ransom funds. In letters pleading for salvation, the slaves themselves depicted conversion to Islam as a real terror, but they also used the threat of apostasy as a rhetorical strategy to stir compassion. From the crown's perspective, the plight of captive French subjects was important but not more important than the glory of France. Louis XIV, at least, showed himself willing to sacrifice individual subjects to the infidel in order to preserve France's power, balancing the fate of Barbary captives against the strength of his navy, his position on the world diplomatic scene and the needs of Mediterranean commerce. Ignoring pleas from consuls, merchants and captives, the king consistently refused to exchange Christian slaves in Barbary for Muslims on his galleys because he did not want to lose any rowers. On the rare occasions that France and a Barbary power, most often Morocco, traded captives head-for-head, the king only authorised the release of invalids who were no longer fit to serve. And when the king did agree to spend royal funds on ransom, he preferred to buy back subjects with use-

---

Paris: Champion, 1879, 33-36. Also see Archives municipales de Marseille (AMM), FF 32, 'Affaire du massacre des Turcs', 14 mars 1620.

13. For documents pertaining to the Muslim cemetery in Marseille in 1723, see AMM EE166; for 1761 see ACCM G6; for 1774-1775 and 1782-1784, see ACCM G6 and Archives départementales des Bouches-du-Rhône (ADBR), C3825. In 1761 an Algerian slave who escaped from the Spanish galleys reported to the dey that Toulon's mosque and cemetery had been destroyed and its cadi put on the chain. The intendant of the Marine in Toulon quickly denied the accusations, swearing that the Muslim cemetery remained intact, and that no mosque ever existed (though Muslims were allowed to gather and pray). The cadi was condemned to the galleys as a common crook. In response to a request from the French consul in Algiers who feared for the 'avanie' of the French nation, the intendant forwarded certificates from Muslims 'qu'ils attestent la liberté qu'ils ont dans l'Exercice de leur religion dans laquelle ils n'ont jamais été interrompus'. Letters from the Intendant of the Marine in Toulon to the Marseille Chamber of Commerce, 18 February and 6 March 1761, ACCM, G6.

ful skills.[14] Finally, most of the late seventeenth-century controls on settlement in the *échelles,* which focused on regulating religious practice, found their basis in economic considerations, namely the desire to ensure that profits generated by Mediterranean commerce flowed back into France.

Efforts to redeem French subjects from Barbary captivity and to extend a French Catholic administrative reach over subjects residing in the *échelles* reflected mercantile concerns and anxieties about conversion to Islam. But the practices of redemption in North Africa also demonstrated uneasiness about whether and how to accommodate the kingdom's Protestant minority. Of the three networks concerned with liberating French slaves, the redemptive orders were the most catholic in their willingness to ransom back captives from other faiths. Before the revocation of the Edict of Nantes, their Christian charity sometimes extended to Huguenots, or so claimed at least one Trinitarian in his published account. Better to rescue Protestants from Barbary than abandon them to Islam, he implied.[15] For the most part, however, Catholics and Protestants before

---

14. Relaying the contents of an *arrêt de conseil* to the Chamber of Commerce in 1690, the intendant of Provence urged the deputies to execute a redemption from Algiers with a cynical rejoinder. 'Je ne sçauroit trop vous exhorter dy satisfaire promptement, non seulement pour le soulagement de ces miserables, et vous eviter les frais qu'on ne pouvait se dispenser de vous faire, mais aussy dans la conjecture presente, ou lon à un extreme besoin de matelots.' Letter from Pierre-Cardin Lebret to the Marseille Chamber of Commerce, Aix, 9 May 1690, AMM, GGL106.

15. In *L'Ordre des Trinitaires pour le rachat des captifs.* Toulouse: Privat, 1903, Paul Deslandres writes that although the Trinitarians generally only redeemed Catholics, 'quand il y a des captifs "de la religion", les protestants leur confient parfois des fonds pour leurs coreligionnaires, ou ils s'occupent eux-mêmes de ce rachat'. Sometimes, French redemptive fathers brought funds from foreign Protestant powers. In 1703, for example, the city of Hamburg sent 300 marks to the Trinitarians, n. 2, p. 388. Trinitarian father Philémon de la Motte writes that he intended to save two Huguenot women before they apostatised: 'Je ne puis omettre que dans Alger, il y a deux femmes de Normandie, l'une de Rouen, et l'autre du diocèse de Lisieux. Elles étaient calvinistes ... Toutes les autres furent rachetées, et celles-ci l'auraient été sûrement si elles étaient pas formées des chaînes qu'on ne peut rompre, ayant renoncé au Christianisme, et s'étant données à des Mores.' François Comelin and Philémon de la Motte, (1703) *Etat des Royaumes de Barbarie, Tripoly, Tunis et Alger contenant l'Histoire naturelle et Politique de ces Pais, la maniere dont les Turcs y traitent les esclaves, comme on les rachete, & diverses avantures curieuses.* Rouen: Guillaume Behourt. Former slave Germain Mouette implies that uneducated Catholics and Protestants in Barbary stood at particular risk of conversion. He witnessed the king of Morocco preach the benefits of apostasy to a new batch of captives. 'Ces jeunes gens qui estoient presque tous valets & garçons de Navires, &

and after the revocation, maintained separate funds and employed different methods to rescue their coreligionaries. Until 1685, Protestant churches in Paris, La Rochelle and Lyon organised general collections in local parishes and then confided the money to Protestant merchants furnished with royal permission to negotiate ransoms. In other instances, relatives went through private channels.[16] After 1685, French refugees continued to collect alms for Protestant captives, and appealed to Dutch and English consuls in North Africa to save their French brethren from captivity. The Ministry of the Marine, however, categorically refused to ransom Huguenots unless they abjured. Learning of an opportunistic Protestant captive, who claimed to be English in the presence of English redemptors and then asked the French consul to attest that he was French, the marine minister ordered the royal envoy in Morocco to start indicating religious affiliation on the lists of captives he sent to Versailles.[17]

par consequence peu instruits dans la Religion Catholique, la plûpart même d'entr'eux heretiques, écouterent les promesses de ce Prince Barbare. & se firent tous Mahometans excepté deux.' Mouette, Germain (1683) *Relation de captivité du Sieur Mouette dans les royaumes de Fez et de Maroc.* Paris: Chez Jean Cochart, 58.

16. Families paid expenses and up to a 22% commission to merchants who redeemed their loved ones from Barbary. For a discussion of the collection of ransom funds by Protestant churches before the Revocation of the Edict of Nantes, and the efforts of French Protestant refugees in England and Holland to redeem relatives held captive in Barbary, see Bonet-Maury, Gaston (October 1906) 'La France et la rédemption des esclaves en Algérie à la fin de XVIIème siècle', *Revue des Deux Mondes*: 898-923. Marcel Delafosse (1948) examines contracts between families and merchants from La Rochelle to ransom Protestant slaves from North Africa, preserved in the notarial records of the Archives départementales de la Charente-Maritime: 'Les Rochelais au Maroc au XVIIe siècle: commerce et rachat de captifs', *Revue d'histoire des colonies* 1st semester, no. 35: 70-83. Charles Serfass, (April-June 1930) 'Les esclaves chrétiens au Maroc du XVIe au XVIIe siècles', *Bulletin historique et littéraire de la société de l'histoire du Protestantisme,* also addresses Protestant redemption networks.

17. Letter from J.B. Estelle to Pontchartrain about Pierre Ballé, Protestant slave, Salé, 29 September 1695, Archives des Affaires étrangères (AAE), Maroc, Consulaire, vol. 2, ff. 254-255 v.; cited in Cenival, Pierre de (ed.) (1931) *Les Sources inédites de l'histoire du Maroc de 1530 à 1845,* 2nd series Paris: Geunther, 4: 358-360. To give an idea of the percentage of Protestant captives, at least in Morocco: Estelle's 1698 census of 254 French slaves held captive in Meknes identifies 9 Huguenots plus another 11 who had abjured in France and then returned to Protestantism in North Africa. AAE, Maroc, Consulaire, vol. 2, ff. 428-429; cited in Cenival, (1931) *Sources inédites,* 2nd series, 4: 630-632. Between 1700-1727, 29 out of 378 French captives in Morocco were Protestant; Cossé Brisse, Philippe de ed., *Sources inédites*, 2nd series, (1960) 6: 13-84.

Sometimes redemptive fathers or administrators made explicit a connection between saving slaves from North Africa and making Catholics in France. According to a Mercedarian in 1663, his order intended processions of redeemed captives to inspire conversion among Huguenots, by showing Catholic charity as the proper response to Mediterranean piracy. A demonstration in Montpellier had its desired effect, recorded the redemptive father. After seeing this demonstration of Catholic fervour, there was no doubt, he asserted, 'que plusieurs Heretiques ressentoient que la conscience leur dictoit que cette-là est la vraye Eglise'.[18] Two years after the revocation of the edict of Nantes, the French consul in Salé made a similar link when he pointed out the hypocrisy of proselytizing to French Protestants, while ignoring the fates of Barbary captives. 'Sa Majesté ... donne les moyens journellement pour ramener les heretiques de son royaulme au sein de l'Eglise', he wrote in a letter back to Versailles. 'C'est le moins que peuvent faire ceux quy sont employez par elle et ses ministres ... travaille[nt] [pour] que ceux de ses subjetz quy sont en esclavittude ne s'en tirent en se resniant'.[19]

If the religious affiliations of French subjects in Barbary and Protestants in France worried spiritual and, at least, some administrative authorities during the mid to late seventeenth century, why did Louis XIV and his ministers stake such ambiguous positions on encouraging conversion among Muslims on French soil? In the years contiguous to the revocation of the Edict of Nantes, a period also corresponding roughly to the conclusion of peace treaties between France and each of the Barbary powers, the drive to purge Huguenots from France and consolidate the kingdom's Catholic identity clashed with military and commercial priorities in the Mediterranean. Certainly baptisms of the occasional Muslim, whether Morisco, merchant or slave, in towns and cities like Bayonne, Cassis, Marseille, Toulon and Rennes during the

---

18. Auvry, Michel (1663) *Le Miroir de la charité chrétienne ou Relation du voyage que les religieux de l'Ordre de Nôtre Dame de la Mercy du Royaume de France ont fait l'année derniere 1662. en la ville d'Alger, d'où ils ont ramené environ une centaine de Chrétiens esclaves.* Aix: Jean-Baptiste & Etienne Roize, 188. For a consideration of religious processions as techniques of conversion, see Luria, Keith 'Rituals of Conversion: Catholics and Protestants in Seventeenth-Century Poitou', in *Culture and Identity in Early Modern Europe (1500-1800): Essays in Honor of Natalie Zemon Davis*, ed. Barbara B. Diefendorf and Carla Hesse (1993) Ann Arbor: Michigan University Press, 65-81.

19. Letter from Périllé to Seignelay, Salé, 27 May 1687, AAE, Maroc, Consulaire, vol. 1, ff. 313-315; reproduced in Castries, (1927) *Sources inédites*, 2nd series, 3: 84.

seventeenth century provided cause for celebration.[20] In the late 1680s, *Le Mercure Galant* published accounts of two Muslim baptisms, along with exhortations to encourage conversion among the few infidels left in Catholic France, and the king's claim that 'le salut d'une âme' meant more to him than 'la prise de beaucoup de vaisseaux'.[21] Conversions from Islam to Christianity apparently occurred frequently enough to warrant a royal ordinance, issued on 25 January 1683, stipulating that Muslims who choose to renounce their religion be instructed only in the tenets of Catholicism rather than the 'fausse doctrine' of 'ladite R.P.R.'.[22]

Pious rhetoric aside, however, preaching Catholicism to the infidel put the cause of religion into conflict with the interests of state. When Muslims on the galleys converted, French authorities found themselves in the uncomfortable position of having to justify the forced labour of Catholics who committed no crime, or else lose their most valuable rowers. Yet throughout most of the seventeenth century, royal policy on oarsmen who embraced Catholicism remained uncertain. Colbert expressed outrage when the intendant of the galleys released a newly-converted Catholic Turk, who had adopted the name of a Marseille merchant Louis Bonneau, and allowed the slave to travel to Paris and petition for his liberation in July 1676. 'De quelle authorité empeschez-vous un Turc qui se porte bien, qui est en estat de servir le roy, de partir en mesme temps que les galères pour servir comme les autres?' he wrote.[23] But later that year the galley intendant had a change of heart,

---

20. See Archives municipales de Bayonne, GG4; Archives communales de Cassis, GG2; Archives communales de Toulon, GG29; Archives départementales d'Ille et Vilaine, 3E/245/1.

21. *Le Mercure Galant*, (October 1687): 387 and (May 1688): 196; cited in Turbet-Delof, *L'Afrique barbaresque*, 150.

22. 'Declaration portant que les Mahométans et idolâtres qui voudront se convertir ne pourront être instruits que dans la religion catholique', Versailles, 25 January 1683 (Registered at the Parlement de Paris 13 February 1683). Reproduced in Isambert, Jourdan and Ducresy, (eds.) (1829) *Recueil général des anciennes lois françaises*, 28 vols. Paris: Verdière, 19: 414r.-415r.

23. Letter from Jean-Baptiste Colbert to Jean-Baptiste Brodart, Versailles, 26 July 1676, AN, Marine, Ordes du roi pour les galères, 1676 [old classification system], f. 90; cited in Clément, Pierre (1882) *Lettres, Instructions et Mémoires de Colbert*, 10 vols. Paris: Imprimerie Nationale, 3: 28. 'This Turk is a very bad man, a great sodomist; he only became Christian to escape ... I beg you not to give [him] his liberty.' Letter from Brodart to Colbert, 1676, AN, Marine, B682, ff. 32-34; cited in Bamford, Paul (1973) *Fighting Ships and Prisons: The Mediterranean Galleys of*

calling Bonneau a sodomist who had converted out of self-interest and asking the minister not to authorise the slave's release. In 1677 Colbert instructed the consul in Genoa to buy as many Turks as possible but warned him to 'prendre garde de n'en acheter aucun qui soit chrétien, S.M. ne voulant pas s'en servir sur les galères'. According to a note in the letter's margin, 'On ne s'est point attaché à cette distinction dans ces derniers temps et l'on a cru même devoir préférer les chrétiens. On travaillait autant que l'on pouvait, quoi qu'assez capricieusement, à faire entrer les Turcs dans la religion chrétienne et l'on donnait un sol par jour aux Turcs qui s'étaient faits chrétiens'.[24] Five of 257 Turks purchased for the galleys between 1685 and 1687 had already been baptised. There are no records of baptisms while serving on the galleys during this period, however, implying either the insufficiency of conversion as grounds for liberation, or, perhaps, a resolution not to publicise the morally dubious practice of holding onto Christianised Turkish rowers.[25]

Concerns about preserving France's good standing in the *échelles*, deemed crucial to the health of Mediterranean commerce, also worked against encouraging Muslims to renounce Islam.[26] When a rumour that the French consul in Tunis had kidnapped a Muslim woman to Marseille and had forcibly baptised her began to circulate in 1685, galley officials rushed to quash it by compelling a Turk on the 'Patronne Marie' to send assurances to the Tunisian dey. 'Seigneur il y a cinq ans que je suis esclave en france et que je demeure à marseille', wrote Aly Abdallah, 'et jamais je n'ay veu ny ouy dire que le consul, ou autre, aye mandé des filles de tunis ou d'autre part à marseille n'y qu'on y ayt fait par force

---

France in the Age of Louis XIV. Minneapolis: University of Minneapolis Press, 217.

24. ACCM, Fonds Arnoul 28 (destroyed in 1944); cited in Masson, *Galères de France*, 28.

25. In 'La chiourme turque des galères de France de 1685 à 1687' (1969) *Revue de l'Occident musulman et de la Méditerrannée*, 6: 53-74, Pierre Boyer analyses a register of Turkish galley slaves held at the marine archives in Toulon (1 O. 106 bis). He postulates that some galley slaves did convert but were not released, based on a court case of a Turk named Chaban, whose condemnation for apostasy in 1700 implies an earlier conversion, of which there is no archival trace. See ADBR, Dépot Aix, B5570 for the arrêt from the Parlement d'Aix.

26. Consuls often paid off local officials to keep up good relations and banished French subjects who sullied the name of the French nation. A 1663 arrêt from the Parlement of Provence, for instance, condemned two men accused of 'the crime of fornication committed against a Moorish woman' in Sidon to pay a large fine, make a public apology and never again step foot in any echelle under Ottoman rule. ADBR, Amirauté, 9B2, ff. 1024-1026.

chrestien aucun turc'.[27] To guard against retribution in North Africa, the Marseille Chamber of Commerce and the Intendant of Provence repeatedly intervened to appease disgruntled Muslims in France, whether to secure right of entry to the Muslim cemetery, or to foot the medical bills for Moroccan and Algerian sailors involved in fights. By the 1770s, the king had charged the Minister of Marine with ensuring that no Muslim in France had any cause for complaint.[28] The royal rationale seemed to be that as long as Muslims lived quietly and separately, their false beliefs did not provide sufficient reason to give up their labour or their goods, or threaten the reciprocal tolerance Christians in the Barbary *échelles* enjoyed. Furthermore, as long as the few Muslims who chose to convert did so quietly, without setting off alarms in North Africa and the Ottoman Empire, and as long as they chose Catholicism over Protestantism as their new religion, their foreign origins did not preclude their membership in the French Catholic Church.

So far this paper has argued that French authorities considered Islam a real threat to subjects residing in Barbary but a mere nuisance to subjects living in France. The possibility of insincere conversion might have been another reason French authorities hesitated to urge Muslims in France to embrace Catholicism. 'Il y a trois mois ... deux Marchands Mahometans deguisés en Chrestiens étoient venus de Bordeaux en cette ville pour passer à Tunis', wrote father Gourdon, a Jesuit priest in Marseille, in a letter to Colbert dated November 1668. Jailed by galley intendant Nicolas Arnoul at the priest's demand, one of the traders confessed to living outwardly as Catholic and secretly as a Muslim and attested to 'un grand nombre [de] Mahometans repandus dans la France surtout en Languedoc en Guienne et en Normandie'. This man had taken a French Christian wife and given saints' names to their numerous offspring, all the while instructing his family in the tenets of Islam. Arnoul's first instinct was to view this so-called 'Chrestien mahometan' in his custody as a perfect subject for preaching the virtues of Catholic faith and charity as, he wrote, 'on fait [pendant] les missions aux Indes

---

27. Copy of a translated letter from Agy Abdalla, slave on the 'Patronne de France', to the dey of Tunis, Marseille, February 1685, ACCM, G50.
28. The Archives départementales des Bouches-du-Rhône preserves a folder entitled 'Police des Levantines', ADBR 2502, with correspondence between the minister of the Marine, the intendant of Provence and the Chamber of Commerce about street brawls that involved Muslims and complaints about insults to the honor of Ottoman subjects.

pour la conversion'. But then worries about the corruption of French women and children crowded out concerns about the soul of a single Muslim. Arnoul promised Colbert he would investigate the merchant's claims, writing that though he was doubtful they had any merit, 'si ce [que ce] miserable dit est vray, la France seroit pepiniere de Mahometans'.[29]

This final example suggests that the locus of French religious identity during the late seventeenth century lay in the person of French subjects and their loyalty to the monarch rather than within the kingdom's fluidly defined geographical borders. Thus the mere presence of Muslims in French territory, a de facto form of religious pluralism, did not in itself threaten to undermine France's Catholic character. And merchants trading in enemy lands did not necessarily compromise their French Catholic allegiances; they might successfully preserve ties to their religion and their ruler in the *échelles* by maintaining connections to his Mediterranean representatives. What did threaten the balance between religious homogeneity and commercial interests in seventeenth- and eighteenth-century France was less the existence of foreign faiths than the possibility of flux, especially among the society's most vulnerable: women, children and slaves. Yet the further French Catholic subjects strayed from their homes and their king, the longer they remained captive in Barbary and, perhaps, the more they interacted intimately with Muslims, whether in North Africa or in France, the closer they moved towards apostasy and treason. The very expression 'turning Turk' insinuates a conflation of religious and sovereign allegiances and implies the impossibility of remaining French while

---

29. Letter to Colbert from Jesuit priest Gourdon, Marseille, 5 November 1668, Bibliothèque nationale (BN), Mélanges Colbert (MC) 149, Correspondance XVIIe siècle, ff. 469-470b; letters from Nicolas Arnoul to Colbert, Marseille, 24 and 27 November 1668, BN, MC149, ff. 615 & 664. In a short article (1984) entitled 'Documents sur la diaspora morisque en France au XVIIe siècle' in *Religion, identité et sources documentaires sur les Morisques andalous* (partie française, espagnole et anglaise), vol. 2 Tunis: Publications de l'Institut Supérieur de Documentation, 163-166, Turbet-Delof proposes that the crypto-Muslim merchants arrested in Marseille in 1668 were the descendents of Morisco refugees expelled from Spain in 1610. Although Jules Mathorez (1919) has pointed to the persistence of a Morisco community in Bordeaux as late as 1636, *Les Etrangers en France sous l'Ancien Régime*, 2 vols. Paris: Librairie Ancienne Edouard Champon, 1: 166, there is no particular evidence to suggest that these men were anything other than Barbary traders who had settled and married in France under the guise of Christianity.

Gillian Weiss

becoming Muslim.[30] If travel and trade did not themselves lead inevitably to the betrayal of king and Church, they did provide the preconditions for captivity and the accompanying risks of defection and spiritual corruption.

---

30. Julie Landweber makes this observation in her paper, 'The Case of the Comte de Bonneval: Conflicts of Gender, Nation and Identity in the Experience of an Eighteenth-Century French Convert to Islam'. Paper delivered at the American Historical Association Annual Meeting, Washington, D.C., 9 January 1999.

ALEXANDRA WALSHAM

England's Nicodemites: Crypto-Catholicism and Religious Pluralism in the Post-Reformation Context

Perhaps no single issue pricked the consciences of early European Protestants more keenly than the problem of how a true believer should behave in the face of persecution. How were the godly to conduct themselves in a hostile Catholic environment? How could they maintain their 'fidelity to the Lord pure and unpolluted' while living amidst the 'horrible sacrilege and Babylonish pollution' perpetrated by the Church of Rome? The question of 'the cohabitacyon of the faithful with the unfaithful' greatly vexed and exercised all the major reformers, but none more so than Jean Calvin, whose own flight from France in 1535 enshrined the vehement rejection of any kind of compliance with idolatry which became a hallmark of his teaching. In a series of uncompromising letters and tracts, Calvin set out to demolish the arguments of those who disguised their inner Protestant convictions behind a façade of outward conformity to Catholic rites and justified it by reference to the biblical figure of Nicodemus, the pharisee who timidly concealed his faith in Jesus through fear. When his sharp strictures against these 'pseudo-nicodemites' met with resistance, Calvin redoubled his attack with the avowed intention of making 'their ears tingle even more severely'. Making no concession to the human frailties of men and women reluctant to embrace exile in a foreign country, he compared dissemblers with the cleaners of latrines so inured to the stench they worked in that they found it inoffensive.[1]

---

1. Notable recent discussions of Calvin's anti-nicodemite writings include Eire, Carlos M. (1986) *War against the Idols: The Reformation of Worship from Erasmus to Calvin.* Cambridge: Cambridge University Press, ch. 7 and Zagorin, Perez (1990) *Ways of Lying: Dissimulation, Persecution and Conformity in Early Modern Europe.* Cambridge, Mass.: Harvard University Press, esp. ch. 4. Quotations in this paragraph are taken from Calvin, John (1844-51) *On Shunning the Unlawful Rites of the Ungodly,* in *Tracts Relating to the Reformation,* trans. H. Beveridge, 3 vols Edinburgh: Calvin Translation Society, vol. iii, p. 361; *Letters of John Calvin Compiled from the Original Manuscripts and Edited with Historical Notes,* ed. Bonnet,

For Calvin, nicodemism presented a fundamental threat to the very survival of the Reformation in his native land: a subtle diabolical snare designed to dilute the Protestant message and gradually extinguish it. His intolerance of any type of camouflage or compromise embodied an attempt to forge a strong sense of confessional identity in a context of unprecedented religious pluralism and to preserve the ideological integrity of a Church under the cross. Dissimulation, in his eyes, savoured not merely of cowardice and indifference but of a hypocrisy which tarnished the external face of a fledgling faith in the process of being emblazoned by martyrs.

The wide dissemination of Calvin's tracts in the 1540s and 50s and their translation into English, German, Italian and Dutch indirectly highlight the role which furtive nicodemite dissent played in establishing the foundations of the Reformation prior to the emergence of clandestine separatist conventicles and the formation of public Churches in each of these regions. Indeed, as Andrew Pettegree has remarked, without the widespread practice of various forms of syncretism and subterfuge which characterised this early fluid period the huge surges of support for the evangelical cause which occurred in France in 1561-62 and in the Netherlands in 1566 would have been quite inconceivable.[2] But conformity was a persisting feature of the contemporary religious landscape: a pragmatic, yet also often a principled response to the pressure exerted by regimes intent on enforcing uniformity and by lay people anxious to expel heresy from their communities. Hence the ongoing complaints in Antwerp about parents who allowed their children to be baptised and married 'in the papist fashion'; hence the Protestants in Paris, Troyes, and Rouen who 'swam between two waters' and 'kept themselves in the favour of the world' by continuing to participate in the Mass and attend confession at Easter; hence the mass abjurations in the wake of the St Bartholomew's Day Massacre when thousands flocked to cathedrals and

---

Jules 4 vols New York: Burt Franklin Reprints, 1972; first publ. 1858, p. 435; Calvin, Jean (1970) *Excuse aux Nicodemites*, repr. in *Three French Treatises*, ed. Higman, Francis M. London: Athlone Press, p. 134. *A Treatise of the Cohabitacyon of the Faithful with the Unfaithful* was the title of a tract by Peter Martyr Vermigli published in Strassburg in 1555.

2.   Pettegree, Andrew (1996) 'Nicodemism and the English Reformation', in idem, *Marian Protestantism*. Aldershot: Scolar Press, p. 106.

parish churches formally to reconcile themselves with Rome – perhaps most of these 'converts' were really nicodemites.[3]

Despite several recent discussions of Continental anti-nicodemite literature, there has been no sustained examination of the practical manifestations of this diffuse, amorphous and multi-faceted phenomenon at the grass roots. No doubt this is due in large part to its inherent invisibility: by its very nature conformity leaves little mark on the historical record. But in this paper I want to suggest, firstly, that nicodemism is a force to be reckoned with in post-Reformation Europe and, secondly, that it played an important role in shaping the nature of interconfessional relations in the second half of the sixteenth and first half of the seventeenth century: in establishing preconditions for the peaceful co-existence of the adherents of rival creeds and also, rather paradoxically, in keeping alive the deadly germ of intolerance deeply embedded in European society. Somewhat perversely, I shall be focusing my analysis on Elizabethan and early Stuart England – a context in which Catholics found themselves in the same unenviable position as the Huguenots, that of a proscribed religious minority. They shared with their confessional enemies the experience of professing dogmas at odds with those of their sovereign and their response to the daily moral dilemmas this posed was remarkably similar. In many cases, they too carved a delicate path between stealth and discovery, equivocation and extirpation, prudence and zeal. They too practised dissimulation, though the nicknames more frequently used to describe them were 'schismatics' and 'church papists'. There was, of course, one vital difference between these English Catholic nicodemites and their French Protestant counterparts: whereas the latter were men and women taking their first faltering steps in a new re-

---

3. See Marnef, Guido (1994) 'Calvinism in Antwerp, 1558-1585', in Pettegree, Andrew Duke, Alastair and Lewis, Gillian (eds), *Calvinism in Europe, 1540-1620.* Cambridge: Cambridge University Press, p. 148; Diefendorf, Barbara (1991) *Beneath the Cross: Catholics and Huguenots in Sixteenth Century Paris.* New York: Oxford University Press, pp. 121, 122, 144; Galpern, A. N. (1976) *The Religions of the People in Sixteenth-Century Champagne.* Cambridge, Mass.: Harvard University Press, pp. 151-152, and pp. 116-117, 121, 130-132; Benedict, Philip (1981) *Rouen during the Wars of Religion.* Cambridge: Cambridge University Press, pp. 128-130, and ch. 5 passim. On nicodemism in the Netherlands, see also Duke, Alastair (1990) *Reformation and Revolt in the Low Countries.* London: Hambledon Press, pp. 92-93, 114-115, 117, 277-278. For Italy, see Martin, J. (1993) *Venice's Hidden Enemies: Italian Heretics in a Renaissance City.* Berkeley: University of California Press, esp. ch. 5.

ligion or negotiating the ebb and flow of persecution which accompanied its halting progress, the former were individuals intent on clinging stubbornly to a set of beliefs which had hitherto held the monopoly. Their behaviour was a way of expressing protest and dissent while maintaining a pragmatic 'toehold within the institutional structure of the national Church'.[4] It was also paradigmatic of the manner in which perhaps the majority adapted to the English Reformation. Indeed, it would not be too much of an exaggeration to say that most of those involuntary Protestants created by the Elizabethan Settlement of 1559 were initially church papists – people, as one preacher complained, with 'a pope in their belly'.[5]

I

This was a stance which was particularly prevalent in the first twenty years of Elizabeth I's reign. As more than one commentator remarked, before 1570 'the Papists made no scruple of coming to our churches': recusancy, or refusal to be present at Protestant services, was rare.[6] This was largely a result of the lack of firm guidance committed Catholics received from the hierarchy of the Church of Rome itself. Although both Pope Pius IV and a committee of the Council of Trent concluded that attendance at heretical services was a mortal sin, their decisions remained poorly publicised throughout this decade, partly for diplomatic reasons.[7] However, widespread conformity was also a consequence of significant continuities at the parochial level: of slow and reluctant enforcement of the official injunctions reforming worship and church interiors and of timeserving Marian priests who catered for the conservative liturgical tastes of their congregations by conducting services bearing a close resemblance to the outlawed mass. This early absence of overt opposition might, moreover, be regarded as a back-handed com-

---

4. Houlbrooke, Ralph (1979) *Church Courts and the People during the English Reformation 1520-1570*. Oxford: Oxford University Press, pp. 249, 257.
5. Dent, Arthur (1610) *The Plaine Mans Path-way to Heaven*. London, edn., p. 125.
6. Quotation from Taylor, Jeremy (1638) *A Sermon Preached in Saint Maries Church in Oxford. Upon the Anniversary of the Gunpowder-Treason*. Oxford, p. 22.
7. See Bayne, C. G. (1913) *Anglo-Roman Relations 1558-1565*. Oxford: Clarendon Press, pp. 163-181, 290-1; Maitland, F. W. (1900) 'Pius IV and the English Church Service', *English Historical Review*, 5, pp. 330-332.

pliment to the Elizabethan regime's cautious and fabian strategy for effecting Reformation. Tactful concessions to time-honoured tradition such as the retention of familiar rituals like the churching of women, of ceremonial gestures such as making the sign of the cross in baptism, and of old clerical vestments including the surplice did much to encourage acquiescence. So did the use of unleavened wafers reminiscent of the Catholic host during communion: in 1580 the Privy Council advised one bishop 'charitabely to tollerate them (that esteem wafer bread), as children, with milke'.[8] These tactics embodied a determination to create an umbrella-like Church which could embrace a wide range of opinions and standpoints, a Church in which the populace would gradually be weaned away from popish habits and persuaded to swallow Protestant precepts. The linchpin of this programme was the Act of Uniformity of 1559: making attendance at Common Prayer compulsory and absence an offence punishable by a shilling fine, it eschewed enquiry into people's inner beliefs in favour of the minimal requirement of outward compliance. The ultimate effect of these policies was a kind of collective haemorrhage towards the status quo: as a Welsh Benedictine missionary reflected half a century later, many 'easily digested the new religion and accommodated themselves thereto'.[9]

However, conformity became progressively less appealing as religious positions began to polarise and as the Calvinist temper of the Church of England and its personnel toughened. The papal bull of 1570 excommunicating and deposing the queen confronted Catholics with a stark choice between allegiance to their monarch and allegiance to the pope. Although widely ignored, it coincided with, and contributed to, the growth of recusancy and its increasing identification by the authorities with political disloyalty. During the 1560s, this form of conscientious objection had been enjoined by a small rump of recalcitrant priests, but the campaign in favour of fully-fledged nonconformity did not really take off until the arrival after 1574 of bands of missionaries trained in seminaries in the Low Countries and Rome. Both in printed propaganda and through their pastoral endeavours in the field, leading Jesuits and secular priests maintained that staunch recusancy was the only stance

---

8. Quotation from Wark, K. R. (1971) *Elizabethan Recusancy in Cheshire*, Chetham Society, 3rd ser. 19, p. 18n.
9. *Memorials of Father Augustine Baker and Other Documents Relating to the English Benedictines*, ed. McCann, J. and Connolly, H. (1933) Catholic Record Society 33, p. 16.

sincere Catholics could adopt. Men and women who inwardly adhered to the religion of their forefathers but outwardly complied with Protestant ordinances were declared to be guilty of the heinous sin of 'schism' and threatened with eternal torment in hell. By halting between God and Baal, they not only led astray the weaker brethren and laid themselves open to infection with heresy; they committed an act of gross hypocrisy and flagrant idolatry. To conform was to shirk one's duty to confess one's faith without flinching in the face of persecution. According to the Counter Reformation clergy, such timorous dissemblers were 'Calvin's excrements' and, like the lukewarm church of Laodicea, they too would be spewed out of God's mouth.[10] The arguments Gregory Martin, Robert Persons, Henry Garnet and other priests assembled to condemn church papists thus closely parallelled those used by Protestant reformers against the nicodemites. They too believed that symbolic segregation from the false religion that surrounded them was essential to their very survival; they too sought to foster a confessional identity rooted in heroic defiance. And in striving to eradicate the cancer of crypto-Catholicism they even made grudgingly approving reference to the teachings and writings of their polemical archenemies. Robert Persons quoted a relevant passage from a catechism by the Frenchman Jean Garnier, remarking 'If errour finde such zeale, what zeale ought truthe to have?' Another tract made use of examples of the stalwart nonconformity of Marian Protestants drawn from John Foxe's 'Book of Martyrs', and Robert Southwell cited Calvin's *De vitandis superstitionibus* and *Excuse à Messieurs les Nicodemites* and the counsels of Philip Melanchthon, Peter Martyr and Martin Bucer, declaring that 'albeit their reasons were misapplyed', 'yet are they very sufficient and forcible to confirme that repayring to a false church in deed, is moste sinnful and damnable'.[11] In an age of militant confessionalism, dissembling behav-

---

10. This summarises the discussion in my *Church Papists: Catholicism, Conformity and Confessional Polemic in Early Modern England.* Woodbridge: Boydell and Brewer, 1993, ch. 2. See also Holmes, Peter (1982) *Resistance and Compromise: The Political Thought of the Elizabethan Catholics.* Cambridge: Cambridge University Press, ch. 6; Zagorin, *Ways of Lying,* ch. 7. Quotation from Hill, Thomas *A Quartron of Reasons of Catholike Religion* (Antwerp [English secret press], 1600), pp. 183-184.
11. Persons, Robert (1580) *A Brief Discours contayning certayne Reasons why Catholiques Refuse to goe to Church.* Douai. [London secret press], fos. 52a-54a; H. B., *A Consolatory Letter to all the Afflicted Catholikes in England* (Rouen [Lon-

iour was intolerable to spokesmen on both sides of the denominational fence.

There was, however, an important contrast between Calvin and these English Catholic priests, and this contrast comes in the guise of casuistry. Trained in this science in the seminaries, the clergy were taught to respond compassionately to the moral predicaments faced by their flocks and permitted to exercise a degree of leniency when dealing with the sin of occasional conformity in the privacy of the confessional. While there was never any question of condoning church papistry *per se* or *en masse*, in practice the uncompromising strictures of the recusancy tracts were mitigated significantly. In part this embodied an astute recognition that some relaxation of the general rule was necessary to secure the commitment and preserve the resources of men who might well form the political backbone of a future Catholic regime. As one Elizabethan Catholic from Essex remarked 'the tyme will come [we] will nede such fellowes'. The wisdom of the serpent could only be sanctioned while hope remained of reclaiming England by means of conspiracy or invasion to the Roman fold. Consequently every effort was made to keep these casuistical concessions tightly under wraps.[12]

But the persistence of church papistry cannot be attributed solely to casuistry. It also testifies to a spirit of lay independence and resistance to policies framed by clerical leaders safely in exile on the Continent. The distaste of many of the gentry and nobility for the treasonous machinations of the Jesuits is well documented; their frustration with the Tridentine hard line on recusancy proceeded from a similar conviction that Persons and his colleagues had no sympathy for the straitened condition of Catholics who had remained in England. As the Suffolk gentleman Sir Thomas Cornwallis exclaimed in exasperation, '[t]hey be out of the way themselves and therefore do not regard what we endure' – a curious echo of words written by the Parisian Antoine Fumée in 1543 in response to Calvin's attack on nicodemism: 'A number of people think your assertions are thoroughly wretched. They accuse you of being

---

don secret press, 1587-1588]), pp. 53-5; Southwell, Robert *An Epistle of Comfort* (Paris [London, 1587-8]), fo. 172r-173r.

12. British Library, Lansdowne MS 33, fol. 148r (referring to the church papist Sir John Petre of Ingatestone, Essex). For the casuists' concessions, see Holmes, P. J. (ed.), *Elizabethan Casuistry*, Catholic Record Society 67 (London, 1981), pp. 49, 50, 51, 84-86, 94-96, 120-121, discussed in my *Church Papists*, ch. 3, and Holmes, *Resistance and Compromise*, ch. 8.

merciless and very severe to those who are afflicted; and say that it is easy for you to preach and threaten over there, but that if you were here you would perhaps feel differently'.[13]

Church papistry, then, seems to have been the *modus vivendi* which large numbers of Catholics reached with the Elizabethan government regardless of the dictates of domineering priests – a way of demonstrating their political loyalty without forgoing their private beliefs. Ironically it was a stance which became ever more attractive as the authorities responded to the rise of recusancy by augmenting the weapons in their legal arsenal. In the face of the statutes of 1581, 1587, and 1593 which imposed crippling fines on persistent offenders, rendered them ineligible for political office and eventually confined them within a five mile radius of their place of residence, it is not surprising that nicodemite Catholicism continued to thrive. A wide variety of ingenious compromises were devised.[14] In many upper class households a shrewd domestic arrangement evolved, whereby the husband and head periodically attended church in order to protect the family's financial security and social respectability, while his spouse and children safeguarded its spiritual health by practising unwavering recusancy. In 1596, for instance, the Sussex JP Edmund Pelham was said to be 'very backward in religion' coming to church 'but slakly' minus his wife (except 'twise or thrise a yeare') and such tactics also helped the Yorkshire families of Babthorpe, Meynell and Vavasour to preserve their fortunes almost intact.[15] Occasional conformity was a duty which some fathers carefully groomed their sons and heirs to assume when they came of age and succeeded to their inheritance.[16] Others attended more regularly but ignored or disrupted the proceedings by noisily clicking their rosary beads, concentrating on primers, missals and other devotional books, or chanting

13. McGrath P. and Rowe J. (1961) 'The Recusancy of Sir Thomas Cornwallis', *Proceedings of the Suffolk Institute of Archaeology*, 28, p. 257. Fumée is quoted in Eire, *War against the Idols*, p. 254.

14. For further discussion of such strategies, see my *Church Papists*, ch. 4.

15. British Library, Lansdowne MS 82, fol. 103r; Aveling, Hugh (1960) *Post Reformation Catholicism in East Yorkshire 1558-1790*, East Yorkshire Local History Society 11, pp. 25-9; 'The Recusancy Papers of the Meynell Family of North Kilvington, North Riding of Yorkshire 1596-1676', (1964) ed. Aveling, Hugh in *Catholic Record Society Miscellanea*, ed Reynolds, E. E. Catholic Record Society 16.

16. See, eg, Foley, Henry (ed.) (1877-84) *Records of the English Province of the Society of Jesus*, 7 vols in 8 London: Burns and Oates, vol. 4, pp. 422-423.

psalms to drown out the execrable tones of heretical worship. In 1577 James Eton, chapter clerk of Hereford Cathedral sat so far away from the preacher that he was unable to hear; a few years earlier one Thomas Stiddy of Yorkshire was presented as 'a disquieter of the minister during divine service' and a vile abuser of the suffragan bishop of Nottingham.[17] Notwithstanding the fulminations of the missionaries, there was nothing remotely lily-livered about church papists of this kind. Many Catholics drew the line when it came to receiving communion, persuading themselves that mere church-going might be stomached but not Calvin's supper. It was by no means unusual for non-communicants to use such occasions to dramatise their disapproval of the Protestant Eucharist. At Egton in 1582 Robert Burton was charged with contemptuously spitting out the wine. Others were less frank about the reasons behind their refusal to receive: a York butcher's wife was discovered trying to make away with the sacramental bread in her hand and a serving maid called Elizabeth Coulson alleged that she had not swallowed it 'by reason of a pain in her side and a cough'.[18]

While it is important not to ignore the psychological discomfort which dissimulation often entailed, we also need to recognise the positive forces which inhibited many Catholics from taking the plunge into total nonconformity: ties of attachment to the close-knit communities in which they resided; a sense of responsibility towards their families and neighbourhoods; the duty of upholding the established social order drummed into them from birth; and the obligation of charity imposed upon every Christian by the Bible. For more than a century after the Elizabethan Settlement, it is very hard to force English Catholicism into the straitjacket of a fully segregated sect. In many respects it is better thought of as semi-separatist.

---

17. 'Diocesan Returns of Recusants for England and Wales, 1577', ed. Ryan, Patrick in *Catholic Record Society Miscellanea XII*, Catholic Record Society 22 (1921), p. 78; Aveling, J. C. H. (1970) *Catholic Recusancy in the City of York 1558-1791*, Catholic Record Society Monograph Series 2, p. 168.

18. Aveling, Hugh (1966) *Northern Catholics: The Catholic Recusants of the North Riding of Yorkshire 1558-1790*. London, p. 102; Aveling, *Catholic Recusancy in ... York*, pp. 195, 197.

II

All this is testimony to the richly pluralistic character of post-Reformation English society. The second part of this paper offers some preliminary and speculative suggestions about the implications which the widespread practice of church papistry may have had in the realm of interdenominational relations. It explores the possibility that conformity may provide a partial explanation both for the apparently impressive capacity of the English populace to tolerate religious heterodoxy within its midst and for the alarming but infrequent spasms of intolerance which rocked the country in this period.

Although anti-popery played a crucial role in the formation of a popular Protestant and patriotic consciousness, historians have found little evidence of sectarian hatred of the intensity and on the scale of that experienced in France during the Wars of Religion. The virulent apocalyptic polemic which streamed from the pens of propagandists and resounded from the pulpits seems not to have had much impact on the behaviour of the populace at the grass roots. Passionate literary denunciations of the machinations of the papal Antichrist were hardly ever translated into active hostility towards individual Catholics. On the contrary, inspired partly by the work of Christopher Marsh, there is currently an emphasis on the considerable capacity of contemporaries to countenance the presence of people with dissenting opinions living within their vicinity. The threatening stereotypes portrayed in Protestant sermons and tracts do not appear to have precluded a significant degree of practical cooperation, not say cordial interaction, between the adherents of the Churches of England and Rome.[19]

In some ways this state of affairs might be regarded as a tribute to the wisdom of Elizabeth I's celebrated refusal to make windows into men's souls: to the pragmatic latitudinarianism of a Church which, de-

---

19. On intellectual anti-Catholicism, see Lake, Peter 'Anti-Popery: The Structure of a Prejudice', in Cust, Richard and Hughes, Ann (eds) (1989) *Conflict in Early Stuart England*. Basingstoke: Macmillan and Milton, Anthony (1995) *Catholic and Reformed: The Roman and Catholic Churches in English Protestant Thought 1600-1640*. Cambridge: Cambridge University Press. For practical tolerance, see Marsh, Christopher W. (1994) *The Family of Love in English Society, 1550-1630*. Cambridge: Cambridge University Press, esp. pp. 14-15, 187-196, 249-250, and Milton, Anthony (1999) 'A Qualified Intolerance: The Limits and Ambiguities of Early Stuart Anti-Catholicism', in *Catholicism and Anti-Catholicism in Early Modern English Texts*, ed. Marotti, Arthur F. Basingstoke: Macmillan.

spite the efforts of puritan zealots to impose more searching tests of doctrinal orthodoxy, demanded only external conformity as a sign of assent. Yet it may also be a consequence of the day-to-day compromises Catholics reached with their heretical enemies, not merely the symbolic gestures of deference to the sovereign and state they offered in the guise of occasional conformity, but the numerous other concessions they made in the spheres of hospitality, commerce, law, local government and personal relations in the interests of maintaining harmony and peace and avoiding confrontation. Here the hypothetical cases of conscience studied by seminary priests in the course of their training are very revealing. They suggest indirectly that many Catholics continued to act as godparents to the infants of Protestant friends and to entrust them with the spiritual welfare of their own children; that they paid their tithes, contributed to repairing the fabric of ecclesiastical buildings, purchased produce grown on glebe land, and even participated in seasonal pastimes involving the floral decoration of parish churches now in the hands of the heretics. As magnates and landowners they held the civil offices of notary, mayor, bailiff, constable, justice of the peace, and even sometimes churchwarden; as patrons they exercised their right to present ministers to benefices. On fast days they served meat to their Calvinist visitors; in assorted company they turned a tactful deaf ear to the sacrilegious prayers and graces which preceded lunch and dinner.[20] It is also clear from parish registers and other sources that both recusants and church papists persisted in utilising other essential services supplied by the established Church, especially with regard to marking rites of passage. They baptised their babies according to the Reformed liturgy to spare them the taint of illegitimacy; buried their dead by the Book of Common Prayer to ensure they were laid to rest in consecrated ground; and celebrated weddings with Protestant ceremonies to prevent rumours of adultery and fornication from spreading.[21] Mixed marriages are another index of the extent to which the stark polarities etched so acidly on paper were softened by the bonds of obligation and love. The matriculation records of the English College at Rome suggest that many novice Jesuits came from families in which parents, children and siblings bal-

---

20. Holmes (ed.) *Elizabethan Casuistry*, esp. part I, sections F, G, H, I, J, K; part II, ch. 2, part 2.
21. *Ibid.*, part I, sections A, C, D; part II, ch. 2, part 2, cases 1, 20. See also Bossy, John (1975) *The English Catholic Community 1570-1850*. London: Darton, Longman and Todd, ch. 6, §iii.

anced their religious zeal against emotional attachment.[22] Bill Sheils'
study of Egton on the North York moors shows that strong kinship ties
ensured that confessional animosities did not disrupt or damage neigh-
bourly relations, while in the Cambridgeshire village of Linton,
Elizabethan Catholics trusted Protestants to witness their wills, appointed them to supervise the distribution of their charitable bequests
and occasionally even left small legacies to their local vicar.[23]

This culture of conciliation and compromise had a mirror image on
the other side of the denominational divide. For instance, when a group
of drunken soldiers plotted to extort money from two Catholic ladies at
Corscombe in Devon in 1626, local people warned the household and
the constable arrested the culprits.[24] In many towns and villages, Protestants evidently reciprocated the gestures of good will made by their
Catholic neighbours, protecting them from harassment by government
pursuivants, respecting their scruples about receiving communion, and
winking at offences they ought to have reported to the authorities. Occasional conformity itself was sometimes an elaborate charade in which
church papists and magistrates acted out pre-rehearsed parts.[25] And, as
the case book of the Stratford-upon-Avon physician John Hall reveals,
anti-Catholic prejudice did not prevent committed Protestants from ad-
mitting papists as patients.[26] There is, then, much to suggest that far
from being isolated and marginalised, early modern Catholics were often
fully integrated members of their communities. Their willingness to
meet the heretics half way must have helped to defuse latent antagonism
and foster a climate in which people of both persuasions felt able to con-

---

22. See Kenny, Anthony (ed.) (1962) *The Responsa Scholarum of the English College,
    Rome: Part One: 1598-1621*, Catholic Record Society 54. See also Holmes (ed.)
    Elizabethan Casuistry, part I, cases C2, C4, D1; part II, ch. 2, part 1, case 13, ch. 2,
    part 2, case 8.
23. Sheils, W. J. (1998) 'Catholics and their Neighbours in a Rural Community: Egton
    Chapelry 1590-1780', *Northern History*, 34, p. 130; Bida, Andrzej 'Papists in an
    Elizabethan Parish: Linton, Cambridgeshire, c. 1560-c.1600'. Cambridge, Diploma
    in Historical Studies Dissertation, 1992, pp. 31-33.
24. See Underdown, David (1987) *Revel, Riot and Rebellion: Popular Politics and
    Culture in England 1603-1660*. Oxford: Oxford University Press, p. 129.
25. But cf. the contrary evidence assembled in Questier, Michael C. (1996) *Conversion,
    Politics and Religion in England, 1580-1625*. Cambridge: Cambridge University
    Press, chs 5-6.
26. Lane, Joan 'John Hall and his Catholic Patients', paper delivered at a conference on
    'Shakespeare and the Warwickshire Catholic World', Stratford-upon-Avon, 19
    Sept. 1998.

done beliefs and observances of which they disapproved. As in seventeenth-century Aquitaine, Catholics and Protestants were enclosed within 'a cocoon of mutual relations'.[27]

Simultaneously, and somewhat paradoxically, however, we need to make room for the possibility that this state of de facto religious pluralism may have served in the long term to heighten rather than inhibit the dialectical process of confessionalisation. In a context in which ideological differences were becoming a permanent, ineradicable and tacitly accepted feature of the contemporary landscape, the cultural practices which distinguished individuals who professed rival creeds probably became commensurately more important. Over time the trend towards social separatism seems to have sharpened and deepened, reminding us of the way in which puritans eschewed 'familiar company keeping' with the 'carnal worldlings' with whom they rubbed shoulders in the Elizabethan and early Stuart Church.[28] As John Bossy has shown, the Catholic community became increasingly insular, endogamous and sectarian in character as the seventeenth century progressed. This accords well with Philip Benedict's recent account of the history of Catholic-Reformed coexistence in Montpellier after the proclamation of the Edict of Nantes.[29]

Turning full circle, it could be argued that these processes encouraged the construction and identification of English Catholics as a deviant

27. Hanlon, Gregory *Confession and Community in Seventeenth-Century France: Catholic and Protestant Coexistence in Aquitaine* (Philadelphia: University of Pennsylvania Press, 1993), p. 12, and ch. 4. This accords well with recent research on Lollards, Familists and Dissenters. See the essays by Plumb, Derek Marsh, Christopher and Stevenson, Bill in Margaret Spufford (ed.) (1995) *The World of Rural Dissenters. 1520-1725.* Cambridge: Cambridge University Press and Marsh, *Family of Love.*

28. Collinson, Patrick 'The Cohabitation of the Faithful with the Unfaithful', in Ole Grell, Peter Israel, Jonathan I. and Tyacke, Nicholas (eds) (1991) *From Persecution to Toleration: The Glorious Revolution and Religion in England* Oxford: Oxford University Press.

29. Bossy, *English Catholic Community*, ch. 6. Philip Benedict, 'Un roi, une loi, deux fois: Parameters for the History of Catholic-Reformed Co-existence in France, 1555-1685', in Ole Grell, Peter and Scribner, Bob (eds) (1996) *Tolerance and Intolerance in the European Reformation* Cambridge: Cambridge University Press, pp. 84-93. Forster, Marc R. (1992) paints a similar picture in *The Counter Reformation in the Villages: Religion and Reform in the Bishopric of Speyer, 1560-1720* Ithaca-New York: Cornell University Press, ch. 7, commenting on the 'mania for differentation' (p. 225) which marked interconfessional relations in the eighteenth century.

other, a body of outsiders who, at times of communal and national emergency, could readily be transformed into scapegoats.[30] It is in these terms that we need to interpret the anti-Catholic scares which periodically swept urban centres in periods of political crisis and the fear and anxiety which flared when tragic accidents and natural disasters occurred – rare but spectacular eruptions of the enmities that lay dormant beneath the surface of everyday life. Thus an outbreak of gaol fever in Oxford in 1577 was blamed on a Catholic bookseller on trial for sedition and plague epidemics were regularly attributed to divine wrath at a society which condoned the polluting presence of papists in its midst.[31] Thus the vicious conduct of the London crowd in the wake of the collapse of an attic in Blackfriars in which three hundred Catholics assembled for worship in October 1623, when unruly mobs went on the rampage, pelting the injured with stones, and attempting to set fire to carriages in which the victims tried to escape from the scene.[32] And thus the rumours about popish conspiracy which proliferated in the turbulent 1640s: Leicester, Lichfield and Ashby-de-la-Zouche kept night watches in the winter of 1641 following talk of 'a plot intended to be done by the Papists upon the Protestants' and in Liverpool a Catholic was arrested after saying that 'the Protestants should shortly have a blow and the papists should have crosses or the like on their hats that they thereby might not be killed'.[33] During these brief moments of moral panic, the possibility that England might experience a St Bartholomew's Day Massacre of its own must have seemed very real. Like puritans, Catholics were also perennial victims of persecution by words, the target of mocking rhymes, scurrilous libels and uncharitable taunts which ostracised them from their peers and temporarily turned up the heat of interpersonal relations.

---

30. See Scribner, Bob 'Preconditions of Tolerance and Intolerance in Sixteenth Century Germany', in Grell and Scribner (eds) *Tolerance and Intolerance*, pp. 39-43.
31. For the Oxford gaol fever, see Batman, Stephen (1581) *The Doome Warning all Men to the Judgemente* London, p. 404. For plague epidemics, see, eg, Gouge, William *A Plaister for the Plague*, in *Gods Three Arrowes* (London, 1631), p. 79; Gloucester Cathedral Library, MS 40, fragment of a letter c. 1630.
32. Walsham, Alexandra (1994) '"The Fatall Vesper": Providentialism and Anti-Popery in Late Jacobean London', *Past and Present*, 144.
33. Clifton, Robin 'Fear of Popery', in Conrad Russell (ed.) (1973) *The Origins of the English Civil War*. Basingstoke: Macmillan, p. 160 and passim, and his 'The Popular Fear of Catholics during the English Revolution', repr. in Slack, Paul (ed.) (1984) *Rebelllion, Popular Protest and the Social Order in Early Modern England*. Cambridge: Cambridge University Press.

In Jacobean Yorkshire, for example, adults and children hissed 'Papist', 'Papist', at an elderly recusant woman set in the stocks in the market place like 'a monster, or an owl in the daytime'.[34] We should not underestimate the potential for such verbal aggression to spill over into action, or for the potent mixture of jingoism, bigotry and xenophobia ritually unleashed during annual celebrations of the nation's providential deliverances from the Spanish Armada and Gunpowder Plot to disturb the delicate equilibrium which generally characterised Catholic-Protestant coexistence. When it converged with other animosities and tensions, anti-Catholicism could turn from a mild allergy into a delirious fever and destructive force.

At such junctures, there are good grounds for thinking that church papists were the focus of the most intense fear and anxiety. Protestants came to see them as far 'more dangerous and hurtfull to the state' than 'symple recusants' who stuck out like a sore thumb and displayed their colours on their sleeve: a fifth column, Trojan Horse, an insidious, unseen enemy within.[35] Emasculated by mounting debts to the Exchequer, recusants posed little threat to the regime, but schismatics who put on the costume of loyal conforming Protestants were denounced as 'deepe dissemblers', 'timeserving hypocrites ... the bane of this lande ... prickes and thornes in our sides'.[36] There was a grumbling worry that many such 'counterfeits' used their conformity as a smoke screen for subversive undercover activity – for spying and collecting intelligence, for housing mass priests whose very presence on English soil was an act of high treason, for insinuating themselves into positions of influence where they could intervene on behalf of their molested co-religionists. This was a phobia fed by the presence of figures like Ambrose Griffith, a Hereford lawyer and 'halfe Recusant' whom the government identified as particularly treacherous in 1604, noting that 'though hee goeth to the

---

34. 'Father Pollard's Recollections of the Yorkshire Mission', in Morris, J. (ed.) (1877) *The Troubles of our Catholic Forefathers*, 3rd series. London: Burns and Oates, p. 452. For one example of a libel, see 'Recusancy Papers of the Meynell Family', ed. Aveling, p. xiii.
35. *Catholic Record Society Miscellanea: Recusant Records*, ed. Talbot, Clare Catholic Record Society 53 (1961), p. 66.
36. Quoted in Wiener, Carol Z. (1971) 'The Beleaguered Isle: A Study of Elizabethan and Early Jacobean Catholicism', *Past and Present*, 51, p. 38.

church, yet hee runneth the Jesuite's courses most violentlye'.[37] In this sense church papists arguably assisted in inflating popery into a spectre and bogey of exaggerated proportions, albeit one that was only occasionally invoked. They instilled a fear of crypto-Catholicism into English society which found its fullest and most dysfunctional expression in alarm about the rise of Arminianism and Laudianism – developments zealous Protestants perceived as a kind of Counter Reformation by stealth and ultimately took up arms to repel.

In conclusion, it is tempting to take up John Morrill's famous throwaway remark that 'the English Civil War was not the first European revolution: it was the last of the Wars of Religion'.[38] Could it be that the pluralism nurtured by the Elizabethan Settlement helped to prevent the outbreak of a confessional war in the mid sixteenth century but created the conditions in which one would ignite eighty years later? To this extent, there may be less of a contrast between early modern England and France than traditional historiography has implied. To borrow phrases from Philip Benedict and Christopher Marsh, both countries were characterised by a paradoxical 'mixture of tolerance and intolerance', by 'an almost schizophrenic religious culture, in which contradictory instincts jostled for supremacy'.[39] It has been the contention of this paper that crypto-Catholicism in a multiplicity of guises was a key ingredient in this compound – an agent of concord and integration and at the same time a recipe for suspicion, mistrust, and even violent dissension. Perhaps Protestant nicodemites in France played an equally ambivalent role; perhaps it is time for French historians to peel away their disguises and coax them out of their closets.

---

37. *Catholic Record Society Miscellanea II*, Catholic Record Society 2 (1906), p. 297; Foley (ed.) *Records of the English Province*, vol. iv, p. 370. See also British Library, Harleian MS 360, fo. 25r.
38. Morrill, John (1993) 'The Religious Context of the English Civil War', repr. in idem, *The Nature of the English Revolution*. London: Longman, p. 68.
39. Benedict, 'Un roi, une loi, deux fois', p. 67; Marsh, Christopher (1998) *Popular Religion in Sixteenth-Century England*. Basingstoke: Macmillan, p. 191.

MARK GREENGRASS

Epilogue: The Adventure of Religious Pluralism in Early-Modern France

The protestant reformation was a volcanic explosion in Christendom. Along the fault-lines of a middle-band of territories in Europe, running from Ireland in the west through central continental Europe to Poland and Hungary in the east, lay the greatest fissures. Here the vents of religious tension generated volcanoes of sectarian tension. They pushed up new states and radically altered the political terrain of others. In the fertile volcanic ash new species of political and cultural expression eventually took root, including more secular approaches to authority, even while older species of irredendist confessional belief continued to flourish. France lay along this fault-line and the volcanic irruption of the reformation left indelible marks on its political and cultural development, as the twenty essays in this collection testify.

The subject of the conference from which these papers derive was not that of religious toleration. The latter implies a teleology that reads the 'rise' of toleration back from the halcyon heights of the Enlightenment *philosophes* who shook their heads in rationalist disbelief at the confessional excesses of the post-reformation age. The *philosophes* sought to trace the development of attitudes and social behaviour that asserted the right of individuals to their own beliefs. In the process, the *philosophes* tended to conflate that right with the legal principle that the state may, in certain circumstances (including those of necessity or political prudence) allow a freedom from persecution (to a variety of limited degrees) to groups that did not subscribe to the faith of the prince or the majority population. The former right may have had its roots in the sixteenth century but it did not make its mark before the eighteenth century. The latter, however, was emphatically the child (a monstrous birth, as many contemporaries saw it) of the sixteenth century. 'Pluralism' – the *de facto* existence of bi- (or multi-) confessional plurality – was abundant in the volcanic craters of the reformation. It was not willed

by choice or welcomed, but extruded in the muddied and muddled practicalities of the reformation.

The pacification at Nantes in 1598 is the emblem of this pluralism in
the history of early-modern France. Commemorations are the stuff of the
heritage industry of the late twentieth century and the edict of Nantes
was second only to the World-Cup in the French national calendar in
1998. There were media-events, memorabilia, conferences and books.[1]
Yet another volume on the pacification of Nantes would be to pile Pilion
upon Ossa. The edict that brought the most violent phase of France's
religious troubles to a close is, however, a starting-point for this volume.
In itself the edict was far from unique, but it lasted longer than its predecessors. It developed an aura of its own, and so it stands as the most
challenging, perhaps the most ambitious, piece of legislation attempted
by the French crown in the ancien-régime. A triumph of the 'justice-
state', the edict also (as David Trim has pointed out elsewhere in this
volume) owed something to the 'military-state' as well. But the latter
was, like the naval administration that Henri IV inherited, only lightly
institutionalised. Alan James shows how Henri IV, despite the traditions
of Huguenot privateering and naval strength in north-west European
waters and his predecessor's efforts to reform the navy, was unable to
create a coordinated and effective instrument of his authority where it
would have counted – in the Atlantic. So Henri IV's martial authority
depended on a projection of an image of personal authority and a willingness to work with individuals with different agendas, prickly senses
of their own honour, and beliefs different from his own.

All changes were negotiated and 'brokered' in the early-modern period. That common-place applies to religious changes as well. The
processes of 'mediation' occurred at every level when it came to the application of the edicts of pacification. As Penny Roberts and Daniel
Hickey demonstrate, they depended on the efforts of the commissioners
for their execution. In divided localities, these commissioners needed
reserves of patience and determination. On the delicate questions upon

---

1. The following is a selection of the latter: Cottret, Bernard (1997) *1598. L'édit de
   Nantes. Pour en finir avec les guerres de religion.* Paris; Wanegffelen, Thierry
   (1998) *L'Edit de Nantes. Une histoire européenne de la tolérance du XVIe au XXe
   siècles.* Paris; Garrisson, Janine (1998) *l'Edit de Nantes. Chroniques d'une paix at-
   tendue.* Paris; *L'Edit de Nantes.* Nantes, Editions de la Réunion des musées
   nationaux, 1998; Joxe, Pierre (1998) (avec la collaboration de Thierry Wanegffelen
   and Jean-Sylvestre Coquin), *L'Edit de Nantes. Une histoire pour aujourd'hui.* Paris.

which they were required to decide, they were, as Hickey stresses, required to invent the necessary jurisprudence where the terms of the edicts did not assist them. Local mediation was dependant on the national settlement being one that did not stretch the limits of local brokerage – as had occurred in the abortive peace of Monsieur of 1576.[2] The pacification of Nantes was successful because it built on previously, and painfully, learned experiences in this respect. But mediation was even more reliant upon finding local notables willing to engage in the politics of pluralism. The local roots of pluralism have recently been stressed by Olivier Christin.[3] Municipal notables were prepared, in certain circumstances to reach their own accords in matters of religion. Sectarian tensions were, at least to some degree, taken off the streets and into the council and court-rooms. These formally sworn, local accords remained exceptional. Yet, in places like Nantes (where the protestants remained clearly a minority), official hostility amongst the local notability to the protestant minority in their midst was tempered by a tacit, unofficial, willingness not to provoke issues of public disorder and make trouble for their communities needlessly.[4] In protestant strongholds, too, the processes of local mediation depended on local notables. As Philip Conner emphasises, the loyalties of the Scorbiac family were of considerable significance, a family whose protestantism and affiliations to Henri IV were held carefully in balance as they manipulated local sentiments in favour of the Bourbon interest.

Such mediation was, of its nature, an ongoing dialogue and process. It involved complex issues – and never more so than in the independent principalities on the frontiers of the kingdom. In Béarn, Lorraine or Savoy, there were additional issues – questions of strongly independent inherited traditions, language as well as complex matters of princely succession. In Lorraine where, as Pierre Chaunu famously argued, the province acted as a frontier of faith – a relatively impervious membrane

---

2. See my earlier chapter.
3. Christin, Olivier (1997) *La paix de religion. L'autonomisation de la raison politique au XVIe siècle*, esp. ch. 3.
4. See Elizabeth Tingle's chapter; Bob Scribner calls this a 'passive (or rather, covert) freedom of belief) and cites examples from the early reformation in Germany – see his chapter in Grell, Ole Peter and Scribner, Bob (1996) *Tolerance and intolerance in the European Reformation.* Cambridge, p. 35.

to the spread of protestantism.[5] The ultimate French conquest of Lorraine in the 1630s undoubtedly helped to change the tempo of the catholic intra-confessional debates in France as well as to alter the confessional balance of forces within the kingdom.[6] But, as Bonney suggests, it was only after 1661 that the terms of trade of the mediation and brokerage of the religious pluralism turned decisively in favour of the absolute monarchy.

We should not, however, exaggerate the extent of the impact of the inter-confessional divides in early-modern France. For many, no doubt, the *plat pays de la croyance* was a landscape marked by familiar rituals and established verities that did not appear noticeably to change during their lifetimes.[7] For others, however, it turned out to be a *bocage* of inter-confessional debates that interplay and interweave with *intra*-confessional hesitations, discussions and divisions. Pluralism existed within and around the confessional *blocs*. The construction of those apparently monolithic confessions (*Konfessionalisierung*, or *Konfessionalsbildung*, as it is known to historians of the smaller states of Germany in the second half of the sixteenth century) furthered intra-confessional dissent, at least in the short-term. This varied patchwork quilt of beliefs (the 'religions of the people' as Galpern entitled his study of them in Champagne) was particularly evident in the widespread anticlerical attitudes that were so dominant in France on the eve of the reformation. These attitudes embraced a popular and visceral anticlericalism that refused to pay tithes and disputed the authority of the church. That anticlericalism included vestigial remains of the Waldensianism in south-east France, from whom the proverb that 'it was better to be shrieved by a worthy man than a worthless priest' acquired a broader resonance that outlasted the formal existence of the heresy itself.[8] But there was also a more fashionable and articulate anticlericalism that was sometimes expressed with a degree of invective that shocked contemporaries. Marguerite of Navarre, for example, shocked the bishop of Carpentras in 1548, Jacopo Sadoleto (himself no traditionalist in church-matters) with her open expression of views that Rome would have re-

5.   Chaunu, Pierre (1962) 'Jansénisme et frontière de catholicité, XVIIe-XVIIIe siècles, à propos du jansénisme lorrain', *Revue Historique* 227, pp. 115-138.
6.   See Kate Currey's chapter.
7.   The phrase is used by Thierry Wanegffelen (1997) in his magisterial study, *Ni Rome ni Genève. Des fidèles entre deux chaires en France au XVIe siècle*. Paris, p. xv.
8.   Cameron, Euan (1984) *The Reformation of the Heretics*. Oxford.

garded as reprehensible on sensitive religious subjects.[9] Brantôme recalled, drawing on his memories and contacts as a young page at her court, her saying that: 'Elle vouloit croire en ce que son Dieu et son Eglise commandoient, sans entrer plus avant en autre curioisté'.[10] Here was pluralism from within, or dutiful dependance, depending on how you chose to read it. It must have appeared threatening indeed in the early, confessionally pre-pubescent years of the reformation. For, like seismic shifts in the earth's crust, there was no clear fault-line, but rather a series of parallel faults, each capable of giving vent of powerful forces from underneath.

Whose God? Whose Church? These were issues that turned into loyalties, into parties, and eventually into institutional formations. The issues were played out in the minds and published writings of the period and, of course, in its 'liturgies' (the word was applied to define ecclesiastical rituals in new, pluralistic ways in the sixteenth century). They formed the stuff of the intra-confessional and inter-confessional tensions of the era of the reformation, notably after the 'beginning of a tragedy' (as Etienne Pasquier foreshadowed) in 1562. The tensions of confessional pluralism, of course, provided an identifiable 'enemy without'. The latter was accompanied by an irredentist sense of the need and desire for unity – represented in the invective against 'nicodemites' from Calvin and the suspicion of 'moyenneurs' from both sides. It recurred in the desire for purification and the spiritual renewal of the earthly city – sentiments that found their echo in the urban elites at the time of the League. It was reflected, too, in the belief that patriotism was an exclusive virtue to one side or the other, and that the 'deviant other' constituted a 'stranger' or 'foreigner'. As Alexandra Walsham has demonstrated, it did not need the sectarian tensions of the French civil wars to create such sentiments. They were equally deep-rooted in peacable protestant England's reactions towards its catholic minority. As Luc Racaut reminds us, the catholic projections of an alien protestant presence in France were remarkably deep-seated. His systematic sampling of anti-protestant literature in the 1560s suggests that it was an even more formidable barrier to religious pluralism than one might have realised. It

---

9. Venard, Marc (1980) *La société ecclésiastique d'Avignon au XVIe siècle*. 5 vols Université de Lille III, 2, p. 416.
10. Brantôme, Pierre de Bourdeille ... de [ed. J. A. C. Buchon] (1888). *Œuvres complètes*. 2 vols Paris, 2, p. 186.

may well be that the political pluralism that emerged towards the end of the sixteenth century rests in part, as he suggests, on a degree of control of the printed word. Whilst not of great efficiency, the modest development of the oversight of what was printed in the wake of the League may well have been capable of restraining and excising from the public domain the more inflammatory components that its publicists were capable of generating.[11]

Yet these rivalries also had curious kaleidoscopic effects within the tunnel visions of the rival confessions. As Lucien Febvre reminded us many years ago, the sixteenth century was prolific in the varieties of its religious expression.[12] These varieties were not immediately exploded by the volcanic irruptions of the reformation. Like Pantagruel in the fourth book of *Gargantua*, individuals had to find their own route between the scylla and charybdis of the 'île Farouche' and the 'Andouilles farfelues'.[13] There were perhaps many individuals who, like Charles Du Moulin and Etienne de l'Hôpital, disliked being confessionally 'pigeonholed'.[14] André Thevet, at any rate, thought so, as Loris Petris points out. Referring to de l'Hôpital, Thevet said that there was 'une infinité de personnes qui l'on a veu vivre à la Catholique: si ce n'a esté de cœur on ne le sçauroit deviner, cela estant un secret, qui n'est revelé aux hommes'. There is always a tendency to attempt to 'lump' together the confessionally detached into one category or another. They become 'Erasmians', 'Gallicans' or 'Moyenneurs'. The labels, however, are less than helpful. The 'Erasmianism' after Erasmus was a delicate aroma. It needs highly sensitive detecting equipment to pick up in France in the second half of the century. It had become detached from any one of Erasmus' works and diffused into a more general habit of mind, a refusal to accept dogmas at face-value and an individual piety that conjoined easily with other

---

11. See also Sawyer, Jeffrey K. (1990) *Printed Poison. Pamphlet Propaganda, Faction Politics, and the Public Sphere in Early-Seventeenth-Century France.* Berkeley, Los Angeles and Oxford.

12. 'Deux religions, la catholique et la réformée? Des religions plutôt, car il y en eut bien plus que deux, et la fécondité d'un siècle élémentaire ne s'est point limitée à dresser face à face umn protestantisme bien coordonnée et un catholicisme bien expurgé' – Febvre, Lucien (1983) *Au cœur religieux au XVIe siècle.* 2nd edition, p. 93.

13. Huchon, Mireille (ed.) (1994), François Rabelais, *Le Quart Livre, 1552* Paris, ch. 30; cf the scintillating analysis in Wanegffelen, Thierry (1999) *Une difficile fidélité. Catholiques malgré le concile en France, XVIe-XVIIe siècles.* Paris, pp. 18-25.

14. 'Ce nouvel article de votre foi qu'il faut être papiste ou huguenot ...', remarked Charles Du Moulin in 1565 (cited Wanegffelen, p. 15).

humanist influences. Gallicanism, as Alain Tallon has sensitively demonstrated elsewhere in this volume, was also very far from a monolithic outlook. There was a royal gallicanism that was prepared to contemplate religious pluralism on prudential grounds so long as it was limited, controlled and determined legally by the crown. But there was also a parlementaire gallicanism that stressed the irreducible unity of the kingdom, and the link between law and religion that sustained it. Fracture the one and you would invariably weaken the sacred force of the other. Then there was an ecclesiastical gallicanism that was more concerned to distance itself from both the French crown and the papacy, yet aware of its dependance on both for its protection. 'Splitting' the confessionally detached, rather than 'lumping' them together as a 'middle group', illustrates the degree to which *intra*-confessional pluralism was part and parcel of the *inter*-confessional tensions of the reformation era.

By the end of the sixteenth century, however, some firm confessional scaffolding was in place in France. It was erected around church structures and architecture, buildings that reflected their doctrinal statements and standpoints.[15] How far, however, had 'confessional exclusivism' entered people's hearts and minds? The evidence often points both ways. Take, for example, the case of Isaac Casauban. The great Huguenot scholar records in his diary that, whilst he was in Paris, he did not dare to enter a catholic church because he felt it to be such an alien and strange environment. If Pierre de l'Estoile was to be believed, the feeling was mutual among catholics; they thought it was more wicked to enter a *temple* than a brothel.[16] Yet there was more to Casauban's hesitancy than an *arrière-boutique* of inherited or imbibed protestant phobias – a *Konfessionalieserung* of the spirit. For Casauban's friends and backers, those who had brought him up from Montpellier to Paris, were catholic royalists in high places. He was the object of the subtle ministrations of the 'convertisseurs'. If his son (who *did* convert) is to be believed, his father wobbled. Behind the confessional constructions, the public façades of the churches, lay a more private domain of family, friendships and conscience. Our difficulty is that it is largely hidden from our investigation. It is, as Thevet said, 'secret' and one of the longer-term effects of the development of confessional exclusivism was

---

15. See above, Andrew Spicer.
16. Cited in Mark Pattison, (1892) *Isaac Casauban (1559-1612)*. Oxford, p. 208.

to accentuate the degree to which religious pluralism, especially in the seventeenth century, went silent and 'underground'.

We must resort to looking for the equivalent of the hands drawn in the margin of protestant Bibles in the seventeenth century, the 'finger-posts' that will point us towards the *terra incognita* of this more private pluralism. Every good conference concludes by setting the agenda for another. The papers selected in this volume begin to delineate this further research agenda. What were the zones and limits of practical pluralism in the period of confessional co-existence in France? The question was posed by puritan preachers in England as regards the catholics in their midst, those who came, as Alexander Walsham points out, 'but slakly' to the established church, created distractions during the sermon, conformed in everything but spirit. Should preachers urge their parishioners to shun them? Social conformities and customary decorum dictated that one should salute one's neighbour in the street, even though a known catholic. Equally, the preachers privately urged the godly not to invite them to join them at their meal tables, or at their family events. Yet what if the catholics *were* family? For all that Calvin's powerful invective sought to draw firm and impervious limits delineating the godly from the godless, it was (in practice) never easy. His pamphlet *Contre les Nicodémites* was, as Antoine Fumée said, 'thoroughly wretched . . . it is easy for you to preach and threaten over there, but if you were here you would perhaps feel differently'. As a later commissioner for an edict of pacification, Fumée would come to know a good deal about the difficulties in practice of confessional clarities.

Inter-confessional marriages created family links that dissolved confessional constructions and provided the basis for local pluralism. We know very little about its extent, but Gregory Hanlon's study of the community of Layrac in south-west France documents the extent to which the non-normative sources have beguiled us into thinking that it was a rarity in the period from 1598 to 1685.[17] Hanlon's study relies on a patient identification of the religious affiliations of the community in question. As a result, he is able to document a good deal more mixed marriages than one had previously imagined and, coupled with them, conversions 'of convenience' on the eve of what would have been

---

17. Hanlon, Gregory (1993) *Confession and Community in Seventeenth-Century France. Catholic and Protestant Coexistence in Aquitaine.* Philadelphia, p. 103 *et seq.*

otherwise a 'mixed marriage'. Cousinage, *voisinage*, friendship, these were the practical solvents of confessional exclusivism and the local basis of religious pluralism. Baif's poetry is filled with their echoes: 'le fils à son père', 'le frère à son frère', 'le voisin au voisin', 'citoyens à Citoyens'. These are the potential victims of creed-rage as viewed by the subtle court poet and disappointed supporter of Henri III's ultimately aborted attempts to broker a Valois pacification on the wreckage of the kingdom in the midst of the civil wars.[18]

The 'finger-posts' are most evident amongst the scholars of early-modern France. They were prepared, at least to some small degree, to reveal their struggles of conscience to us, in their private letters. The latter were written in the privacy of their studies, a world where (as one seventeenth-century divine put it) 'my conscience is free'. Isaac Casaubon's pluralism lay in his study. To lose an hour in the day to activities outside his books was to be lamented and offered to God in supplication. On his shelves were the works, cheek by jowl, of catholic and protestant reformation apologists; Bellarmine next to the Centuries of Magdeburg. The same eclectic pluralism was true for more modest protestant pastors too. The Breton pastor, Philippe Le Noir, sieur de Crevain documents for us his reading habits and library from his students days onwards. He read the new science (Gassendi and Descartes) as well as the controversial theology on the sacrificial character of the Mass. He knew the works of the classical historians, took a liking to geography and also had a Koran on his shelves, judging that 'the work contained many excellent things'.[19] A century earlier, de l'Hôpital's subtle and complex Latin poetry was also the product of his humanist study and reading.[20] Not intended for publication, these writings permitted him the freedom to imitate humanist criticisms of religious hypocrisy and blend them with the Gallican onslaught on Romish corruption. They allowed him to enter a world of surrender before the grace of God, in whose hands alone lay salvation.

To invade a scholar's study was to violate a fundamental dignity and freedom. Hugues Sureau Du Rosier, for example, was outraged that his

---

18. See above, Yvonne Roberts.
19. I owe these details to Philip Benedict's fascinating recreation of this pastor's reading habits in 'The Owl of Minerva at Dusk: Philippe Le Noir de Crevain, Pastor of the Era of Louis XIV, Historian of the Reformed Churches of the Sixteenth Century', a paper that is to be published shortly.
20. See Loris Petris's chapter.

fellow ministers took advantage of his absence from Orléans in 1566 to force his study door and confiscate the letters that he had received from Jean Morély in order to incriminate the latter for his unorthodox views on the rights of the pastorate to represent the community of believers.[21] The offence contributed to Sureau's celebrated protestant abjuration a few years later. The form of the 'letter of spiritual advice' was one where a private pluralism was encouraged because the latter was essential to the nourishing of a tender conscience. Marguerite of Navarre had been so nourished in her private, prayerful and mystical relationship with God in her correspondence with Guillaume Briçonnet.[22] The same would be true for Mère Angélique a century later. 'There is nothing wrong, it seems to me, in gathering from several flowers the nectar that we cannot find in just one' François de Sales told her.[23] St-Cyran invited her to 'un silence de gémissement', a kind of 'ablative absolute' pluralism of the spirit within that could be translated into a striking and effective passive resistance to blandishments from her family, or from the ecclesiastical hierarchy, when circumstances demanded it.

Religion is the pursuit of truth. Herein lay the problem. There was only one truth (on that there was universal agreement), but the validation of that truth lay in institutions that claimed it exclusively as their own, and social norms that preferred one claim to truth over another. Historians of science have recently taught us that there is a 'social history' of scientific truth.[24] Historians of religion would also say that religious truth was validated by more than ecclesiastical frameworks in the reformation but also by their worshipping communities, and by the notability that acted as their natural social leaders. This gave the latter some latitude for choice in the reformation; and choice implies pluralism. Timothy Watson's Lyon municipal elite in Lyon did not want the reformation to make windows made of their souls; they were only gradually persuaded of the protestants as an alien, hostile and potentially subversive element within the city. Catherine de Médicis exploited the role of these natural social

---

21. Kingdon, Robert (1961) 'Genève et les réformés français: le cas de Hugues Sureau dit Du Rosier (1565-1574)', *Bulletin de la Société d'Histoire et d'Archéologie de Genève* 12, pp. 77-87.

22. Veissière, M. (1975-77) *Guillaume Briçonnet et Marguerite d'Angoulême*, correspondance 2 vols Geneva.

23. See Daniella Kostroun's chapter.

24. Shapin, Steven (1994) *A Social History of Truth: Civility and Science in Seventeenth-Century England*. Chicago.

leaders during her voyage around Midi France in 1578-79. As she visited towns, she organised for their elites to swear mutually to obey the peace of Bergerac, accept *mi-partie* consulate arrangements and the authority of the *chambres mi-parties* established in the edict of 1577. She shrewdly harnessed the social bases for pluralism against the potential forces for confessional exclusivism and the lesson would not be lost upon Henri IV and his advisors.

This volume has concentrated on the French experience. But, as Gillian Weiss reminds us, Islam was a force to be reckoned with close to France's southern seaward frontier, another religion embodying another civilisation. It posed, as Weiss points out, complex problems for French diplomats, statesmen and churchmen. On the one hand, captured Christians should be ransomed and redeemed by their coreligionists. This did not extend, however, as she points out, to ransoming Huguenot captives unless they agreed to abjure. On the other hand, there was the anxiety that French subjects would, like the Hungarians, 'prennent le turban aussi facilement qu'un bonnet de nuit'. Yet commercial *Realpolitik* dictated contact, commerce and toleration of a kind that would be officially denied to protestants after 1685.

So we should widen our horizons – not least because contemporaries, when looking at France from outside, were inclined to point to the examples of pluralism elsewhere. Listen, for example, to the oration of Franciotto to Charles IX in the wake of the St Bartholomew's massacres in 1573. Orazio Franciotti was a merchant of Italian extraction resident in London. He was horrified by recent events in Paris and elsewhere in France. He had 'observed in all lands men make a difference between a good Christian and a good subject, and [that] there is a toleration of sundry religions so they follow the laws'.[25] The ancient Romans 'allowed the service of all sorts of gods'. The Turks give 'Christians exercise of all religion, even to the very monks that are in Pera'. Various Christian princes, and even the Pope himself, tolerate the existence of a Jewish minority in their lands, although Jews openly question the virginity of Mary and express other blasphemies. In Germany, 'people of different religions live peaceably and contribute equally and with like affection to

---

25. The document is reported in *Calendar of State Papers, 1573* (London, 1880), pp. 425-27. Although the document is apparently dated '1597' the internal evidence suggests that it is correctly calendared. For further details on Franciotti, see *Calendar of State Papers Foreign* (1583 and addenda) ed. A. J. Butler and S. C. Lomas (1913), pp. 269-270.

the charges of the wars and demands of their superiors'. In Muscovy, the Grand Duke accepts the Tartars as his subjects and they fight under his banner, despite the fact that they are the coreligionists of his enemies. In Poland there are 'Latin and Greek churches, French Protestants, Jews and Tartars that are idolaters, quietly living together with all reverence to their prince'. It was not difficult to point to pluralism in other places in Europe at any stage from the onset of the French civil wars onwards.

Yet there was a very variable geometry to these officially tolerated 'pluralisms' in practice. They were not always what they seemed. The rigid bi-confessionalism in a city like Augsburg after the peace of Westphalia in 1648 was not, in reality, a genuine confessional co-existence. Lutherans and Catholics had access to political posts in the city in equal measure but, in the city at large, the communities were segregated and quartered, there was no intermarriage. Each community was an autonomous element within the city, possessing its own school, its own college and hospital and its own financial means for running them. Each community had its own coextensible parishes with the Lutherans harbouring resentments against the Catholics for garnering the rich heritage of ecclesiastical structures in the city to themselves. What looks like a well-found degree of confessional harmony from the outside looks rather different when more closely analysed.[26]

In any case, the lessons of one pluralism were not readily transmutable from one political culture to another. And, as France's travellers discovered when they left the confines of Christendom, this was still more the case between one civilisation and another. Their travels led them sometimes to pose uncomfortable questions about their own society and culture; but the questions were more often occluded within senses of cultural incompatibility and the sense of the exotic afforded by distance. By Louis XIV's reign, such lessons were more easily able absorbed but, at least immediately, less relevant. As France's colonial portfolio accumulated, confessional absolutism took root after 1661. As it did so, Jansenism became another underground pluralism in France's 'commu-

---

26. François, E. (1993) *Protestants et catholiques en Allemagne. Identités et pluralisme. Augsburg, 1648-1806.* Paris. Leszek Kolakowski has also reinterpreted the case of Polish pluralism (albeit on different lines) in *Chrétiens sans Eglise. La conscience religieuse et le lien confessionnel au XVIIe siècle* (Paris, 1969 – translated from the 1965 Polish edition).

nities of belief'.[27] Despite the efforts of episcopal visitations and the ministrations of a more active clergy, there was still room for pluralism at a parochial level. And in the nascent 'Republic of Letters' lay the beginnings of a more powerful and secular pluralism that, in the eighteenth century, would adopt the transforming ideologies of toleration and liberty.

---

27. Briggs, Robin (1989) *Communities of Belief. Cultural and social tension in early modern France.* Oxford, subtly links these two elements – see esp. chs 5 and 6; cf Adam, Antoine (1968) *Du mysticisme à la révolte. Les jansénistes du XVIIe siècle.* Paris.

List of Contributors

REVD RICHARD BONNEY is Professor of Modern History, Head of the Department of History, and Director of the Centre for the History of Religions, Inter-Faith Dialogue and Pluralism at the University of Leicester. His recent books include *The Limits of Absolutism in ancien régime France* (Variorum, 1995); (ed. and contributor), *Economic Systems and State finance* (Oxford University Press and European Science Foundation, 1995); and (ed. and contributor), *The Rise of the Fiscal State in Europe, c.1200Ι815* (Oxford University Press, 1999). He is the editor of the Oxford Journal *French History*.

KEITH CAMERON is Professor of French and Renaissance Studies at the University of Exeter. He has specialised in critical editions of French texts, the history of the Reformation and satire and polemics against Henri III. Relevant recent publications include *From Valois to Bourbon* (Exeter University Press, 1989); *Ethics and Politics in Seventeenth-century France* (ed. Keith Cameron & Elizabeth Woodrough, Exeter U.P., 1996); Bernard Palissy: *Œuvres complètes* (ed. Marie-Madeleine Fragonard, Keith Cameron, *et al.*, Mont-de-Marsan, 1996).

PHILIP CONNER is currently undertaking a doctoral thesis on Huguenot culture in Languedoc at the Institute for Reformation Studies in St Andrews, Scotland.

KATE CURREY was awarded her doctorate, 'The Political and Social Context of Court Festivals in Lorraine 1563-1624', in 1997. She holds two visiting lectureships at the University of the West of England, Bristol and the University of Plymouth.

MARK GREENGRASS has a personal chair in History at the University of Sheffield. He specialises in the history of sixteenth-century France and Europe as well as intellectual history in the seventeenth century. His *France in the Age of Henri IV: the struggle for stability* has recently appeared in a revised, second edition (Longman, 1994) and his *Longman*

Companion to the European Reformation appeared in 1998. He is currently completing 'Governing Passions: the reformation of the French Kingdom, 1576-1586', a monograph on the difficulties of governing France in the period of the civil wars.

DANIEL HICKEY, professor of History at the Université de Moncton (Canada), has produced two books in previous fields of research: *The Coming of French Absolutism* (1986) and *Local Hospitals in Ancien Régime France* (1997). He is currently working on the pacification of France, 1598-1630.

ALAN JAMES is a temporary lecturer and tutor in History at the University of Sheffield. He received his PhD from the University of Manchester in 1997 and is currently preparing a book on French sea power in the seventeenth century.

DANIELLA J. KOSTROUN is a PhD. candidate in History at Duke University and is working on a dissertation entitled 'Undermining Obedience in Absolutist France: The Case of the Port Royal Nuns, 1609-1709'. She is currently a fellow at the Erasmus Institute at the University of Notre Dame.

LORIS PETRIS is 'chargé de cours' at the University of Neuchâtel, Switzerland. He has published two articles on Michel de L'Hospital (*Bibliothèque d'Humanisme et Renaissance*, 1998 and 1999) and is preparing an annotated edition of the discourses of Michel de L'Hospital between 1560 and 1562.

LUC RACAUT successfully completed his PhD on 'The Portrayal of Protestants in the Polemic of the French Wars of Religion' at the Institute for Reformation Studies in St Andrews in 1999. He has been appointed lecturer in History at Crichton College, University of Glasgow.

PENNY ROBERTS is lecturer in History at the University of Warwick. She is author of *A city in conflict: Troyes during the French wars of religion* (1996) and various essays on the social and religious history of sixteenth-century France.

YVONNE ROBERTS was awarded the degree of PhD. for her thesis, *Jean-Antoine de Baïf – Poet to the Court,* at the University of Exeter in 1996. She has since published articles on the relationship of Baïf with the Valois dynasty and her monograph on the poet's political involvement has just been published by Peter Lang.

ANDREW SPICER is a Research Fellow at the University of Aberdeen and teaches at Stonyhurst College. His research looks at the impact of the Reformation on church architecture and he is currently editing 'Society and Culture in the Huguenot World', (Cambridge).

ALAIN TALLON is 'maître de conférences' at the Université Paul Valéry-Montpellier III. He has recently published his thesis on *La France et le concile de Trente (1518-1563)* (Rome: Ecole française de Rome, 1997). His current research focuses on Gallicanism in the sixteenth century.

ELIZABETH TINGLE is Senior Lecturer in History at University College, Northampton. She has researched industrial organisation and artisans and women's work in eighteenth-century France. Currently, she is working on society, economy and authority in Nantes in the later sixteenth century. Recent publications include: articles on building industries and on women's work in Brittany and in eighteenth-century Nantes; a study of pottery-producing artisans in rural Saintonge (13th-18th centuries).

DAVID J. B. TRIM is lecturer in History in the Department of Humanities, Newbold College, Bracknell. He is the author of a number of articles or chapters in scholarly journals and volumes of essays on aspects of European religious and military history during the era of the Wars of Religion

ALEXANDRA WALSHAM completed her PhD at the University of Cambridge in 1995 and is currently lecturer in History at the University of Exeter. Her research interests focus on the cultural impact and repercussions of the Reformation in Europe, particularly England. She is author of *Church Papists: Catholicism, Conformity and Confessional Polemic in Early Modern England* (Boydell Press, 1993; paperback 1999) and of *Providence in Early Modern England* (OUP, 1999).

TIMOTHY WATSON has recently completed a doctoral thesis at the University of Oxford entitled 'The Lyon City Council 1525-1575: Politics, Culture, Religion'. He has recently been appointed lecturer in History at the University of Newcastle.

GILLIAN WEISS is a doctoral candidate in Early Modern European History at Stanford University and is writing a dissertation on the captivity and liberation of French subjects in North Africa during the 17th and 18th centuries.